AF378390

Somerville 140
1879–2019

A Celebration of
Somerville College, Oxford
in 140 Objects

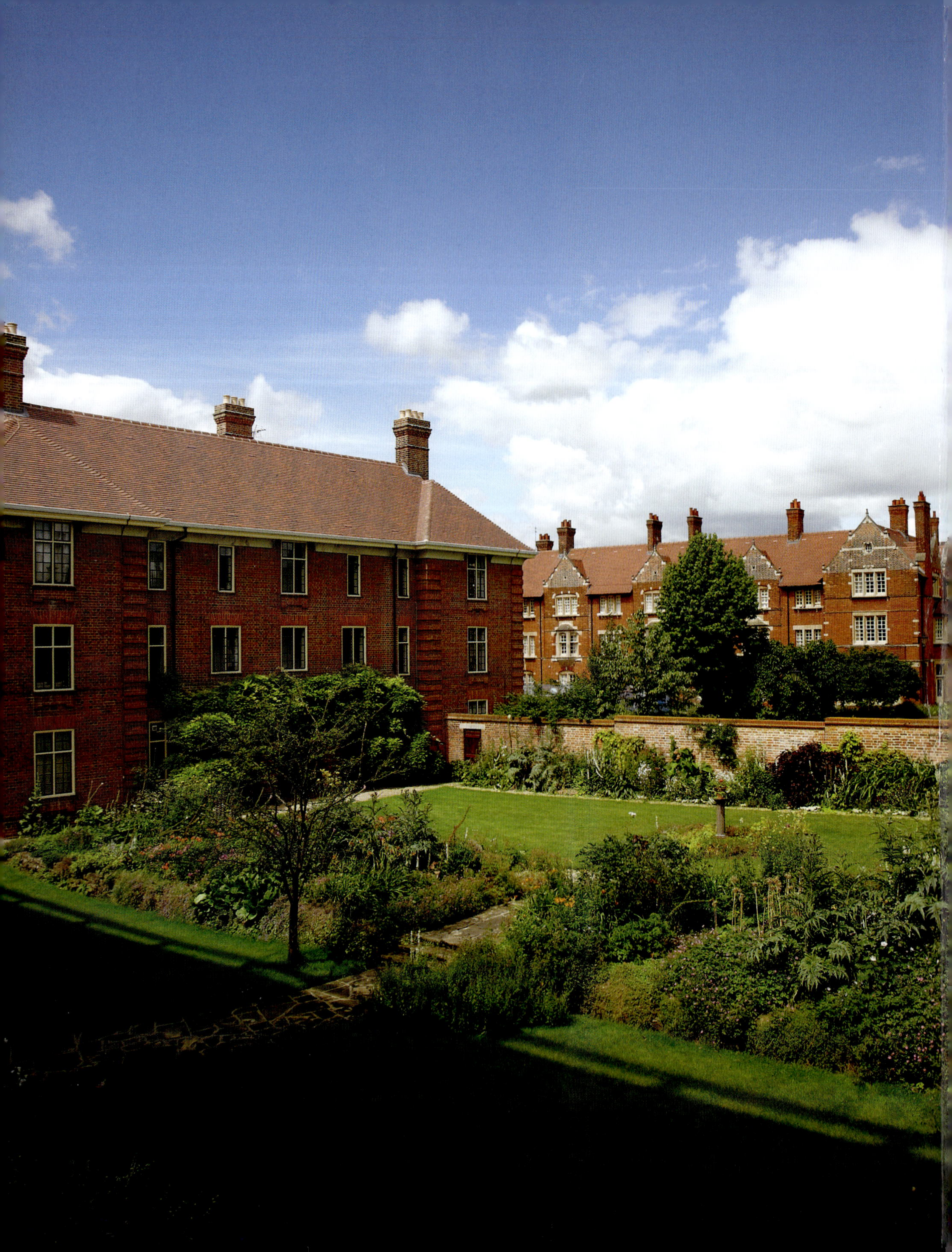

Somerville 140
1879–2019

A Celebration of
Somerville College, Oxford
in 140 Objects

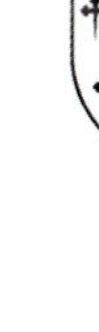
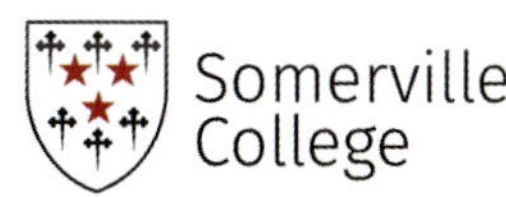

Somerville
College

SCALA

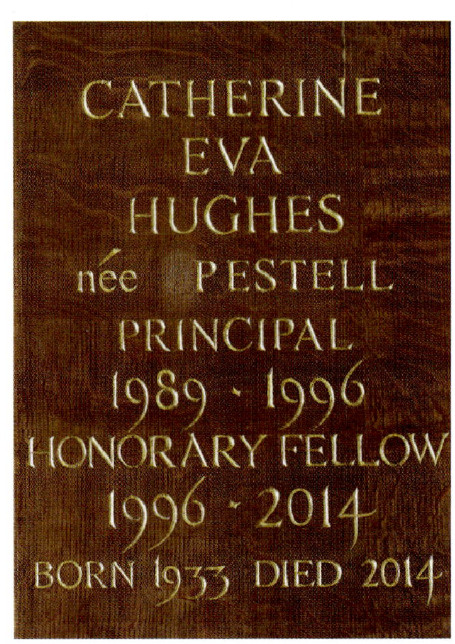

CATHERINE
EVA
HUGHES
née PESTELL
PRINCIPAL
1989 · 1996
HONORARY FELLOW
1996 · 2014
BORN 1933 DIED 2014

Contents

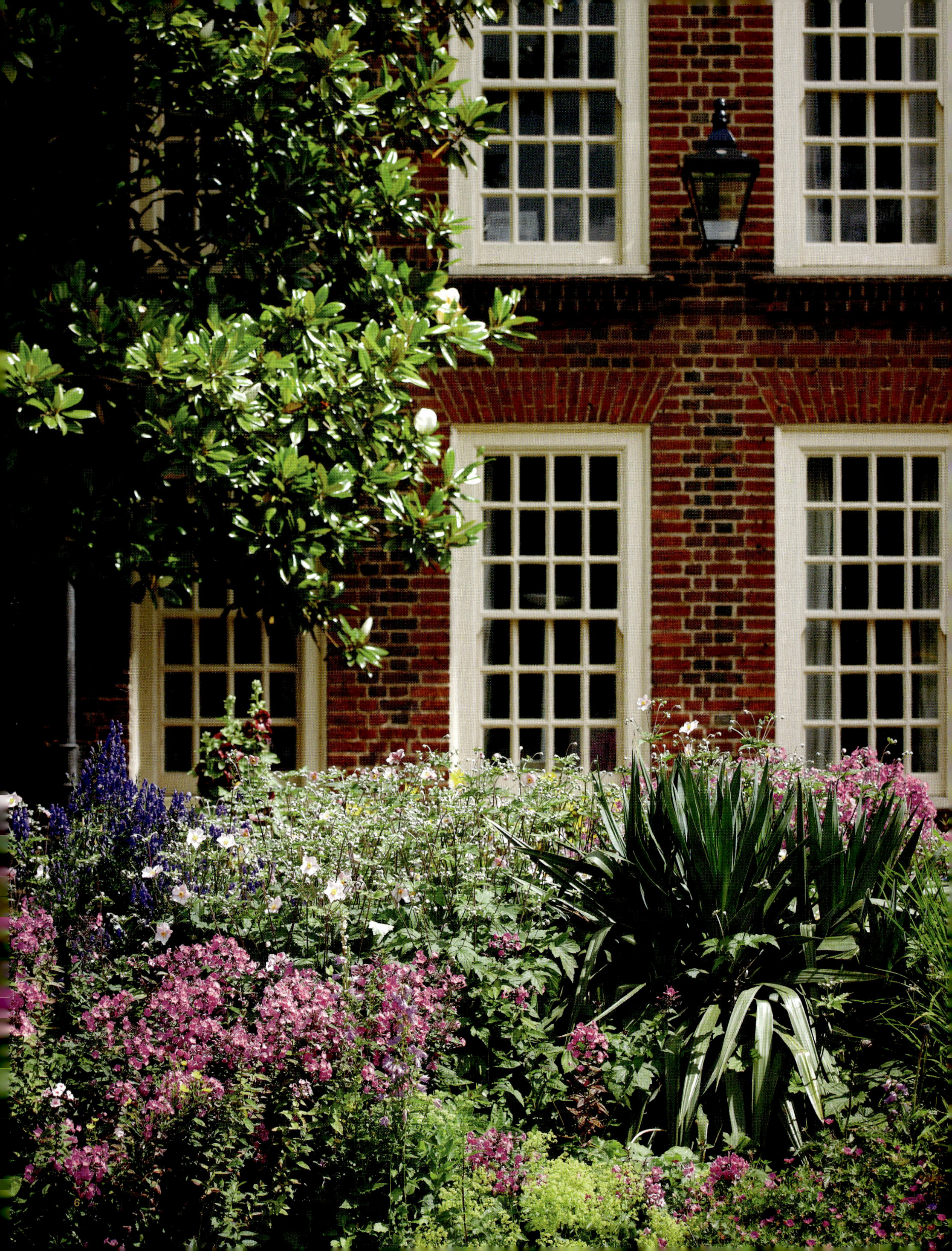

Foreword

Baroness Williams of Crosby, CH, PC
Honorary Fellow of Somerville

When I first arrived, in the spring of 1948, at Somerville to be offered a scholarship, I was in a thoroughly bad temper. I was convinced that I had only been offered a scholarship because my mother was a Somervillian (I did not appreciate that this was not Somerville's style and never had been). I much preferred my own choice to go to the LSE. I remember walking into the Principal's office and telling her that I rejected the bloody scholarship, and then I turned to leave. Faced with that, anyone else would have let me go, with a strong sense of Good Riddance, but this was the inimitable, unforgettable Janet Vaughan. She was intrigued rather than offended: 'Come and tell me why you are so bloody angry', she said, and sat down on the floor. So I did, and sat down next to her. Our conversation was the main reason I eventually accepted the scholarship.

From this incident I learned something about Somerville. Somervillians are intrigued by events rather than shocked by them. They are intelligent, and they have a candour that can sometimes be bracing. They are not always likeable: so be it. They have a yearning for public service that is both bold and radical (no matter what their politics) that may sometimes seem at odds with today's world. An Oxford education is, at its best, a fine training for the mind, but a Somerville education brings something else over and above that: a tenacity and persistence that gets things done.

Reading the celebration in this book of Somerville's first 140 years, it is easy to see how these qualities emerged in a place that had to fight so hard to exist and then to survive. This is not just a book of Somerville's history. It is a treasure chest of people and objects, a rich source of recollections. To appreciate the stories here is to find that unusual balance of careful thought and bold action that Somerville seems to specialise in: Emily Penrose, whose brilliance as a classicist was matched only by her

skills as a diplomat for women's education; Eleanor Rathbone, the first
Somervillian elected to Parliament, who never stopped looking for the
issues that needed to be brought to light and did so regardless of their
consequences for herself; and, of course, for me especially, but for many
others too, my mother, Vera Brittain, whose powerful writing led us
all to reflect on the agonies of war.

It is more than nostalgia for me to encounter Somerville in these pages,
to meet again my mother and her great friend, the writer Winifred Holtby.
I was lucky that to me, and to my brother John, she was 'Auntie Winifred'.
I was unlucky – we all were – that she died so young, when I was only five
years old. When I was older, I read *South Riding* and came to love it, not
least for the way it made local politics come alive, for its characters and for
me. In other words, I grew up in a world already tinged with Somerville's
ethos and its values, although at the time I did not really appreciate that.

I know now how unusual my own experience has been. I was fortunate
when young to hear people talk about politics, social issues, war and peace
and our responsibility to build a better world. As a result, I believed I could
do and be whatever I wanted. I know that is unusual. But what has always
impressed me about Somerville is that it brings a sense of confidence to
its students, no matter what their background.

I came up to Somerville in September 1948, when Oxford was filled
with young men who had come from the war rather than straight from
school. Like the rest of Oxford, Somerville was an austere place at that
time, not least in its food (potato cakes and dried milk featured heavily,
I recall), but it was nonetheless full of opportunities. I enjoyed acting as
well as politics. I made friends at Somerville who are still my beloved
friends now.

When I returned to start my second year, it was made clear to me that
my priorities needed to be altered: Somerville expected its undergraduates
to put academic work first. I read PPE ('Modern Greats' as it was then
known), and was fascinated by politics and economics, though at that
time I found philosophy devoid of interest, and I fear I was little match for
the philosophic mind of my tutor, Philippa Foot. I remember her looking
at a sofa in my first tutorial and asking whether it could be both red and
green all over. I have wonderful memories of my college (not least of the
occasional climb over the wall to get back in late at night), but, far more
than that, I have had a lifelong relationship with it. Somerville keeps hold
of its members: we come back, we keep up with the place, and there is
always something new to be enjoyed alongside what we remember.

For me, the lessons of a childhood shared with a great Somervillian,
and of a life lived and shaped by Somerville, are these: think, write and read,
always; live and work vividly, and bring your mind to bear on everything,
from the tiniest practical problem to the widest social issue; respect the

views of others, and of the past, but don't let that stop you being awkward when you need to be. Argue for what you believe, and do it well.

Somerville is a rare place, and I think that in today's world, the college's ethos matters more than ever. 140 years after it was founded, it continues to educate its members to the point where they can challenge untruth and shape the world. Pursuing truth is a fundamental objective of education. The founders of Somerville knew that education matters: that's why they fought so hard for it. Women in these 140 years have become more self-confident, braver, more ready to lead. The societies we live in reject prejudice and discrimination, as Somerville has done throughout its history. To read that history here, and the stories of those who make Somerville so remarkable, makes me proud to be part of this tradition.

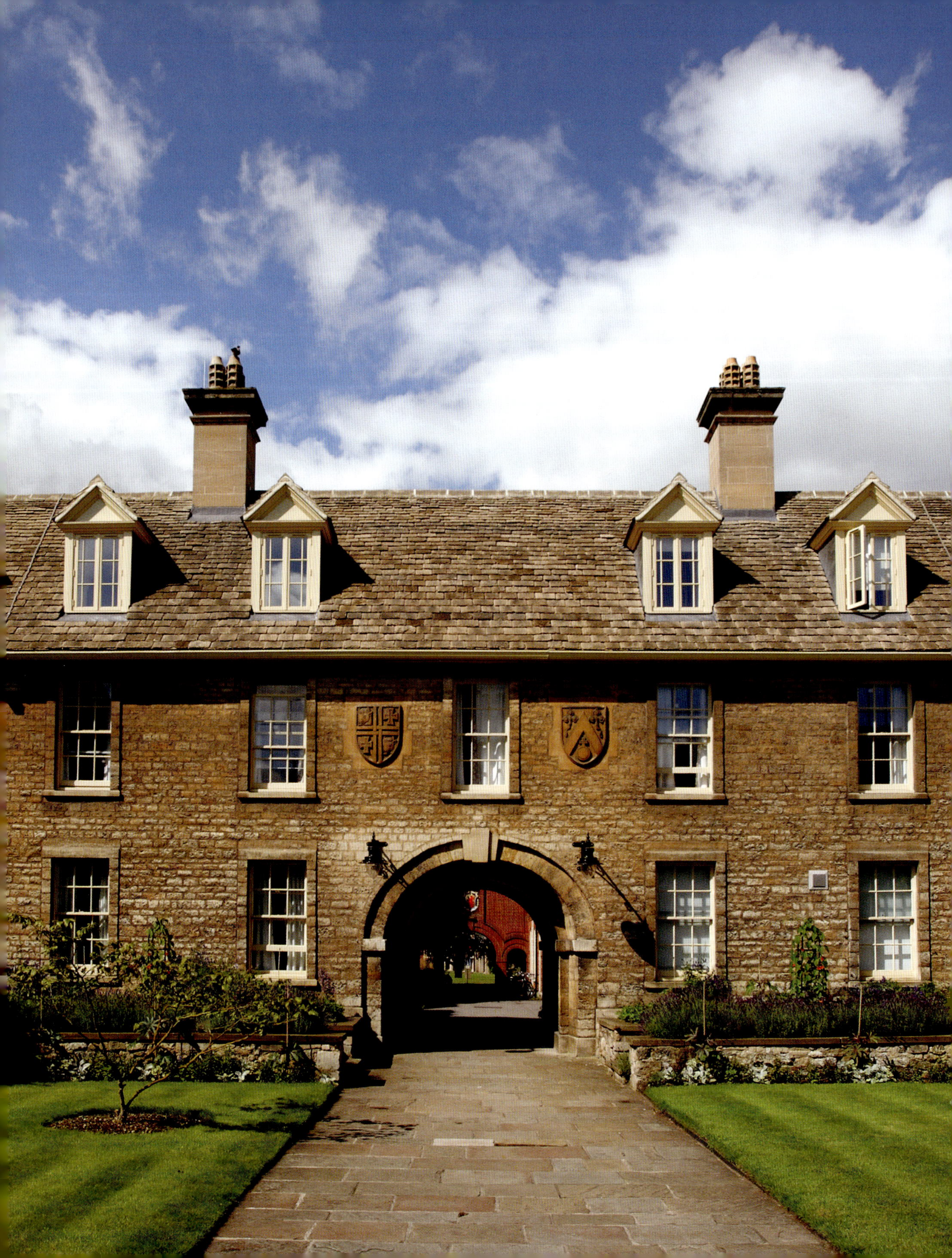

'a rare and valuable thing'

Baroness Royall of Blaisdon, PC
Principal of Somerville

What *is* a college, really? For the individuals who are also part of Somerville, it is perhaps above all a place of memories: the remembrance of intellectual habits formed and of friendships made. Rooms, weather, food and gardens are some of the frames in which those memories exist. And while every generation of Somervillians lives in a new way, their preoccupations, their interests and the spaces in which they find themselves are not so very different from those that have gone before.

Somerville was founded in 1879, 'for the reception of women desirous of availing themselves of the special advantages which Oxford offers for Higher Education' (as a Council meeting of 1878 phrased it). It was, from the start, a place determined to break down barriers, a place in which it was agreed that there would be 'no distinction between students'. In its early years, the question of distinction was about religion: Somerville was set up without any religious denomination, and deliberately so. As time went by, the college became a pioneer in setting aside other forms of distinction too, welcoming students in every academic discipline, from every background, and from across the world. From this rich mixture has come an extraordinary roll-call of the distinguished and brilliant: philosophers, mathematicians, scientists and writers, including the only British woman (to date) to win a Nobel Prize for science and the UK's first woman Prime Minister.

The college is, and has always been, a deliberately international institution. From its early years it welcomed women from outside the UK, and it has continued to be at the forefront of offering practical support as well as a warm welcome to international students (and particularly to international graduate students). It has an especially deep connection with India. Cornelia Sorabji [24], who came to Somerville in 1889, was the first Indian woman to study at a British university and also the first woman to study Law at Oxford. Indira Gandhi (Nehru) [109] studied here in 1937

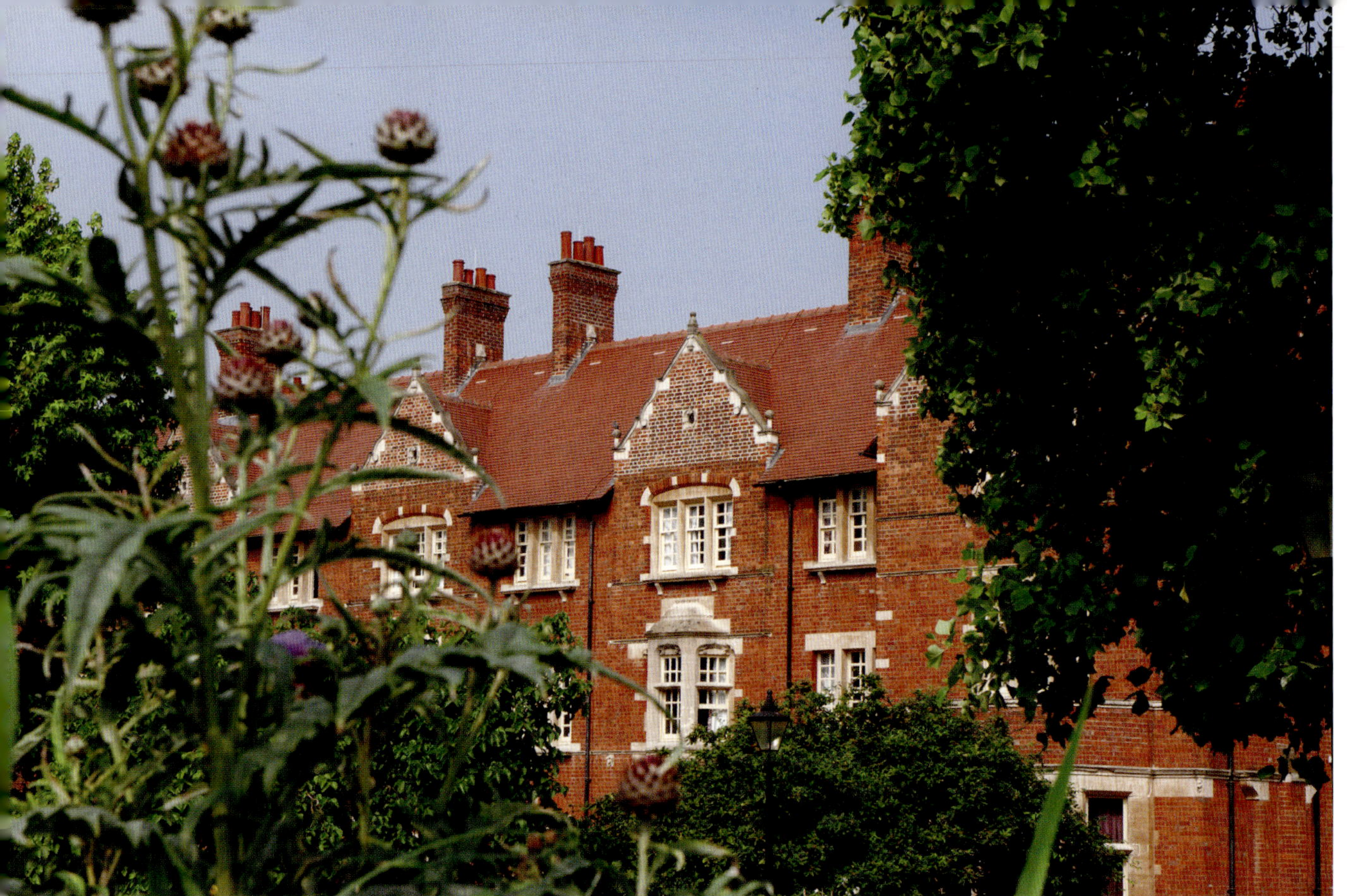

and went on to become India's first woman Prime Minister. Fitting, then, that the college has now become the home of the Oxford India Centre for Sustainable Development and of a programme of scholarships for talented Indian students.

Somerville has always included the excluded. It was set up to do so, and it is still known as one of Oxford's most liberal, diverse and outward-looking colleges. Partly this comes from an early engagement with the world beyond Britain. Including the excluded has taken many forms over the course of Somerville's history, from allowing women to study at Oxford, to offering a home to Jewish refugees in the 1930s and 1940s, to helping to make Oxford less white, less English and less middle class: Somerville has been, and must be, a continuing experiment in radical change.

How do we approach the history of such a place? Fortunately the job of providing a detailed written account has already been done for us, and done admirably. The very first history of the college, by Muriel St Clare Byrne and Catherine Hope Mansfield, chronicled the early part of Somerville's life, up to 1921 (it was in the preface to this that Gilbert Murray wrote: 'A college like Somerville is a rare and valuable thing'). Pauline Adams, in *Somerville for Women*, has set out the college's history from the time of its foundation to the decision in 1992 to admit male fellows and students. Adams undersells her history of Somerville when she calls it 'essentially a domestic history'. In fact, *Somerville for Women* covers every aspect of Somerville's story, and sets it carefully into the wider context of the early debates surrounding women's education in Oxford (and elsewhere). It also understands the financial origins and maintenance of the college and University in a way that would repay study for those dealing with the current crises in higher education. A brief note of the college's history is included at the end of this introduction, but if you have not already done so, I would urge you to read Adams. In addition to *Somerville for Women*, there has been *Breaking New Ground* by Anne Manuel, looking at how the buildings of Somerville came into being, and bringing us up to 2013. And it is no coincidence that Adams and Manuel are the college's former and current Librarians respectively. For Somerville, perhaps even more than for other colleges in Oxford, the library is the guardian of the college's history and purpose, and it is also therefore the home of many of the objects included in these pages.

Faced with the happy task of thinking about how to commemorate the 140th anniversary of Somerville's foundation, and with such sound historical work already in place, we have allowed ourselves to float free of a traditional approach. Here we offer something that we hope will appeal to those (Somervillians and others) who might instead enjoy a book to 'dip into', a book that shows what a wonderful and powerful combination of things goes to make up Somerville's identity. In large part it simply illustrates what others have already described in black and white, and it shares with its predecessor volumes the urge to explain what a college is, what draws people to it, and what they most remember about it.

Why have we chosen to commemorate our 140th anniversary in particular? 2019 falls between three other major anniversaries, anniversaries of events that shaped Somerville and also grew out of its history, and it therefore seemed right to us to celebrate Somerville's history at this time. The end of the First World War prompted the world to reflect on the catastrophe of loss, and one of the most famous Somervillians, Vera Brittain, was at the forefront of that reflection when she wrote *Testament of Youth*. The Representation of the People Act in 1918 gave the first votes to women, something for which many Somervillians had fought and fought hard. And in 1920 Oxford University awarded the first degrees to women. Now Somerville really could give women all 'the advantages which Oxford offers for Higher Education'.

In choosing to put together a history of Somerville in 140 objects we have of course taken our inspiration from Neil MacGregor's wonderful 2012 work, *A History of the World in 100 Objects*. It was a book (and a radio series) that brought a particular way of doing history vividly into all of our imaginations. Not that a history of a college can be compared to a history of the world, of course. To its members, though, Somerville is a kind of world, and those who have studied and lived here will surely remember the 'bubble' of full term (especially in the days before mobile phones and social media), when it wasn't unusual to go through eight weeks without really knowing or caring much what was going on outside the round of tutorials, lectures and labs that gave shape to the day.

The objects here have been chosen for many reasons: for their historical importance (to Somerville and to the history of education more broadly, especially the education of women); for their rarity and their beauty; for the everyday memories of living here that they evoke. To choose is also, of course, to exclude. When the project began there was, briefly, a concern that it would be hard to find 140 objects. Very soon we realised we had the opposite problem. By the standards of many institutions Somerville is not large, nor does it have great age. However, perhaps because it was such an unusual institution at the time when it was founded, it seems to have inspired an especially strong degree of loyalty and affection in its members and, along with that, an equally fervent collecting spirit. The early members of Somerville were aware of themselves as pioneers, and they knew that it was important to keep things that would attest to the college's mission and its first years. Later they also began to give things that they valued to Somerville. This awareness of identity, of history, of specialness, wasn't in any way grand or pompous. The decision to change the college colours (abandoning the original choice because it was 'so trying to many complexions') gets a place in the records, just as much as the struggle for women's suffrage or for women to be granted degrees.

Many of the objects here have been chosen because they are those that Somervillians will remember seeing as they went about their everyday lives here: walking past the clock in Darbishire or seeing the portraits as they queued up the stairs to Hall. There are also those that have been chosen here precisely because they won't have been seen before. Then there is the vexed question of what counts as an 'object'. Something you can pick up or hold (a book; a teapot) is easy to categorise. But what about a building? Or a view? We have taken as our definition that each object here should, however loosely, be a part of Somerville, a physical thing built into or held within the college (or in one case, visible from it). That is, of course, to exclude many things outside the environs of the college which also have great significance for Somerville's intellectual and social history (the door through which women readers were permitted to enter the Bodleian, for example, or the room where the decision was finally made to award degrees to women). Most of all, we have tried to choose those things that say 'Somerville' to Somervillians, throwing in a few curiosities for good measure.

To make our selection we first simply walked around the college, seeing what caught our eye. In some cases the choice came from seeing anew

'it seems to have inspired an especially strong degree of loyalty and affection in its members'

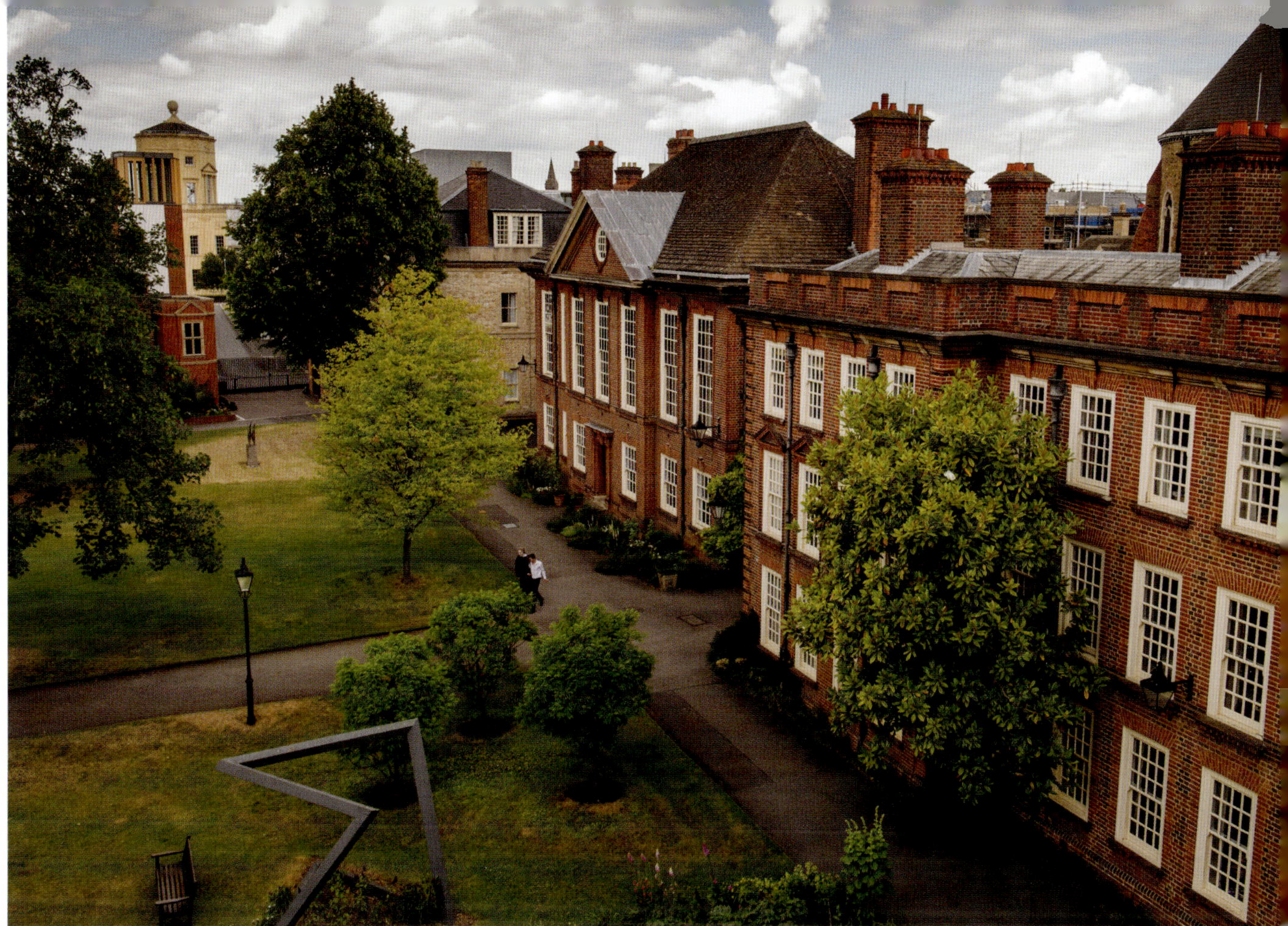

the things that are so much part of our picture of Somerville that we long ago stopped noticing them (the richly coloured floor tiles in House; the inscription over the entrance to the chapel). Then we talked to those in Somerville about what they remembered. And sometimes, faced with an embarrassment of riches, we frankly cheated, putting more than one object under a heading because we wanted to show off as many as possible of these intriguing things.

Finally, we took the decision to order our list of objects chronologically, and to do so by grouping them in the timeframes of the college's 12 Principals. Does the figurehead chosen by an institution reflect what the place is, or does she set the tone? The answer isn't always clear, and of course, both can be true at the same time. If you try to consider Somerville in terms of its history, you find that its Principals are definitive: they reflect the pressing issues of the day (inside and outside the college's walls) and they can also be seen shaping the agenda. This is our 140th year, so it seemed only right to let readers meet, at the beginning of each part, the women who have guided and sustained Somerville for those 140 years. The portraits of our Principals therefore introduce each part, with the exception of my own, which has yet to be arranged.

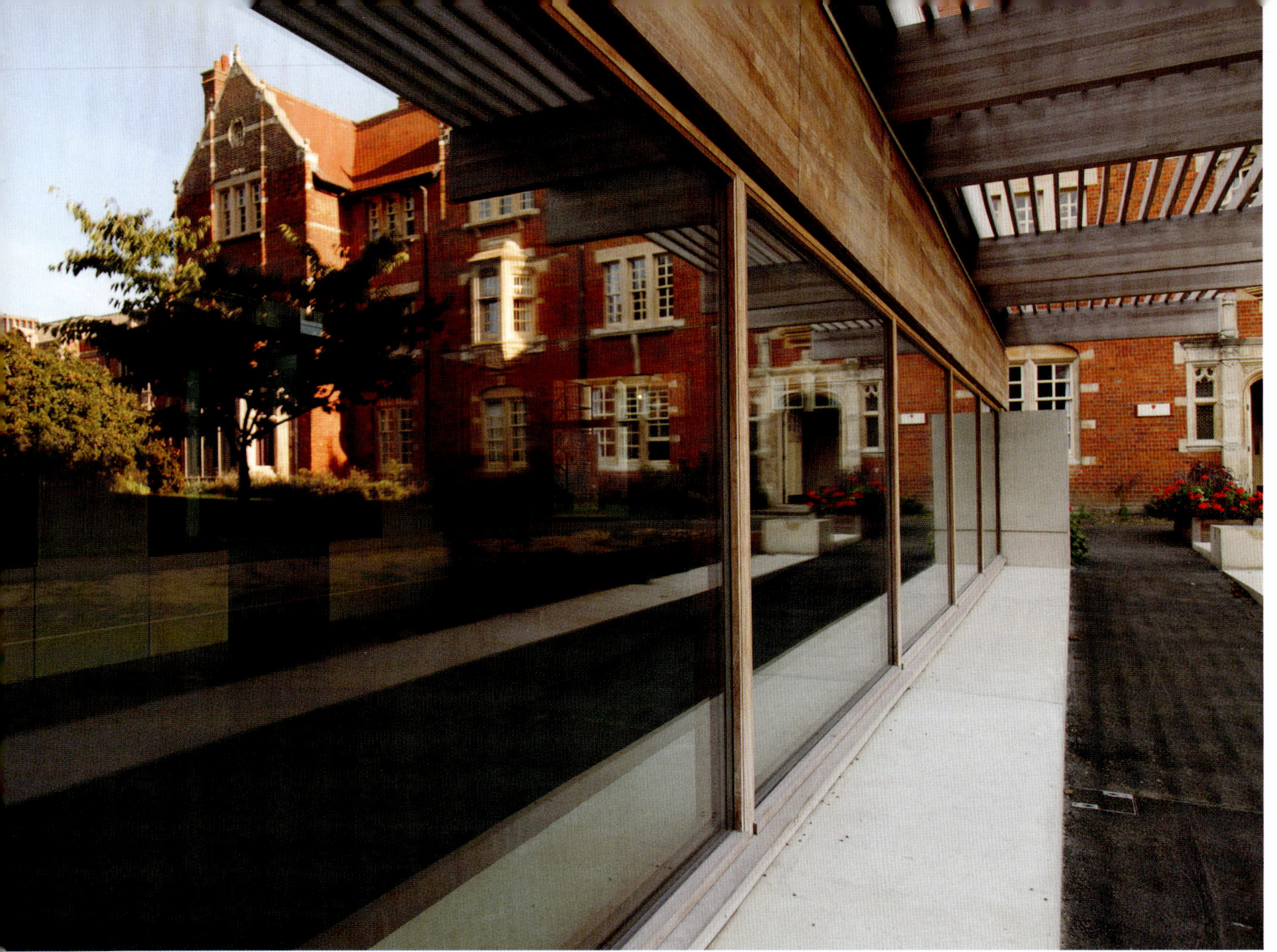

What is to an extent missing from this collection of objects, except obliquely, is the thing that is the whole point of Somerville: the life of the mind, the academic work, the scholarship, teaching and research that make it such an extraordinary and exciting place. These are the things that draw people to become members of the college in the first place. Of course, there are flashes of it: editions of books from the many Somervillians who became writers; the desks in the library that were used by so many students and still are. Many of the objects here are part of the frame in which the academic picture exists.

It is in the nature of Oxford's intellectual life that you can't understand it just by reading about it. As a student here you find yourself quickly working at a level you never would have thought possible while you were at school. As a tutor and researcher here you are, by the standards of most people, academically and intellectually stratospheric. So a college's fabric, the gifts it is given, the curiosities it produces: all these things can only point to that level of mental activity. We can show you Dorothy Hodgkin's Nobel Prize Medal [104], but we can hardly explain the protein crystallography work with which she won it. We can read Cocteau's note to Enid Starkie [100],

'One of the features of life in Somerville is how comfortably and successfully the present sits alongside the past'

but we can't convey anything more than a hint of the depth of knowledge she had about French literature.

As any Somervillian will tell you, though, the things around and about you in college become woven into your intellectual experience of an Oxford education: the view from the window of your room as you struggle with the most difficult question on your problem sheet; the welcome sight of the tables and chairs in Hall when you've had a day of work and want to talk to your friends about something completely different; the lanterns reflecting the trees and the buildings as you head for your tutorial on a darkening winter afternoon. The life of the mind is still lived in a body, and the intellectual life of a college depends as much on its buildings, its books, its food, its trees and its bike racks as it does on its tutors and its students.

We have tried, wherever possible, to tell the academic story behind an object. We have also concentrated particularly on objects that have been seen seldom, or not at all. These are, by their nature, things that may be tangential to the everyday life of the college, but what they often reveal is the social networks that went to make that everyday life possible: the surprising connections between Somervillians and other scholars, travellers, writers, artists and scientists. Of course, many of the things included here are parts of the college's history, but almost as many take us to places and people far outside Somerville. Tracing the links back to the college is part of the purpose of this book. Its main task, though, is to offer visual entertainment and nuggets of information.

One of the features of life in Somerville is how comfortably and successfully the present sits alongside the past. The college is, thank goodness, very far from being a museum. To walk around Somerville – past a sculpture, under a tree planted to commemorate somebody's life, and then perhaps to the nearest coffee machine – is to understand that the college is still now what it was at the very beginning: a place to come if we are 'desirous of availing' ourselves 'of the special advantages which Oxford offers for Higher Education'.

It is, too, a lesson in how very many personal stories are contained within this extraordinary place. Because the history of Somerville is really the history of Somervillians: what they take out to the world, and what they do there, and how all of this is shaped by the time they have spent in the college living, thinking and, not least, forming friendships that last a lifetime. The objects here are often the result of the brilliant and groundbreaking things that Somervillians have done, and point outwards as well as inwards. We know that this is how it will be for another 140 years, and then another, and then another. As the college motto has it (a little cryptically, but then what would life be without an intellectual challenge?), Somerville will be here, people and objects, *donec rursus impleat orbem* ('until the orb is filled again').

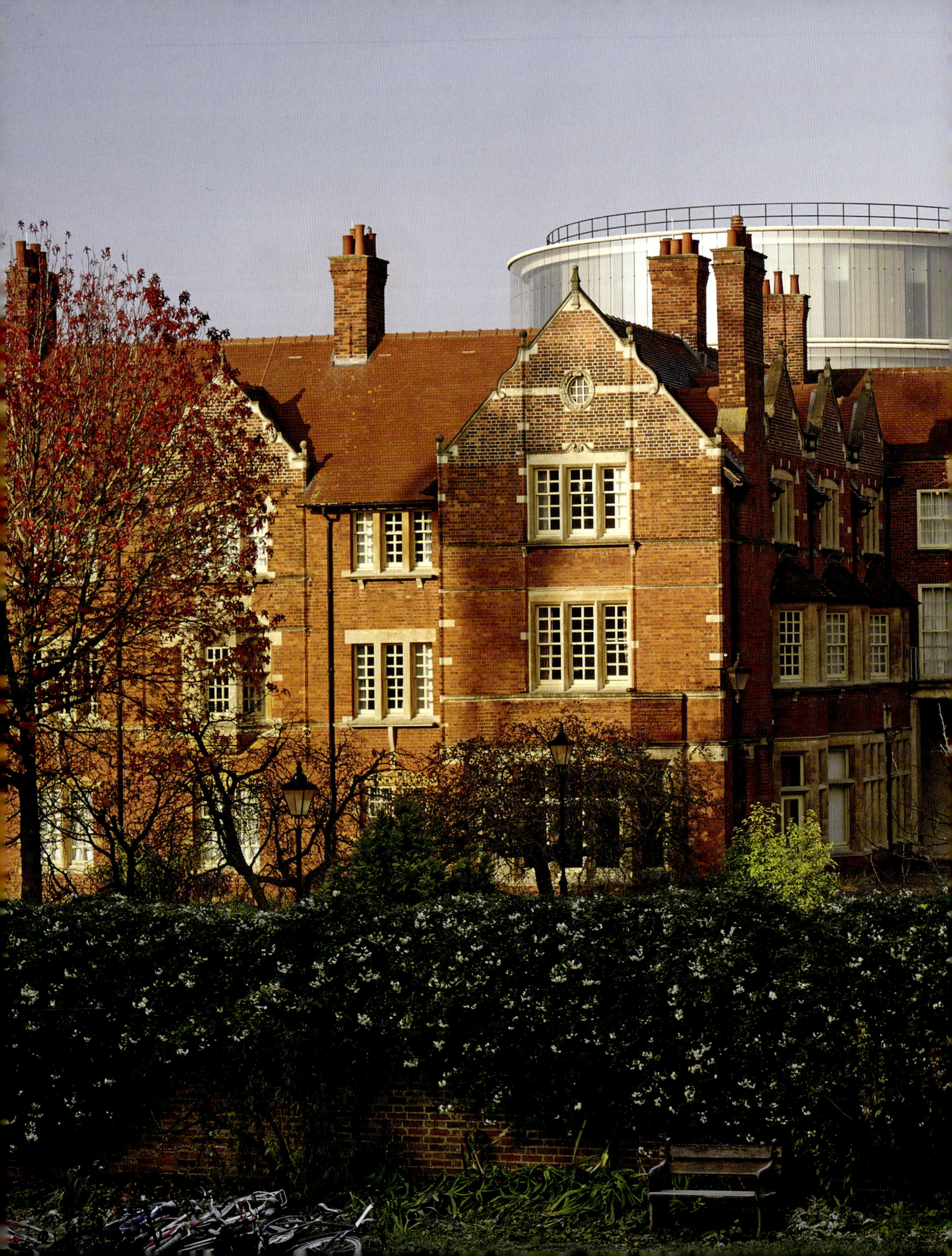

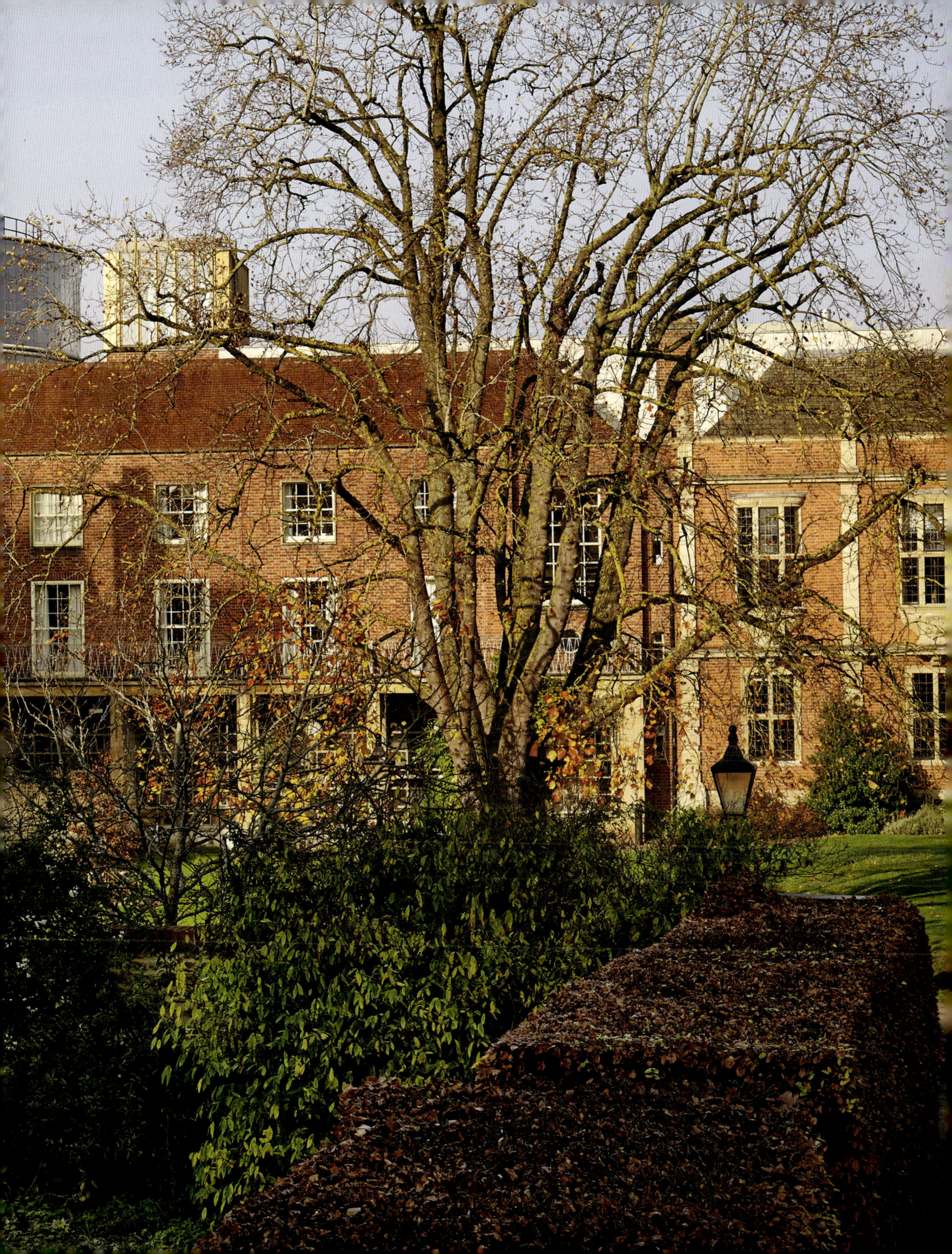

A brief history of Somerville

Somerville was founded in 1879 as Somerville Hall in the north of the city of Oxford, as part of a determined movement to gain university education for women. It began with 12 students: a place where women could live while they followed the courses of instruction offered in Oxford by the Association for Promoting the Higher Education of Women (AEW). Somerville Hall was named in honour of Mary Somerville (1780–1872), the Scottish scientist and mathematician. In 1894 Somerville took the decision to call itself 'Somerville College', in recognition of the fact that it wanted to be known as more than a hall of residence. For the duration of the First World War Somerville's buildings were requisitioned as a military hospital. The students and tutors of Somerville moved for that period to St Mary Hall, part of Oriel College.

In 1920 the University of Oxford granted women full membership of the University and women at Somerville (or 'Somervillians', as the members of the college are known both during and after their studies) were finally awarded degrees for which they had worked. During the Second World War a smaller part of Somerville was once again requisitioned as hospital accommodation (it became known as the 'Isle of Man'). During the 1950s, 1960s and 1970s Somerville increased its numbers of students (expanding to admit many more graduates) and fellows, and continued to grow in its reputation as an academic powerhouse.

Somerville remained a college for women only until 1993, when the first male fellows (tutors and researchers) were admitted. The first male students arrived in 1994. Somerville has been honoured to be the college of many brilliant individuals, among them the first woman to become Prime Minister of India, the first scientist and first woman to become Prime Minister of the UK and the only British woman thus far to win a Nobel Prize for science.

Note on the text

Objects are here ordered by the date at which they came to Somerville. This creates some oddities (an Egyptian mummy mask listed within a few pages of the First World War, for example, or Degas appearing next to Cocteau). Occasionally objects are grouped where they seem to have most relevance, even if their date of acquisition or appearance means that they should appear elsewhere. It is usual in Somerville's publications to include the matriculation year and subject of study when a Somervillian is mentioned by name. To avoid confusion for non-Somervillian readers we have not observed that convention here, but we have tried to ensure that the year in which each Somervillian came up, together with her/his subject, are recorded when the name is first introduced. Where women are referred to by their married name, their maiden name is normally given in brackets.

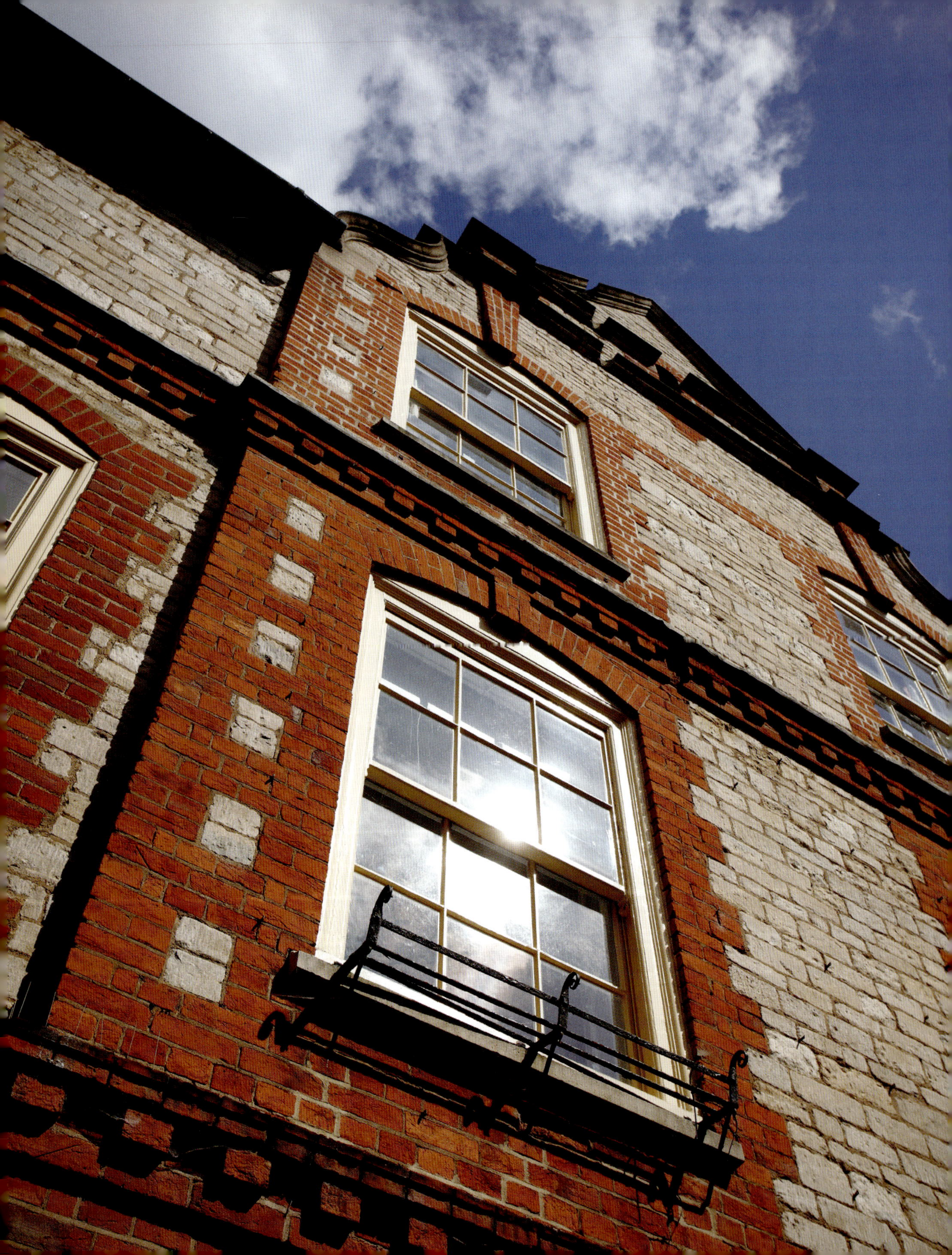

1780–1872
'in memory of the late Mary Somerville'

I t may seem odd to start with somebody who died before Somerville was founded. However, the suggestion recorded in an 1879 Council minute that the hall 'be called Somerville Hall, in memory of the late Mary Somerville' was definitive. In part this was because Somerville herself was extraordinary: a self-taught expert in, and writer on, science and mathematics, she was called 'the queen of science' in one obituary. It was also because, by choosing her, Somerville's founders were making a very particular statement about the sort of institution Somerville was to be. Mary Somerville was a devout Christian but she was known for her scientific work, not for her religious good works. The choice of name was therefore made in deliberate contrast to Lady Margaret Hall (named for Lady Margaret Beaufort [1443–1509], whose first act of munificence to a university was to found a Professorship of Divinity at Cambridge in 1502).

Mary Somerville

So who was Mary Somerville? Born in Jedburgh, Scotland, into
a comfortable family, Mary Fairfax had little by way of formal
education. She was allowed to follow her own interests in
arithmetic and algebra a little way, but her parents discouraged
her from studying (even taking away her candles). In her *Personal
Recollections* (1874), Somerville remembered the aunt who had
discovered her reading Shakespeare. The young Mary was soon
packed off to the village school so that she could be taught
sewing instead. 'I was annoyed', she recalled, 'that my turn for
reading was so much disapproved of, and thought it unjust
that women should have been given a desire for knowledge if
it were wrong to acquire it'. Mary Fairfax married in 1804 but
found herself a widow three years later, with sufficient means
and time to pursue her love of mathematical and scientific work.
She married again in 1812 (she became, eventually, the mother
of six children), having found a husband, William Somerville
(1771–1860), who was supportive of her interests.

From 1825 she began to carry out experiments, working on
magnetism. Her paper 'On the Magnetizing Power of the More
Refrangible Solar Rays' was presented to the Royal Society a
year later, and was only the second by a woman to be read in
the Royal Society. Her first book, *The Mechanism of the Heavens*,
brought the advanced methods of calculus developed by
French mathematician Pierre-Simon Laplace (1749–1827) to a
wider British audience, while her later work *The Connexion of
the Physical Sciences* examined physical phenomena. By this
stage Somerville was widely recognised and distinguished by
her fellow scientists, having been elected an honorary member
of many learned societies, including the Royal Irish Academy,
the Royal Astronomical Society and La Société de Physique et
d'Histoire Naturelle de Genève. She went on to publish two
more books, *Physical Geography* and *Molecular and Microscopic
Science*. She would read mathematical and scientific works 'for
four or five hours in the morning' of every day and continued
revising her unpublished book on the differential calculus into
her 91st year.

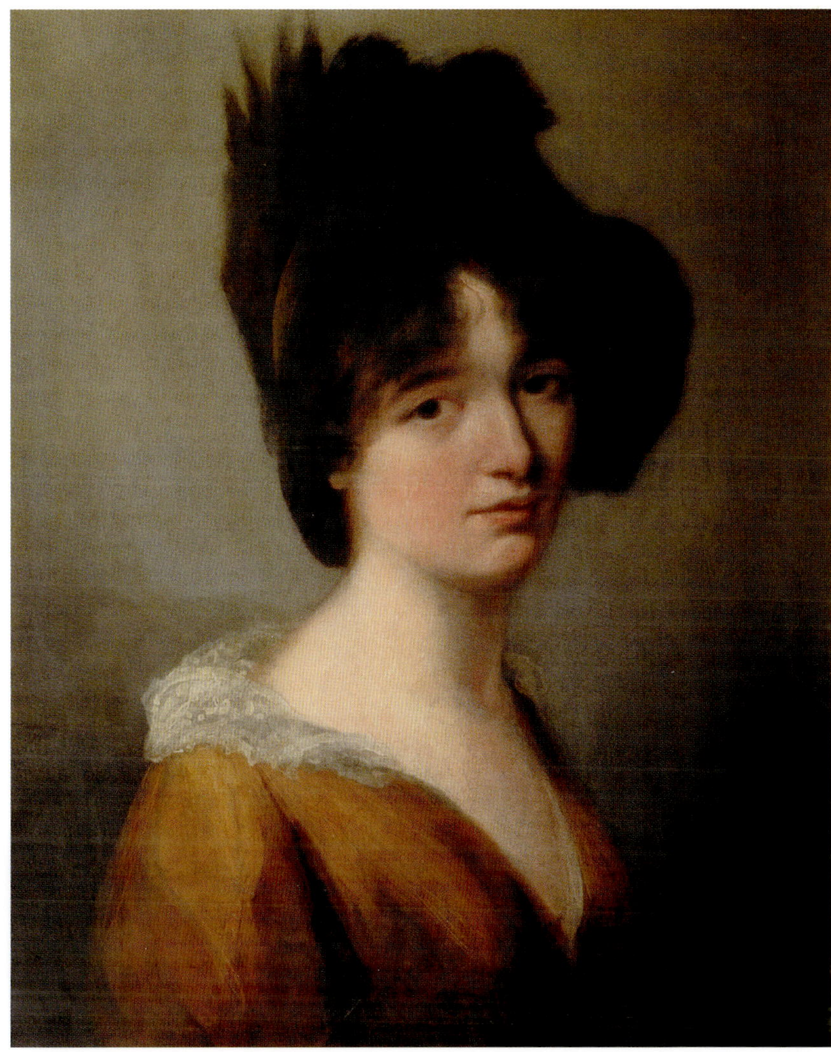

1

Portrait of Mary Somerville

This is the portrait of Mary Somerville that was chosen to hang in the college's new Maitland Hall [52] when it opened in 1913. Indeed, the panelling for the hall was specifically designed to fit around the painting, which was given to the college by an anonymous donor in 1911. Somerville holds a number of portraits of the woman after whom it is named, including a self-portrait, but it seemed right that we should begin our selection with the image to which Somervillians chose to give pride of place. The portrait was painted by John Jackson (1778–1831), who began his working life as an apprentice tailor (his father opposed his artistic ambitions) but then established himself as a painter of miniature portraits. His talent soon earned him powerful patrons, including Frederick Howard, 5th Earl of Carlisle (1748–1825), and by 1807 his fame as a portraitist had been established. In 1819 Jackson travelled through Europe with his friend the sculptor Francis Chantrey (1781–1841) [6]. He went on to paint a number of important figures, including the Duke of Wellington (1769–1852). Although we do not know the date of his portrait of Mary Somerville, the fashions and the age of the sitter suggest that it almost certainly comes from the time before Jackson fully established his reputation, and probably when his subject was still Mary Fairfax.

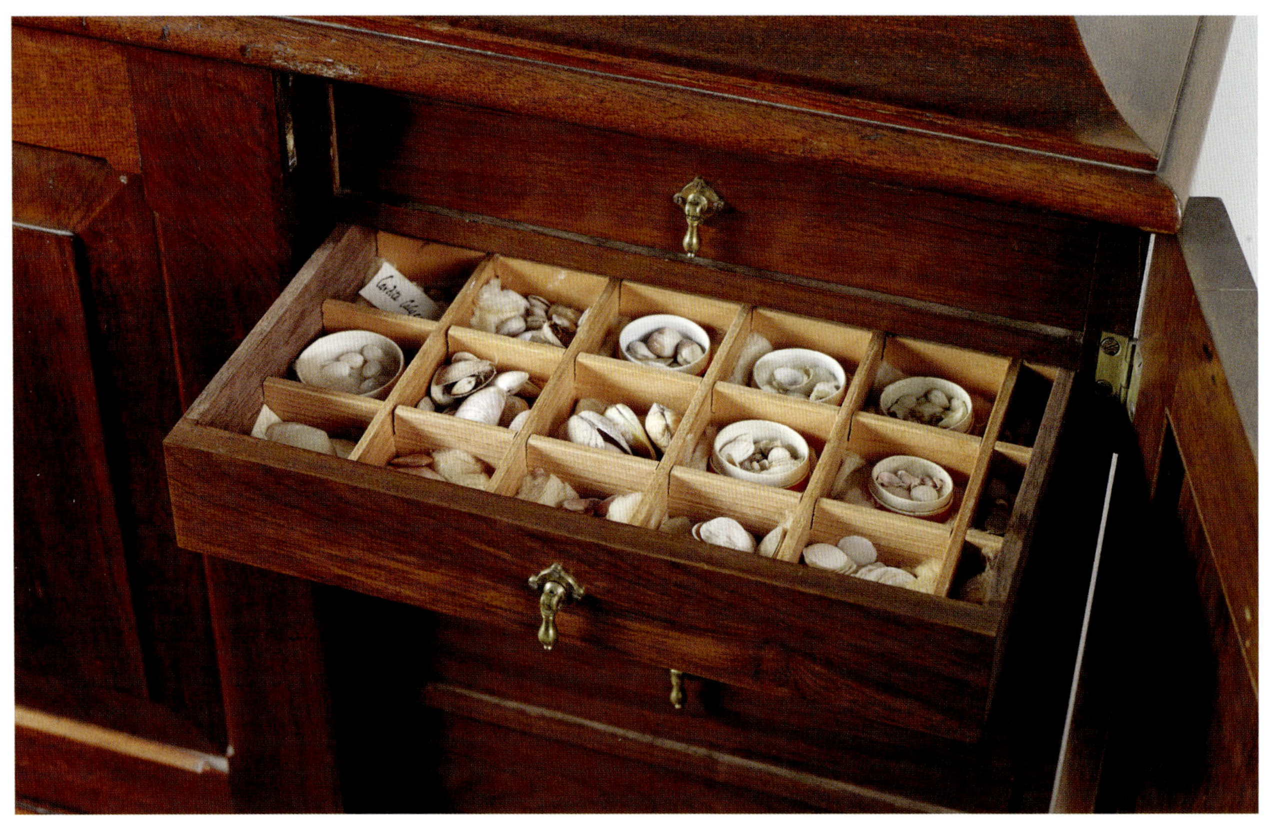

2

Shell cabinet

Collecting shells from the beach might feel like a rather everyday thing for a child to do, and so it is. For the young Mary Somerville it was the beginning of her study of the science and mathematics of the natural world. She also collected examples of limestone, which she took, along with her shells, back to what she called her 'repository'. As she grew up she continued to develop her interests in geology, mathematics and astronomy (and learned Latin), as well as maintaining the social life and accomplishments considered appropriate to her class and gender. Somerville's awe of nature, which began during her solitary explorations of the Burntisland beaches, stayed with her throughout her life. Enabled by mathematics to predict the appearance and paths of comets, in La Spezia in 1861 Somerville ventured out in a small rowing boat to see 'the clear starlit heavens with [a] beautiful comet reflected, nay, almost repeated, in the calm glassy water of the gulf'. This cabinet was given by the descendants of Mary Somerville, who remembered being allowed to look at the contents, but never to touch!

3
Mary Somerville
Castle by a Lake

Mary Fairfax studied painting with Alexander Nasmyth (1758–1840), who had opened an 'academy for ladies' in Edinburgh. She recalled that she was not taught to draw but was given a painting to copy: 'Though I spoilt the canvas, I had made some progress by the end of the season'. Nasmyth was principally a painter of landscapes (though he is also famous for his portrait of his friend Robert Burns [1759–96]). He had a particular interest in architecture and engineering, and Somerville claimed that overhearing Nasmyth talking about perspective was what led her to read Euclid's *Elements*. Her own paintings very much recall Nasmyth's romantic, expansive and luminous style. Although she was modest about her painting, others admired it a good deal. Dr Hugh Blair (1718–1800), minister of the High Kirk of Edinburgh, wrote to her in 1796 that he was 'persuaded that your taste and powers of execution in that art are uncommonly great'. 'I was delighted with the letter', Somerville later recalled, 'and not a little vain of the praise'.

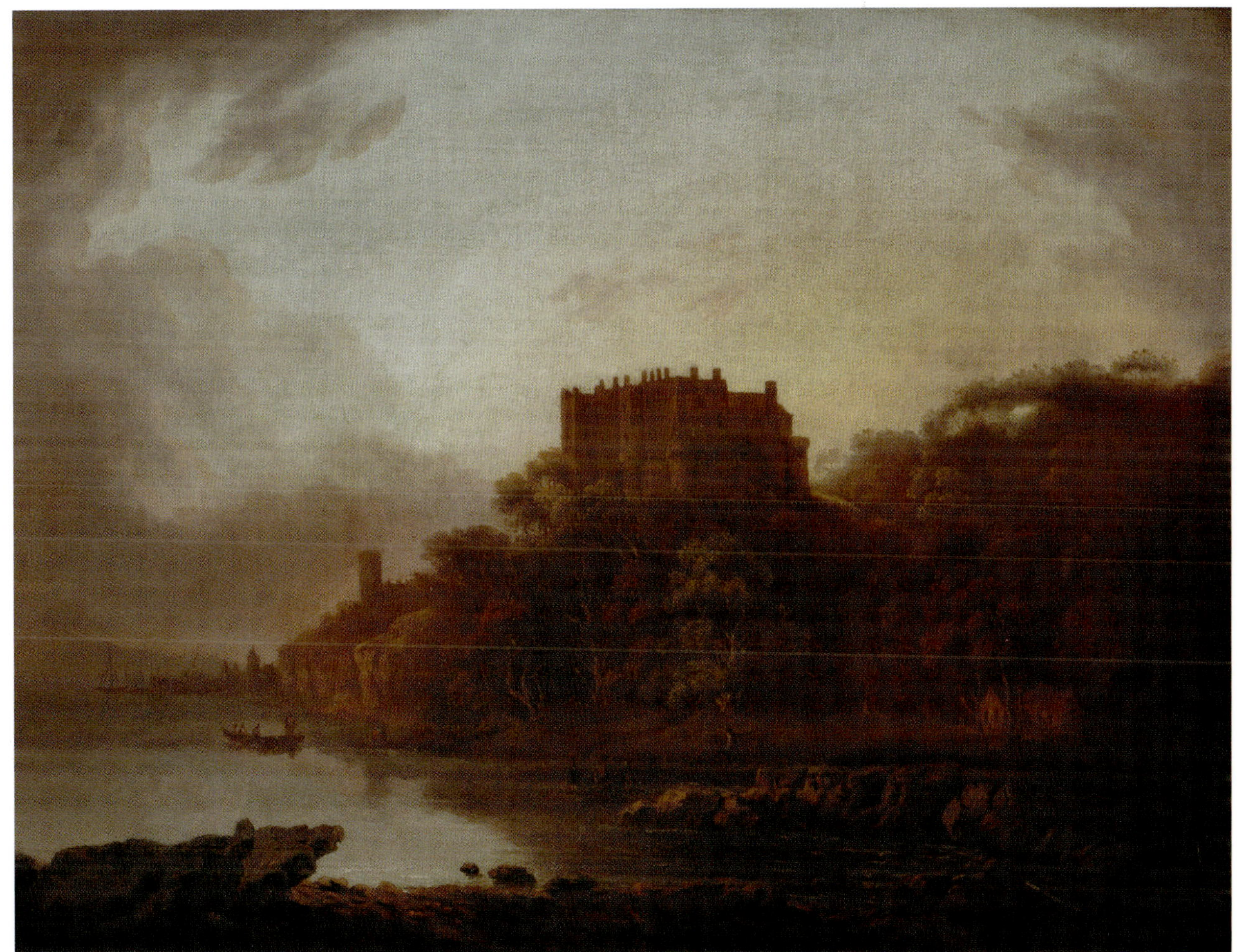

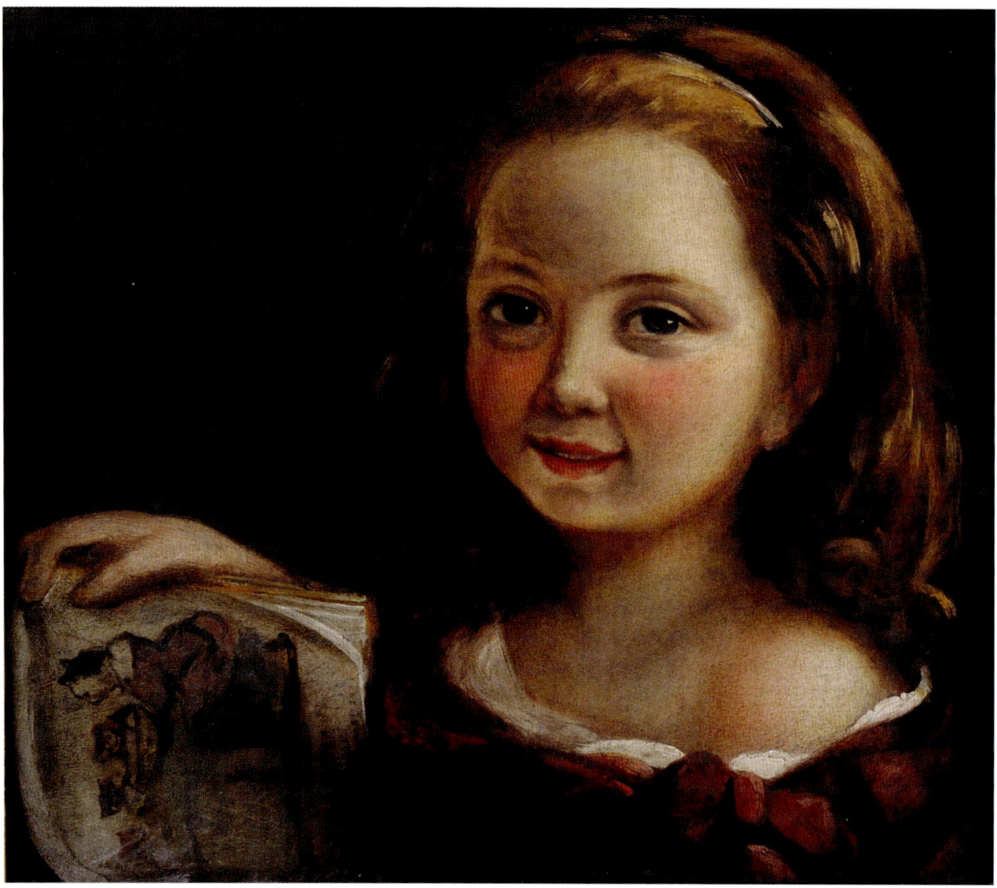

'It was by my advice that she studied mathematics'

4

Portrait of Ada Lovelace

The mathematician Ada Lovelace (1815–52) is renowned for her 1843 paper on the applications of Charles Babbage's (1791–1871) designs for calculating machines, and thus for her contribution to the science of computing. Lovelace was the daughter of the poet Lord Byron (1788–1824), though she and her mother were abandoned by him a month after she was born. This portrait of Lovelace as a child was painted by Alfred d'Orsay (1801–52). Lovelace's education in mathematics and science spoke to her natural talents – 'I believe myself to possess a most singular combination of qualities exactly fitted to make me pre-eminently a discoverer of the hidden realities of nature', she later wrote to her mother – although it was also contrived as an antidote to the study of poetry (Lovelace's mother feared that Byron's wildness would come out in his daughter unless her mind was trained in non-poetic disciplines). In 1833 Lovelace met Mary Somerville and they became mathematical correspondents and lifelong friends. Lovelace's early mathematical studies were guided by reading suggested by Somerville, to whom she would write letters when she met with difficulties.

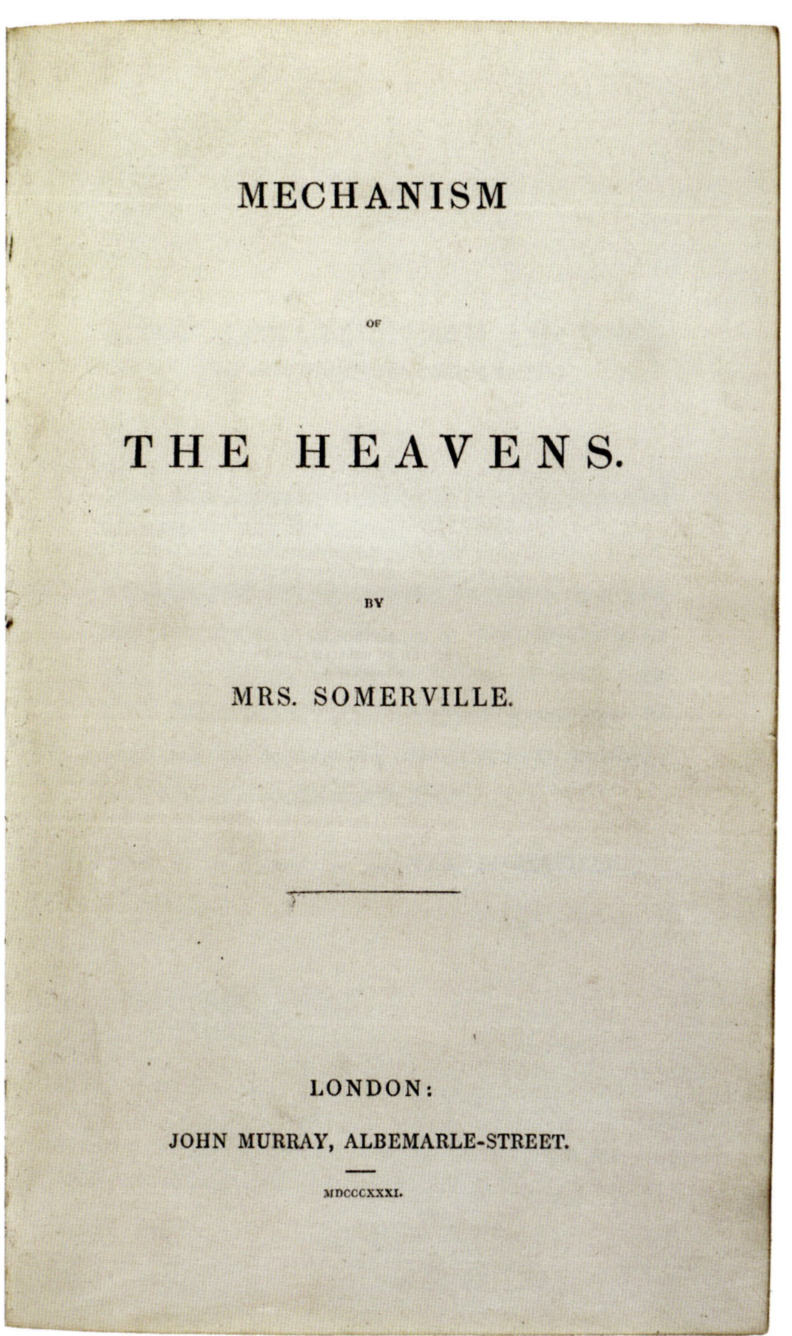

5
Mary Somerville
The Mechanism of the Heavens

Mary Somerville cultivated a strong, vibrant social network through meetings and correspondence with the most notable mathematicians and natural philosophers of nineteenth-century Europe. In 1824 she received a letter from Pierre-Simon Laplace, in which he recognised her deep understanding of analysis (studying relationships through manipulation of mathematical formulae), cementing her reputation as an accomplished mathematician. Subsequently Somerville was commissioned by Henry Brougham (1778–1868) to write a translation and exposition of the mathematical concepts of Laplace so that a broad audience could understand them. *The Mechanism of the Heavens* was the result, although Somerville only agreed to write it on the understanding that the project would be kept secret until she could be sure it was any good. Published in 1831, it was far better than that, going on to become a recommended text on the subject at Cambridge University. 'I felt in my own breast that women were capable of taking a higher place in creation than that assigned to them in my early days', Somerville wrote in later life. And through Somerville herself, and the hall named for her, the cause of this 'higher place' was advanced.

6

Bust of Mary Somerville

This plaster bust of Mary Somerville is a cast of the marble original displayed in the Royal Society. The bust was made by Francis Legatt Chantrey and its cool, classical style recalls earlier marble likenesses similarly displayed. Chantrey was famous for this sort of work, and later Royal Society worthies such as James Watt (1736–1819) were modelled, for the sake of consistency, in the same style. It was one that Ada Lovelace [4], for one, did not like. The marble bust of Mary Somerville had been funded by subscription and cost £200 in total. Chantrey himself probably made up the shortfall between the subscribed amount and the final cost. The story has a coda, which reminds us that while sculptures might have been equal at that time, their subjects were not. Mary Somerville's scientific paper 'On the Magnetizing Power of the More Refrangible Solar Rays' was published in the 1826 *Proceedings of the Royal Society*. Because women could not be fellows of the Royal Society, Somerville was not permitted to read the paper herself. Furthermore, she was not able to access the extensive libraries of the learned societies, even those that had elected her an honorary member. Her husband, Dr William Somerville, thus provided a vital role in her research by using his own membership of these societies to source texts in libraries and by reading her results to the Royal Society.

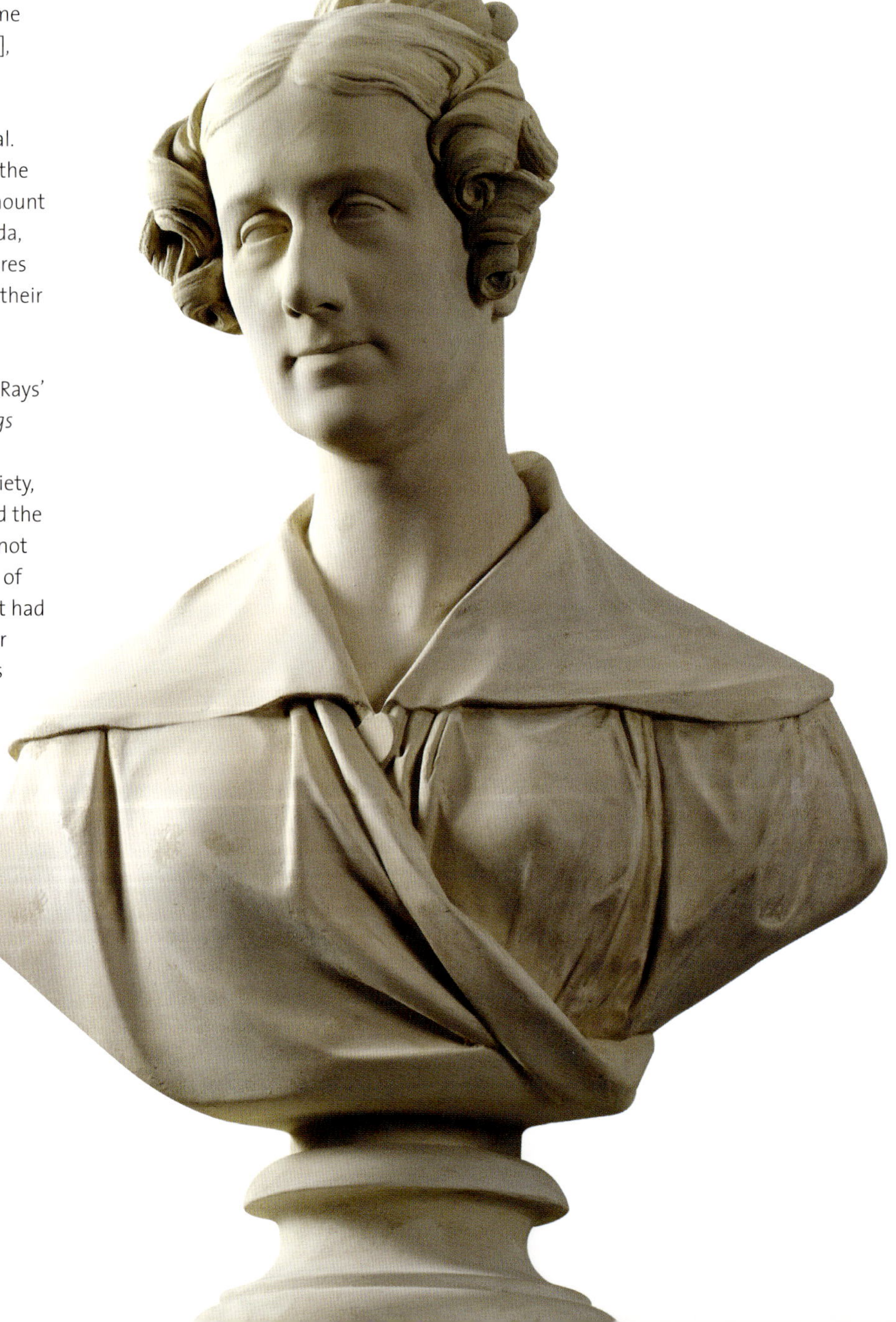

ON

THE ORIGIN OF SPECIES

BY MEANS OF NATURAL SELECTION,

OR THE

PRESERVATION OF FAVOURED RACES IN THE STRUGGLE
FOR LIFE.

By CHARLES DARWIN, M.A.,

FELLOW OF THE ROYAL, GEOLOGICAL, LINNÆAN, ETC., SOCIETIES;
AUTHOR OF 'JOURNAL OF RESEARCHES DURING H. M. S. BEAGLE'S VOYAGE
ROUND THE WORLD.'

LONDON:
JOHN MURRAY, ALBEMARLE STREET.
1859.

The right of Translation is reserved.

7
Somerville's copy of *On the Origin of Species*

In her *On the Connexion of the Physical Sciences* (1834) Mary Somerville gathered and presented the recent advances made in the study of astronomy, geology, botany, chemistry and physics. Building on her first book, *The Mechanism of the Heavens* [5], Somerville used *Connexion* to further encourage British mathematicians to adopt the French methods of analysis, which she claimed would soon 'embrace almost every subject in nature in its formulae'. The work proved a hit, running to ten editions and over 9,000 copies, and one reviewer even had to reach for a new word – 'scientist' – to describe its author (given that 'man of science' was hardly appropriate). The book's publishers, John Murray, only bettered their performance with an 1859 work by Charles Darwin (1809–82), *On the Origin of Species*, of which this is Mary Somerville's copy. Murray himself inscribed this copy 'to Mrs Somerville with John Murray's kind compliments'. Diagrams of orchids from Darwin's later work appear in Somerville's final book, *Molecular and Microscopic Science*, an occurrence that 'delighted & honoured Darwin'. Mary Somerville's scientific writings and papers are owned by Somerville and held by the Bodleian Library.

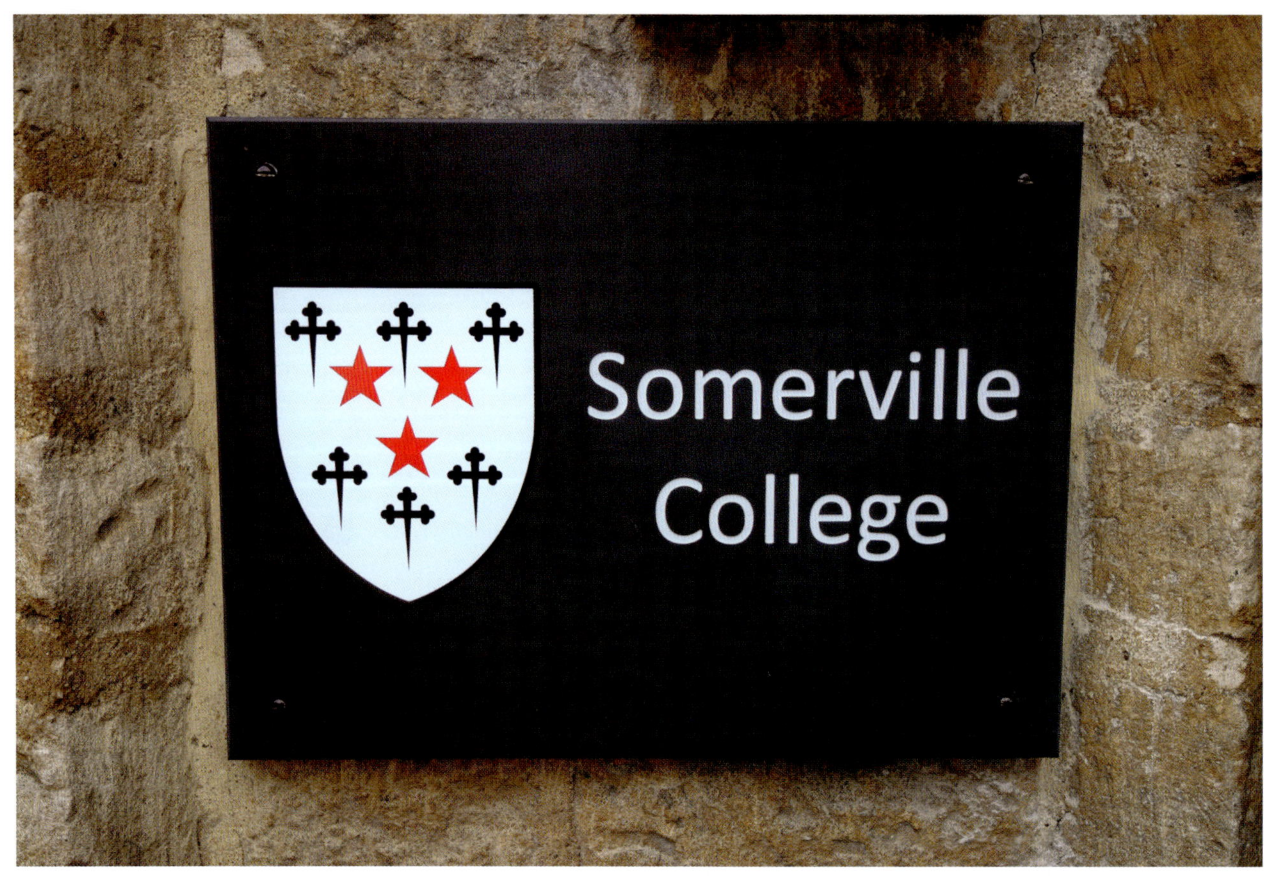

8
Coat of arms

The college's coat of arms and motto come from the family of Mary Somerville's second husband (and cousin), William. The Scottish branch of the Somerville family is said to have descended originally from William de Somerville, a follower of King David I of Scotland (who ruled from 1124 to 1153). The current coat of arms and motto are undoubtedly far more recent than that, though to decipher them you still need to be able to understand both heraldry and Latin. The official description is 'Argent, three mullets in chevron reversed gules between six crosses crosslet fitched sable'. 'Argent' means a light silver (here the background colour). A 'mullet' is a starlike shape with straight-sided rays and 'in chevron reversed' refers to the layout of these shapes. 'Gules' ('throats' in Old French) means a red colour, and the 'sable' (black) crosses are 'crosslet' (with their edges formed into further crosses) and 'fitched' (the vertical bar ends in a point). The original colours of the Somerville family coat of arms were in fact gold and blue, but Somerville Hall soon abandoned these in favour of red and black [21, 134]. The motto – 'Donec rursus impleat orbem' [129] – translates, roughly, as 'until the orb is filled again'. The hand on the crest holds a crescent aloft (and is known by some college members, it must be confessed, as 'hand holding a banana').

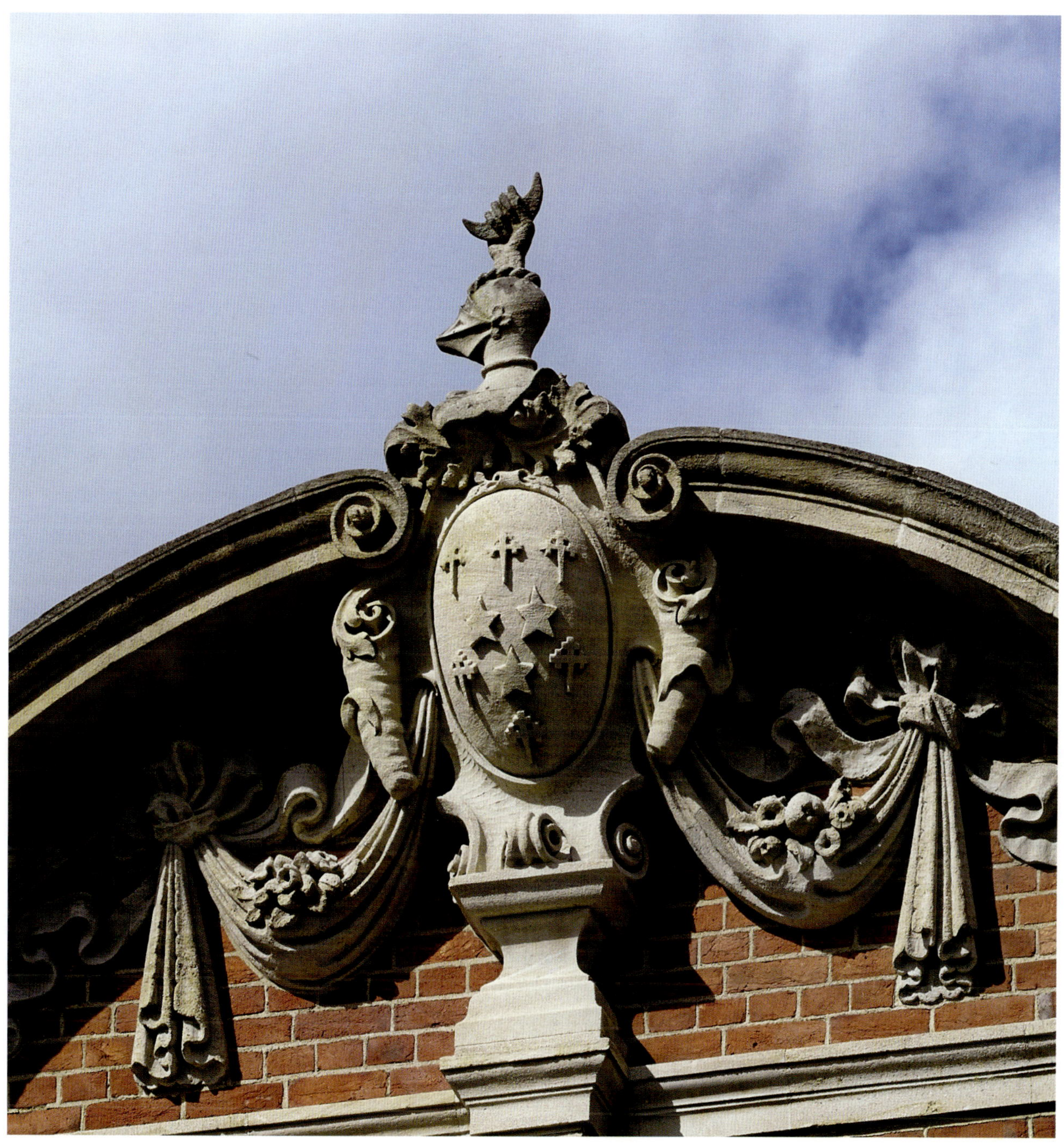

'*Donec rursus impleat orbem*'

Motto of Somerville College

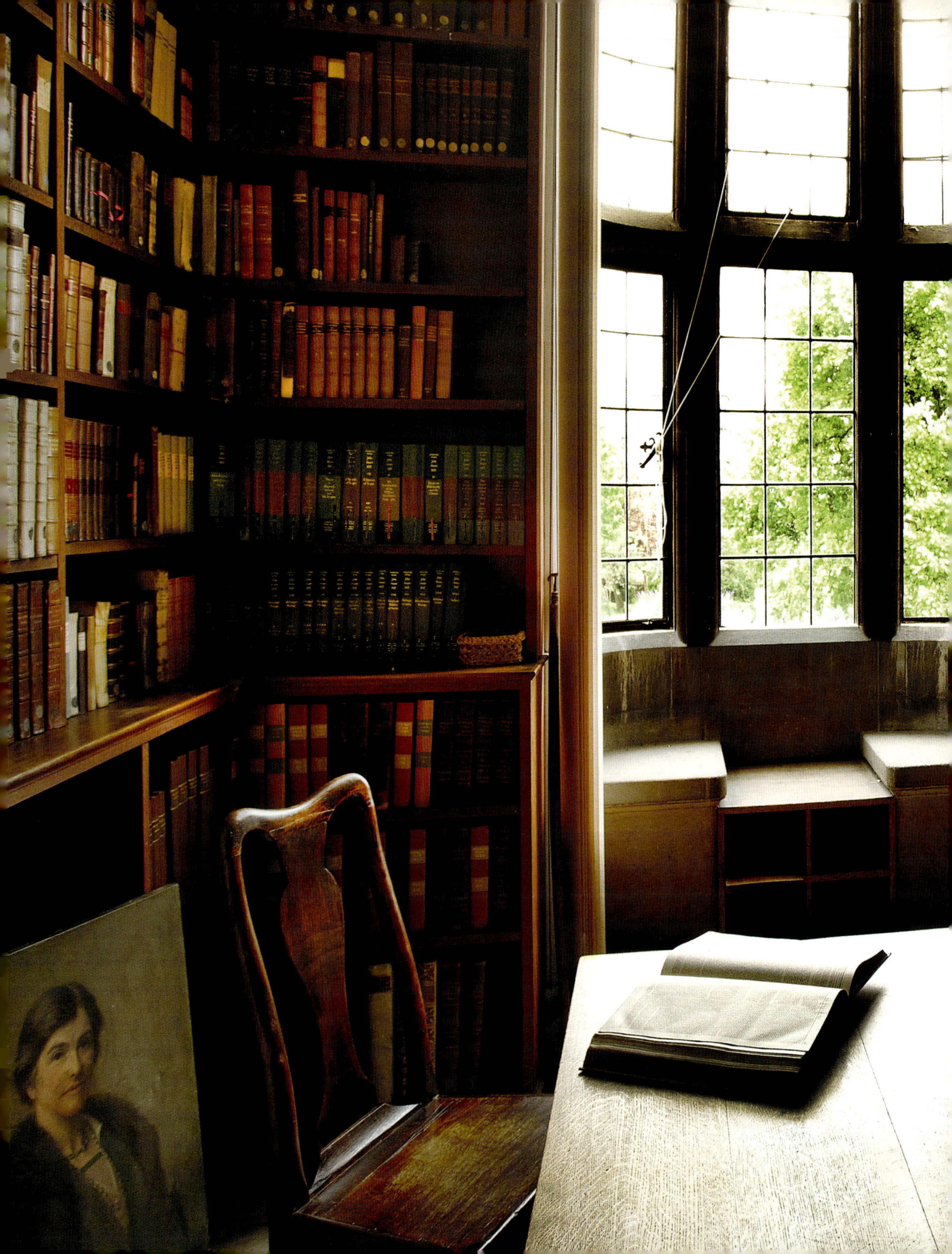

1879 – 1906
'the life of an English family'

Neither of Somerville's first two Principals had any particular training in what Oxford would have recognised as an academic subject. There was very little of that sort of formal education available to women at the time (hence the need for Somerville at all). What they did have, and what Somerville needed more than anything else, was social acceptability. The women of Somerville were part of an extraordinary social experiment, and one that could have been snuffed out at the first hint of impropriety.

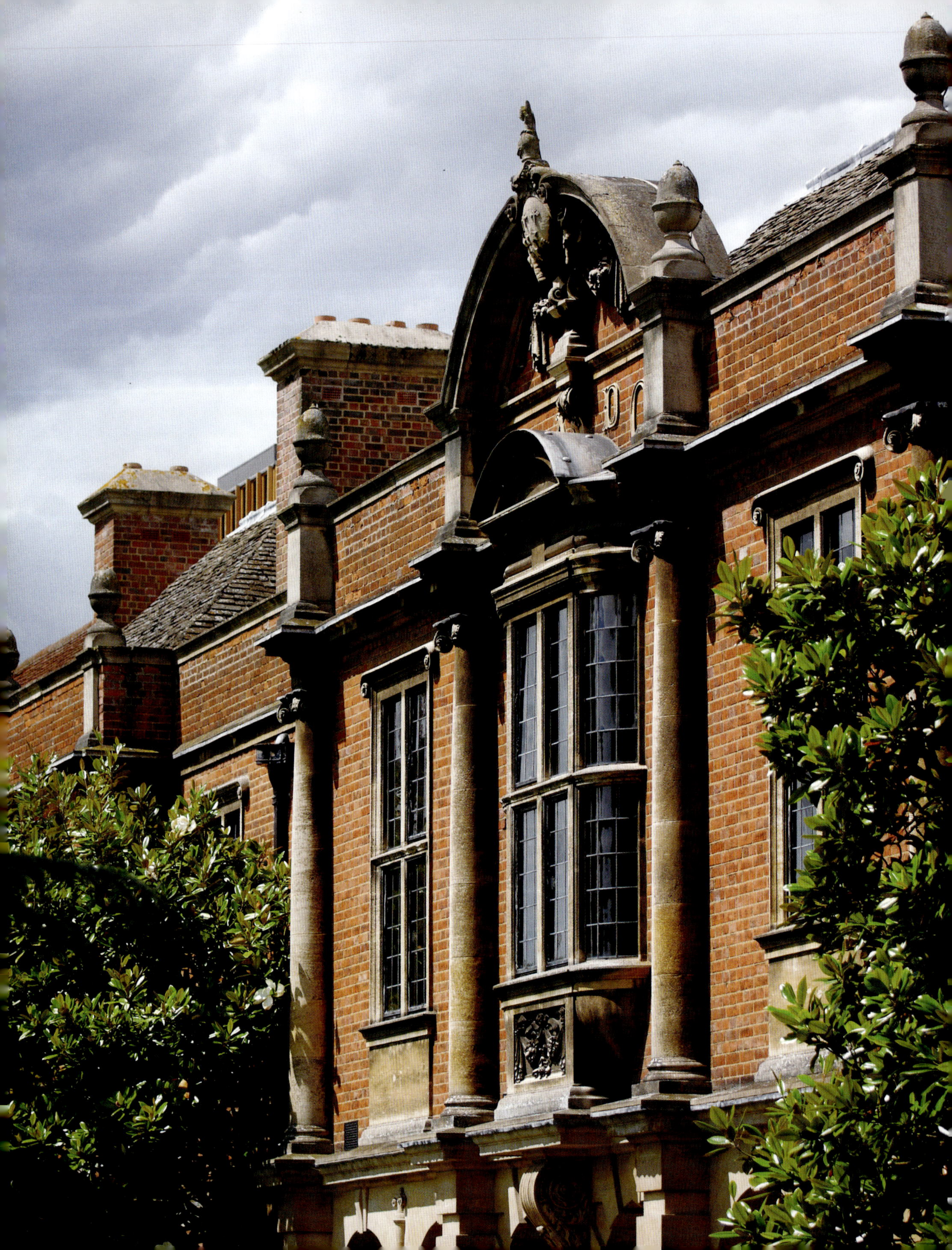

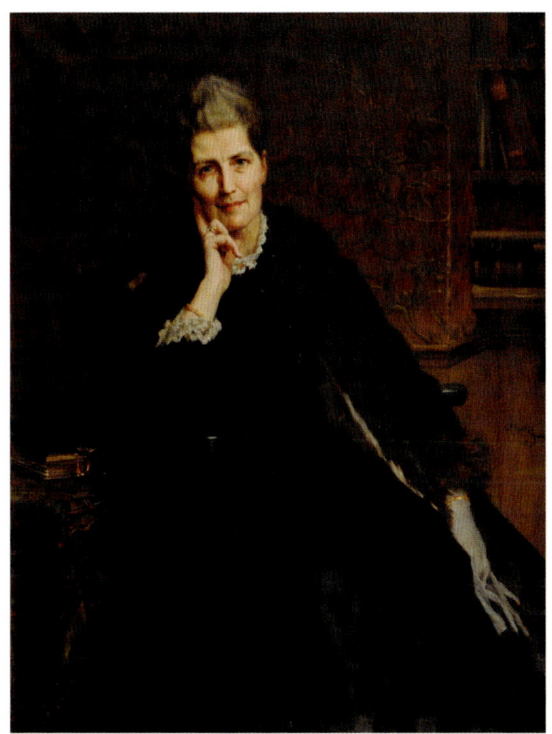

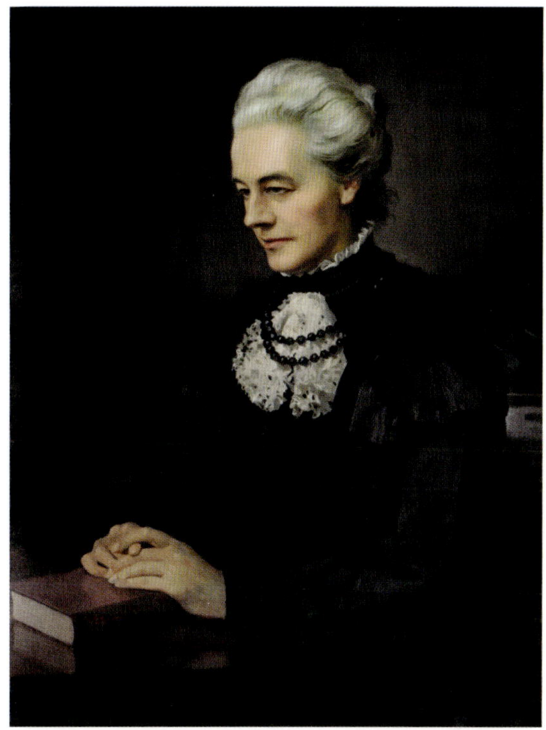

1879–1889
Madeleine Shaw Lefevre

Madeleine Shaw Lefevre (1835–1914) was chosen by the
Somerville Committee for her courteous manners and
her unimpeachable family connections. Under Lefevre,
Somerville existed as a family, and not an enormously large
one by Victorian standards (there were only 12 students
in Somerville's first year, and numbers fluctuated as
students came to and left this new and unusual place). It
also cultivated some powerful and important friends. The
Lefevre family connections brought visitors to Somerville
Hall including William Gladstone (1809–98) and Octavia Hill
(1838–1912), and Madeleine Shaw Lefevre's own considerable
talents brought new friends and supporters, not least John
Ruskin (1819–1900) [14]. She also established the rules of
conduct that made Somerville work (in every sense) in those
early years. Even when numbers grew, Shaw Lefevre insisted
that students should live and eat in small groups, fulfilling
the wish of Somerville's founders that the women who
studied there would live 'the life of an English family'.

1889–1906
Agnes Maitland

Agnes Maitland (1849–1906) came to Somerville Hall as its
second Principal in 1889. Her background was in domestic
science (she had acted as an examiner of teachers trained by
the Northern Union Schools of Cookery) and her published
works included *The Afternoon Tea Book* (1887). Her knowledge
of domestic economy made her the perfect person to take
the reins from Madeleine Shaw Lefevre. Miss Maitland was
also a good deal less shy than her predecessor, and she was
an experienced public speaker. Perhaps the most important
quality she brought to the college was her own ethic of public
service. It was one that was to become strongly characteristic
of Somervillians. Margery Fry said of Maitland that 'from first
to last, education in all its grades appealed to her most strongly
as a preparation for the conduct of affairs and for the business
of ordinary life'. While at Somerville she continued with her
work in public service more generally, pressing, for example,
for more school inspectors. Domestic economy for Maitland
was not about cosiness, but about improving life. She also set
about the task of regulating teaching more effectively, not least
by ensuring that tutors were recruited on a longer-term basis.
Under her Principalship Somerville more than doubled in size,
from 35 students to 86.

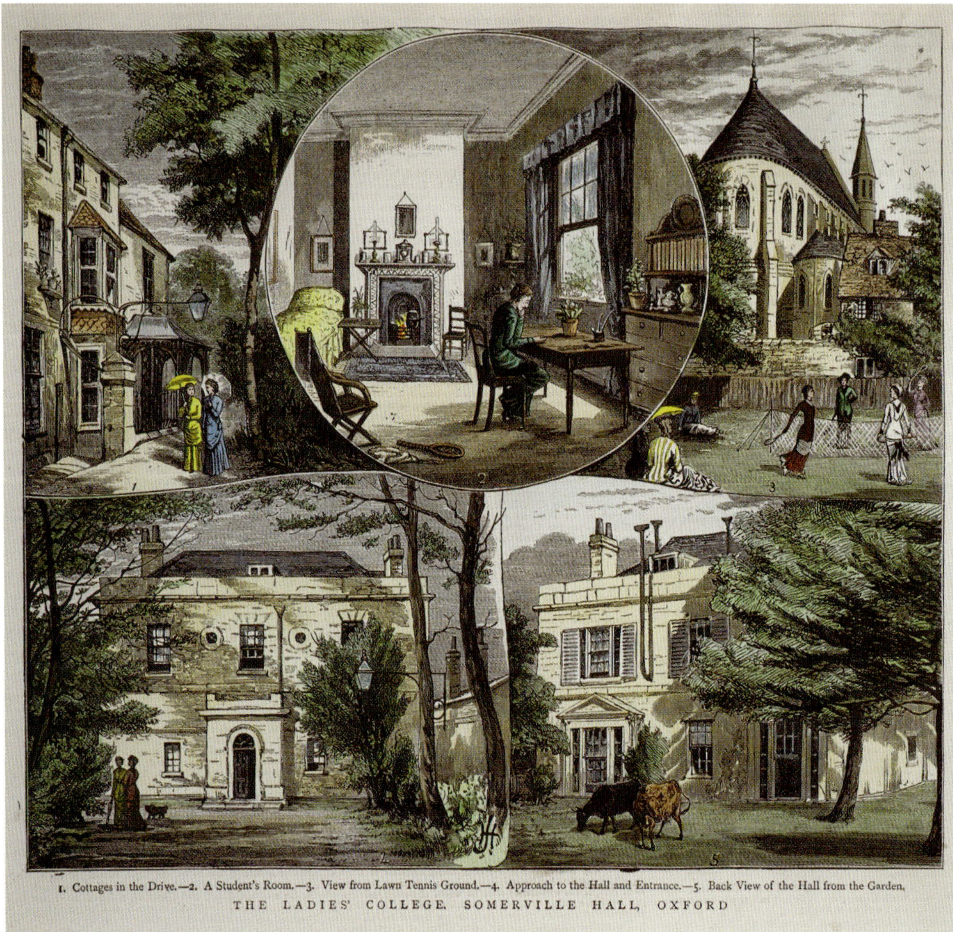

'The grey square stone house covered with wisteria and other creepers had a very countrified aspect'

Madeleine Shaw Lefevre

9
Illustration from *The Graphic*

Well, the one thing you might expect a college to look like is a college. But this is a quiet country house, the sort of place you might find middle-class Victorians spending the weekend with one another. And that is exactly the point. Walton House (just 'House' to Somervillians now) was chosen precisely to be a place where the daughters of the English middle classes would feel at home. It was also far enough from the centre of Oxford not to alarm the men's colleges. There were no grand new buildings and no bold architectural declarations of intent. Instead, when the first Somerville students arrived in October 1879 they arrived as though staying for a country house visit. The illustration here comes from *The Graphic* (a weekly illustrated newspaper). Despite its appearance, Walton House was no bucolic idyll: before the students could take up residence, the drains had to be completely overhauled and numerous changes made to the rooms to ensure that there was sufficient light and air. Even after they had moved in, problems with dry rot and leaking gas pipes continued to plague Walton House.

Gift book

Meticulously completed from the first, the record of gifts given to Somerville remained in use until it was superseded by spreadsheets and databases. Here we see the listing for the very first item given, a Broadwood piano, the gift of Miss M. Ewart (Mary Ewart [1830–1911], who also left a bequest that initially funded undergraduate scholarships and is now used for junior research fellowships). It was very much in the spirit of Somerville's foundation that these first gifts should be to furnish and make comfortable the house in which Somerville's students would live the 'life of an English family'. Indeed, the first pages of the gift book read rather like a wedding list: tablecloths, pottery, vases, a 'bread platter and knife', as well as things for the garden [11].

Here, too, is a note on the donation of the bust of Mary Somerville (a copy of the original by Chantrey, still in the Royal Society today [6]), and there is also a record of the gift of a portrait of Caroline Herschel (1750–1848), who was, jointly with Mary Somerville, the first woman to be elected to honorary membership of the Royal Astronomical Society.

1879	Presented by
Piano. a new trichord Cottage by Broadwood.	Miss M. Ewart of Coneyhurst
2 Sets of 3 Etchings one by Whistler framed	Professor & Mrs T H Green
2 Dutch Etchings by Gravesande framed	Mr & Mrs Humphry-Ward
"Chill October" by Millais autotype framed	F. H. Peters
2 Heads of Children & Madonna, Raphael. ⎱ framed	Mrs Arthur Acland
3 Pictures of Saints. Memling framed ..	R. W. Raper Esq
Jar. Flemish. Pottery	Mr Arthur Johnson
Curtain Poles. black & gold. 4 sets & 2 Fiji Mats	Hon. Lady Gordon
Table-cloth . drawing-room 1	Mr Henry Pelham

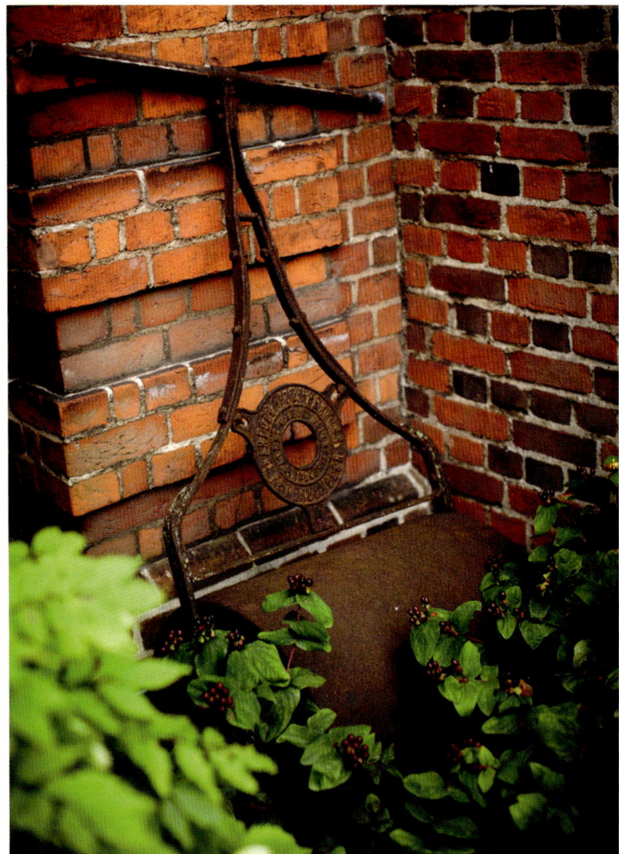

Item	Presented by
Garden Roller _ _ _ _ _	Mrs Arthur Sidgwick
Portrait of Mrs Somerville (framed)	Frances Power Cobbe
3 Flemish Vases	Lady Constance Shaw-Lefevre
St Paul. autotype _ framed and Scinde Rug	Mrs Humphry Ward
Portrait of Caroline Herschel (framed)	Dowr Lady Herschell
Bread Platter and Knife	Mrs Turnbull
Plaister Cast of the Bust of Mrs Somerville by Chantry - The original is in the Hall of the Royal Society	Mr Hamilton - late Dean of Salisbury to whom it had been given by Mr W. Greig Mrs Somerville's Step-son

'the rural effect of the place'

11

Garden roller

Propped against a wall of the Fellows' Garden is a rusted turf roller, fading into the brick so that you hardly see it. This is like something out of an old-fashioned country house garden. It was given to Somerville in 1879. The donor, Mrs Arthur Sidgwick (1853–1924), was one of many who rushed to furnish Walton House and its three acres of grounds before Somerville's first students arrived for Michaelmas Term in that first year. Somerville Hall's founders had deliberately chosen the site and the house as appropriate for their new venture [9]. Other early gifts included a grand piano and other items befitting the 'life of an English family' [10]. Somerville's first Principal, Madeleine Shaw Lefevre, later recalled the setting of Walton House, its 'large garden well planted with fine old trees', and how 'the field beyond bright with buttercups and the apple trees in blossom added to the rural effect of the place'.

This box of cameos from Italy would have been the height of fashion when it was collected by Margaret Lindsay, Lady Huggins (1848–1915). She and her husband, William Huggins (1824–1910), were pioneers in the field of spectroscopy in astronomy, and it must have been this link with Mary Somerville's work in astronomy [5] that prompted Lady Huggins to make a gift of these to Somerville. Neoclassical representations of the historical and cultural great and good (the box includes Dante, Petrarch and Machiavelli), these were clearly cameos designed for collectors. They sat safely in a cupboard in the library until they were rediscovered in 2010. That they were overlooked is understandable: the marbled paper on their presentation box makes it look exactly like a reference volume.

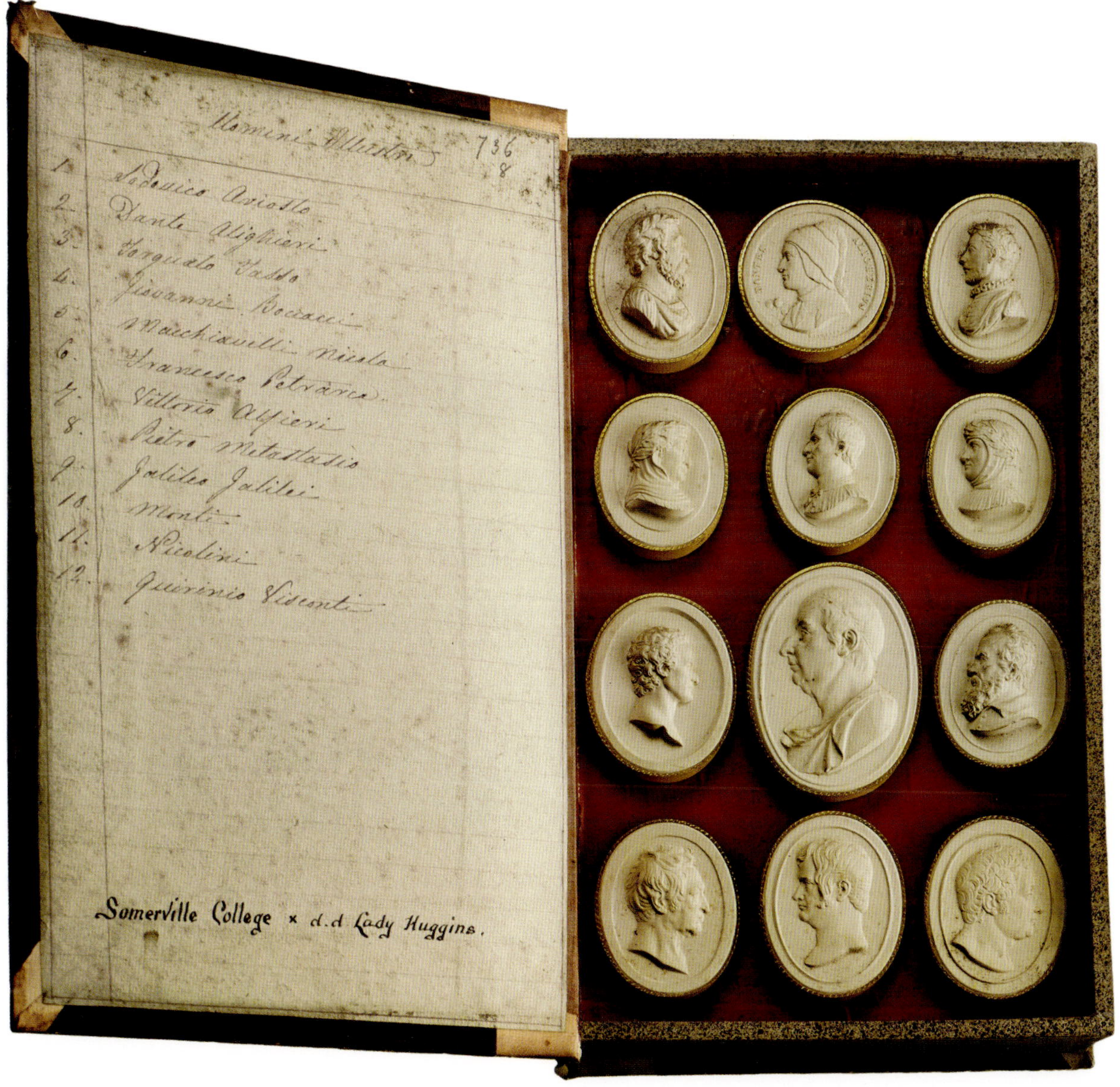

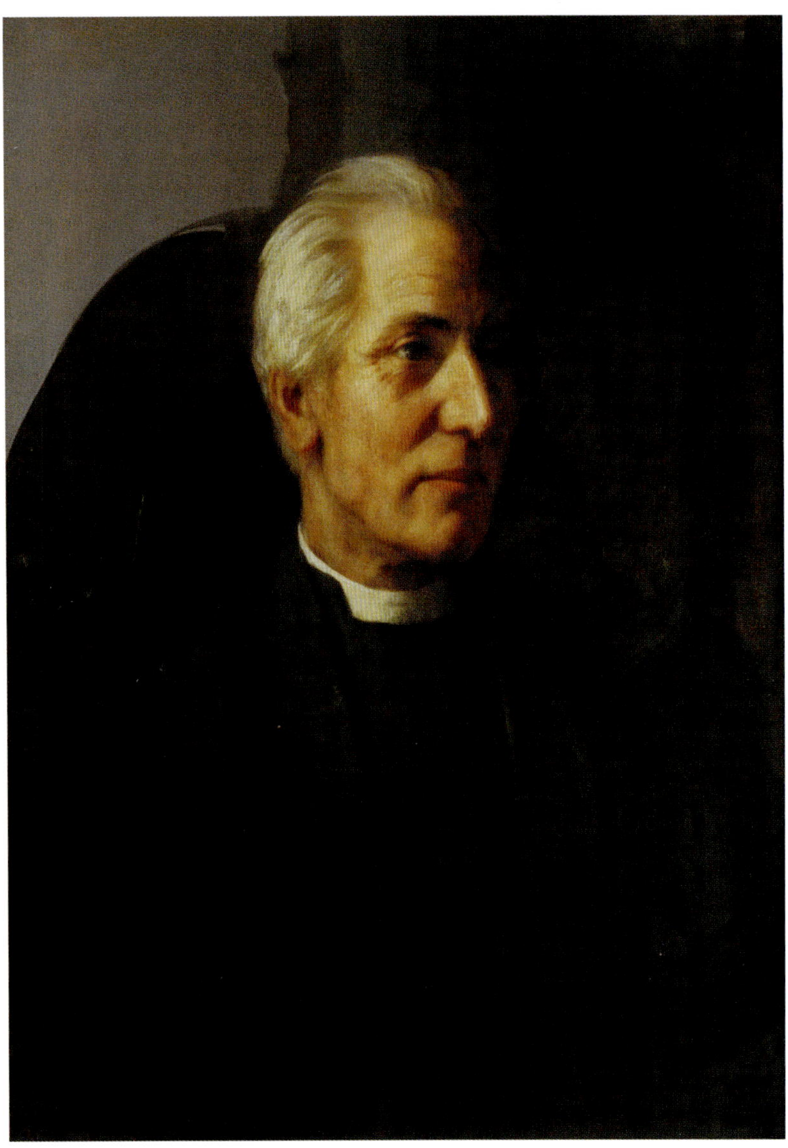

13

Portrait of John Percival

It was in the nature of Somerville's foundation that it was deeply indebted to men as well as to women for its success. All the founders of Somerville Hall knew that their establishment would need to appear respectable, unthreatening and as well connected as possible if it were to survive and to thrive. The contacts that men could bring were especially valuable in this regard. Dr John Percival (1834–1918), the first Chair of Somerville's Council, was a bishop as well as the former headmaster of Rugby and of Clifton College, and he had been instrumental in founding University College, Bristol. In 1879 he became President of Trinity College, at the heart of Oxford's establishment. This portrait was painted by his daughter, Mrs Basil Johnson (b. 1864). Ranged alongside Percival in the group of men who helped to found Somerville were the idealist philosopher Thomas Hill Green (1836–82) and another future President of Trinity, historian Henry Pelham (1846–1907) [23, 35]. They shared a liberal philosophy of equality of opportunity, with a particular emphasis on education. Fervently Christian, they were just as passionate in their commitment to a non-denominational hall for women.

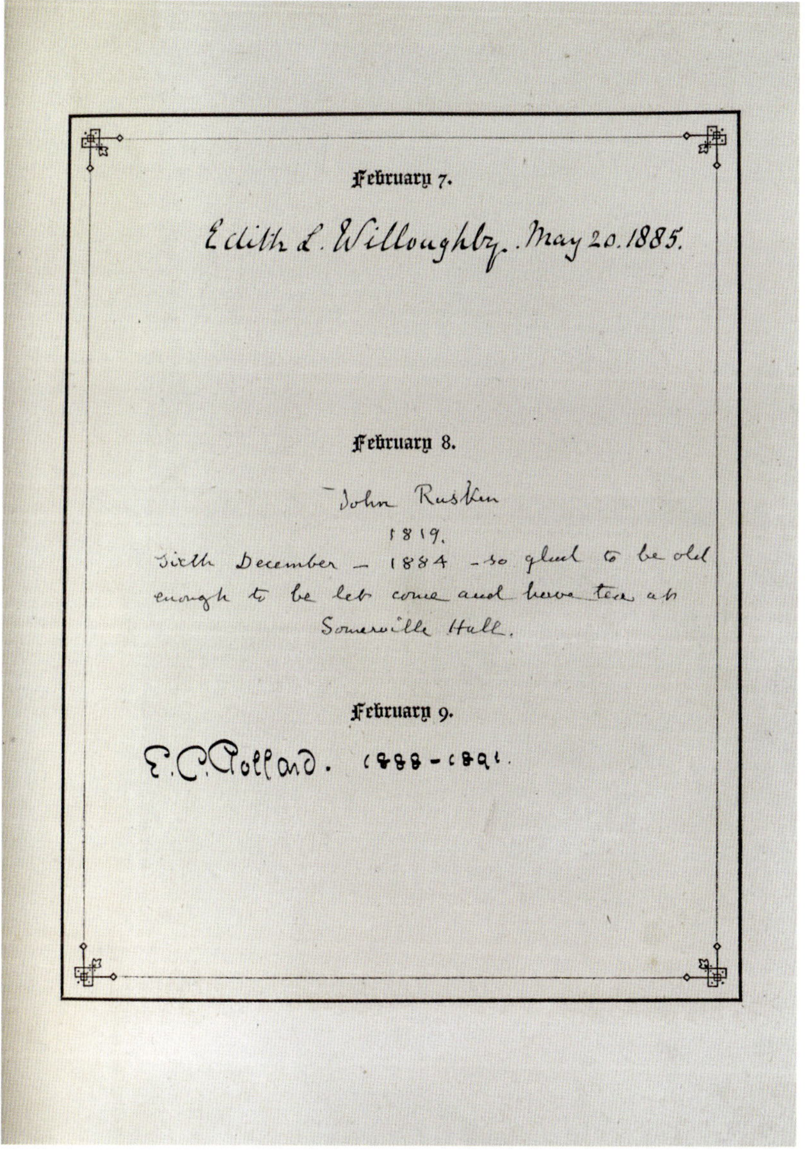

14
Ruskin birthday book

The 'birthday book' was greatly in fashion in Victorian England, and remained so well into the twentieth century. It was a kind of autograph book, in which you would be expected to sign or write a short note under the date of your birthday. John Ruskin gave this one to Somerville when he visited in December 1884, and noted under his own birthday (8 February) that he was 'so glad to be old enough to be let come and have tea at Somerville Hall' (in other words, he was of a sufficient age that students did not require a chaperone [65] when meeting him). Ruskin had come to Somerville at the invitation of the Principal, Madeleine Shaw Lefevre, whom he had met at a dinner party in November 1884. She later recalled:

> I was told he was not much in favour of women's colleges – but I persuaded him to come and see Somerville … several of the Students having joined us as we went along, he sat down in one of their rooms and discoursed to them in his delightful way while they gathered round him and literally sat at his feet.

The birthday book continued in use for a good many years, gathering the signatures of, among others, Queen Mary, Queen Elizabeth and Indira Gandhi [109].

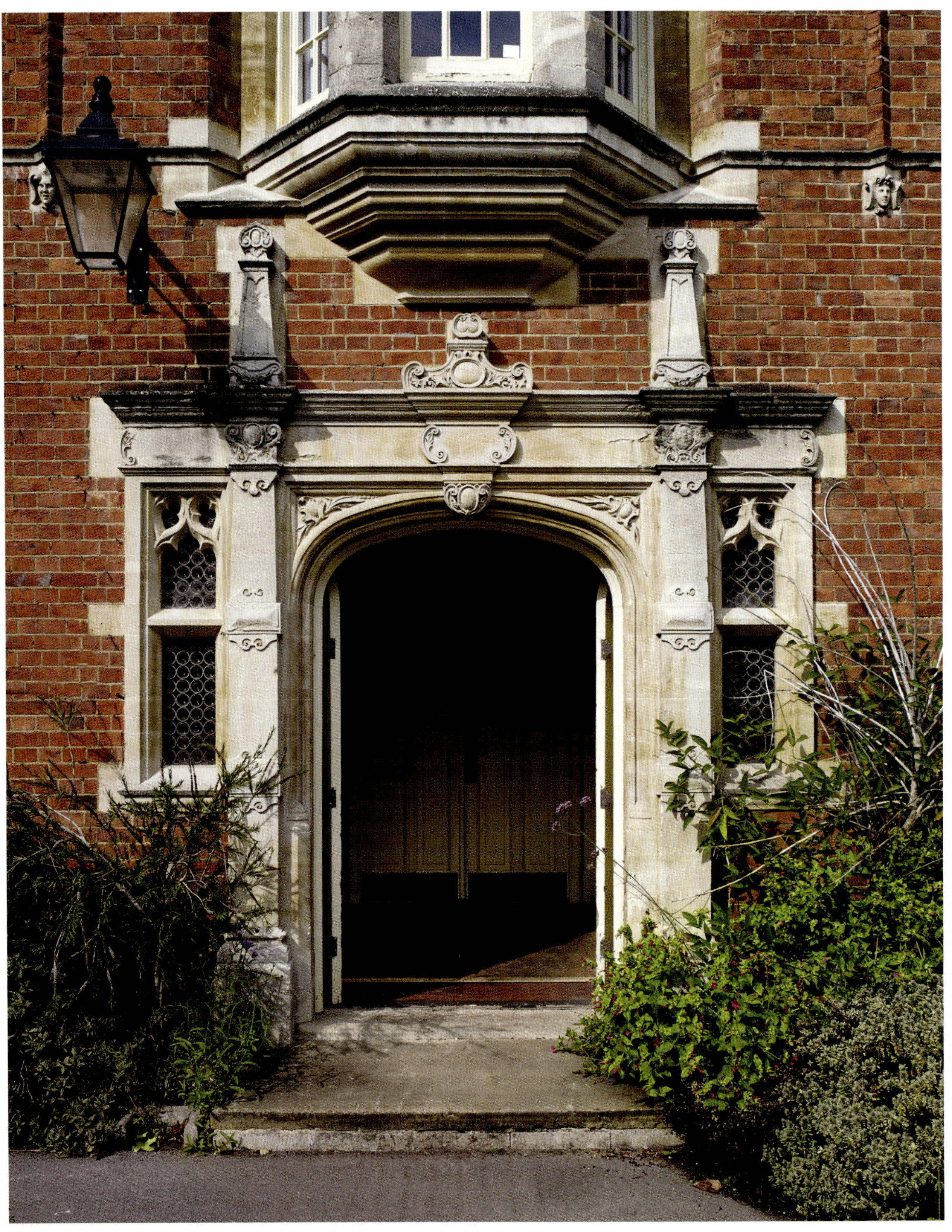

15
Entrance to 'the West'

Originally known as 'the West Buildings', 'the West', or just plain 'West', Park was renamed for Daphne Park, Baroness Park of Monmouth, Principal of Somerville from 1980 to 1989. At the western side of the site, West was built in 1885 as Somerville Hall outgrew Walton House. It was designed by H.W. Moore (1850–1915), known for his work for St John's and on the houses in the new suburb of North Oxford. Where that work was Gothic in inspiration, West was modelled on an Elizabethan house, with a central staircase and a wide door with ornate glass worked into its archway. The point of the design was to sustain the principle of replicating family life by establishing a separate house with a separate head (the Vice-Principal). Problems arose when West and House effectively became rival establishments [20]. The solution came with the construction of Maitland Hall in 1913, where the growing number of students could finally gather in one place to meet and eat [52]. Today the entrance hall of Park houses something else to make students feel at home: a vending machine.

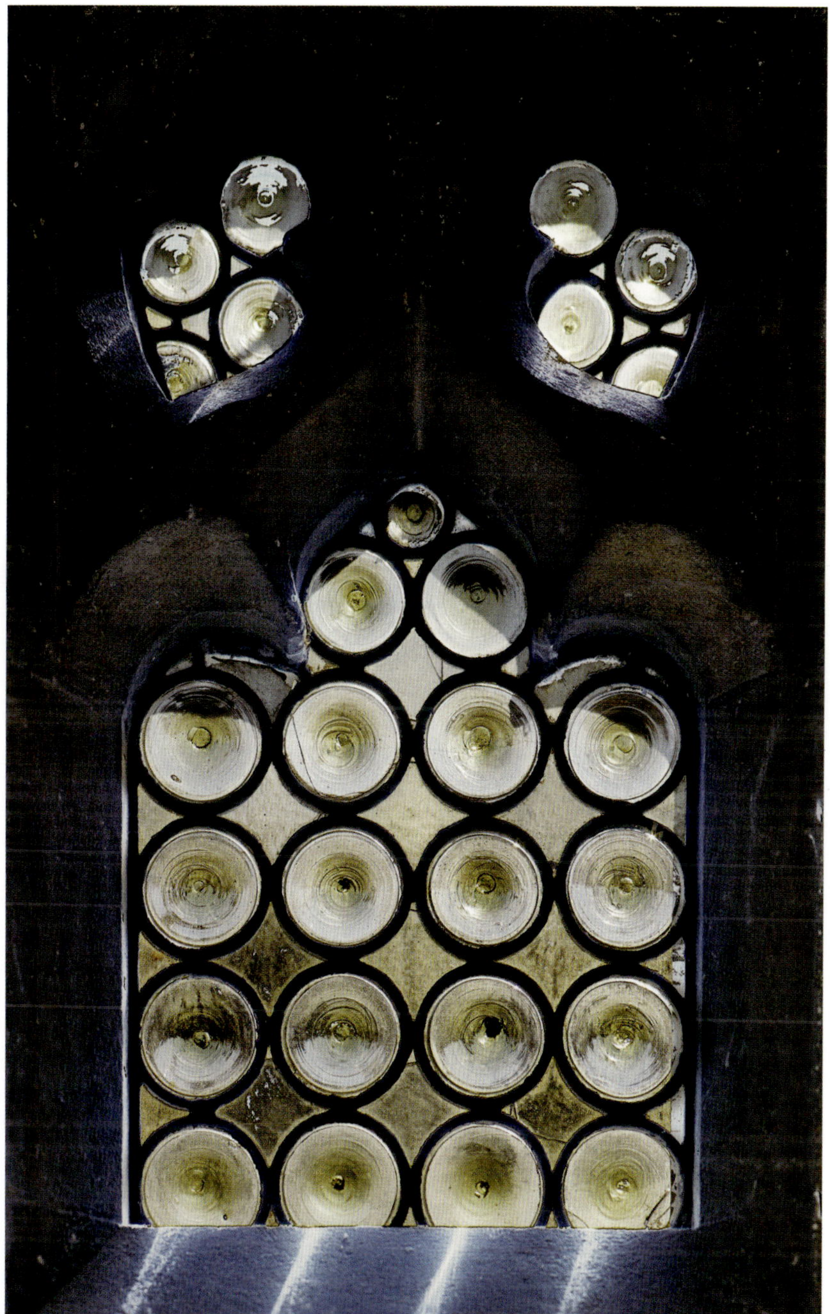

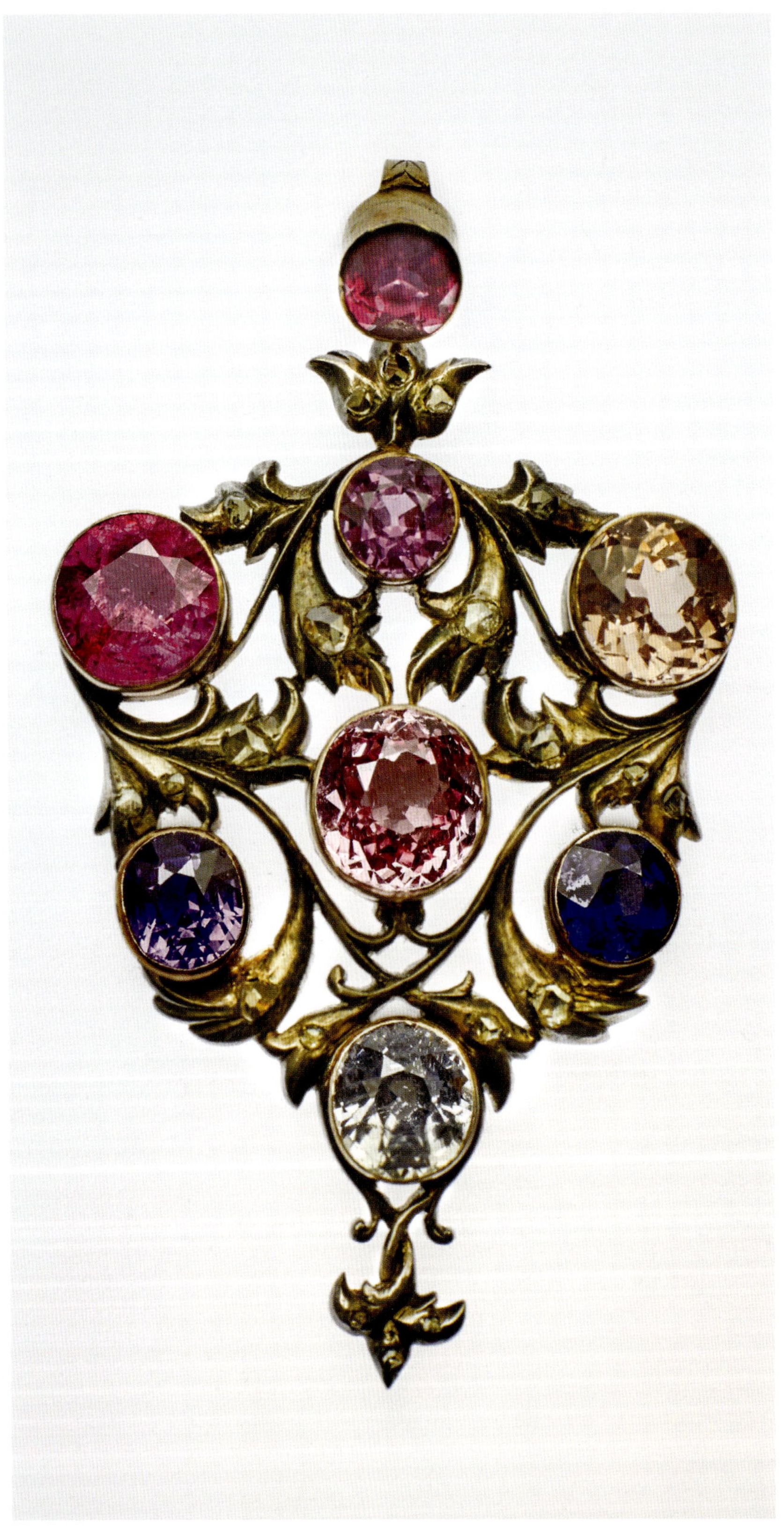

Principal's regalia

These jewels did not arrive in Somerville as we see them now. The pendant in which they sit was paid for by subscription by a group of Somervillians in 1921. The sapphires had already been used in other settings and became known as the Principal's 'regalia'. They were given by John Ruskin as part of a series of gifts he made to Somerville. When Ruskin first came to Somerville he was charmed by both Shaw Lefevre and her students [14], and shortly afterwards he sent a box of uncut stones. Shaw Lefevre, ever scrupulous, soon returned them to him on the assumption that they had been a loan. He sent them back to her, explaining that he wished them to be a permanent gift of 'regalia'. So far, so respectable; but unfortunately Shaw Lefevre was forced to return the box of stones to a London diamond merchant when it became apparent that Ruskin had never actually paid for them. When Ruskin sent these sapphires in 1887, Shaw Lefevre was particularly careful to retain clear evidence of the gift, lest questions should be asked at a later date.

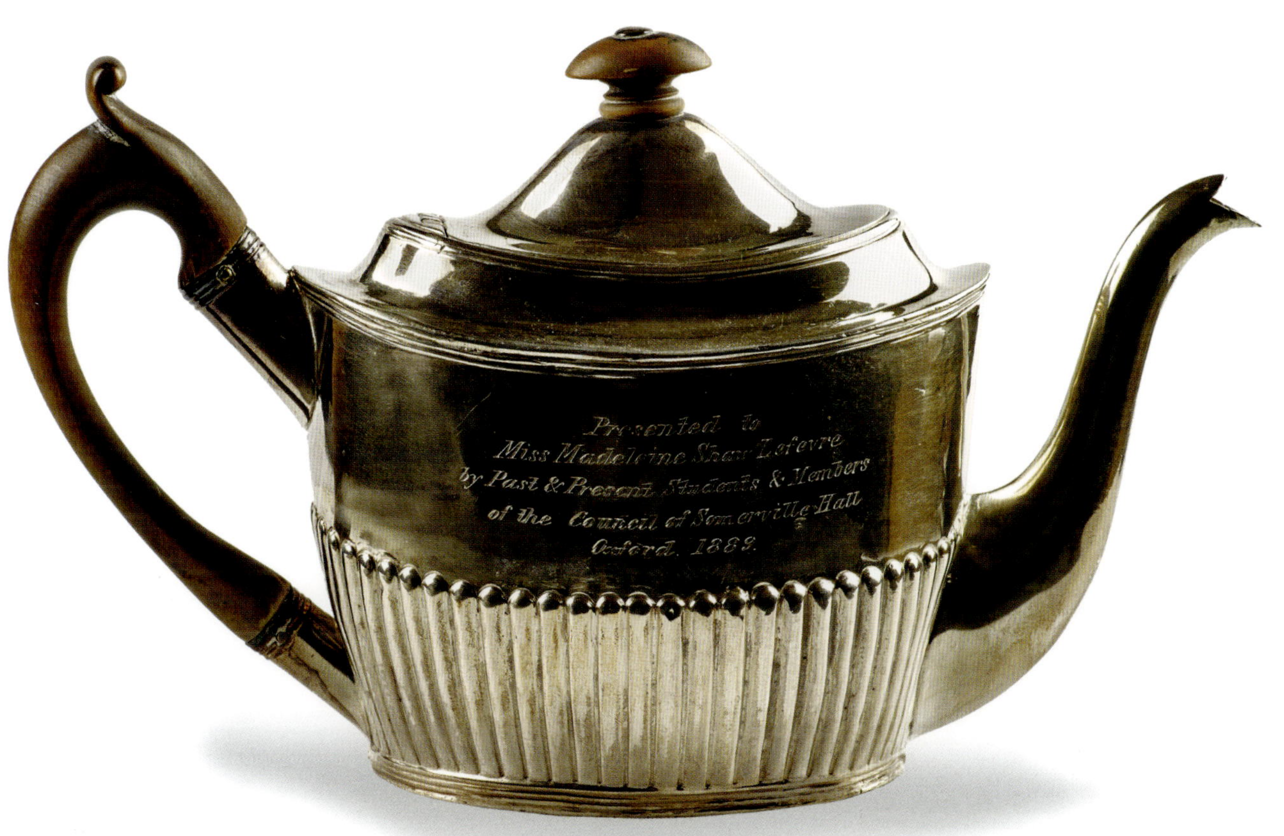

17
Silver teapot

Somerville's mode of living was set up to provide 'the life of an English family'. That might sound twee now, but in 1879 it was a rather daring statement. The other women's halls in Oxford would look to 'the life of the Christian family' as their model. Somerville was different, but the rhythms of English family life still prevailed. It had been the custom for some centuries for Oxford men to donate silver tankards and drinking cups to their colleges. Fitting, then, that this gift of silver from Miss Shaw Lefevre's students and from Somerville's Council should come in the form of a George III silver teapot of 1802 (made by the London firm of Peter, Ann & William Bateman). Gifts of silverware continued to be given by students well into the twentieth century. Tea and coffee pots were favoured choices, along with candlesticks and cutlery, although Art Deco wine coolers and an electroplated crumb scoop also feature. Like a real 'English family', then, albeit one of a particular social standing, Somerville soon found itself with a relatively large and sometimes idiosyncratic collection of silver. These days some of the more impressive specimens (candlesticks in particular) still come out for special occasions.

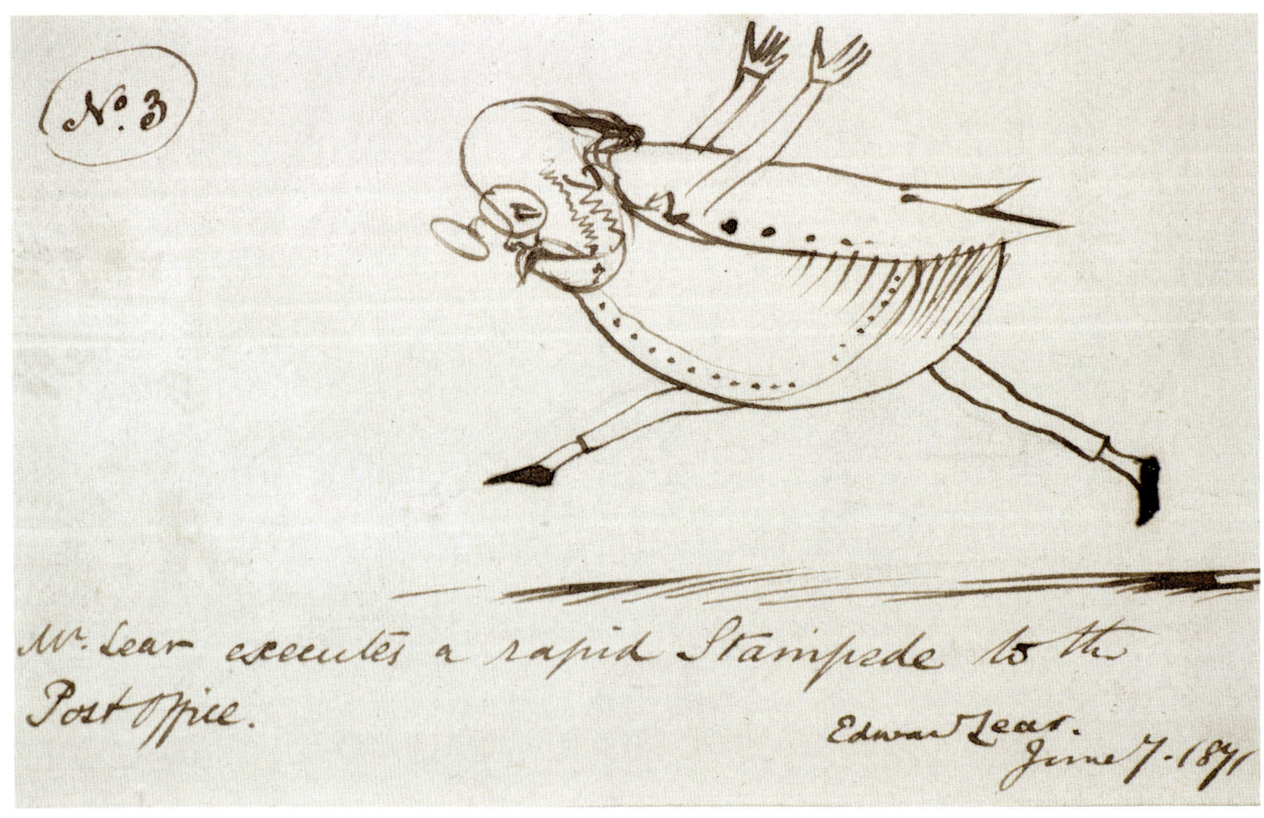

'Mr Lear executes a rapid stampede to the Post Office'

18
Edward Lear cartoon

This cartoon comes from an illustrated letter of 1871 written by Edward Lear (1812–88) to his friend Marianne North (1830–90). In it he makes fun of his own refusal to accept North's letter ('insufficiently stamped') and draws his subsequent quest to retrieve it. North was a renowned botanical artist whose stated ambition was to paint every known tropical plant in its natural habitat. She donated her botanical paintings to the collection at Kew and gave the funds to build a special gallery for them. North was a friend and correspondent of the novelist and Egyptologist Amelia Edwards (1831–92), and this letter was part of the Edwards bequest [41–7]. The college also has a later connection to Lear: Vivien Noakes (1937–2011) came up to Somerville in 1992 to read for a DPhil in English and later taught at Somerville. She had initially studied sciences, and it was her discovery of Edward Lear's paintings of birds that led her to look at his writings. In 1968 Noakes published a biography of Lear, *The Life of a Wanderer*, and she went on to publish anthologies of his work. Her research notes were given to Somerville by her husband, the painter Michael Noakes (1933–2018), in 2016.

19
West Lodge

The lodge on Walton Street was constructed in 1891, around the same time that an additional 19 rooms were added to West. The fact that West had its own entrance and its own lodge and porter added to the sense that Somerville was growing into two establishments rather than one at this time [20]. With the decision to construct a new, larger hall [52], West became simply a block of accommodation rather than a house in its own right, and the West Lodge gave way to the Woodstock Road entrance [80]. One imagines that it may have remained a favoured spot for climbing back into college after curfew. A good number of Somervillians can still recall their preferred patch of wall for late-night/early-hours ingress, although at least one of the trusty spots (at the back of Penrose) has now been built over. Rumour has it that in Somerville's early years, when Jericho was rather less genteel than it is now, one of the ladies of the night on Walton Street ran a profitable sideline charging to give Somervillians a leg-up over the wall.

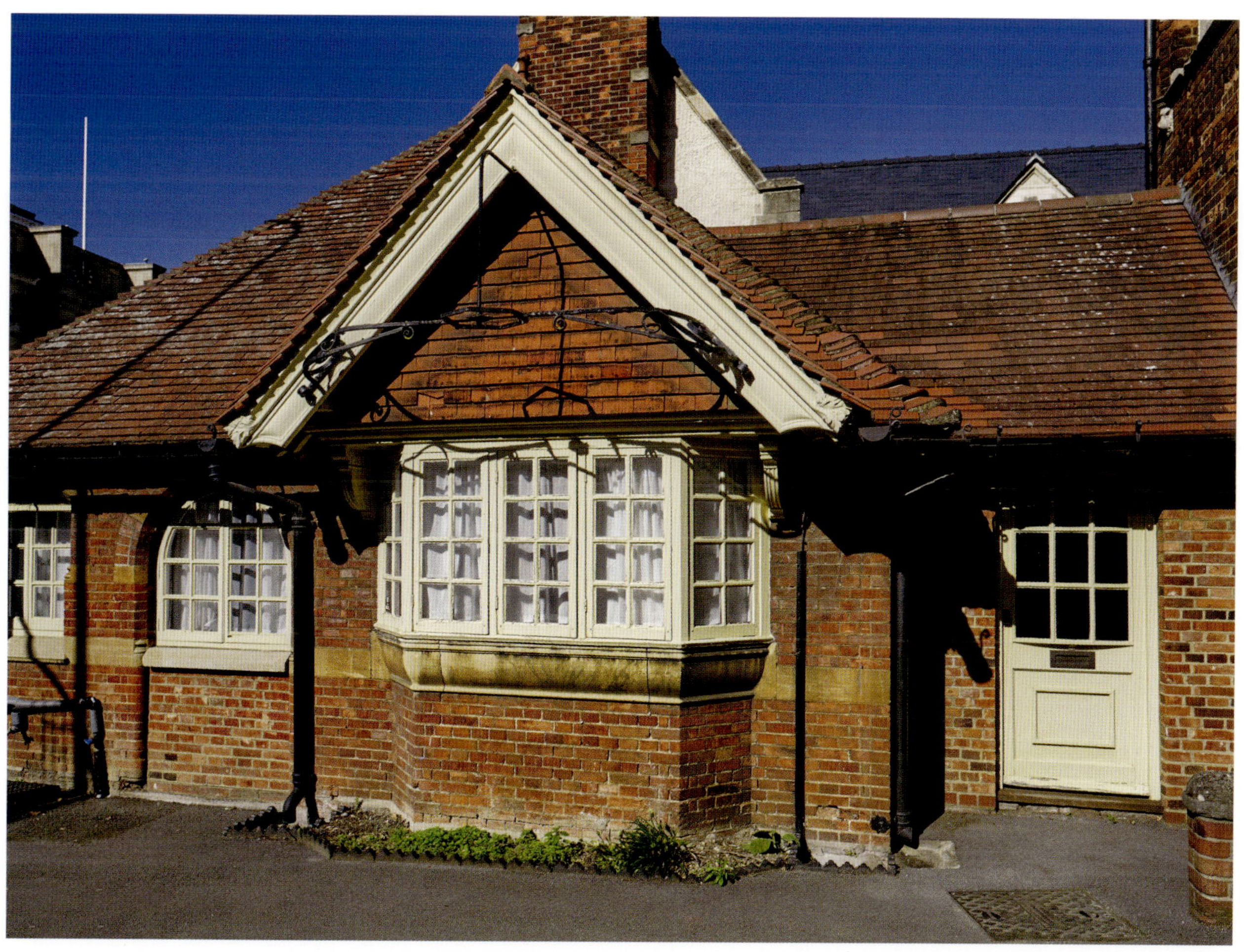

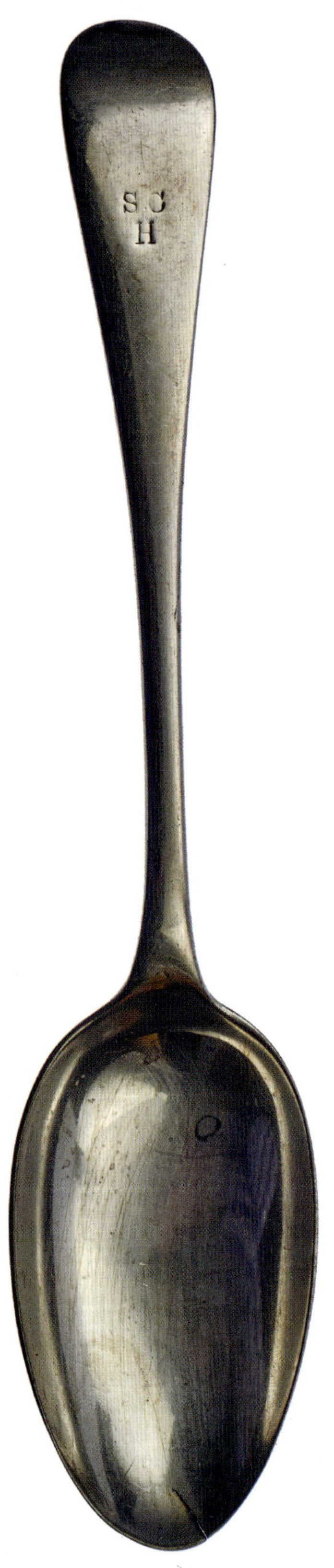

20
'House' and 'West' spoons

These spoons date from a time when there were effectively two establishments in Somerville. The first Principal, Madeleine Shaw Lefevre, had insisted that Somerville should mimic a household and not have a large dining hall to ape the men's colleges. This was all well and good until student numbers began to increase. With the building of 'the West' (now Park) in 1885, another household, with a separate dining room and even its own cutlery ('W S C' for 'West. Somerville College' and 'H' for 'House'). 'House' and 'West' gradually developed an unhealthy rivalry, and it was partly this that prompted the inclusion of a large hall in the plans for the new 'Wrenaissance' building (later called Maitland) to be designed by Edmund Fisher (1872–1918). The opening of the Maitland Hall [52] banished the rivalry but the cutlery remains, turning up from time to time to proclaim allegiance to 'House' or 'West'.

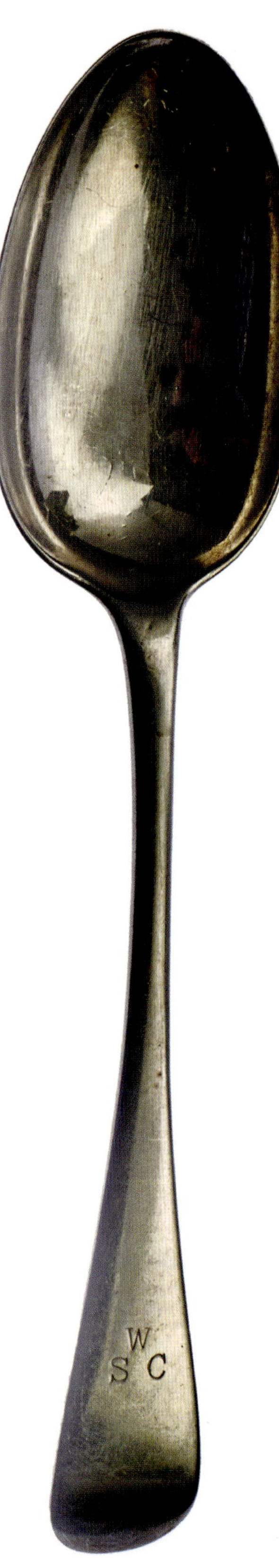

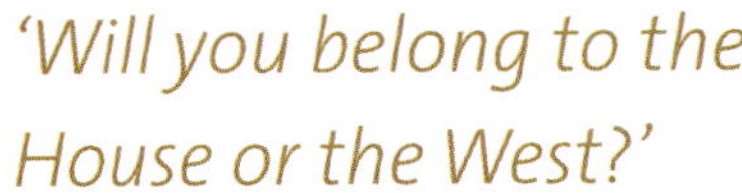

'Will you belong to the House or the West?'

Miss Penrose to Vera Farnell, 1911

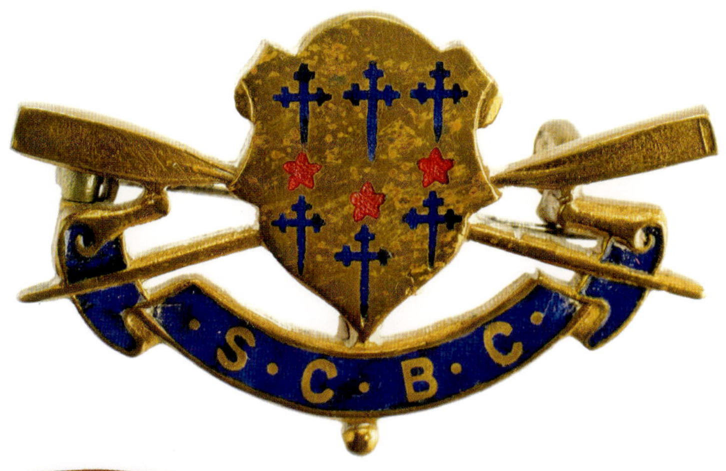

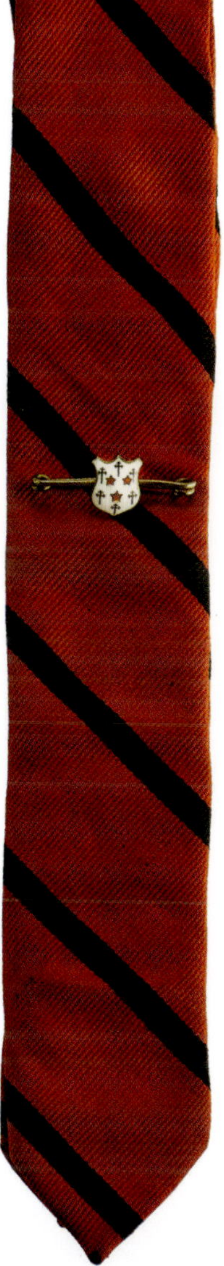

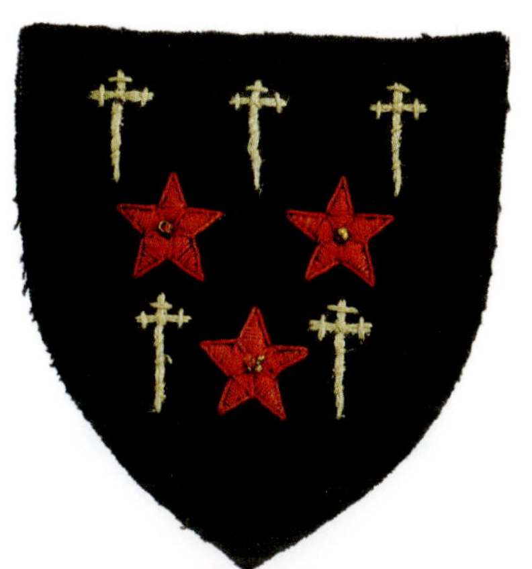

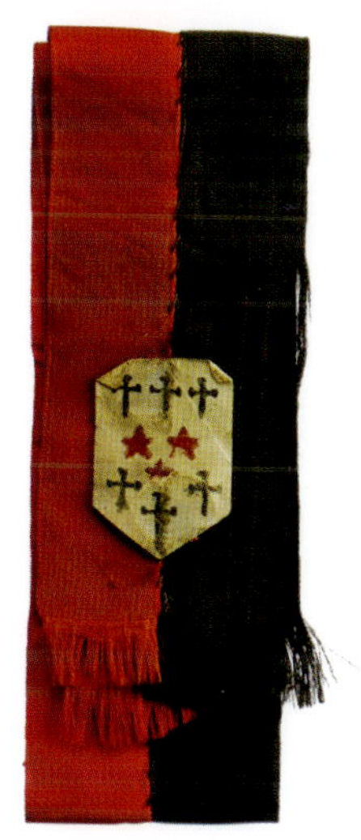

21

Colours

Here it is: that hint of the girls' boarding
school, with a tie to accompany the
Edwardian blouse, the long skirt and
possibly the hockey stick too. In 1892
Somerville's Council agreed to the
students' request for 'a crest or badge and
motto'. Somerville Hall therefore adopted
the 'buff and blue' of the Somerville
family coat of arms [8], and this is what
we see in this early boat club pin. In the
same year it was reported that Somerville
had abandoned buff and blue, 'which
were so trying to many complexions', and
plumped instead for the red and black
that is still so much a part of Somerville's
identity [134].

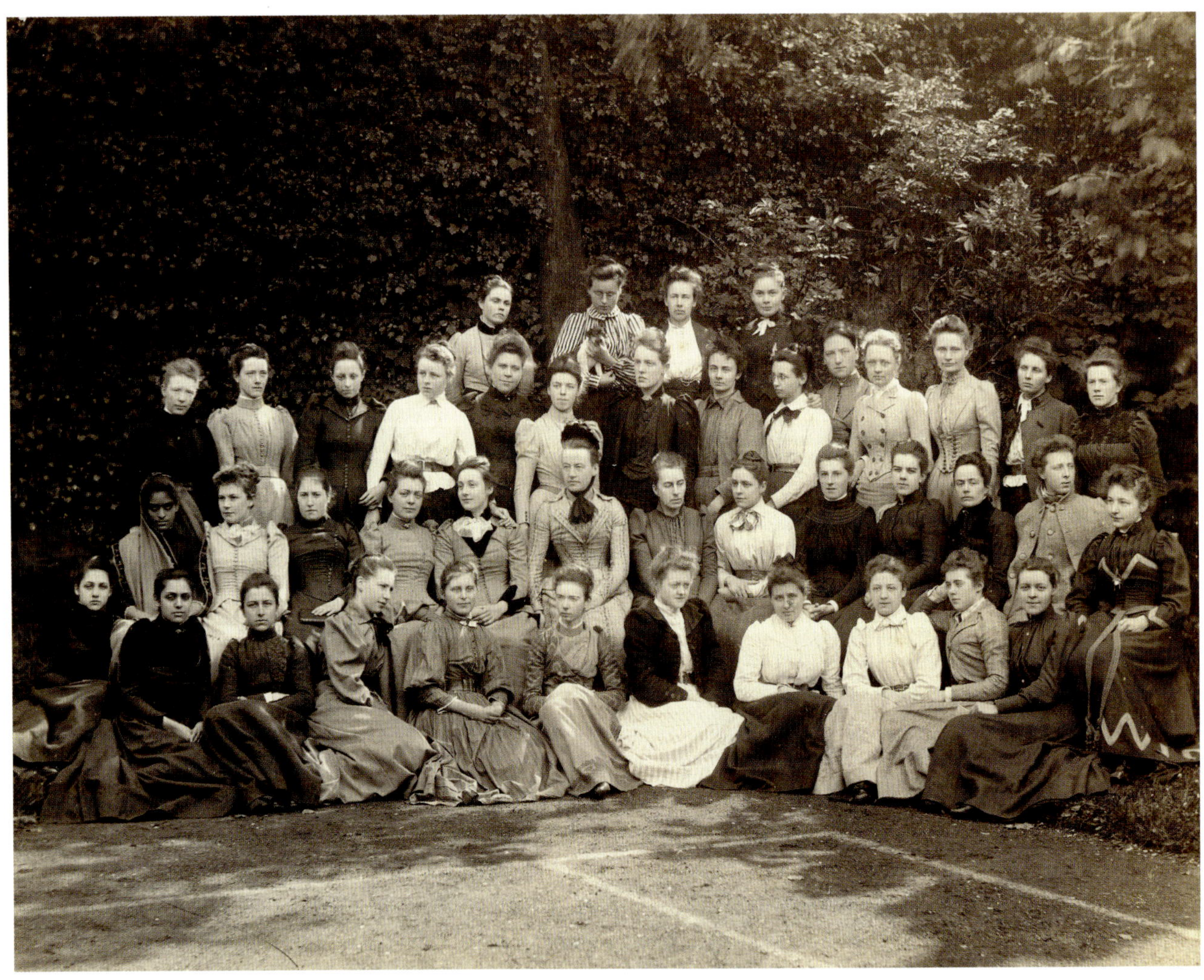

College photograph

Every Somervillian remembers their own college photograph. At the start of Somerville's life the college was still small enough that photographs were of all students together. Before very long that ceased to be practical, and what is now known as the 'matriculation' photograph was born. We could have chosen here the one that includes Dorothy L. Sayers (1893–1957 [87]) or the one with Margaret Roberts (later Thatcher; 1925–2013 [113]). The 1891 photograph (still of the whole college at this stage) is surely worthy of special note. Here in the centre, in her black bonnet, is Principal Agnes Maitland. Third from right in the second row from the back is a future Principal, Emily Penrose [60]. At the far left of the second row from the front is Cornelia Sorabji, the pioneering Indian lawyer [24], and in front of her sit princesses Bamba (1869–1957) and Catherine (1871–1942) Duleep Singh; Catherine went on to become an activist in the suffrage movement. Quite a roll-call for a photograph of only 42 students and for a hall only opened 12 years earlier.

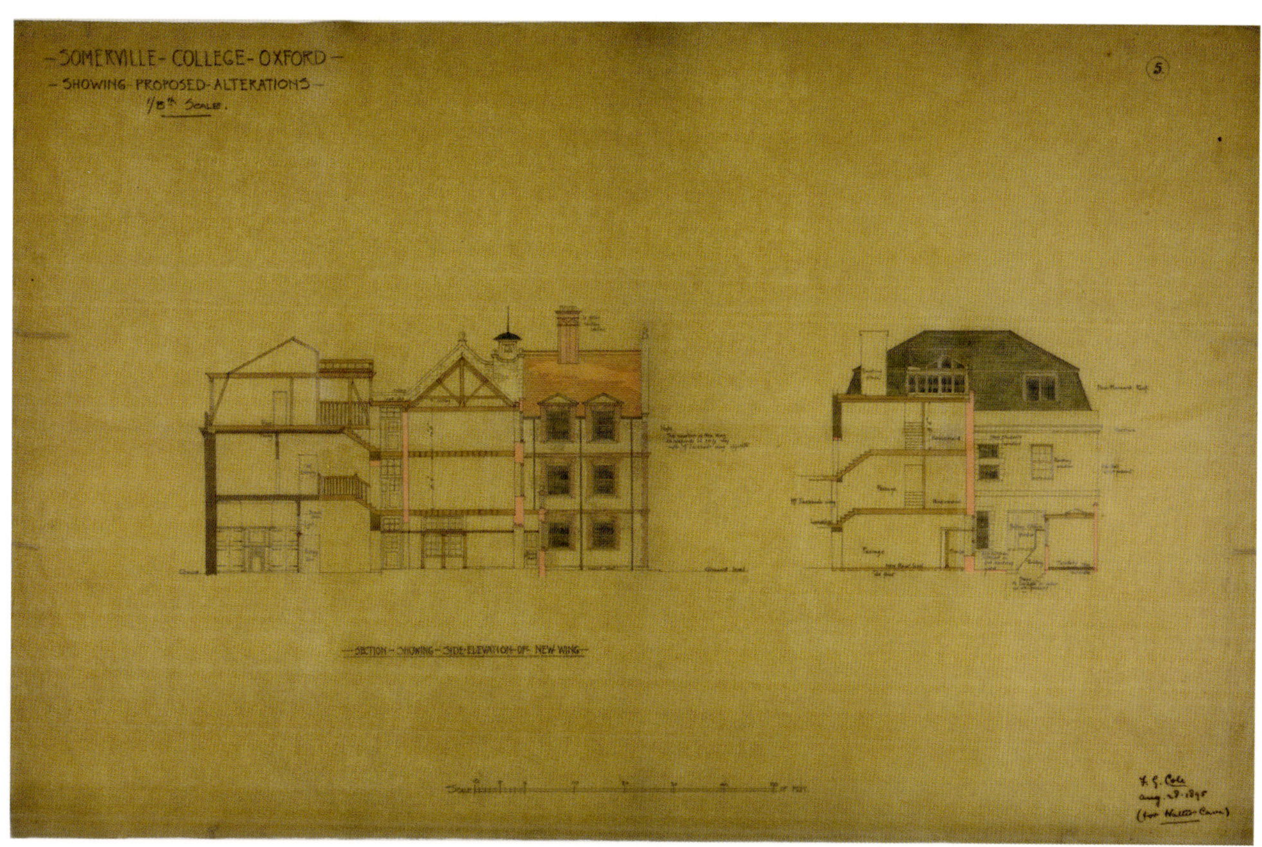

23
Belfry and bell

The bell and belfry at the top of House were given by Henry Pelham [13, 35] (by this time President of Trinity College, Oxford) in 1896. The cost – £21 – is recorded in the gift book [10] between entries for 'a set of plush curtains' and 'two easy chairs' from other donors. Pelham was a member of the first Somerville Committee, and had been particularly active in fundraising for Somerville Hall. As time went by his views were sometimes at odds with the women who ran Somerville on a day-to-day basis. When one tutor consulted him about her research he informed her that she would not need to do any, as teaching in the advanced subjects would be supplied by tutors from the men's colleges. He undoubtedly benefited the college in many ways, though: as well as giving his time and generous gifts, he also suggested to a young Emily Penrose [22, 60] that she should study at Somerville. The bell was restored in 2017 but the belfry was deemed too weak to hold the weight of the bell until it, too, can be restored; so for now the two remain apart.

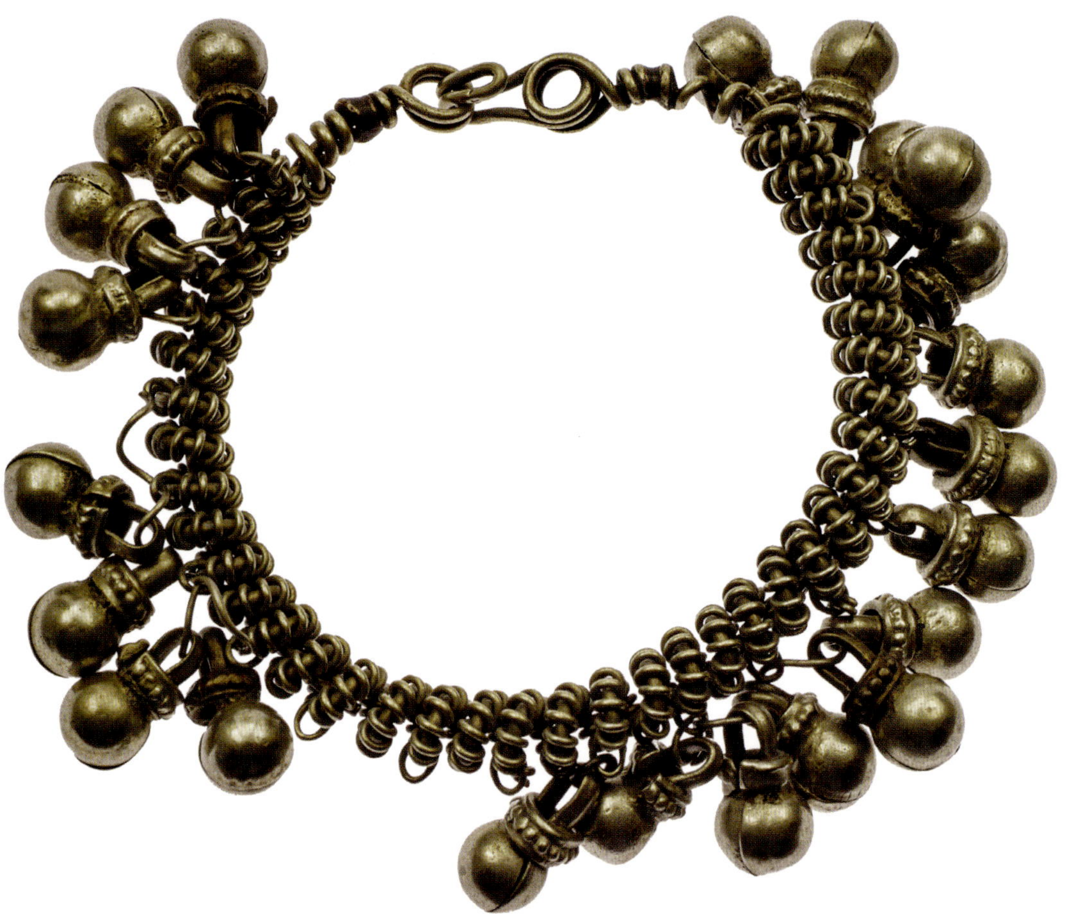

24
Cornelia Sorabji's anklet

It is perhaps inevitable that when we look at the list of Somervillians the word 'pioneer' keeps coming to mind. If we were to nominate the pioneer of pioneers, surely Cornelia Sorabji (1866–1954) would take the prize. Sorabji's life story is a series of firsts: the first woman to graduate from Bombay University (where the male students slammed the doors of the lecture hall in her face, but where she went on to take first-class honours nevertheless); the first woman to study Law at Oxford; and one of the first women to practise law at the Bar in both India and the UK. As a child Sorabji found herself moved by the appalling life stories of the women who lived behind the 'curtain' of purdah. When her mother

asked her, 'What are you going to do for India when you grow up?', she decided that the most practical way to help was to learn the law.

Sorabji wrote in her 1934 *Memories* about her intense memories of her time in England: 'the dark wood of trees in early spring bursting with swollen buds, or powdered with blossom ... chestnuts alight'. At Oxford, she said, she learned 'that difference of opinion need not affect friendship or personal appreciation, and that one could be a zealot and yet open-minded'. Sorabji's first love remained India – 'Dawn at Darjeeling with the snows coming alive with colour'. She gave this Indian anklet to a friend at Somerville, who then gave it to the college as a

memento of this extraordinary woman. When she finished her degree in 1892, Sorabji returned to India and worked with women living in purdah. She helped them with legal issues of rights and property, and also pushed to improve their access to education and social care. Sorabji was eventually admitted to Lincoln's Inn in 1922, and to the English Bar in 1923. When she retired in 1929, she chose to return to England.

In 2016 Somerville and the Oxford Faculty of Law launched the Cornelia Sorabji Graduate Scholarship programme, made possible through generous donations from Somerville's alumni and friends, and from members of the legal community in India and the UK [123].

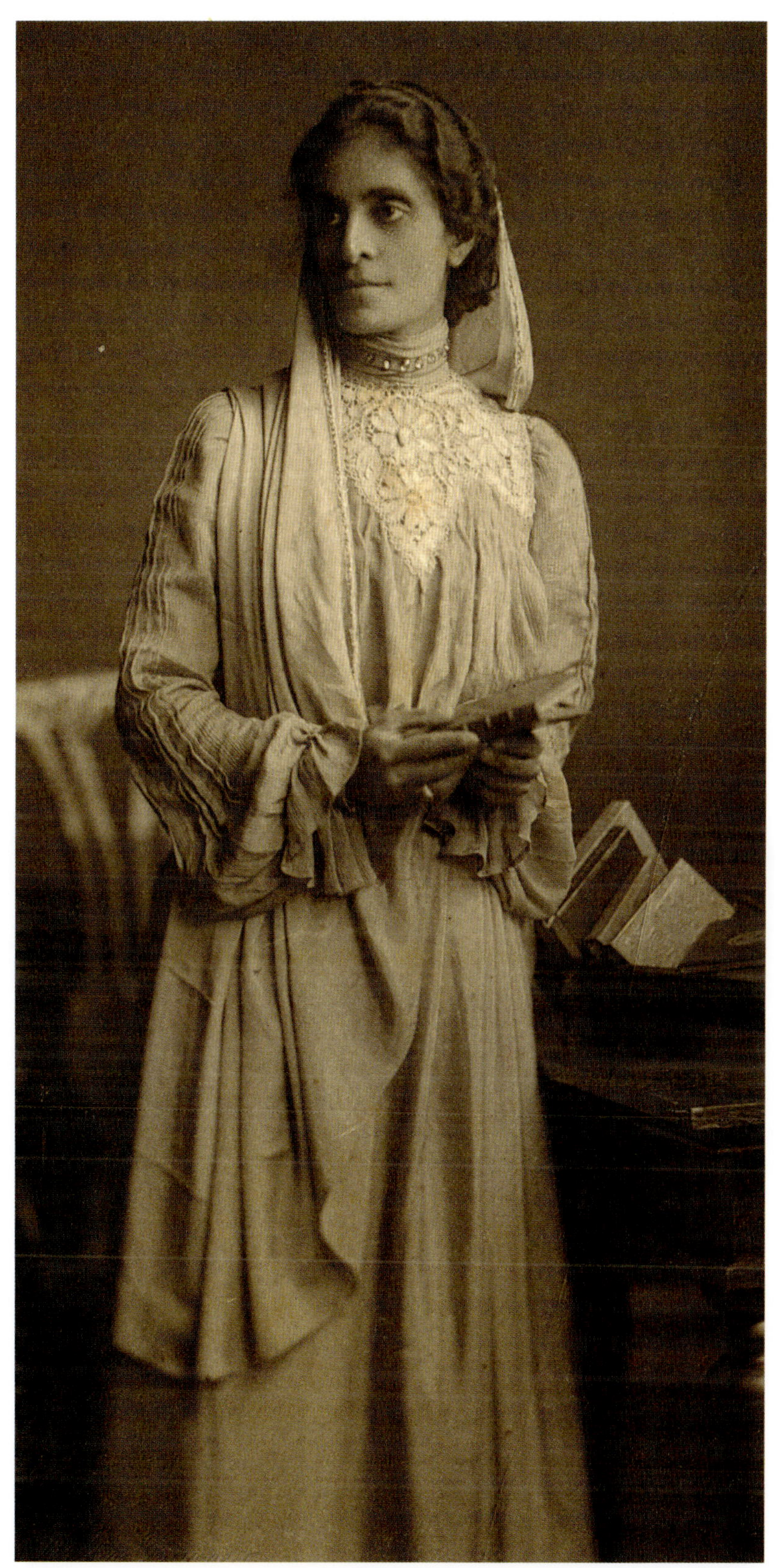

'*difference of opinion
need not affect
friendship or personal
appreciation*'

Cornelia Sorabji

4) L. Lawson & E. T. Joseph gave a brief sketch of factory legislation fr. 1802 – 1892, tracing gradual extension of its operation to all forms of trades & all workers, & summarised the resulting advantages & disadvantages. It seemed to be the opinion of the meeting that the necessary further steps were rather the enforcement of legislation than extension of legislation, but it was pointed out that domestic industry was yet unregulated –

M. K. Pope
Clerk

Meeting XXIII
held in E. Rathbone's room, 15/3/96

Members Present
S. M. Fry, E. Joseph, L. J. Tapworth, M. K. Pope. H. Oakley
L. Lawson, E. Rathbone, & Miss Kay Shuttleworth.
Minutes of preceding meeting were read & adopted.
Clerk announced election of H. Oakley.
It was decided to elect a member to fill the place of L. Lawson, who was going down. Votes were taken & M. Suttell declared elected.
Miss Shuttleworth read a paper on coeducation. She pointed out that in elementary schools there was a tendency in some places to introduce Coeducation, In Secondary Schools Coeducation

25
Minutes of 'The Associated Prigs'

Somerville was a great place for societies: groups were formed and re-formed to talk about academic subjects, literature and the political and social issues of the day. The discussion might be serious, but Somervillians were never po-faced about it. Often the names of these groups poked fun at their pretensions (the 'Mutual Admiration Society', for example, a literary group started by Dorothy L. Sayers [87]). Eleanor Rathbone (1872–1946), who would later become the first of many Somervillians to be elected to Parliament, was one of the founding members in 1894 of 'The Associated Prigs', which met on Sunday evenings for 'collective talk on social subjects'. Topics ranged from school boards through Poor Law administration to the punishment of criminals, and this page records 'a brief sketch of factory legislation'. The group restricted itself to having only seven members at any one time. Margery Fry became the keeper of the Associated Prigs' minute book, returning it to the college later in her life with a note reading: 'I think finally this book might repose at Somerville … or is that swank?' The final meeting of the group was held in 1899, and soon afterwards the Somerville Parliament (which was open to all members of the college) became the place for debate of this kind [37].

26

Portrait of Mrs Humphry Ward

Mrs Humphry Ward (1851–1920) was an extraordinary individual in her own right. She also serves as a useful warning against the danger of making lazy assumptions. Mary Ward (born Mary Arnold, the niece of the poet Matthew Arnold) was a popular and successful novelist (though who has heard now of *Miss Bretherton* or *Lady Rose's Daughter*?) and also worked to advance social causes, including women's education. She was, jointly, the first secretary of the Somerville Council, and she proposed that the hall should be named for Mary Somerville. Yet Ward was also fiercely opposed to the women's suffrage movement, becoming President of the National Anti-Suffrage League and writing in *The Times* in 1909 that legal, financial, military and international problems were ones that only men could solve. Her views in this sense were strongly at odds with those of most Somervillians, but her championing of the causes of education and social reform more widely sat easily with the college's founding ethos. Ward's work lives on today in the Mary Ward Centre for adult education in London.

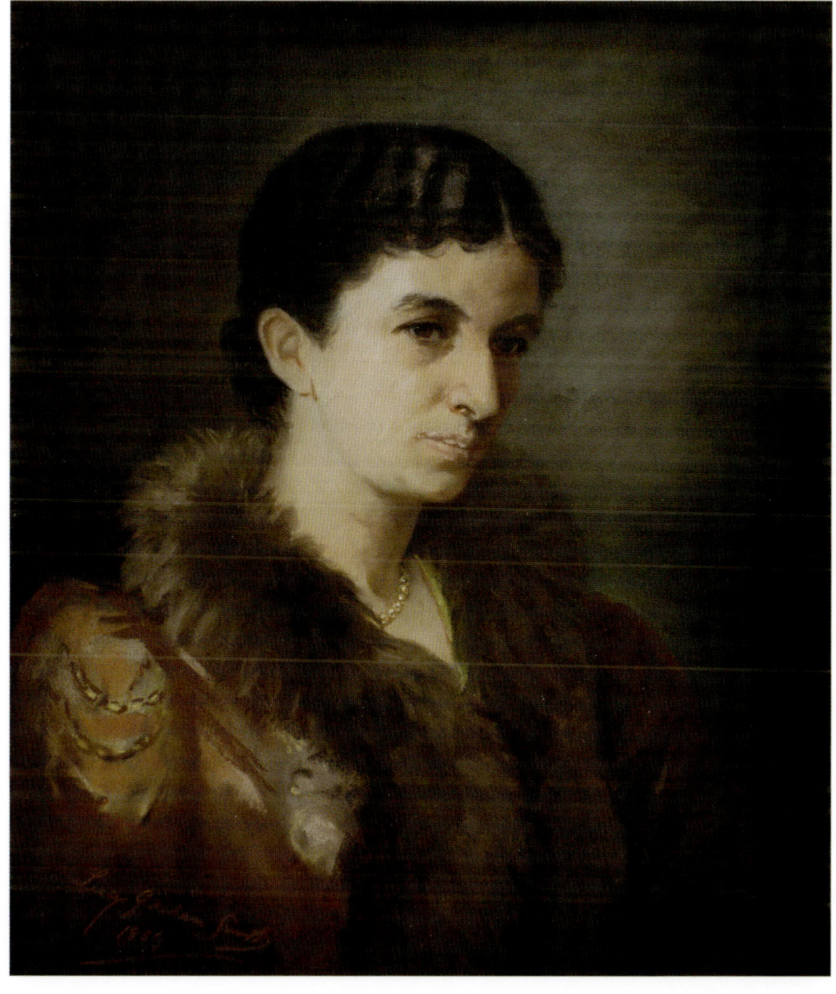

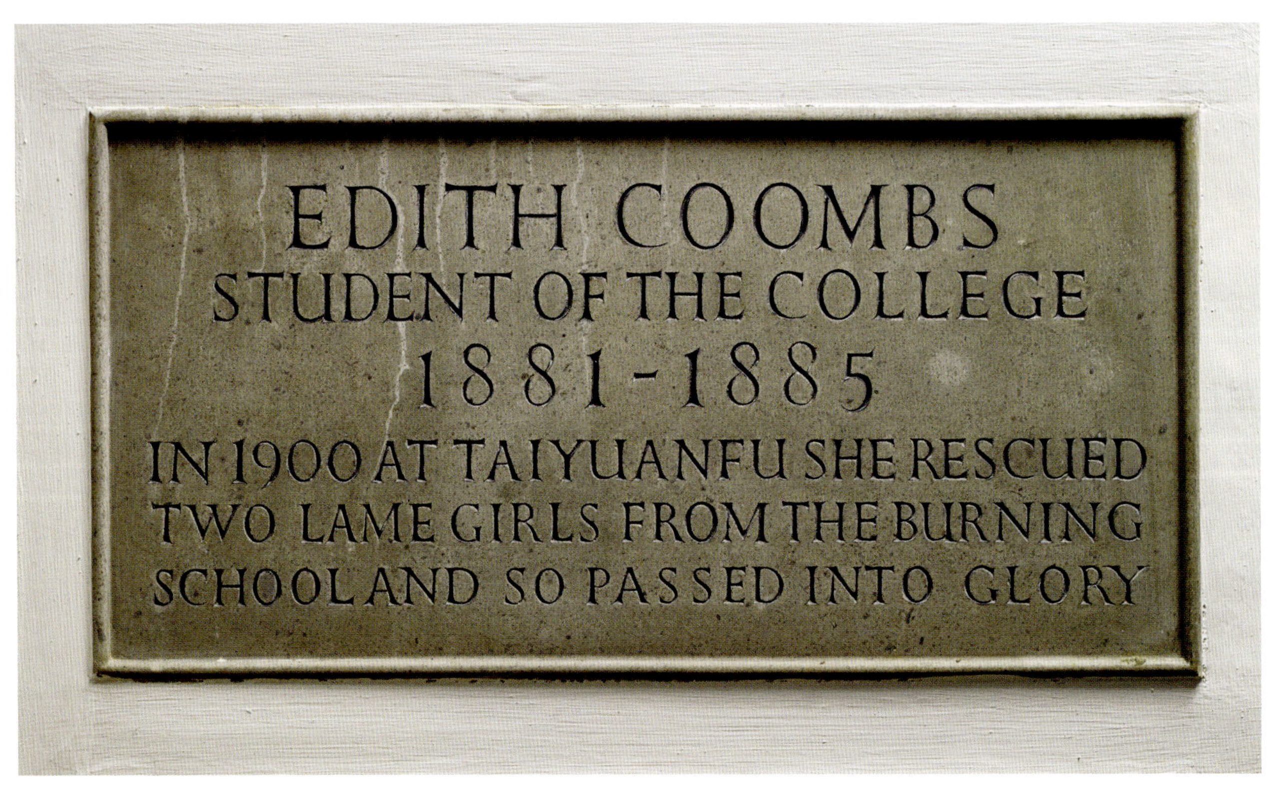

'She rescued two lame girls from the burning school and so passed into glory'

27

Plaque to Edith Coombs

When it comes to Edith Coombs (1862–1900), you have to choose which version of her story you think is the most plausible. Coombs came up to Somerville in 1881 to read Modern History. Later she travelled to China to teach. One account has it that she was captured during the 1900 Boxer Rebellion as she fled from the mission compound in Taiyuan, and that she was beaten and then burned to death as she successfully tried to protect two students from attack. Then there is the official version from a state history of China published in the late 1990s: that Coombs waved a pistol and provoked the rebels, that she was a missionary and an agent of a foreign power. In fact, Coombs was a teacher in a mission compound. A near-contemporary account of her life and death is hagiographical: as a child, it says, 'her conduct was uniformly all her parents could desire', and she became 'the first Christian martyr of Shanshi'. Whatever the truth, there can be no doubt that Coombs showed a zeal and courage that was unusual even in Somervillians. In the academic year 1900–1 her father endowed a scholarship in her memory.

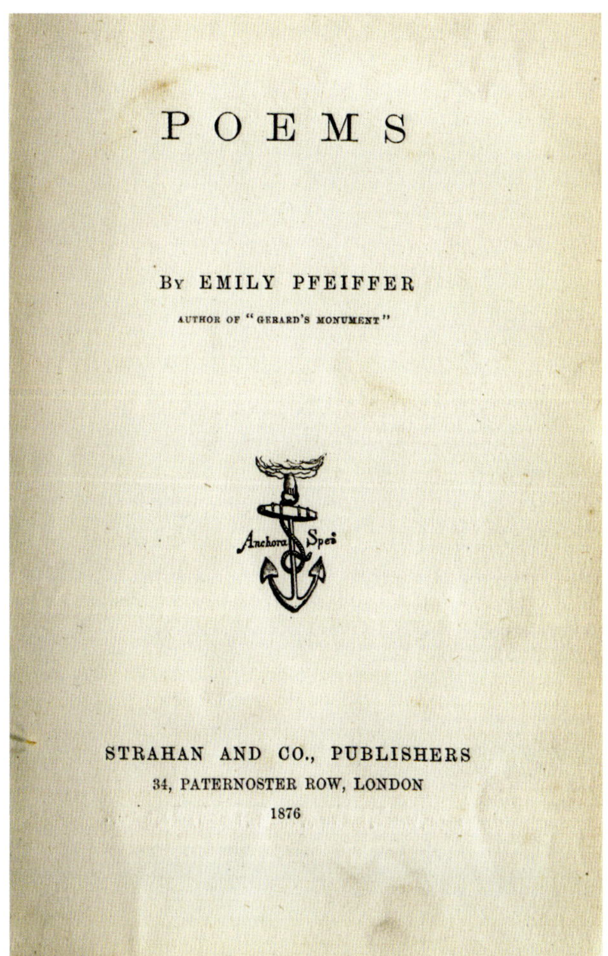

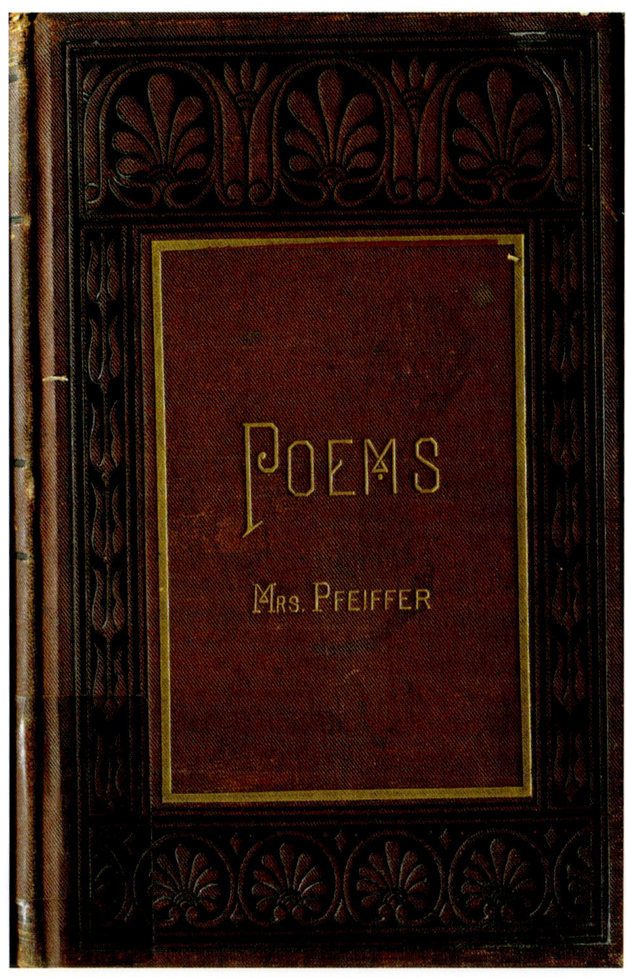

Emily Pfeiffer, *Gerard's Monument*

28
Emily Pfeiffer, *Poems*

Emily Pfeiffer (1827–90) was a poet and philanthropist. Born Emily Davis in Wales, she grew up in Oxfordshire and published her first poems in 1842. She continued to publish throughout her lifetime, gaining popular success with her 1873 metrical romance, *Gerard's Monument*. Her marriage to wealthy tea merchant Jürgen Pfeiffer, and their joint interest in promoting women's education, led to the establishment after their deaths of the Pfeiffer Trust to support the education of women. A number of institutions benefited from grants made by the Pfeiffer Trust, most notably Cardiff University (whose constitution from its beginning in 1883 had stated that 'Female students shall be admitted to attend any of the courses of instruction established at the college'). During Miss Maitland's time as Principal, Somerville had already begun to appreciate the need for a new library and to understand the level of funding that it would require. An application to the Pfeiffer Trust in 1892 brought in an endowment of £2,500, initially used to fund scholarships and then diverted to support the building of the library [32].

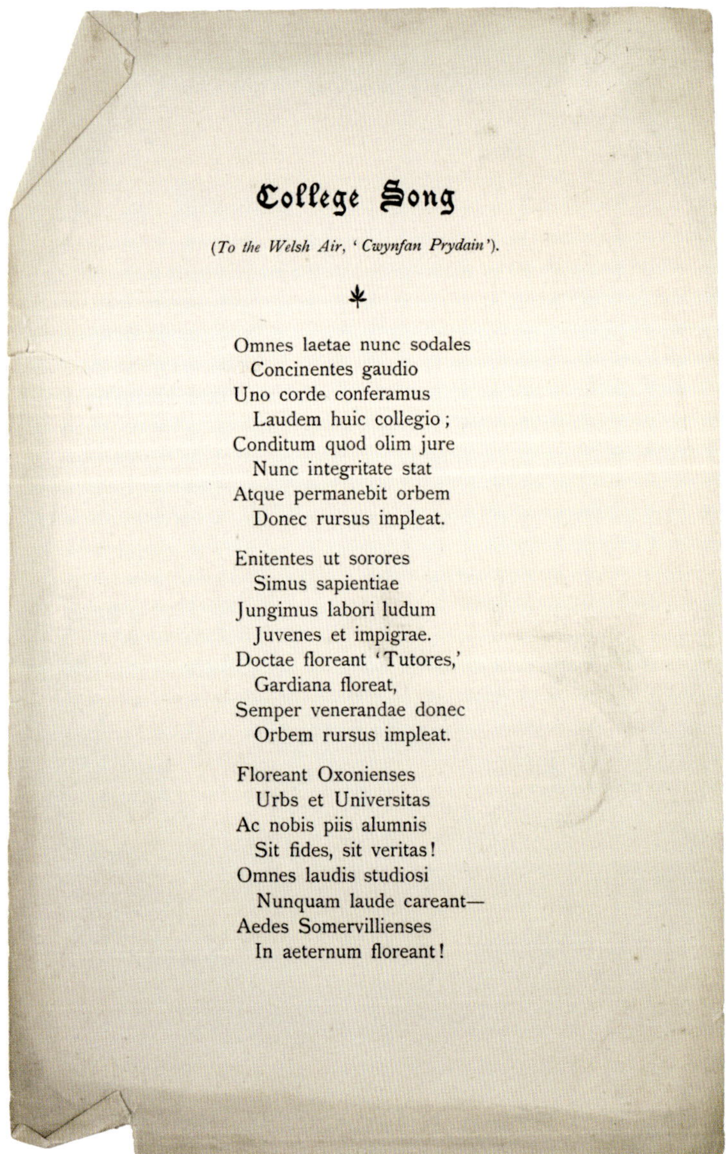

Comrades all in joyful union
Singing loud with common cheer,
Let's with one accord now offer
Praises to this college here;
Which once lawfully established
Sound in status does remain,
And will last and long continue
Till the orb is filled again.

While we earnestly endeavour
Wisdom's sisters to become,
Being young and lively women
Mix we with our studies fun.
May our learned tutors flourish,
May our Principal long reign,
Ever to be venerated
Till the orb is filled again.

Oxford City flourish also
And its University
And in us, its staunch alumni,
Be faith, be integrity!
May each one, renown pursuing,
Never unrenownĕd be –
And may Somerville, our college,
Flourish in eternity!

*'Aedes Somervillienses
In aeternum floreant!'*

29
College Song

Flourishing, rejoicing and truth abound in the Latin lyrics of Somerville's College Song. Written in 1903 by Helen Darbishire, Margaret F. Moor (1880–1959) and Margaret Robertson (1882–1967), it has to be admitted that it is neither a musical nor poetic triumph. The sense of a school song was not one that even a later change of tune could remove. The song's first tune – 'To the Welsh Air, "Cwynfan Prydain"' – was later abandoned in favour of something much easier to sing: music for a lovely hymn written in 1797 by Joseph Haydn as an anthem for the Emperor Francis II's birthday. Unfortunately it was later used for the German national anthem and in the 1930s became particularly identified with the Nazi regime ('Deutschland, Deutschland, über alles…'). A rendition of the Song, recently returned to its first tune, forms the closing part of the college's annual Foundation Dinner, begun in 1994 to honour Somerville's history.

30
Sporting trophies

These early trophies were awarded to the victors in Somerville's in-college sculling and tennis competitions. Pauline Adams, Somerville's Librarian and also the author of *Somerville for Women*, the history of the college from its foundation to 1993, noted there that sport was always 'a minority interest' in Somerville. With typical modesty she fails to mention that she herself rowed at bow in the women's blue boat in 1965, and in recent years sport at Somerville has come rather more to the forefront of college life. The college boat club has enjoyed considerable successes, proudly displaying blades in the bar [137], and Somervillians have appeared again in the women's blue boat as well as in the men's varsity rugby match. As yet, however, there is no suggestion that the tennis court that was once outside the library should be reinstated.

from the College Letter for 1926–7

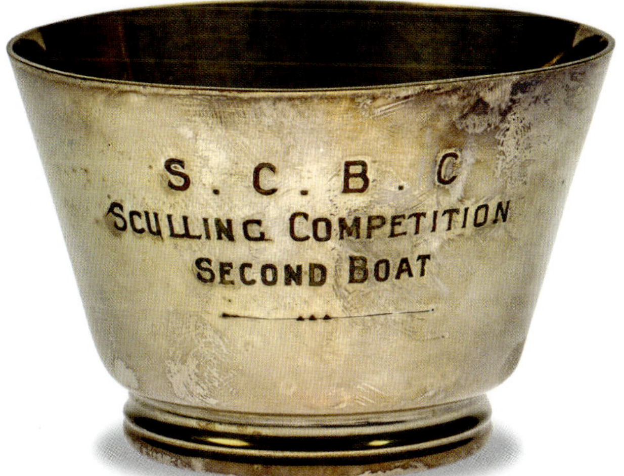

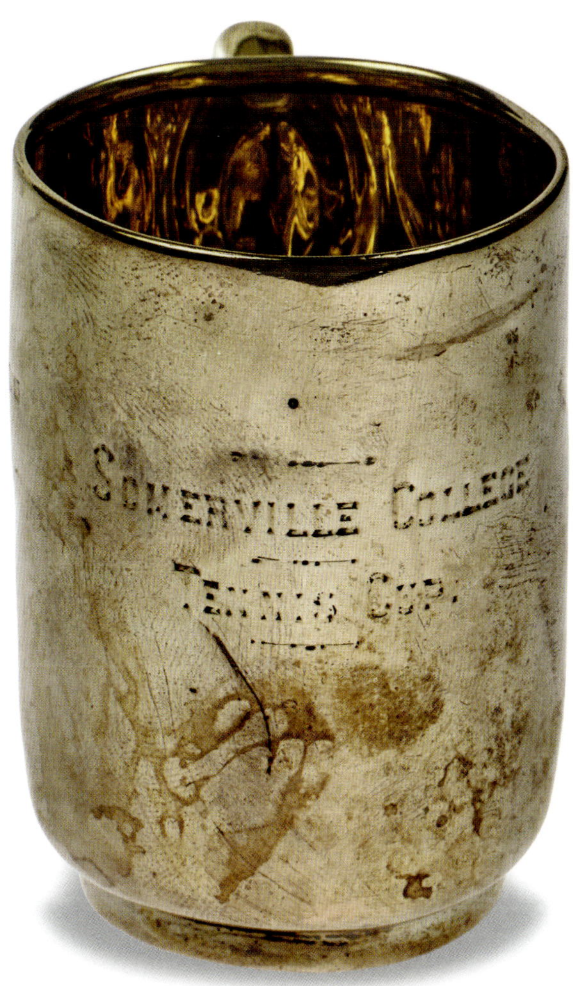

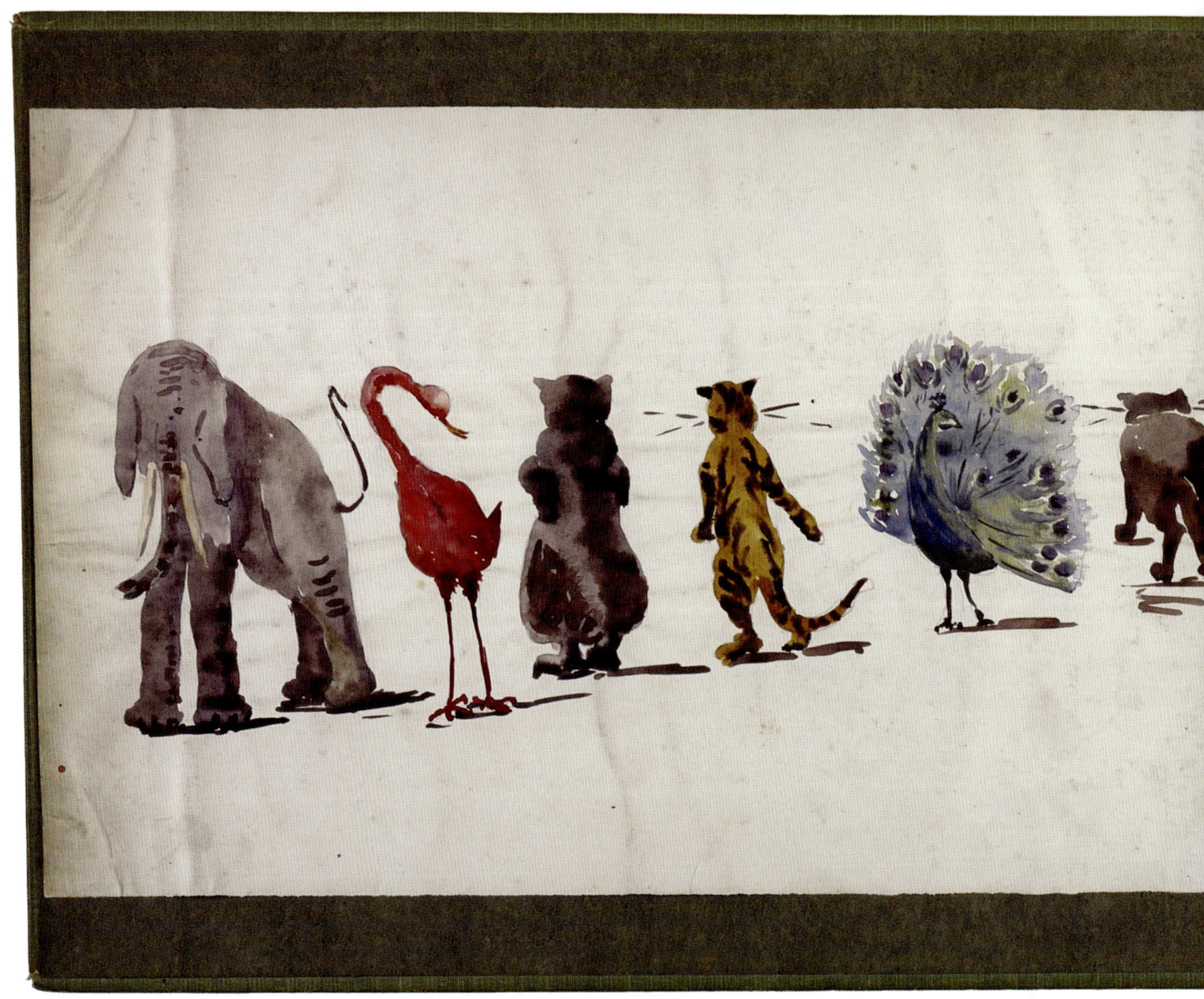

Going Down Play

The 'Going Down Play' (or just 'GDP') was a Somerville tradition, a kind of revue put on by final year students, and the 1903 production was accompanied by this beautiful and funny set of illustrations and descriptions. Each animal represents a member of the college, and later in the book every one gets its own lengthy description. The twist? Each person chose the animal she felt best represented herself. After proffering the general view that 'the old grey sheep' is considered wise, Helen Darbishire goes on to note: 'Let the scientific fact be recognized once and for all that the animal's head is chiefly composed of wool both inside and out'. Darbishire went on to become Principal of Somerville, and although photographs do suggest something woolly about her appearance, no one could accuse this internationally recognised authority on Wordsworth and Milton of being fluffy.

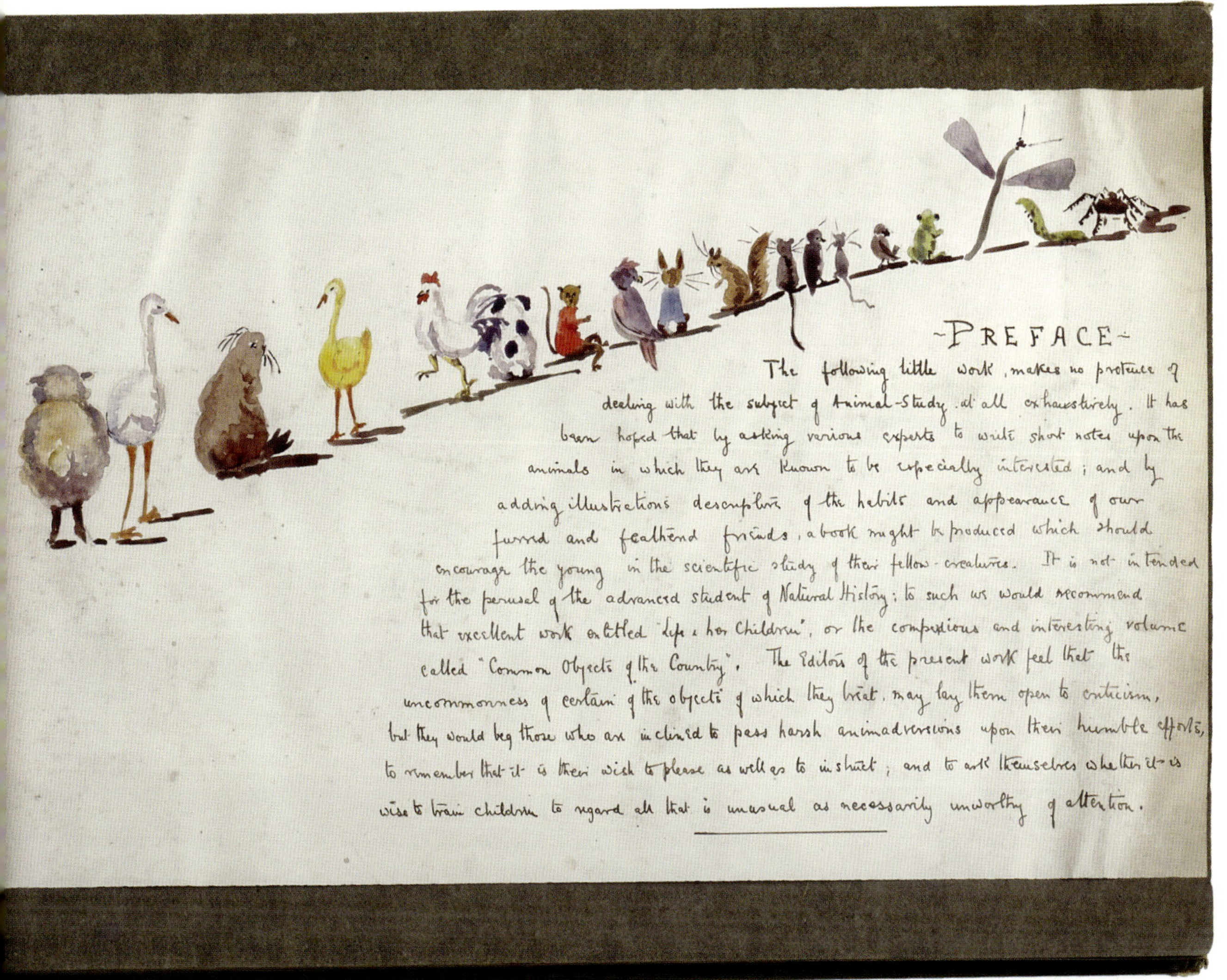

'There seems to be a current belief taking its rise no doubt from a general recognition of the large size of this animal's head, that the old grey sheep is wise.'

The Old Grey Sheep (Miss H. Darbishire)

The chief haunts of this animal are the fields, but it has been seen browsing in the Parks. There seems to be a current belief taking its rise no doubt from a general recognition of the large size of this animal's head that the old grey sheep is wise. Let the scientific fact be recognized once and for all that the animal's head is chiefly composed of wool both inside and out. Its brain is in fact so small that a very little work tires it and its natural instincts quickly drive it out to the fields for refreshment.

One instance however of the exceptional foresight which characterizes this animal and distinguishes it from others of its kind, is its habit of carrying food and other necessaries in a bag, which is green in colour so as to match the grass. This is one of the most successful instances of the instinct of self-colorization which prompts animals to protect themselves from observation. As soon as the Sheep has got into the grass the bag becomes invisible against a background of its own colour, and the animal is safe from the attacks of other animals which might be attracted to steal the contents. By very bold observers bread-and-butter and a pocket Milton have been detected inside the bag, and it has been conjectured upon this very slender evidence that these form the staple food of the animal. It does not like to be shut up in the Menagerie, but strays whenever it can.

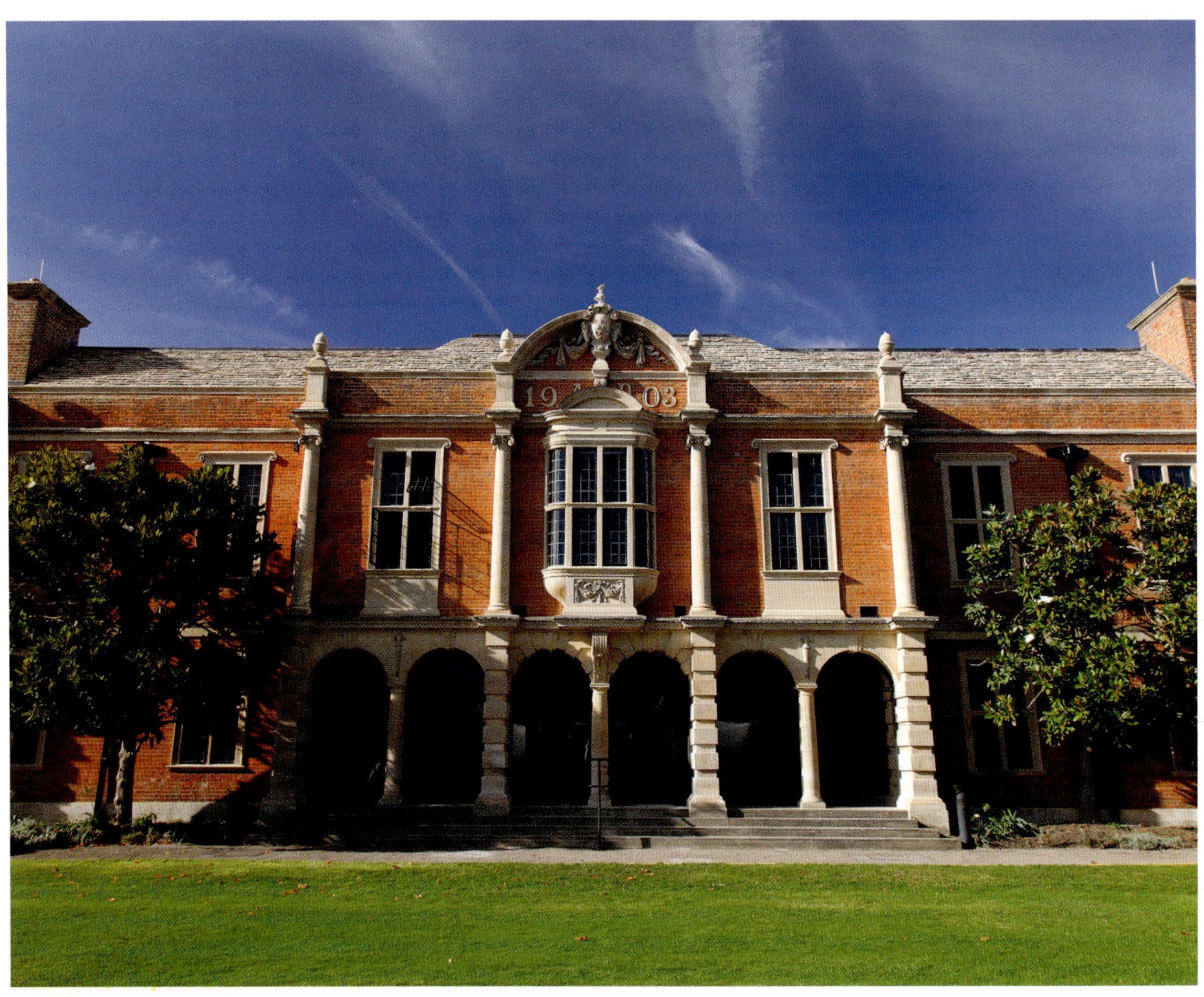

Somerville's heart is surely its library. One of the biggest undergraduate libraries in Oxford, it now contains more than 100,000 volumes. Its superb provision is, in fact, a product of discrimination. Women students were not permitted to use the Bodleian Library independently until 1920. Before that they might, with advance permission and a chaperone, be admitted to look at specific volumes, but as any student will tell you, that's no way to get your essay written.

Books were among the first things ever given to Somerville. Mrs Stephen Winkworth (1839–1909), one of the earliest subscribers to the fund for Somerville Hall, donated 72 volumes, including Gibbon and Macaulay. Somerville was conscious of the importance of its collection of books, and in 1894 it established a library committee but it had no dedicated room to house its collection. In 1899 Miss Maitland secured the

services of a former Somerville student, Margery Fry, as Librarian. Fry found the college's books on shelves in the dining rooms and in the corridors, and their numbers were ever-growing. She began to sketch elevations of a possible library building, and shortly afterwards a fortuitous series of bequests and a successful application to a trust [28] allowed the plans to become reality. The new building was to link the two parts of the college together, with

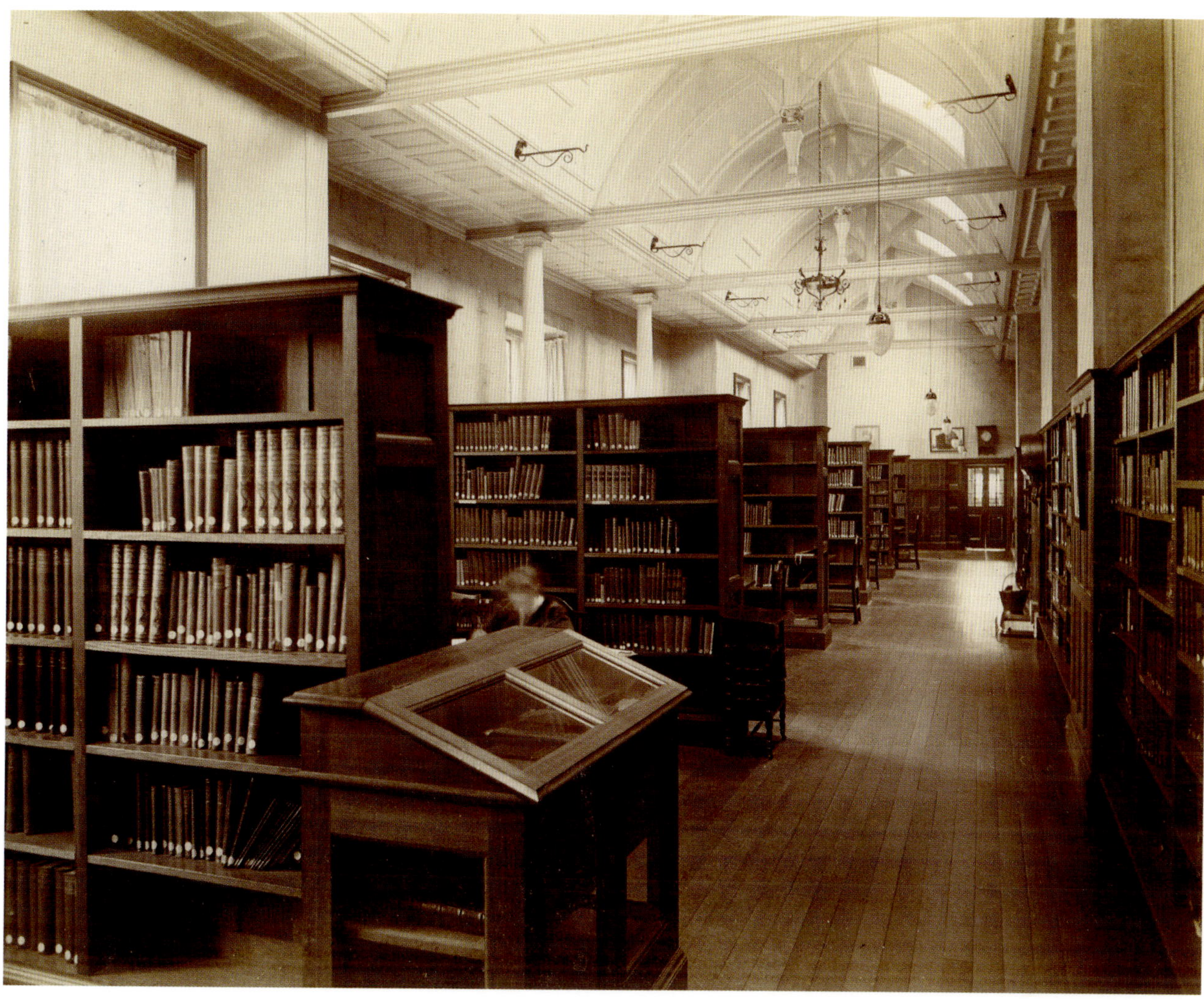

accommodation on the ground floor and the library on the upper floor. It was the first library to be built by a women's college in Oxford, and where the men's colleges often had small medieval libraries designed with fellows in mind, Somerville's library was, from the beginning, for its students as well. There were some difficulties: the architect of the library, Basil Champneys (1842–1935 [112]), chose to pick out the college's motto in white bricks along the front of the building. Margery Fry was horrified at how it looked: 'I could weep at the sight of those horrid white words', she said, and she and Miss Maitland agreed that the motto would have to go. Champneys complied, though grudgingly. A grand opening ceremony, complete with its own masque [33], gave the library a flying start and gifts of furniture were made [34]. The library had been put up just in time: two huge bequests of books came to Somerville shortly afterwards. One was from Amelia Edwards [18, 41–7], who had insisted that her collection must remain together, so a special room in the library was set aside for it. The other was the library of John Stuart Mill (1806–73 [38–40]), whose stepdaughter, Helen Taylor (1831–1907), gave the collection without condition, so that it was simply absorbed into the stock of books, increasing it by almost a third [38].

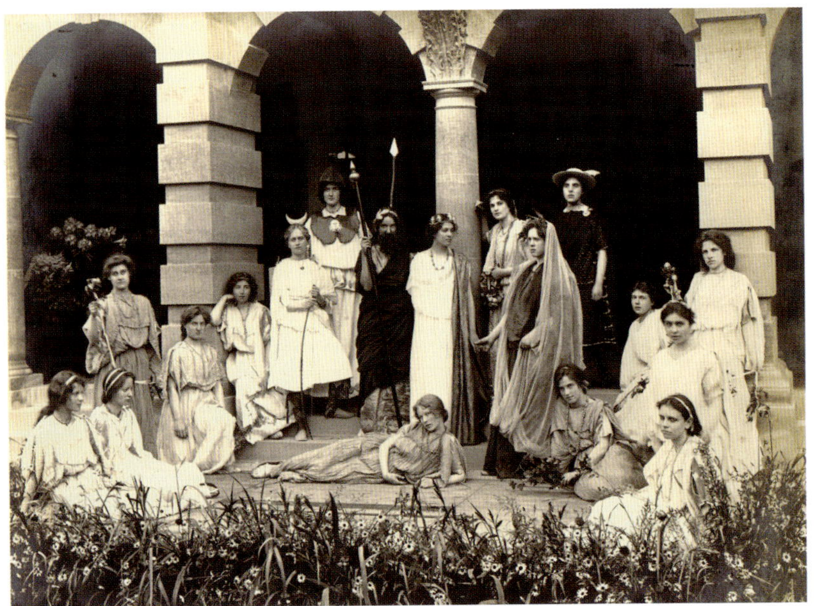

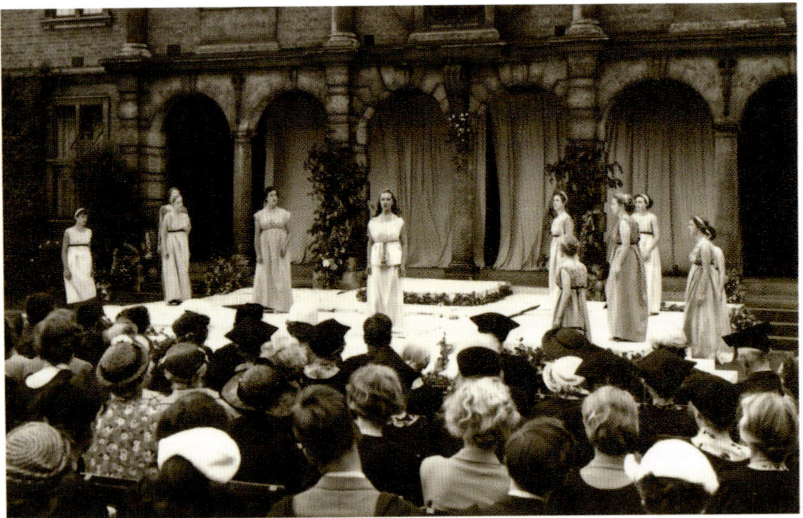

33
Photographs of *Demeter*

The work of Robert Bridges (1844–1930) is out of fashion at present, but at the turn of the nineteenth and twentieth centuries his fame was growing and in 1913 he was made Poet Laureate. Parry, Holst and Finzi set his poems to music, and he wrote and translated a number of familiar hymns (including 'All my hope on God is founded'). In his notes for the 1905 edition of *Demeter*, Robert Bridges wrote: 'This mask [*sic*] was written in 1904 at the request of the ladies of Somerville College, Oxford, and was acted by them at the inauguration of their new buildings in that year.' The largest part of the 'new buildings' was the library [32]. The choice of subject matter for the masque may have been suggested by Margery Fry (she almost certainly approached Bridges, who was married to her cousin). Demeter, the goddess of grain and harvest, was the mother of Persephone, who was taken to the underworld by Hades and only released when Demeter caused the crops to wither and die. Zeus tricked Persephone, forcing her to return to the underworld for part of each year, when Demeter mourns and winter comes. Music to accompany the performance was composed by Sir William Henry Hadow (1859–1937, brother of Grace Hadow [34]). The production was revived in 1954 to mark the jubilee of the library.

34

Exhibition cabinet

Grace Hadow (1875–1940) came up to Somerville in 1900 but was already connected to the college: her brother, Sir William Henry Hadow (who had been Dean of Worcester College), was a member of the Somerville College Council. Hadow and her brother would therefore have seen at first hand the building work for the new library, opened in 1904 [32]. It was William Henry Hadow who wrote the music played at that opening, and it was to the library that Grace Hadow gave this handsome exhibition cabinet, which can be seen in the earliest photographs of the library [32] and which is still the centrepiece of the library's displays today.

Hadow herself remained closely involved in education all her life, with a particular focus on adult education. There was talk of her becoming Principal of Somerville but she refused to stand against Margery Fry. In 1929 Hadow became Principal of the Society of Oxford Home-Students (later St Anne's College).

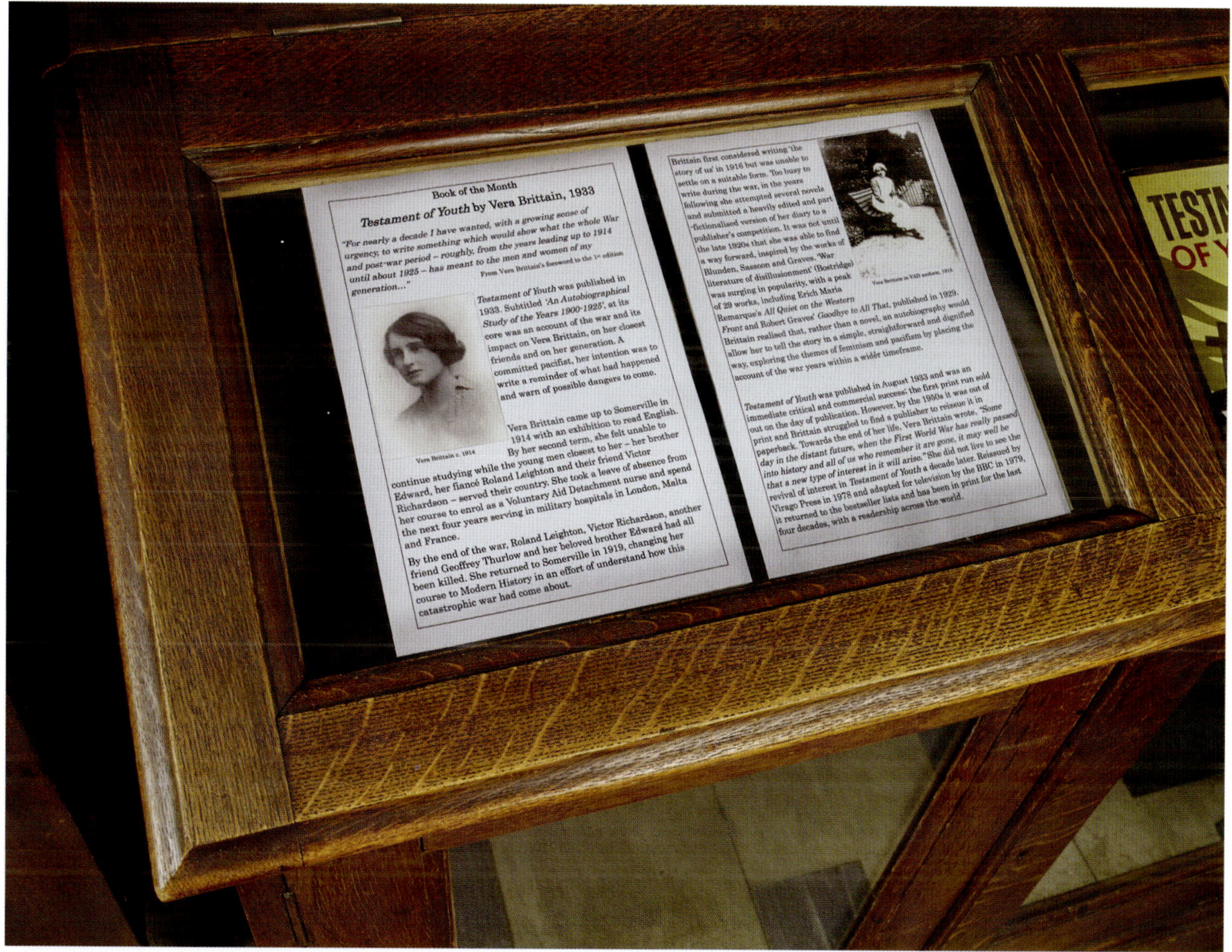

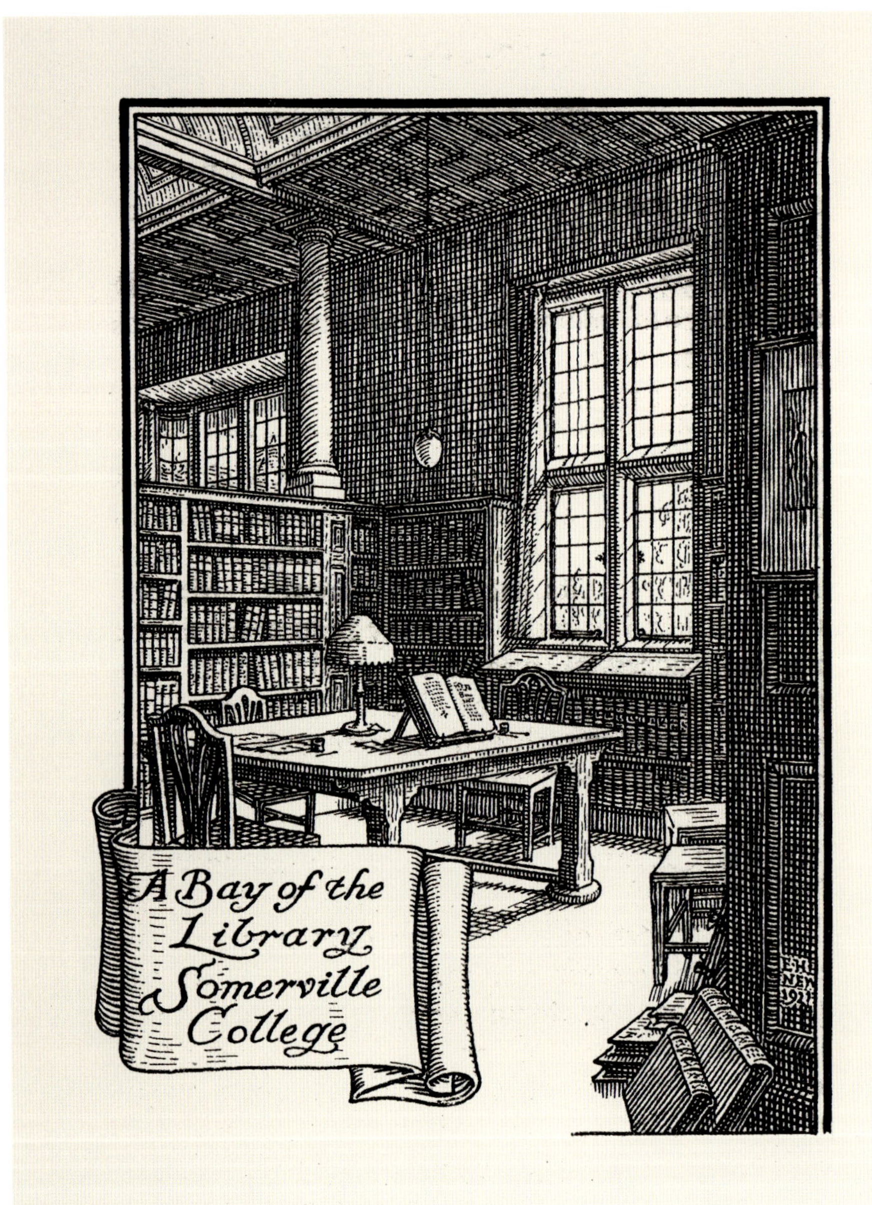

35
Desk and easel

A piece of furniture whose utility has stood the test of time, this library desk with pull-up easel remains popular with students taking notes, even if their notebooks have now become laptops. A number of the tables in the library were given either by or in memory of Henry Pelham [13, 23], Camden Professor of Ancient History and later President of Trinity College, and also a member of the first Somerville committee. This may have been one of them, although the gift book [10] also notes that in 1894 (before the new library was built), Mr W. Rathbone gave 'A Set of Library Furniture', which could have included this kind of piece. Whatever its origins, the table was considered such a feature of the library that it was included as an engraving by Edmund New (1871–1931) in the first history of Somerville, published in 1922. Somerville's library continues to ensure that its working spaces keep up with the newest developments [136].

The ground floor of what is now the library was originally divided into student rooms, each with its own fireplace. The plaster designs echo the decorative stonework on the outside of the building, substituting an 'S' for 'Somerville' in place of the coat of arms. This example was in the room once occupied by Indira Nehru (later Gandhi [109]). Despite its presence, she still found the room freezing cold. When the library was renovated in the later part of the twentieth century, Somerville displayed sensible practicality in the face of the urge to beautify. An adviser on artistic restoration suggested that the plaster fruits and flowers around the fireplaces might be picked out in 'fleshy tones'. The then Library Fellow was heard to repeat the phrase, slowly and witheringly. The plaster remains unpainted.

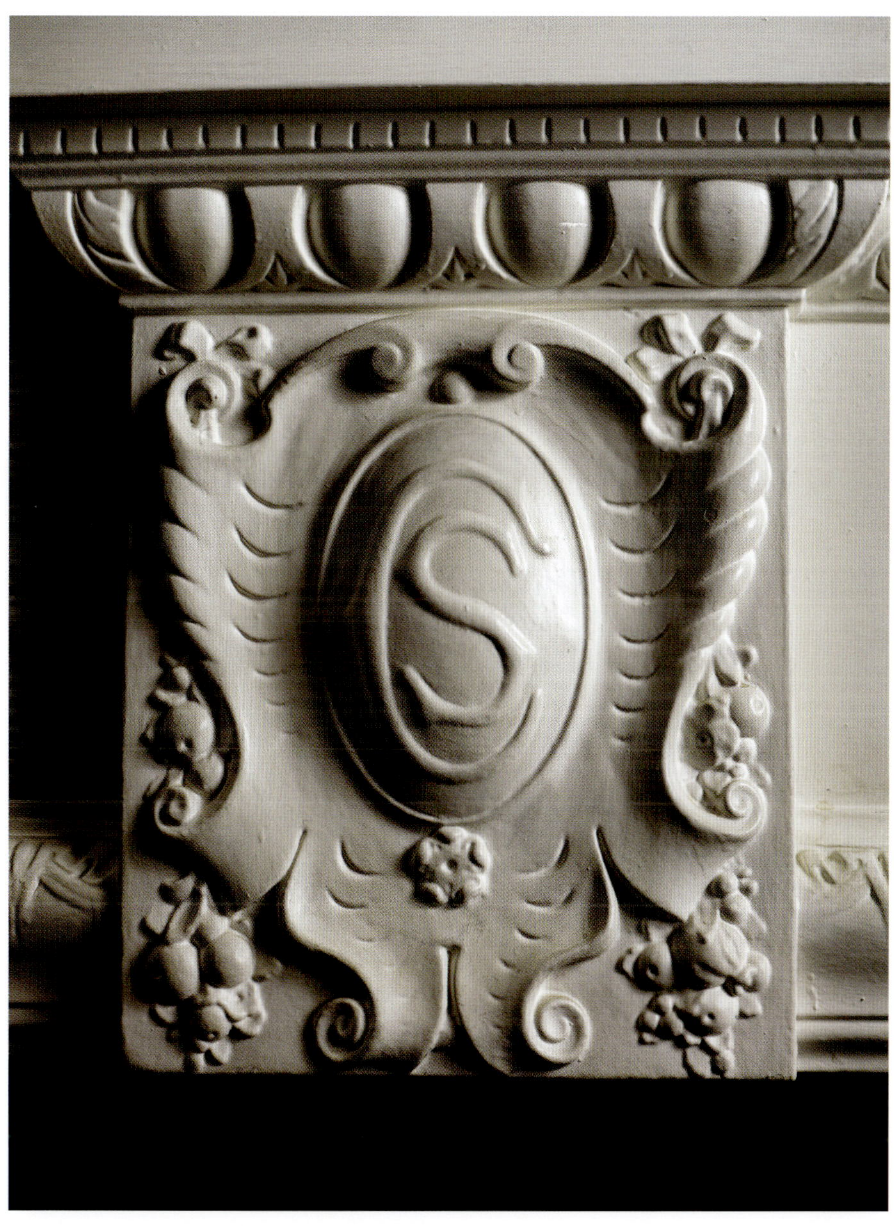

37
Parliament Book

The Somerville Parliamentary Debating Society (which quickly became known as plain 'Parliament') was, by the beginning of the twentieth century, the college's main debating society. It was automatically open to all members of the college, and modelled itself on a similar society in Newnham, Cambridge. Parliament introduced bills and passed legislation, following the strict rules of parliamentary behaviour (including referring to each member in discussion as 'The Honourable Gentleman') and tracking the hot social and political issues of the day, from Home Rule to the Poor Law. It soon became a star player in cross-college debates. There was occasional levity (the impeachment of 'Baron Fry', aka Margery Fry, for bribery and corruption, for instance), but debate was usually so relevant that Somerville's Parliament had an unnerving habit of foreshadowing real bills at Westminster.

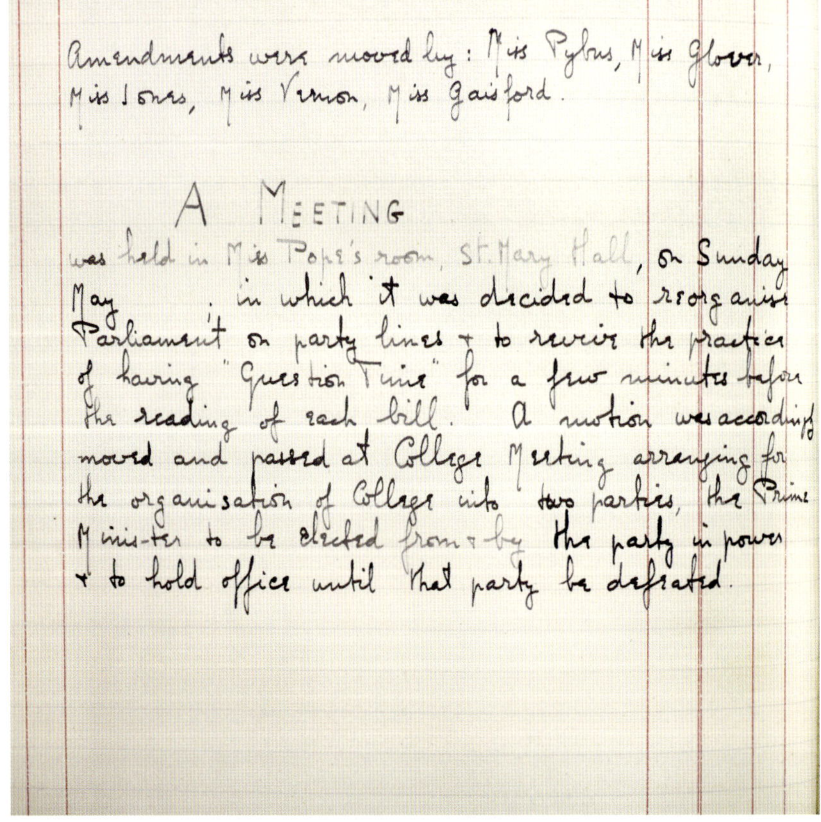

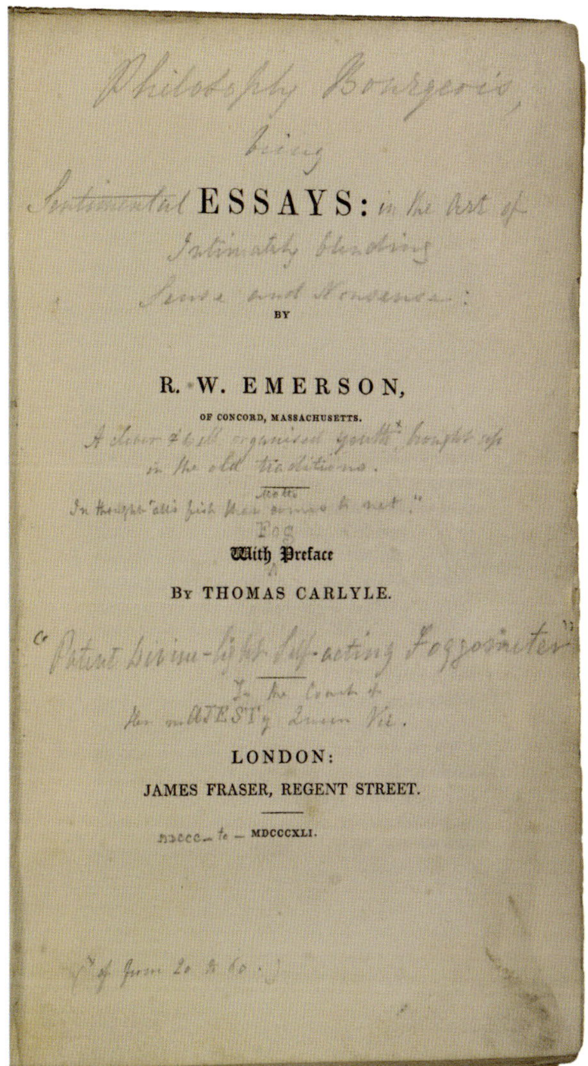

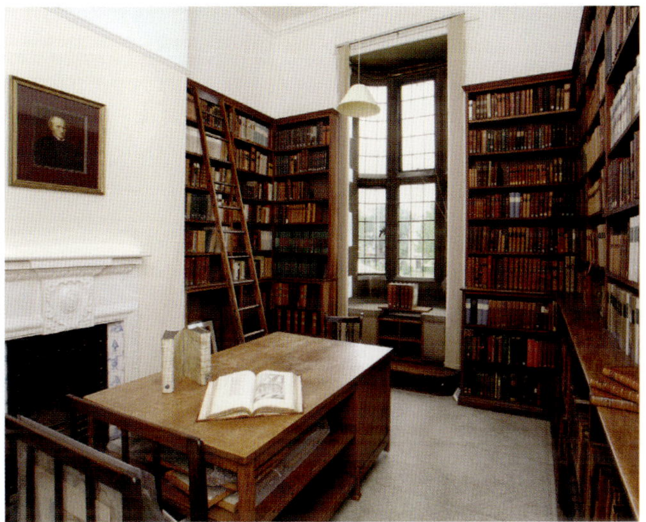

38
John Stuart Mill's copy
of Emerson's *Essays*

Somerville has held the 1,674 volumes of John Stuart Mill's library since they were given to the college by his stepdaughter, Helen Taylor, in 1905 [32]. Alongside his many accomplishments in the fields of philosophy and political economy, Mill was also a writer of comments in the books he owned, and it is these marginalia that are now the subject of a digitisation project, in partnership with the University of Alabama. Somerville is also home to a project to restore many of Mill's books. Much of the library comes originally from Mill's father, James, an economist and political philosopher, and the annotations of both father and son can be found on their copies of everything from Smith's *The Wealth of Nations* to Emerson's *Essays* (published in 1841). When Frank Prochaska, now a Senior Research Fellow at Somerville, looked into the volume in 2013, he discovered a sharp dismissal from Mill, who rewrote Emerson's title as 'Sentimental Essays in the Art of Intimately blending Sense and Nonsense'.

ENFRANCHISEMENT

OF

WOMEN

BY

MRS. STUART MILL

Reprinted from the 'WESTMINSTER REVIEW' for July, 1851.

LONDON

TRÜBNER AND CO., 60, PATERNOSTER ROW.

1868.

Price One Penny.

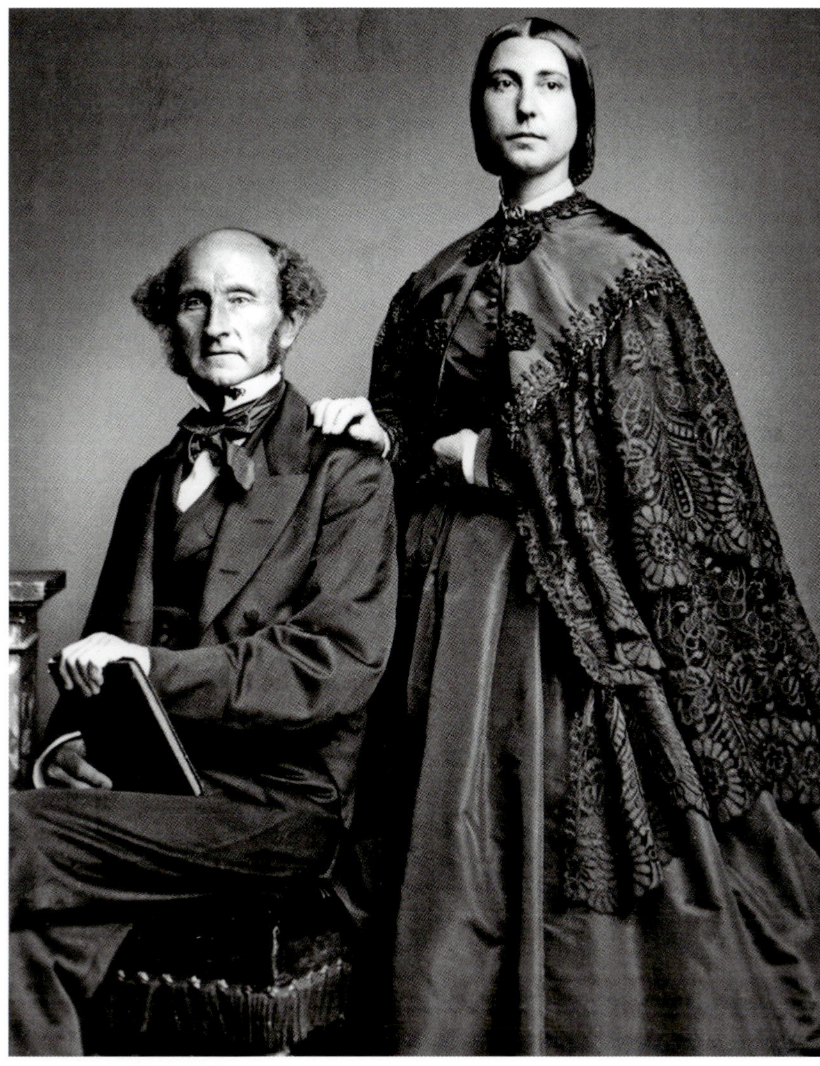

39
Harriet Taylor Mill,
The Enfranchisement of Women

Harriet Taylor Mill (1807–58) grew up with a strong interest in social reform and the equality of women. Her long friendship with John Stuart Mill began in part because the two shared an interest in women's rights. He inspired her writing and she inspired his. After her first husband died, she married Mill, and it was Helen, Harriet's daughter from her first marriage (shown here with Mill), who gave books from Mill's library to Somerville. In 1851, Taylor Mill published 'The Enfranchisement of Women' in the *Westminster Review* and in 1868 it was published as the monograph we see here. Inspired by the movement in the United States to secure the vote for women, the essay called for full equality for women in political, civil and social life and for equality before the law 'without distinction of sex or colour'.

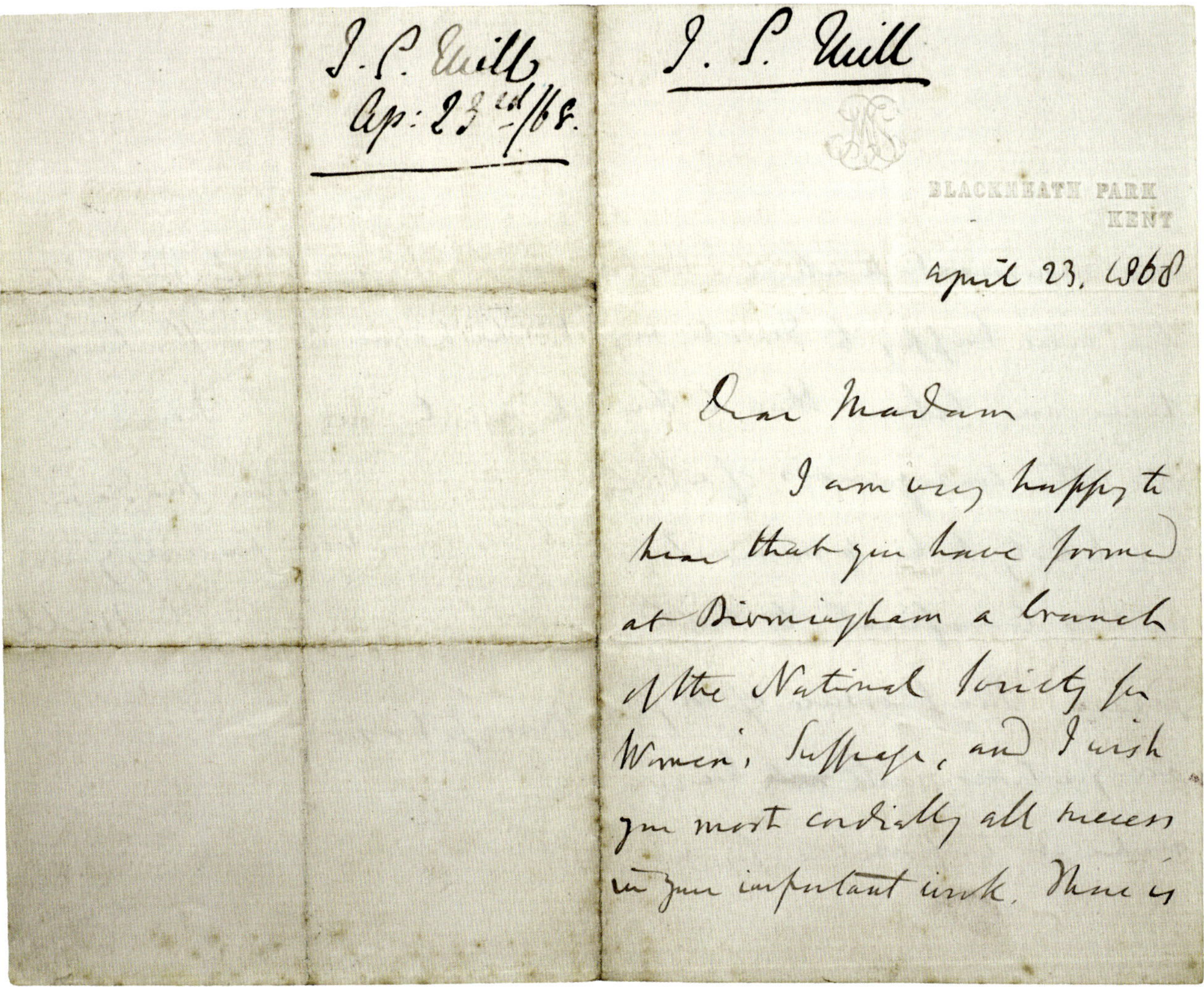

40
John Stuart Mill, letter

Fifty years before the Representation of the People Act gave the first votes to women in 1918, Parliament was already being asked to consider the question of women's suffrage. In 1866, and again two years later, John Stuart Mill put before Parliament signed petitions calling for equal suffrage for women. For both petitions he had deliberately sought out Mary Somerville [1], asking her to be the first signatory on the 1868 petition. In that same year he wrote this letter in response to an invitation to attend a meeting of the newly formed Birmingham branch of the National Society for Women's Suffrage. Though Mill had to concede that the 'pressure' of his 'occupations' made him unable to take up the invitation, he wrote that 'there is no movement to which I should be more happy to devote my time and labour than to this one, the consequences of which are likely to be so momentous and so beneficial to both sexes'. The letter was acquired for Somerville in 2018, with help from the Friends of the John Stuart Mill Library.

no movement to which I should
be more happy to devote my
time and labour than to this
one, the consequences of which
are likely to be so momentous
and so beneficial to both
sexes. The pressure of my
occupations will, however,
make it impossible for me

to be present at the meeting
to which you do me the honour
to invite me. I am

Dear Madam
very sincerely yours

J. S. Mill

Mrs Johnson

'there is no movement to which I should be
more happy to devote my time and labour'

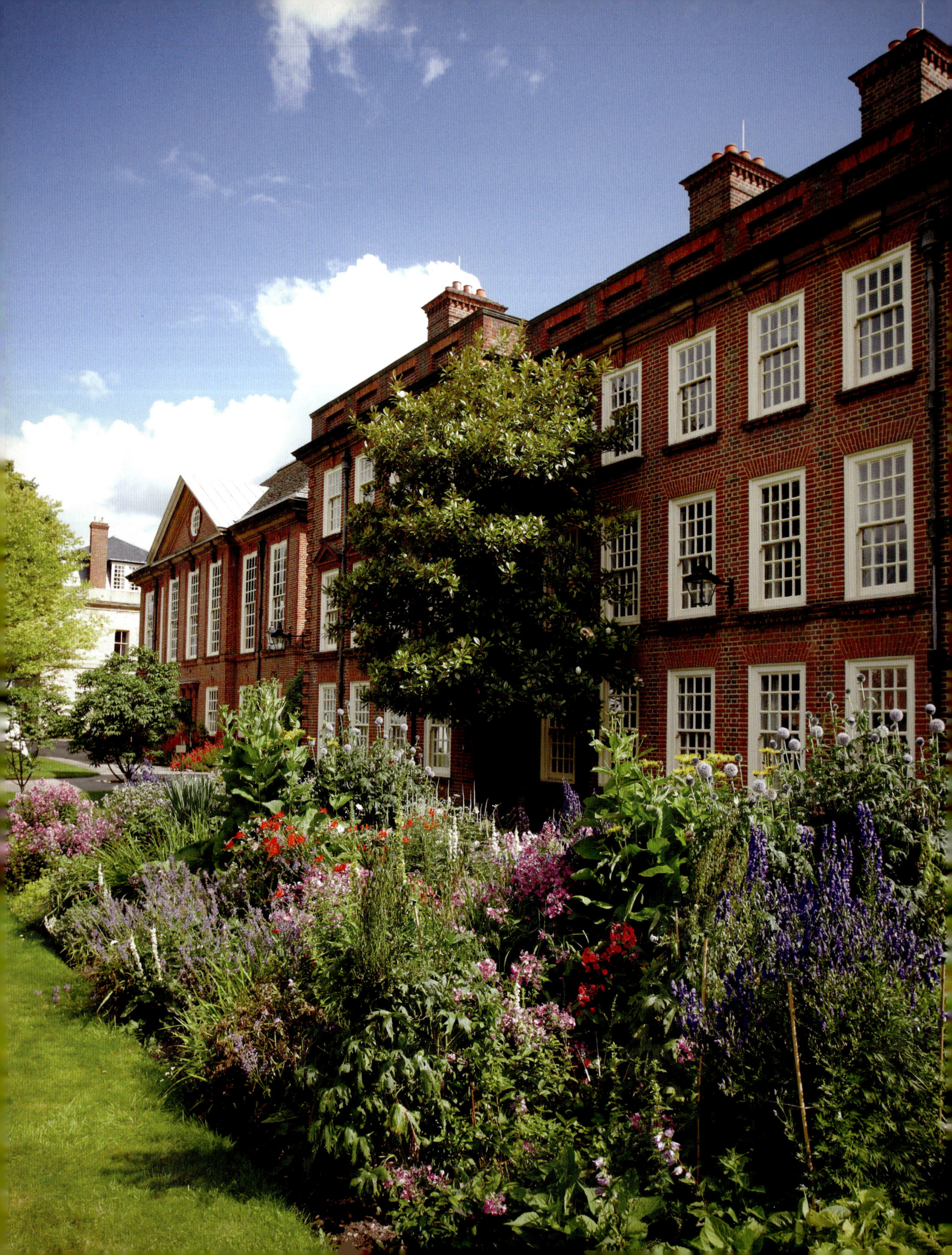

1907–1945
'our entry within the charmed circle'

The First World War meant that the college had to move, temporarily, into accommodation elsewhere in Oxford. But this was no mere interlude. In Somerville, as everywhere else, the War changed everything. The first votes for women came alongside greater freedom for female students, and in 1920 Oxford awarded the first degrees to women. Somerville might have entered the 'charmed circle' (as the Annual Report of 1920 put it), but full equality was yet to be achieved. The tensions of the period – memories of the horrors of the War alongside the hopes of future change – inspired Somervillians to produce works of literature that caught the public imagination (and, in one case, brought much-needed funds to the college).

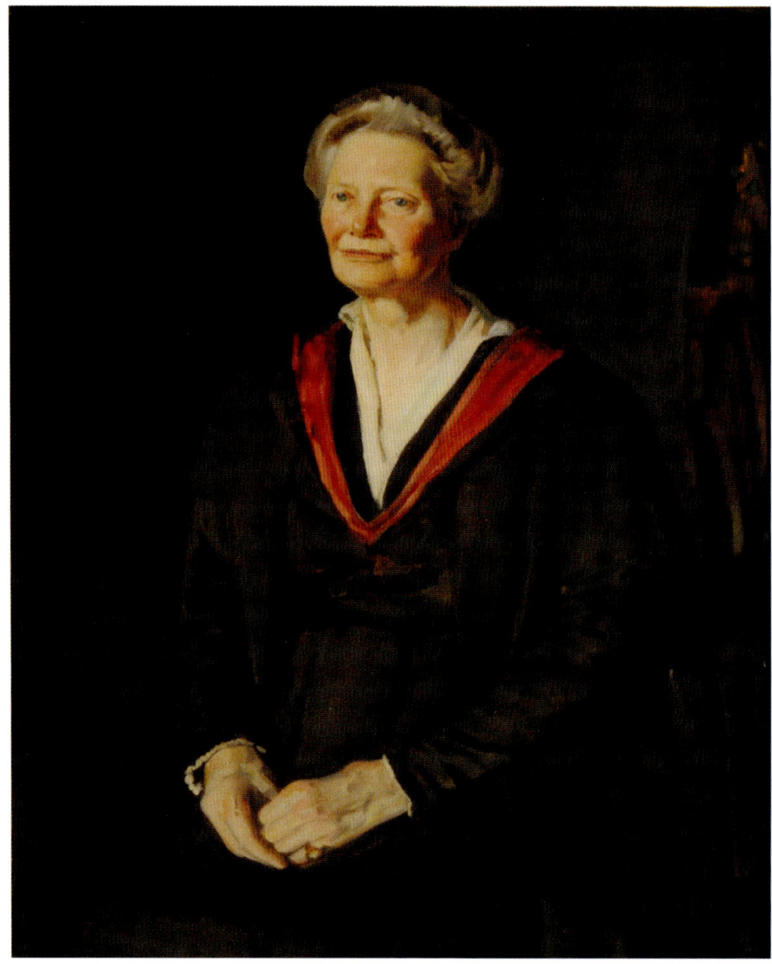

1907–1926
Emily Penrose

Under its third Principal, Emily Penrose (1858–1942), Somerville moved into a different phase. Penrose was 'home grown'. She came up in 1889 and was the first woman to get a First in Literae Humaniores (or 'Greats', covering Latin and Greek language as well as classical history and philosophy). She had also already been Principal of two London colleges before she came back to Somerville. Penrose had the talent and determination to help the college, and the University, look to a new goal: the admission of women to membership of the University. She oversaw arguably the most turbulent and also the most groundbreaking period in Somerville's history. The world was at war, the UK granted its first votes for women and Oxford, eventually, awarded degrees to women. Penrose handled it all with intelligence, strength of will and kindness, as well as a firm degree of practicality (not least when dealing

with loutish behaviour by male students [58]). She also tackled a growing problem: the separation of the college into 'House' and 'West' [20]. Madeleine Shaw Lefevre had written to Agnes Maitland as early as 1889, acknowledging that 'There is a tendency to become separate. I sometimes thought whether it would answer for them to change rooms for a few nights!' Penrose found the solution: the college that eats together works together, and just works. Somerville got its hall, together with new accommodation, and it began to look and feel like a quadrangled Oxford college rather than a collection of private residences. Penrose's overarching achievement was the raising of academic standards at Somerville: her firm insistence that women should take the full degree course in a subject even when they were not allowed to take the actual degree made Somerville a powerhouse of intellectual achievement.

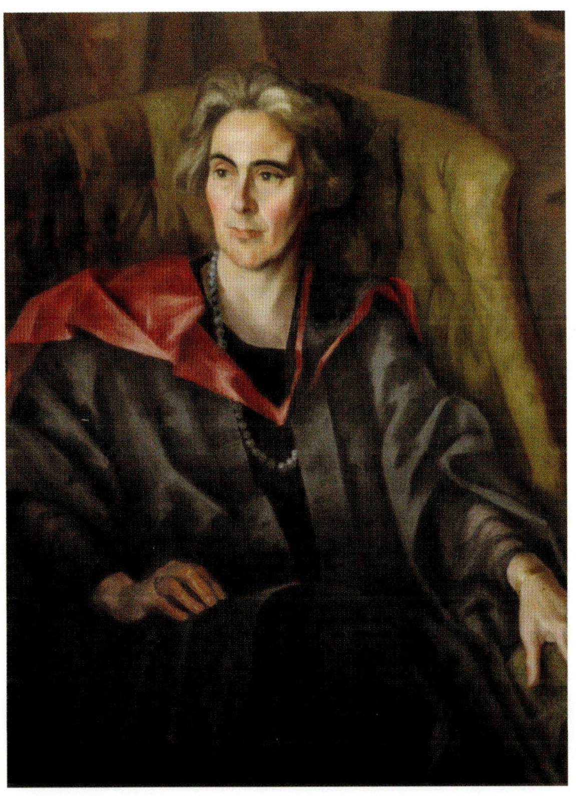

1926–1931
Margery Fry

Penrose was succeeded by Margery Fry (1874–1958), who had been also been a student at Somerville and, for a time, its Librarian [32]. Though Principal for only four years, Fry had a major effect on Somerville in two ways. First, she built on Miss Maitland's interest in public service, going on to lead the cause for prison reform after her time at Somerville. Second, she drew the influence of the Bloomsbury group into the college. Her brother, Roger Fry (1866–1934), was a hugely important figure in the formation of the taste of the English middle classes in the years before the Second World War, and a number of his paintings have been given to the college [76]. One Somervillian recalled how nice it was to hear Margery Fry talk: 'she is so direct, vigorous and sincere'.

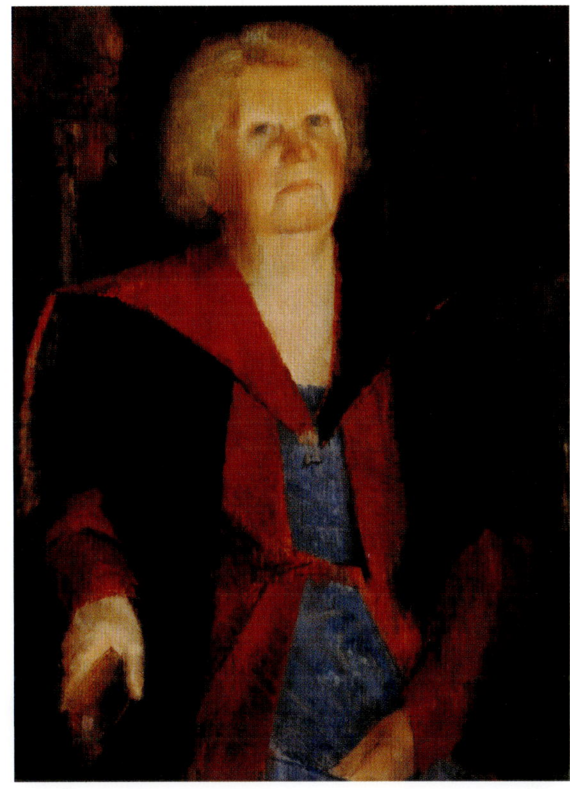

1931–1945
Helen Darbishire

The appointment of Helen Darbishire (1881–1961) as Principal caused consternation among some Somervillians. She was a renowned expert on Wordsworth, and there were those who felt that she was too academic, too narrow, and not sufficiently acquainted with the world beyond Oxford. There was even correspondence in the press about the matter. The undergraduates of the time thought this was in poor taste, and as a result they treated Darbishire with particular respect and affection. She brought a much-needed eye for detail, a warmth of personality and a zest for building works that proved energising for Somerville. She had no difficulty at all in maintaining her academic research alongside her Principalian duties: when an item of college business required urgent attention, a messenger would take the necessary documents to Miss Darbishire's customary seat in the Bodleian.

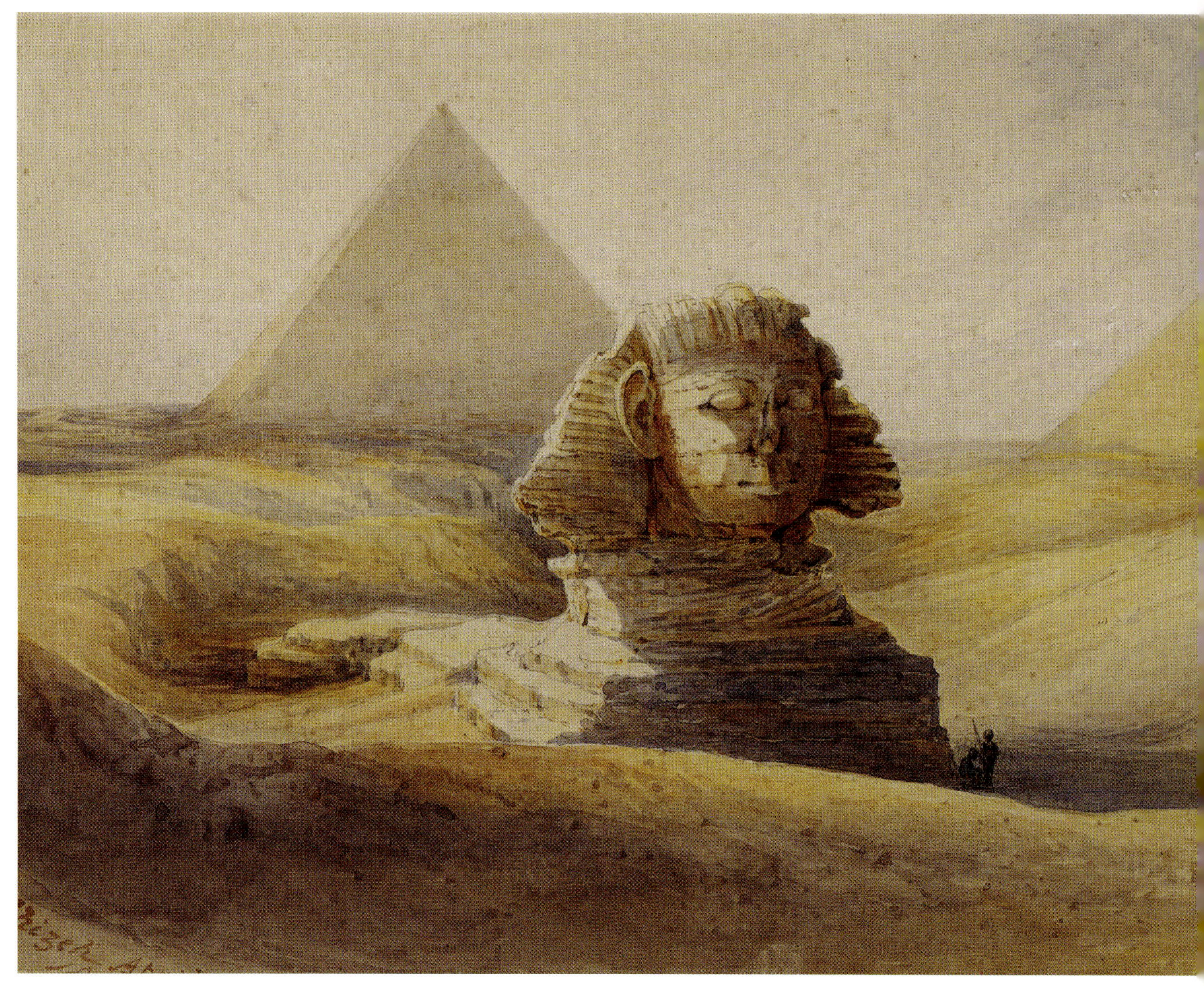

41
Amelia Edwards
A Thousand Miles up the Nile

What is a Victorian bestseller about Egypt doing in Somerville? Its author, Amelia Blandford Edwards, was already well known for her fiction (her 1864 work, *Barbara's History*, was especially popular) when she published her travelogue about a voyage along the Nile, illustrated with engravings after her own watercolours, one of which is shown here. She began to travel extensively during the 1850s, but it was a trip to Egypt in 1873 that left her not only with a new interest in Egyptian history, but also concerned about the neglect with which Egyptian historical artefacts were being treated. She quickly became an admirer of Sir William Flinders Petrie (1853–1942), who was one of the first to introduce scientific principles and ethical protocols to archaeological excavations. Edwards's bequest to University College, London (UCL), to set up a chair in Egyptology included the stipulation that Petrie should be the first holder, and in the later part of Edwards's life Petrie sent her numerous gifts of artefacts. Egypt became an obsession for Edwards, and she was one of the co-founders of the Egypt Exploration Society. She received no formal education herself and espoused the cause of women's education and equality throughout her life, becoming friends with Madeleine

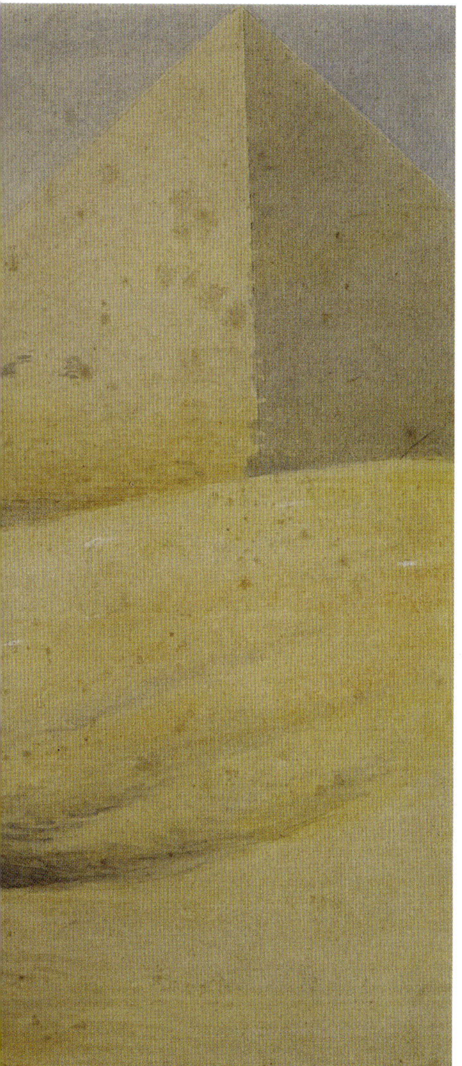

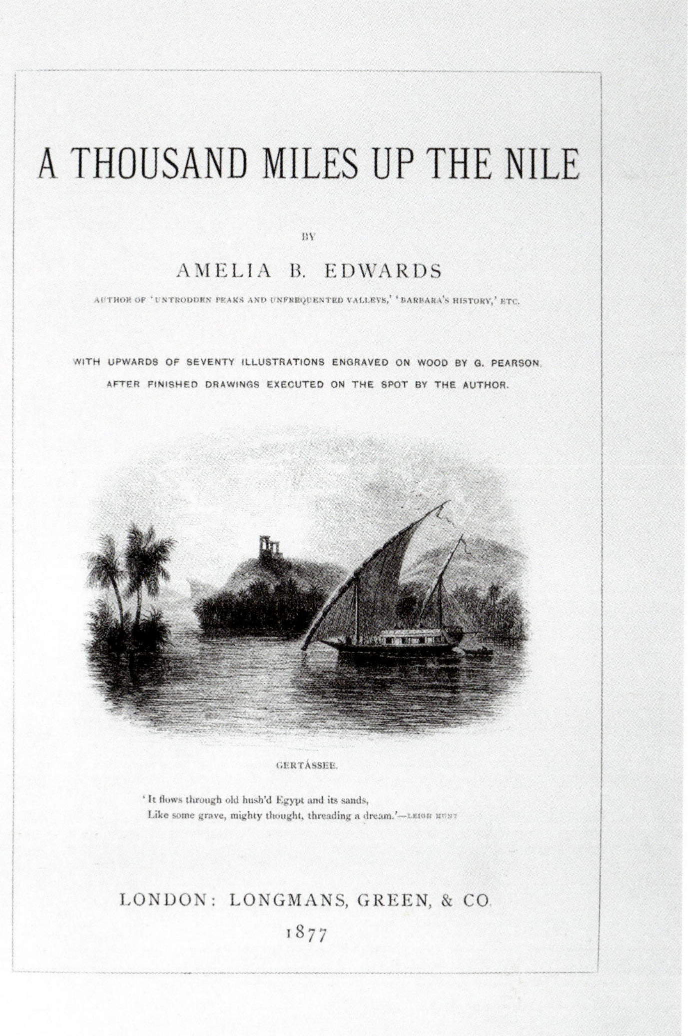

Shaw Lefevre and Agnes Maitland (both of whom were also members of the Egypt Exploration Society). She left the bulk of her library and her collection of Egyptian antiquities to UCL, but also bequeathed to Somerville about two thousand volumes, a selection of her papers and watercolours and a collection of 32 antiquities. The library's note on these ancient objects describes them as 'extremely heterogeneous'; a cataloguing of the collection was made possible by the generous gift of John Wells, a former College Lecturer in Physics. For a time a selection of artefacts from the bequest was displayed in a glass case outside Hall, but the theft of a number of the Graeco-Roman items in 1988 led the college to remove the collection to a more secure location. An article in *Trace* magazine led to the return of five of the stolen pots.

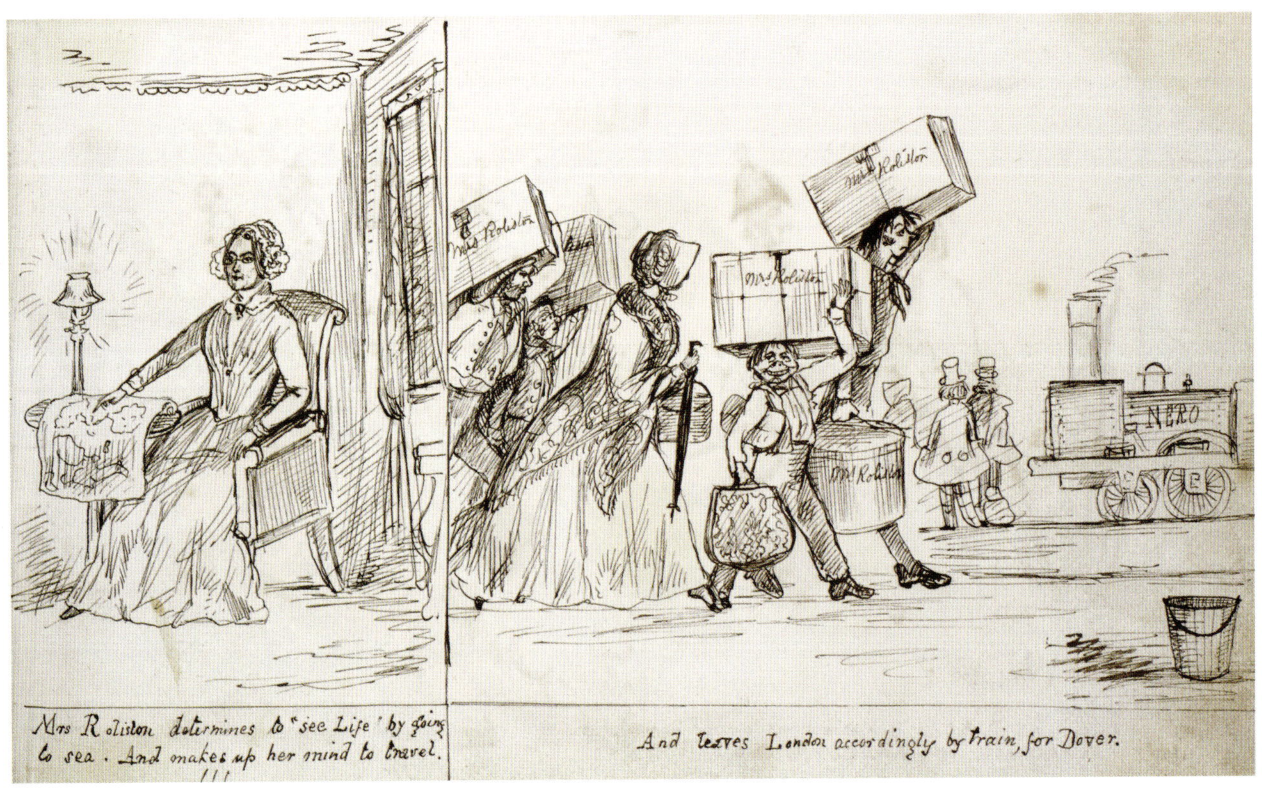

Mrs Roliston determines to "see Life" by going to sea. And makes up her mind to travel. !!!

And leaves London accordingly by train, for Dover.

42
'Mrs Roliston's Travelling Adventures'

Drawn by Amelia Edwards when she was 17, this wonderful book of pen and ink sketches tells the story of the intrepid Mrs Roliston, who 'makes up her mind to travel. !!!'. She abandons her chair, lamp and embroidery, and 'leaves London accordingly by train, for Dover', surrounded by servants and suitcases. As a child Edwards's artistic talent had been noticed by the illustrator George Cruikshank (1792–1878), who offered to teach her, but her parents considered that the life of an artist was not sufficiently respectable. Amusing and accomplished in its own right, 'Mrs Roliston's Travelling Adventures' also prefigures Edwards's own life. She began to travel extensively in the 1870s, and she used her artistic talents to make a record of her journeys [41]. The volume has recently been the subject of a crowdfunding campaign in Somerville which will enable it to be digitised by the Bodleian Library.

These 'mummy masks' may well have been part of the collection of objects sent by William Flinders Petrie to Amelia Edwards [41, 42, 44]. They are made from wood covered with 'cartonnage' (layers of linen that have been stiffened with gesso, a white paint mixture consisting of a binder mixed with gypsum) and then lavishly painted with white slip and red and black pigment. The mask would have been worn over the face of a wrapped head of a mummy, attached with pegs. The purpose of these masks was to provide protection for the head of a mummy as well as offering an idealised version of its appearance. The ancient Egyptians believed that the spirit would survive death and leave the tomb. The mask was a way for the spirit to recognise its host when it returned. This example probably dates from the period c.664–332 BC. Its provenance is unknown.

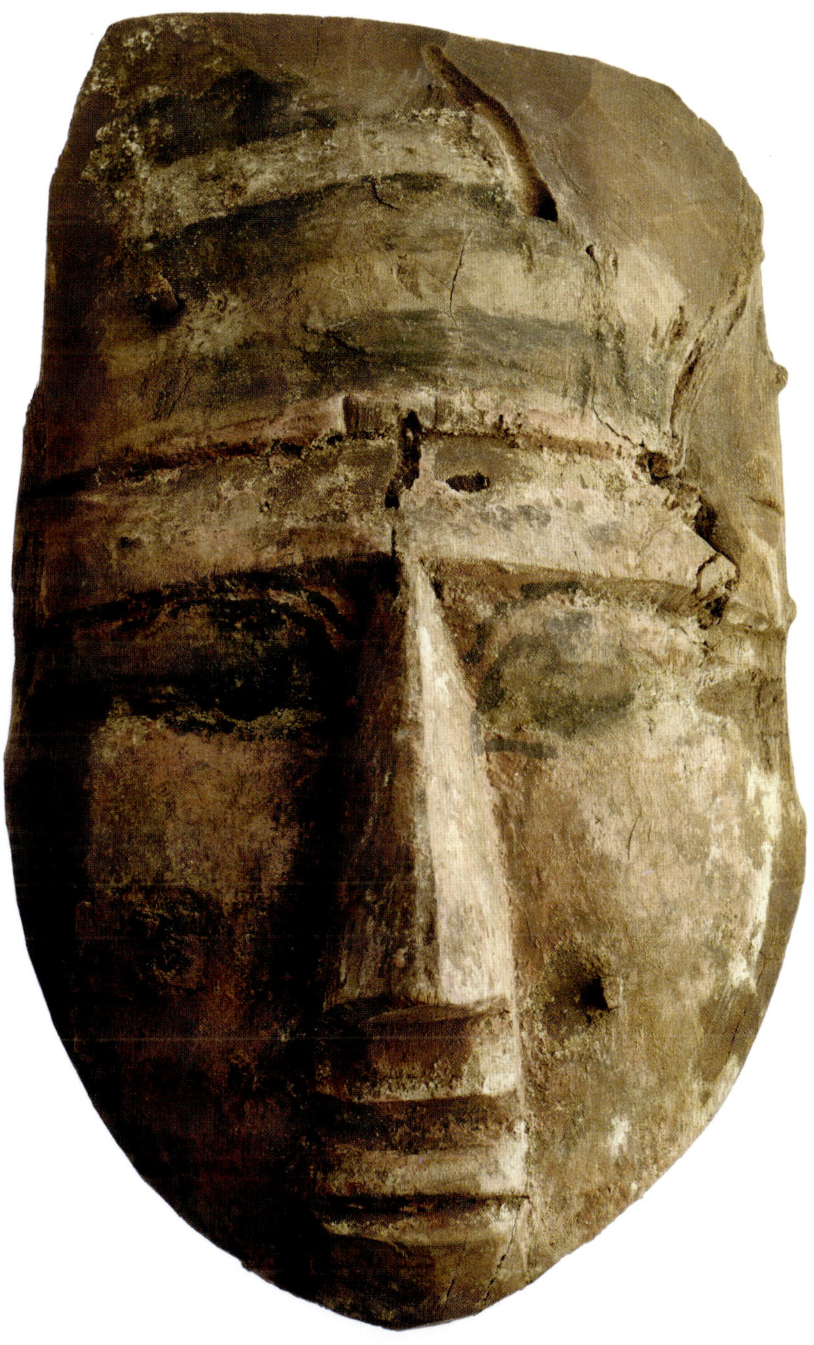

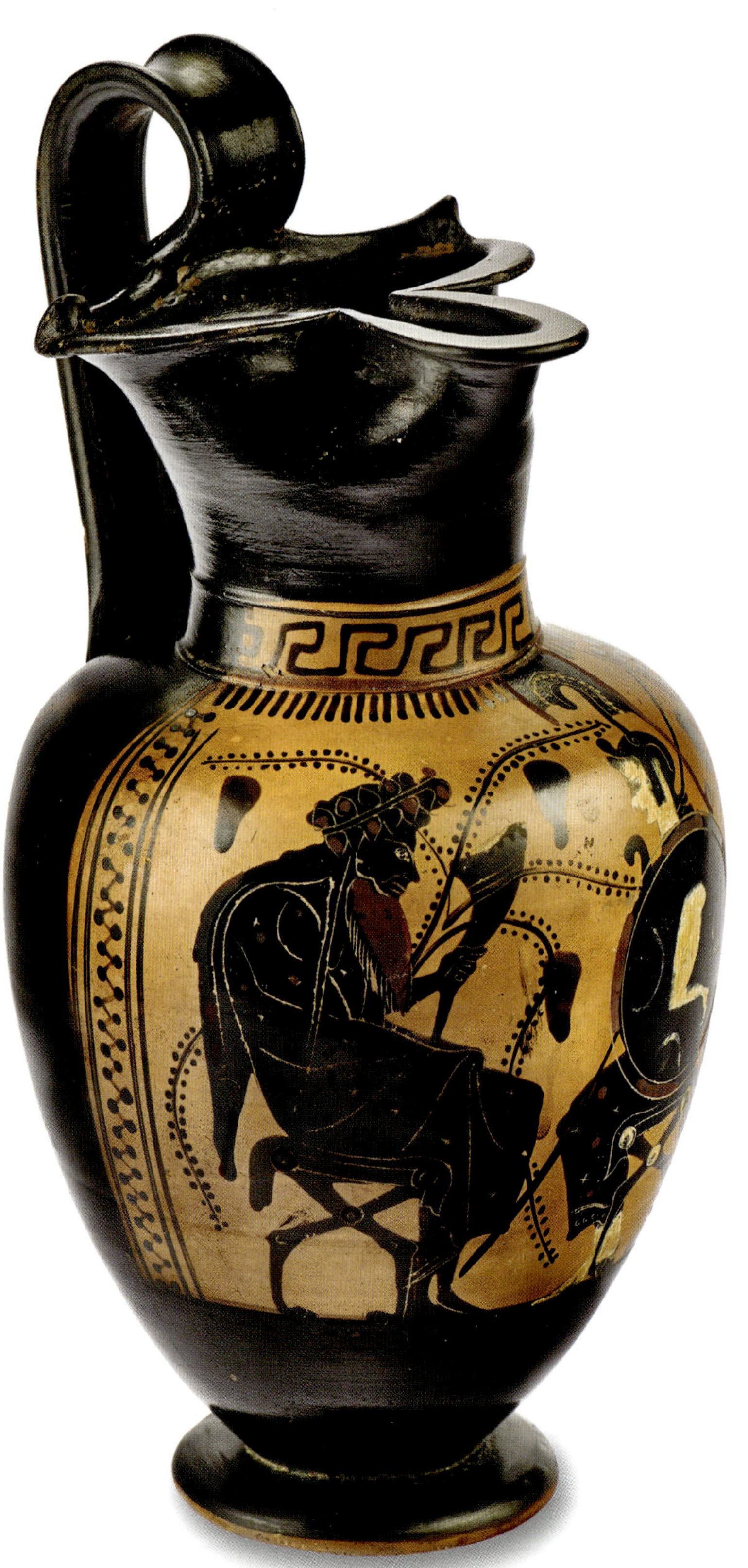

44
Greek vase

This particular shape of terracotta vase is known as an 'oinochoe' or wine jug. It is part of the collection of objects bequeathed to Somerville by Amelia Edwards, and was one of those items that were stolen and later returned to the college [41]. The subject of the painted scene on the piece (Dionysus with drinking horn and grapevine, seated opposite the goddess Athena) underlines its practical function. Like other forms of Greek vessel, the oinochoe could also function as a grave offering. This piece was one of those examined by Sir John Davidson Beazley (1885–1970), Professor of Art and Archaeology at Oxford from 1925 to 1956, who specialised in the classification of Attic vases. On the basis of its style Beazley attributed the painting of this vase to the Leagros Group, a workshop of painters who decorated pottery in Athens from about 525 to 500 BC, using what is called the 'black-figure' technique. Contours were incised into the paint before firing, with details then picked out afterwards in opaque colours.

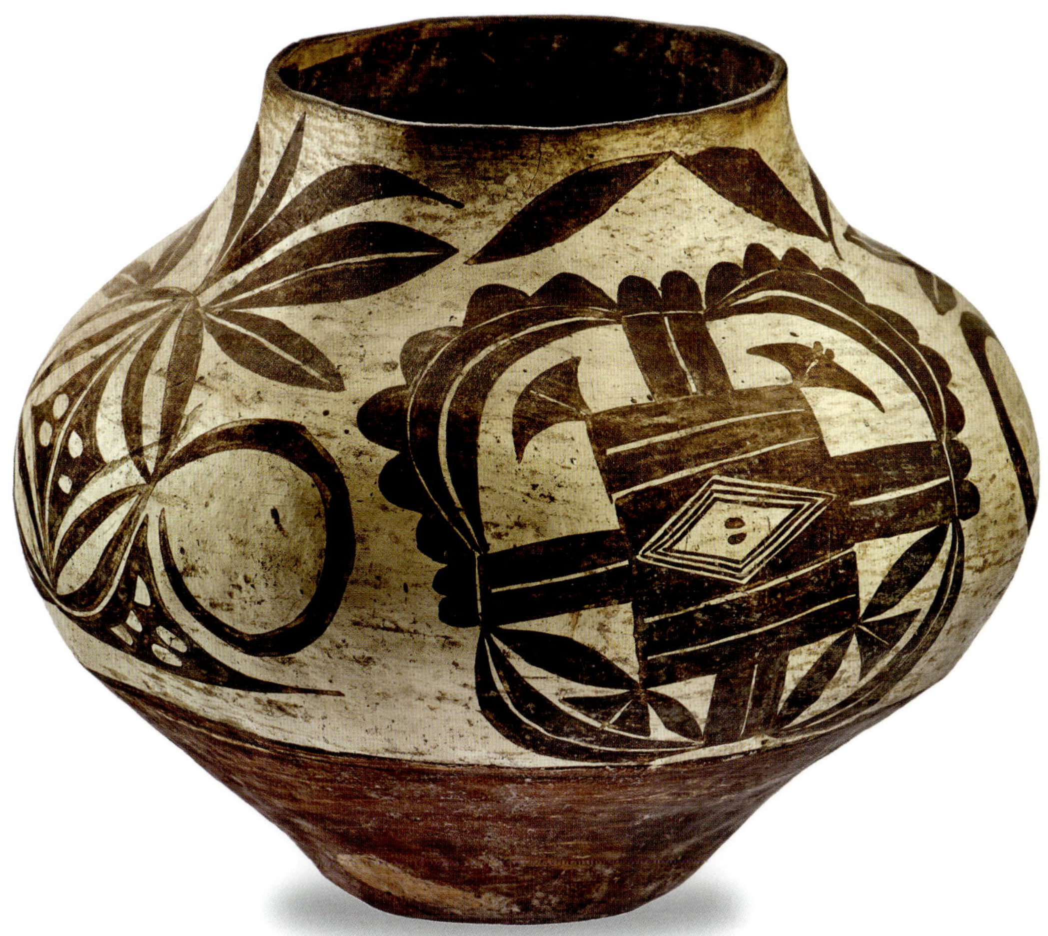

45
Zuni Indian pot

This pot was almost certainly acquired by Amelia Edwards [41] during her American lecture tour of 1889–90 and was probably made in the 1880s in New Mexico. Pots of this shape were used for water storage, often with hide coverings stretched over them to keep the water cool. Traditionally the women of the Zuni tribe would have collected clay and finished each pot by hand before firing them in open fires. Originally each clan in the area would have decorated their pots with their own particular symbols, but as the railroads opened up the area in the 1880s, trade and tourism led to the sharing of designs. This is one of two Zuni Indian pots in the Edwards bequest, and we know that they were displayed in her study. When they came to the college, both spent some years in the room of a Somerville tutor; they are now housed on top of one of the several mahogany bookcases that were also part of the Edwards bequest.

46
Marble torso

Probably from the Hellenistic or
Ptolemaic period, and almost certainly
from Amelia Edwards's collection, this
torso of a male figure is made from
Parian marble, highly prized by sculptors
for its fine grain and semi-translucence.
Not that you would have guessed this if
you'd encountered the sculpture before
it was restored recently: in fact, it was so
dirty that you might have been forgiven
for thinking it was made from onyx.
Now pristine, and with its own specially
designed stand to show off the stance
of the figure (weight held on the right
leg as the left leg moves forward), the
sculpture is affectionately known by
library staff as 'Nigel'.

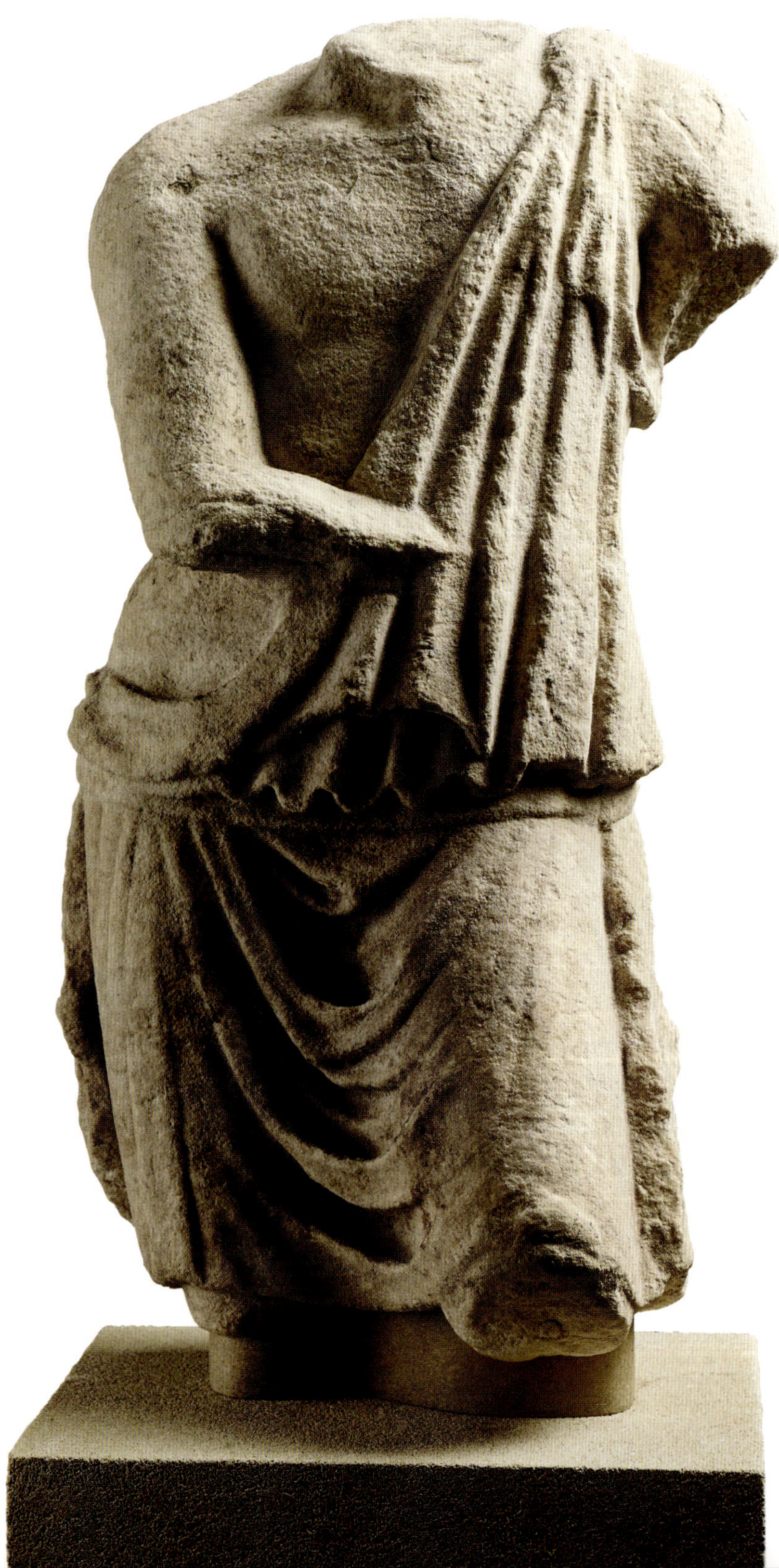

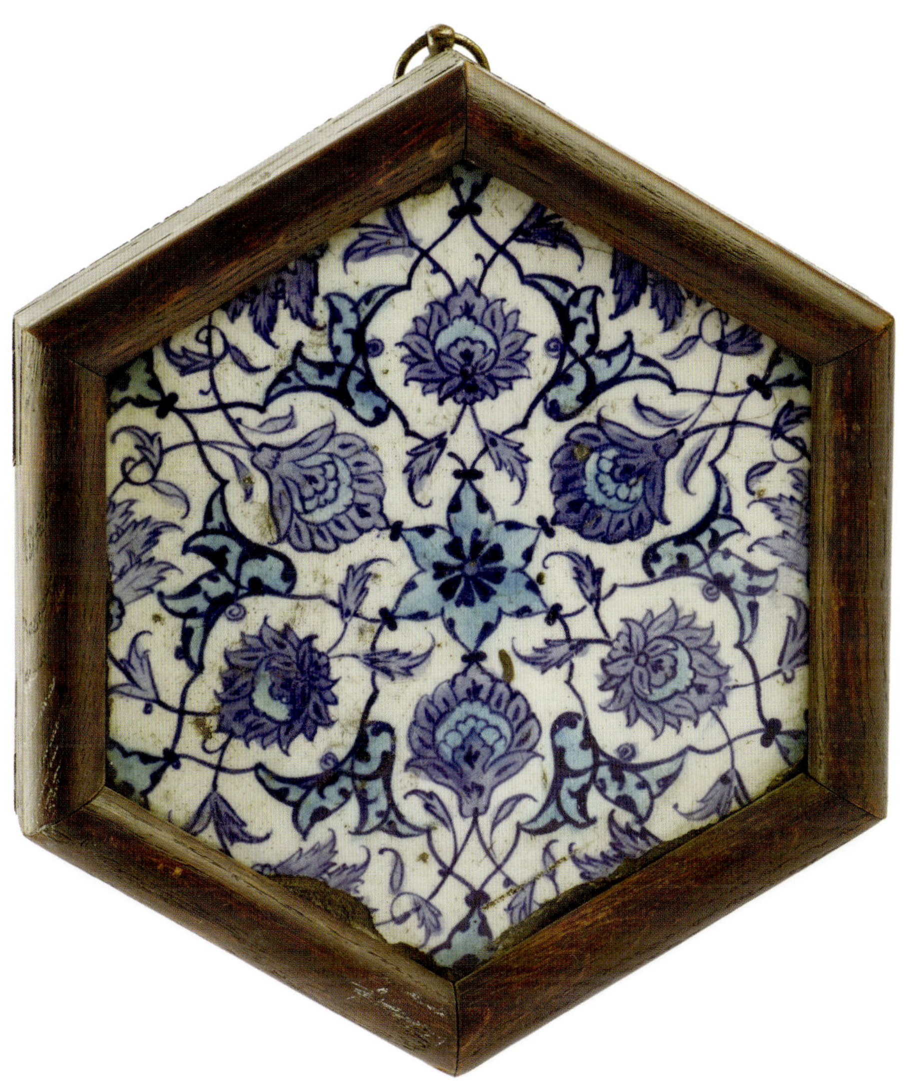

47
Iznik tile

The fireplace surrounds in the library [36] boast a wonderful selection of tiles, from Delft to the stylised florals of William Morris (1834–96) and William de Morgan (1839–1917) or, more likely, their imitators, but these are of a different order. Crouched over your weekly essay in the library or checking a reference, it's easy to miss these beautiful hexagonal tiles, or to notice them and assume that they're just another piece of pretty Edwardian decoration. In fact they almost certainly date from the sixteenth-century Ottoman Empire and were produced in Iznik (south of Istanbul) as part of the new fashion for added colour – turquoise as well as the more traditional blue and white – and Chinese-style designs. These tiles were probably part of the Amelia Edwards collection; similar examples can be seen in the Ashmolean Museum.

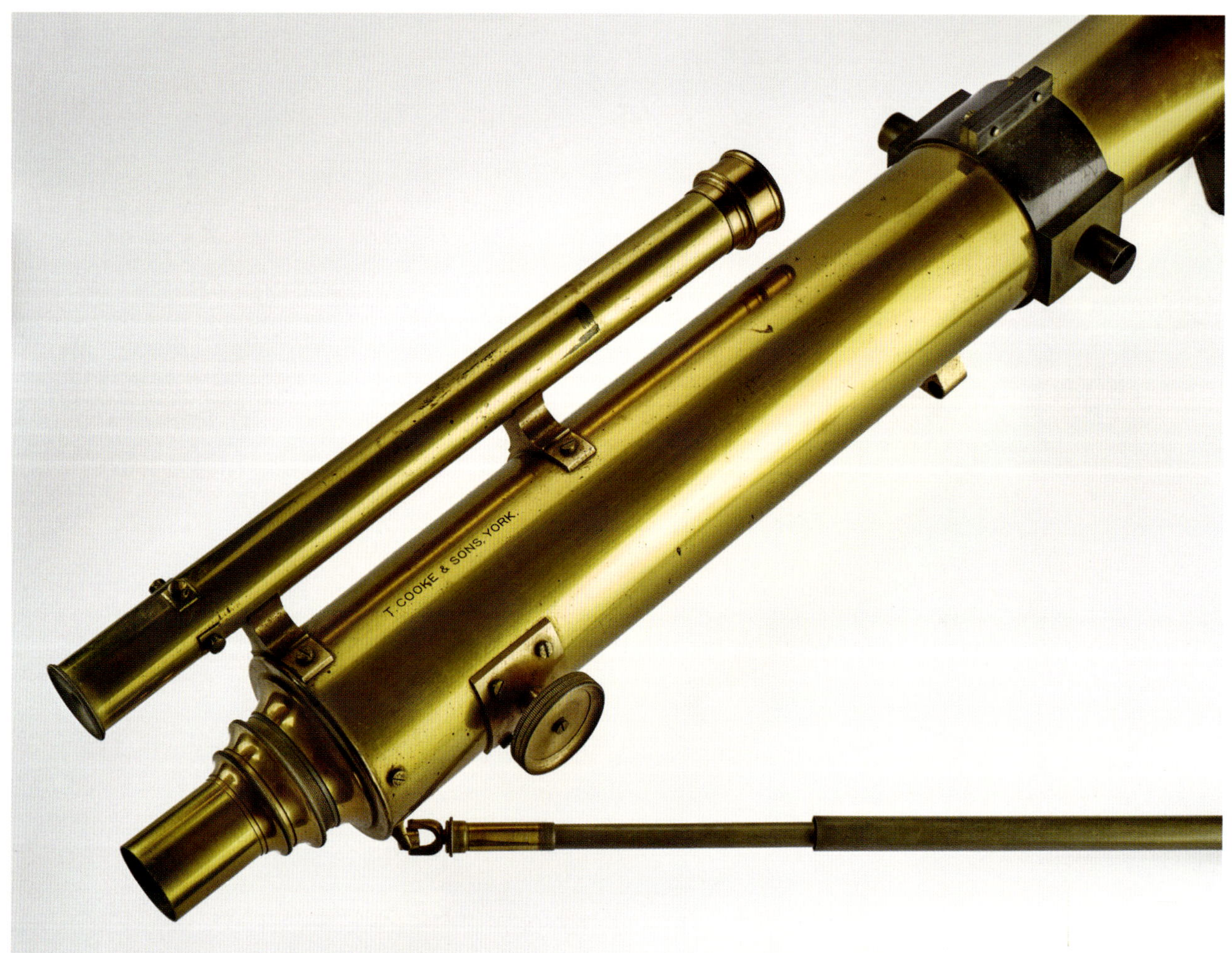

*'the courses of the planets have been observed for ages
with a degree of perseverance that is astonishing'*

Mary Somerville, *The Mechanism of the Heavens*

48
Brass telescope

Sometimes we have to indulge in speculation. This handsome telescope was found in the loft of Penrose: no Somervillian name or story attaches to it. It is tempting to think that it might have been used by Somerville's early students to enjoy a little stargazing – all the more tempting given the scholarly interests of Mary Somerville. Astronomy was one of Somerville's particular areas of scientific focus [5] and she was – jointly with Caroline Herschel [10] – the first woman to be nominated for honorary membership of the Royal Astronomical Society. This telescope was made by T. Cooke & Sons of York, a firm established in 1837 and renowned for the quality of its scientific instruments. We know, for example, that it made the mount for one of the telescopes used by Lord Huggins in his work [12]. By 1922 T. Cooke & Sons had been bought and merged with another maker.

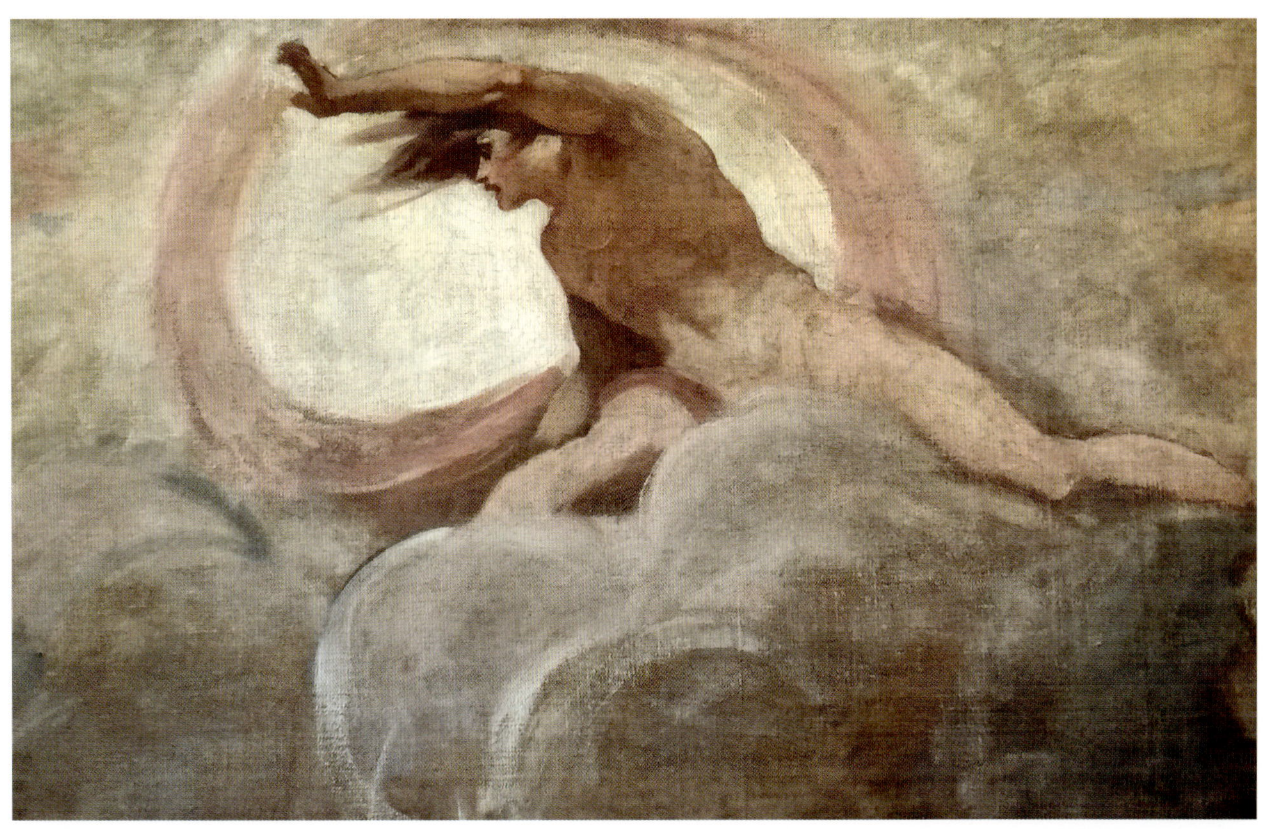

49
George Romney, *Ariel*

What is a muse? Here it may well be Emma Hart (later Emma Hamilton, 1765–1815), whom the National Portrait Gallery describes on its website as 'attractive and ambitious', and whose other claim to fame was as the mistress of Horatio Nelson (1758–1805). From 1792 she became the great inspiration for society portraitist George Romney (1734–1802). He drew her from life and her 'poses' informed his paintings of figures from history, myth and literature: her guises included Miranda, Circe, Bacchante, Cassandra and Mary Magdalene. This picture shows her as Ariel and was given by Sir William Bousfield (1842–1910) as part of a generous bequest that came to the college in 1932, and included paintings, drawings, engravings and 147 books. Bousfield had been the Clothworkers' Representative on the college's Council from 1900 until his death in 1910.

50
Margaret Kennedy,
'Suffragets' March'

Solemn and rousing, this poem by
Margaret Kennedy (1896–1967) was
written when she was a child. It has
all the seriousness (and the charming
misspellings) of Daisy Ashford's *The
Young Visiters* (1919) and it makes
clear the powerful impression that
the suffrage movement made on her.
'So up with the banners and down
with the men', it reads: 'Oh Suffragets,
leave Despotism behind you'. And at
the end, a 'W' clumsily turned into a 'V'
to begin the final phrase on the page:
'Votes for Women'. Kennedy came up
to Somerville to read Modern History
in 1915, three years before the first
'Votes for Women' were granted by
Parliament. She went on to become a
renowned novelist, whose bestselling
work *The Constant Nymph* (published
in 1924) was considered shocking for
its sexual content and its portrayal of
bohemian values.

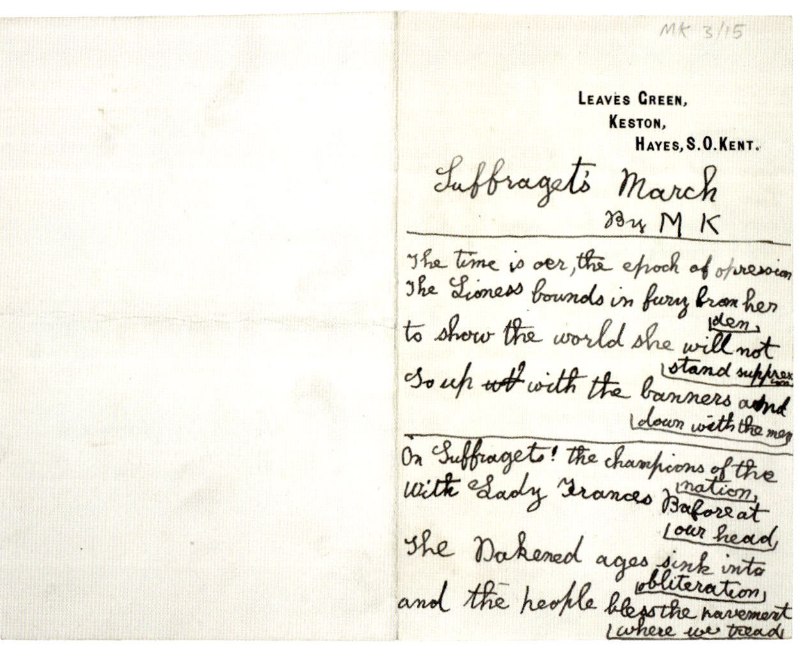

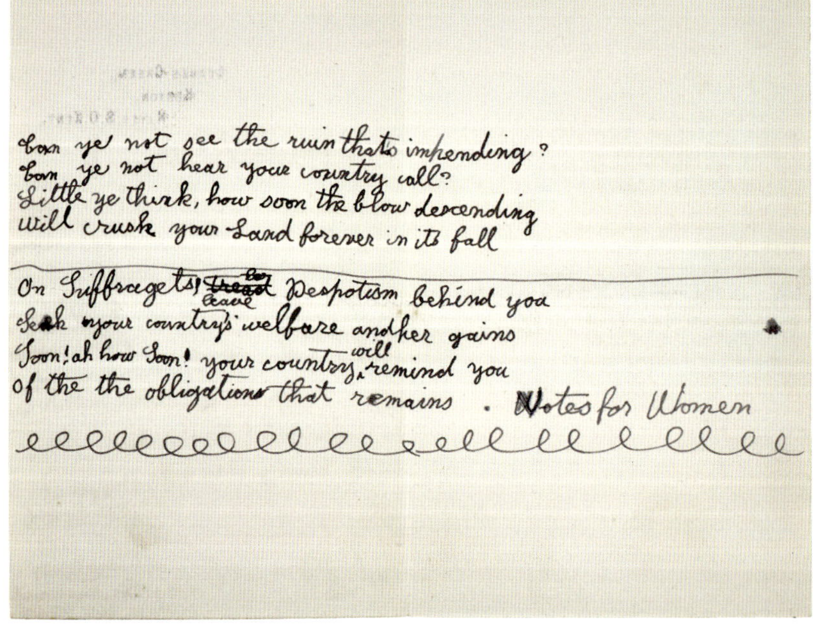

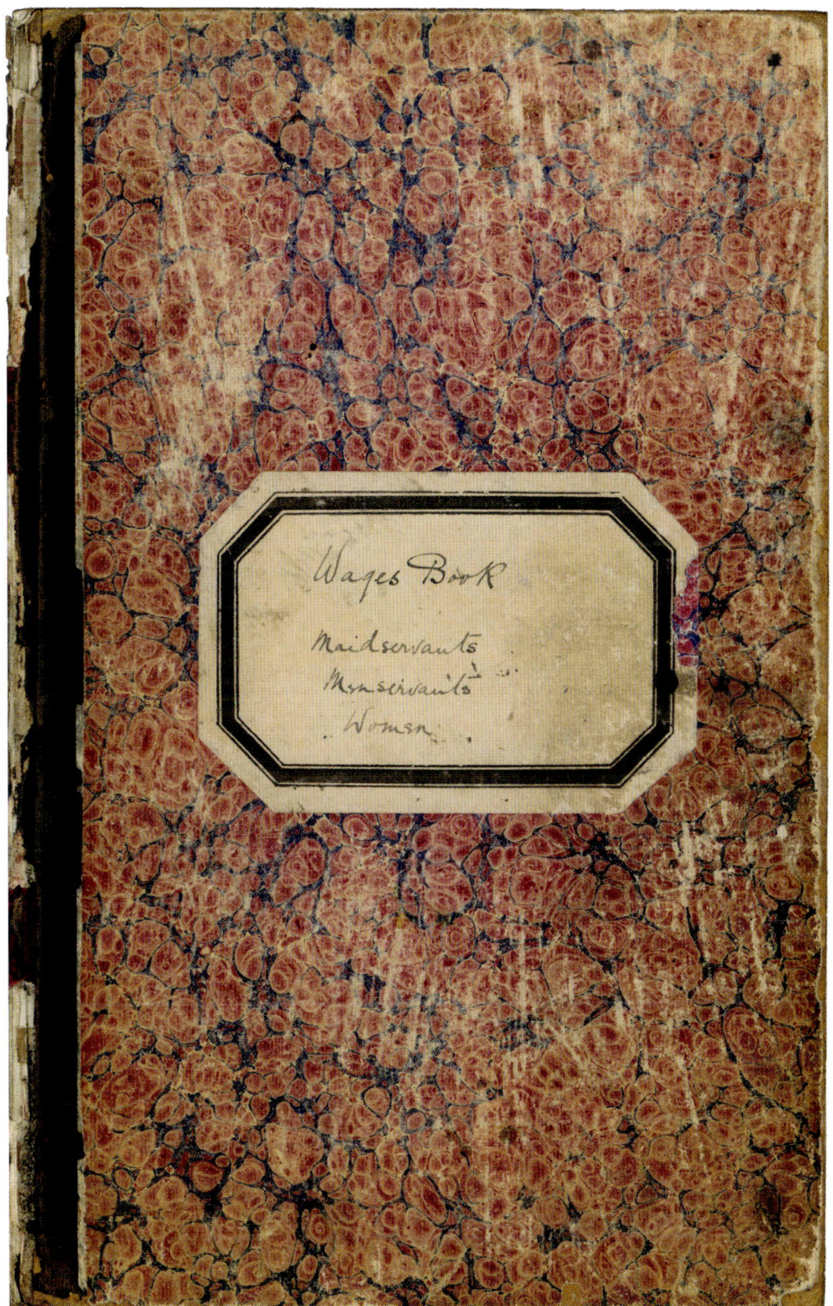

51
Wages book

College histories seldom focus on the sheer number of individuals it takes to keep the life of the mind washed, fed and looked after, but the women (and some men) who lived and worked in Somerville as servants were as much members of the college as the students, not least in their lifelong sense of connection to the place. In 1978, when Somerville wrote to its old members asking for funds, the appeal came to the attention of May Drew, who had arrived at Somerville as a servant in July 1911, on the day she left school. 'I left school at almost 4.30 … and left home at 5.30 PM for Somerville – It was not fair to College or to me as I knew nothing of course – We were paid 5 shillings a week and that quarterly in arrears'. Drew wrote to send money to the appeal ('My mite seems almost too small to share – but I should like to feel I had a tiny share') and to contribute her memories of a Gaudy: 'I can still smell the sweet peas on the little tables in the marquee – and feel the pain in my poor feet'.

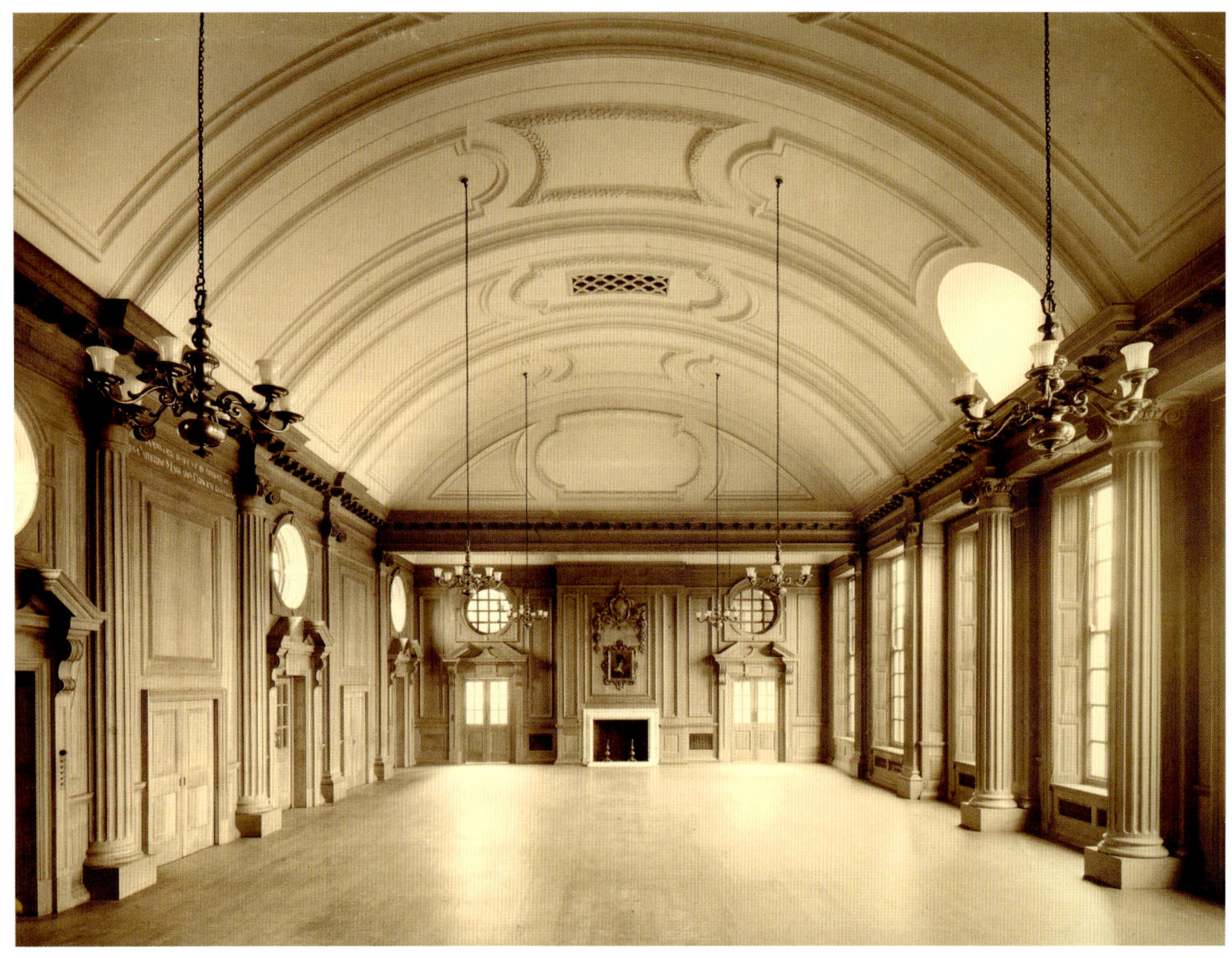

Gilbert Murray, speaking at the opening of the Maitland Hall, 4 October 1913

52
Maitland Hall

'West' (now Park) and 'House' had been kept as separate houses, with separate dining rooms, in order to retain the country-house manners that the founders of Somerville had envisaged [9 and 20]. What had started as a sense of family quickly grew into a sense of division [15], and the decision was eventually taken to break from this principle and opt instead for a model akin to the men's colleges, with one large dining hall for all. The commission was in fact for a range of buildings to offer more residential accommodation as well as space for a new kitchen, private dining room and senior common room along with the longed-for hall where all students and tutors could meet and eat together. Early occupants of the new Maitland accommodation (named for Agnes Maitland, who had died in 1906) included Dorothy L. Sayers [87] and Vera Brittain [79]. The architect selected, Edmund Fisher, was the brother of the historian and politician H.A.L. Fisher (1865–1940), who served as President of Somerville's Council. Edmund Fisher opted to design in what was called the 'Wrenaissance' style, of which the building in Somerville is his most significant example. He was killed during the First World War.

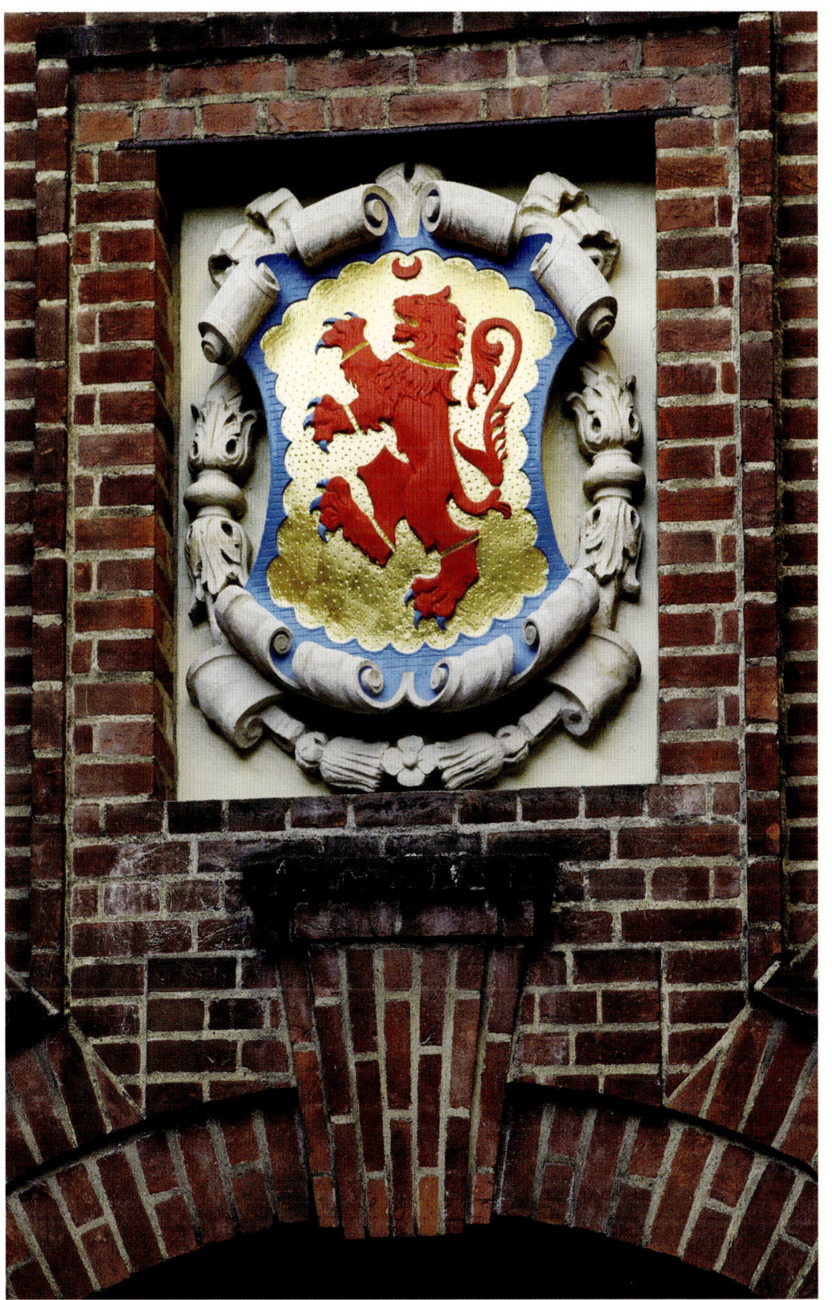

Arms of the Maitland family

What are we to make of the large and colourful coat of arms embedded in the archway between House and Maitland? Most Somervillians probably don't make much of it at all. The archway is where you turn left to lock your bicycle or right to get to Hall: seldom much time to look up. If you were to, you would find a 'lion rampant' (a reference to the lion's position – rearing up – rather than its mood), but also 'couped in all points': bluntly, its paws have been cut off. It is said that this is a pun on the French name from which Maitland derives: 'Matulant', so 'mutilated' in war. Medieval heraldry seems a rather long way from a progressive hall for women. Coats of arms meant respectability, however, and for women's colleges in Oxford respectability was a vital precursor to acceptance. The habit of adding the coats of arms of figures associated with Somerville continued into the 1930s, when the arms of the Shaw Lefevre, Percival [13] and Darbishire families were added to the stonework of the new East Quadrangle (now Darbishire Quad).

'for the Principal at the new high table'

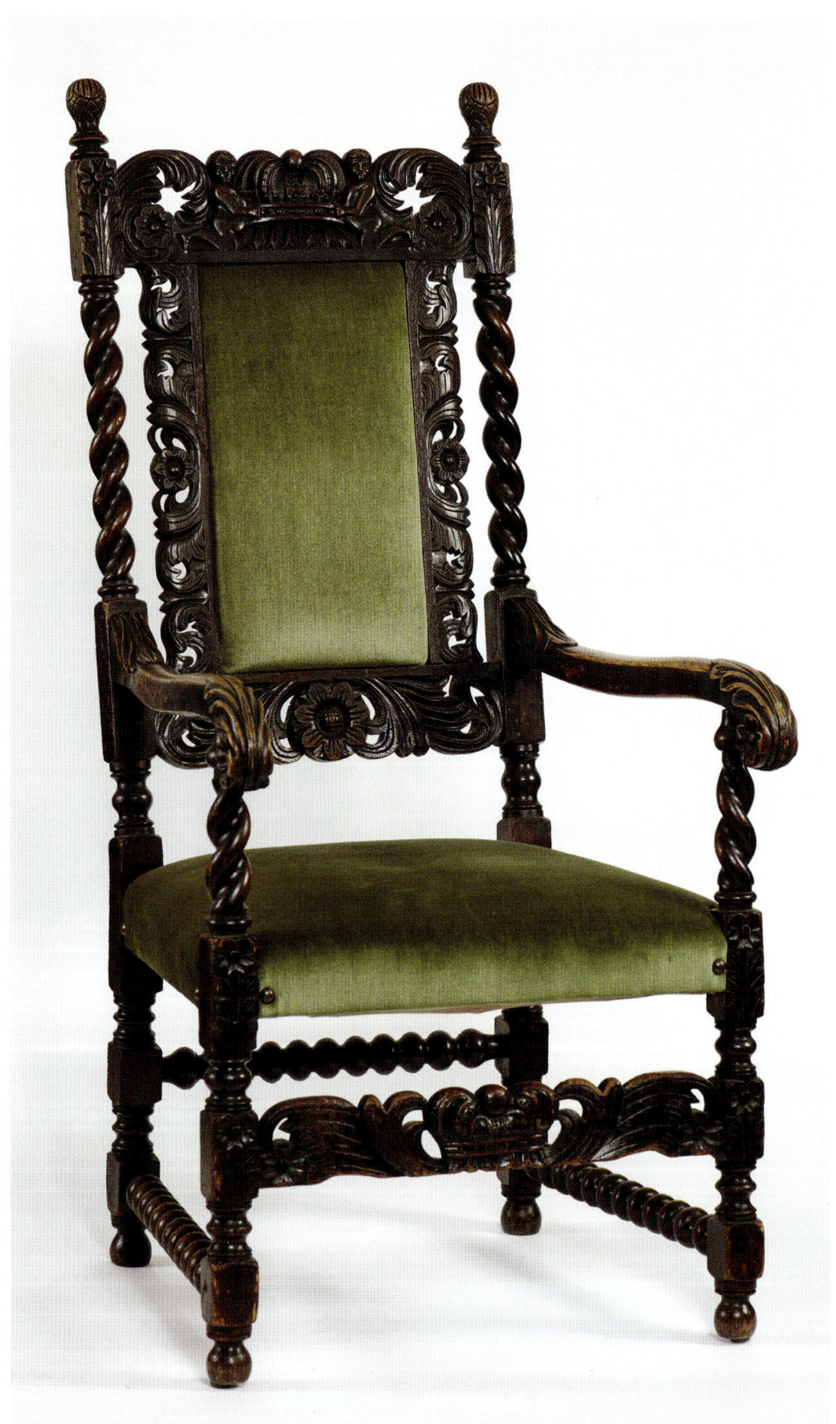

54
Principal's throne

The gift book [10] records that this 'Jacobean chair for the Principal at the new high table' was given by 'Old Somervillians resident in Oxford' in 1913, to celebrate the opening of the new Maitland Hall [52]. So far, so good. To some later generations of Somervillians the notion of a 'Principal's throne', as it began to be called, sat uneasily with Somerville's liberal history. There have been numerous occasions on which it has been banished, sometimes by the JCR (Junior Common Room), sometimes by the Principal herself. Somerville's current Principal, Janet Royall, confesses that she finds it both physically and ideologically an uncomfortable object.

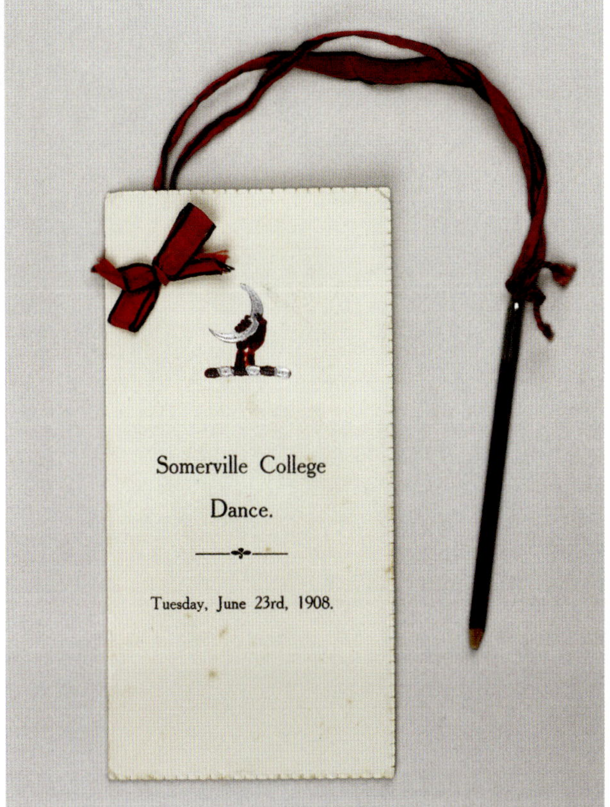
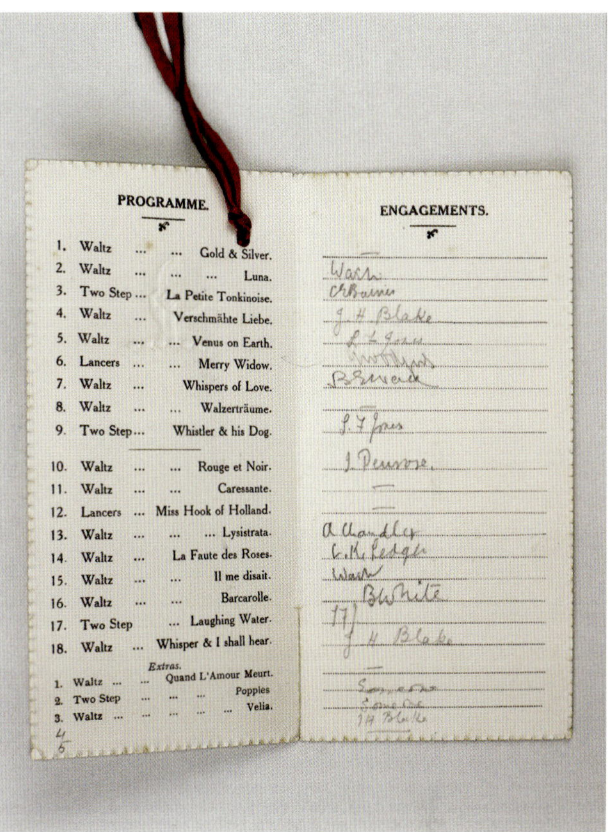

55
Dance card

The inside of this dance card from 1908 carefully records the names of partners for the evening's busy schedule of the Waltz, the Two Step and the Lancers (a form of Quadrille). Six years later, on 22 June 1914, a commemoration ball was held in the Maitland Hall, a proud celebration of a new phase in Somerville's history. The JCR had lobbied for a dance in the new hall as soon as it was finished, but the Council decided that it should wait until the summer. So a committee was formed and the necessary preparations undertaken: two hundred tickets at 8 shillings each; Herr Moritz Wurm and his Blue Viennese Orchestra; refreshments and ices to be served on the balcony at 9 p.m. to the 90 dancing couples; a photograph of those who managed to stay up until dawn. By the same time the following year the hall had been requisitioned for use as a military hospital [56].

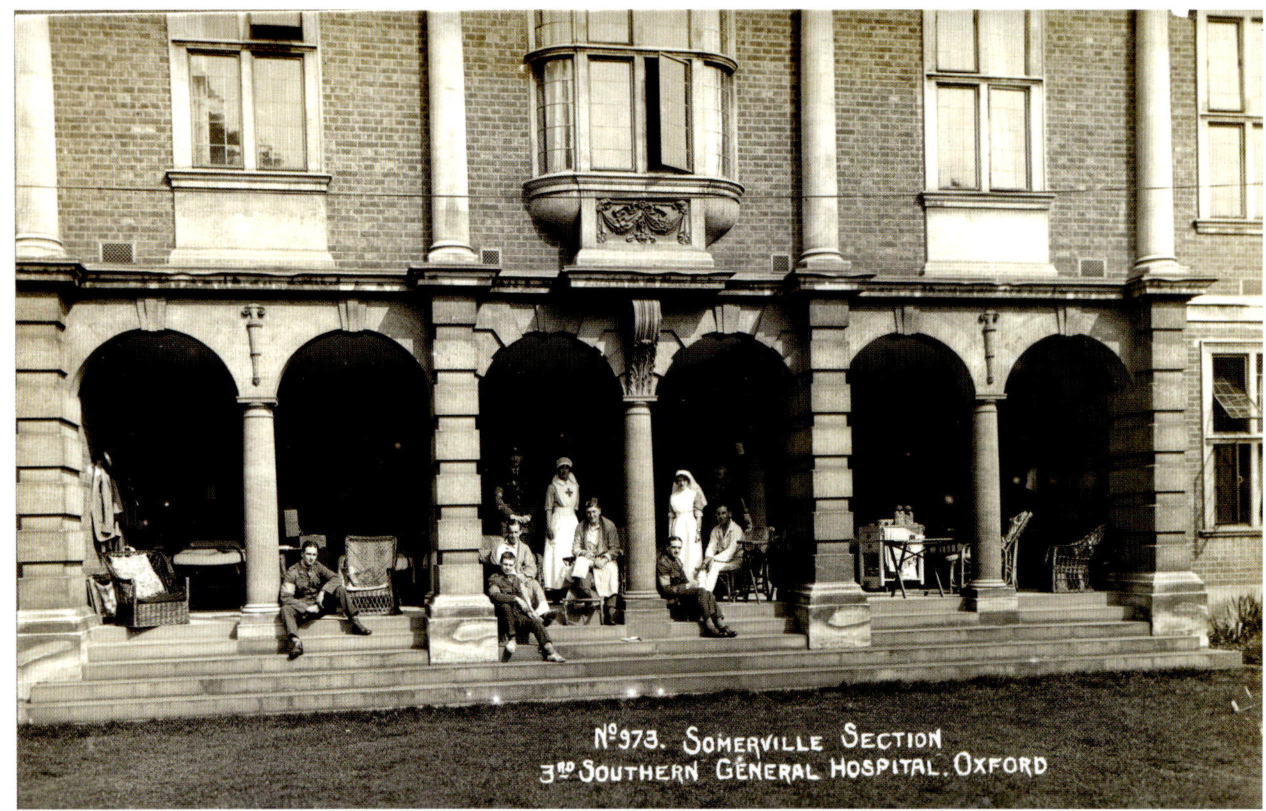

*'for the first few days,
very much like Paradise'*

Siegfried Sassoon

56
Photograph of 3rd Southern General Hospital

The new phase for the Maitland Building [52] was short-lived. By December 1914 *The Fritillary* (the journal of the women's colleges in Oxford) was already noting that 'It seems a long time since the Ball' [55]. Then, in April 1915, Somerville's buildings were requisitioned for use as a military hospital, as the college was next to the Radcliffe Infirmary. The hall was first a ward for officers and then the officers' mess. Among the patients were Robert Graves (1895–1985) and Siegfried Sassoon (1886–1967), the latter recalling in 1945 that 'to be lying in a little white-walled room, looking through the open window onto a college lawn, was for the first few days, very much like Paradise'. Students and tutors decamped to Oriel [58], and soon Somerville was allocated for the exclusive use of officers. The library remained off-limits, although the downstairs loggia was used for those convalescing. When the buildings were returned to college use after the war, a notice was found in the hall: 'Officers are requested not to throw custard at the walls'.

57
College seal

Although it is not clear exactly when this sealing machine (complete with miniature padlock) arrived in Somerville, the official minutes of the college Council make numerous records of 'Authority for the use of the College Seal', and these give an interesting insight into the practical concerns and operations of the college. November 1933, for example, notes that authority was given for the seal's use on an 'Agreement with University College regarding the passage of a drain from the chapel across a corner of its property' and also for 'Dividend Mandates for West Riding and London Transport Stock'. Now, the seal is kept in the Principal's room, and is largely admired for its decorative properties rather than its authority, but it is still used to mark the college's seal on official documents.

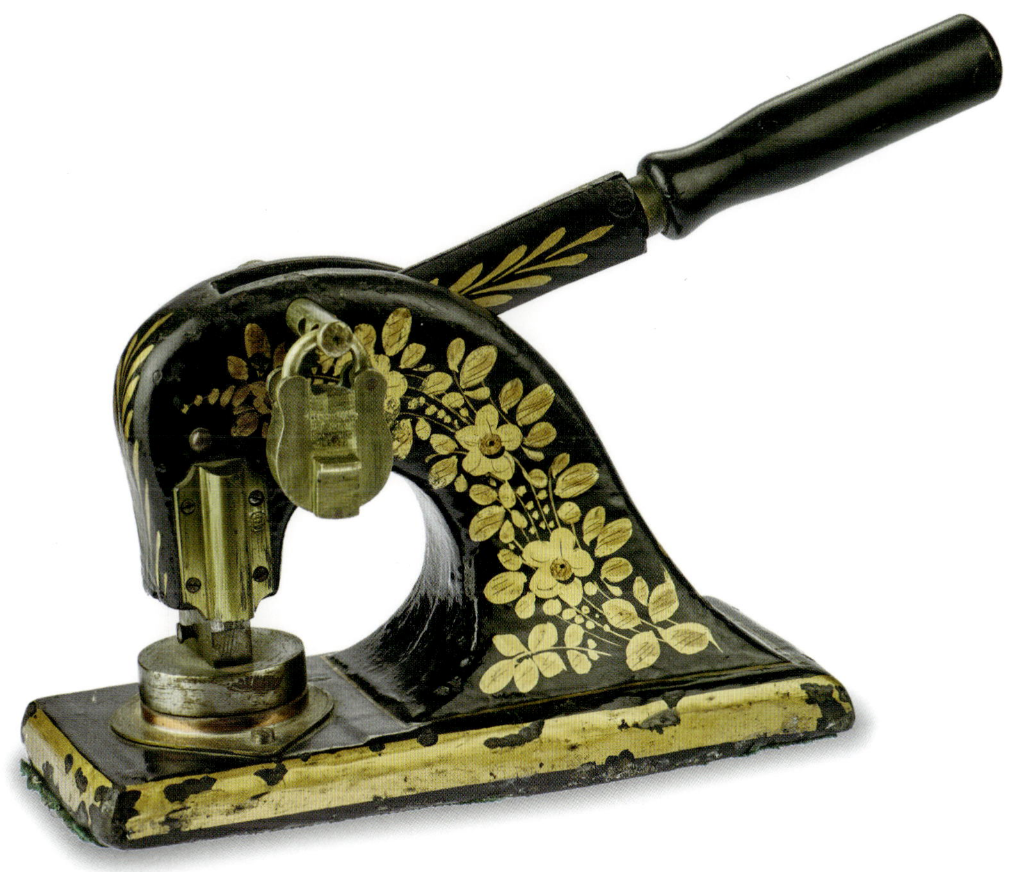

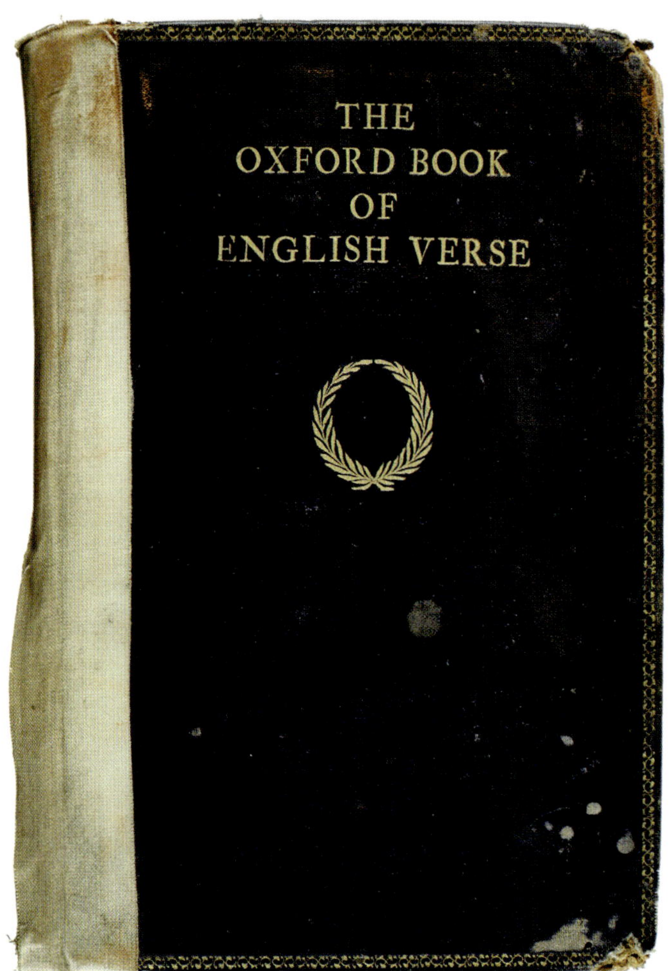

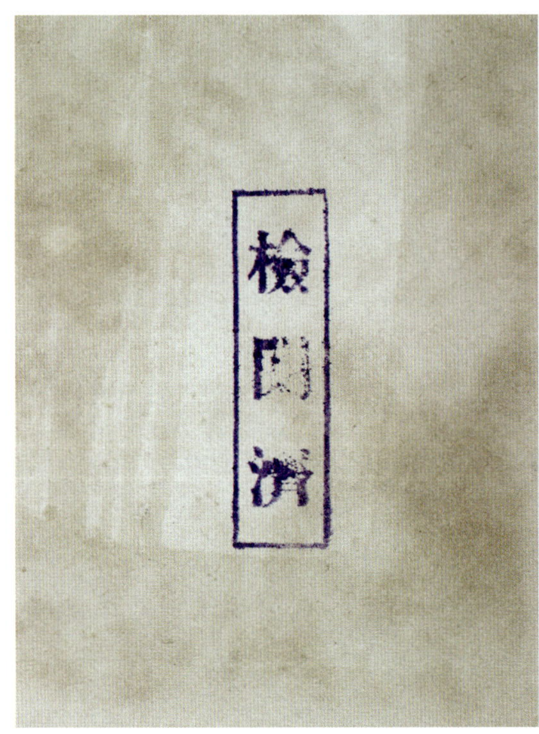

Somerville Log Book, June 1919

58
Oxford Book of English Verse

When the college's buildings were requisitioned as hospital accommodation during the First World War [56], Somerville chose to rent St Mary Hall from Oriel. A special wall was built to ensure separation, but it was not proof against the high spirits (literally: drink had been taken) of Oriel men returning to their college after the end of the War. The Somerville Log Book [63] takes up the story: 'On the night of Thursday June 19th certain members of Oriel JCR expressed their desire to return to St Mary Hall in a somewhat unusual but practical manner. After prolonged bombardment on the intervening wall a breach was effected through which several undergraduates jumped into the quad.' Hilda Lorimer (1873–1954), the Classics tutor, told the men to 'return to your own quarters without delay'. They did so, and Somerville's SCR took shifts to guard the hole in the wall throughout the night. A student, Cicely Williams (1893–1992), lent her copy of the *Oxford Book of English Verse* to the Principal, Miss Penrose, to read during her shift. Williams kept the book throughout her life, taking it with her as she travelled the world, and even managing to retain it when she was a prisoner of war, which is how it came to acquire a stamp from Changi prison in Singapore [95].

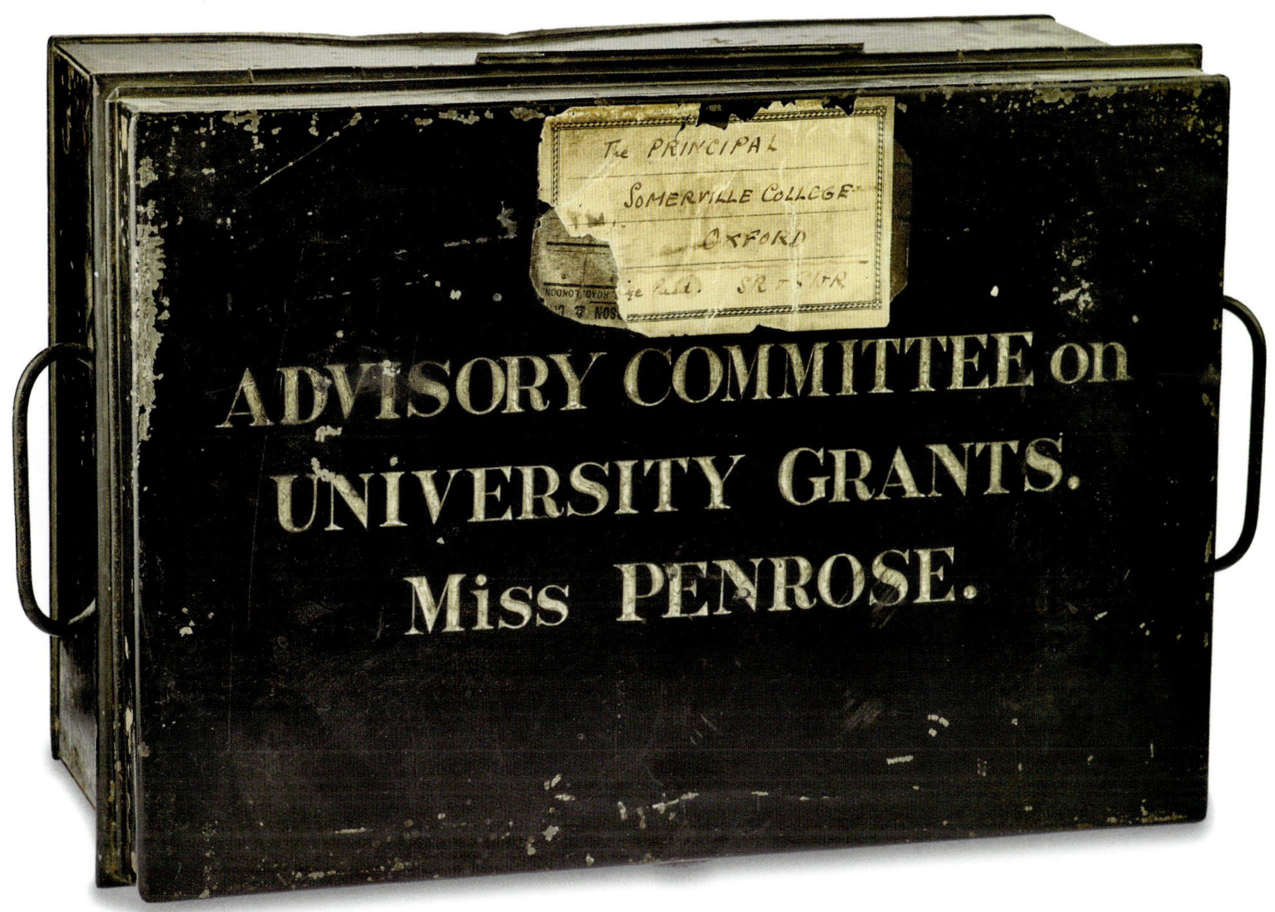

59
University Grants
Committee tin

It looks a little like a school tuck box, but it is, in fact, a rather radical tin. It was owned by Emily Penrose, the third Principal of Somerville and the first to have studied at Somerville herself. When she took up the post at Somerville, she had already held the Principalships of both Bedford College and Royal Holloway College, London. Penrose was a consummate diplomat as well as a talented financial administrator, and it was her gradual and careful navigation through the university system that served eventually to win membership (including the right to matriculate and to take degrees) for women at Oxford. Penrose had already served on the Senate of London University, although she was not the first woman to serve on the Advisory Committee on University Grants (that honour went to Margery Fry). The Committee had been established in 1919 to allocate Treasury funding as 'block grants' to universities. It kept tight control of which universities were given access to funding, and money was only granted for current expenditure (new buildings and other such additional costs had to be funded by means of philanthropy). We assume that the tin was issued to members to hold their meeting papers.

60
Photograph of Emily Penrose with Gilbert Murray

This photograph was taken on 14 October 1920, the day that the first degrees were granted to women by the University of Oxford. Somerville's Council had been at the forefront of the campaign for degrees for women, and one of the chief arguments was about representation: if some women could now vote for the University's representatives at Westminster (Oxford and Cambridge's university constituencies were only abolished in the late 1940s), why could they not be granted degrees? The immense upheaval of the First World War had also played its part (with women lecturers standing in for men in Oxford). However, it was the skill of Emily Penrose in reconciling the many different constituencies in Oxford that was in large part responsible for bringing about the welcome conclusion to this decades-old debate. Vera Brittain, who was not a great fan of Penrose personally, nonetheless recognised that 'no woman living would have done it so well'. Gilbert Murray (1866–1957) was Regius Professor of Greek at Oxford from 1908 to 1936 and was elected to serve on Somerville's Council from 1908. Penrose found him a source of wise counsel, and he may have been the person who suggested her appointment to serve on the Royal Commission that considered the question of degrees for women at Oxford and Cambridge.

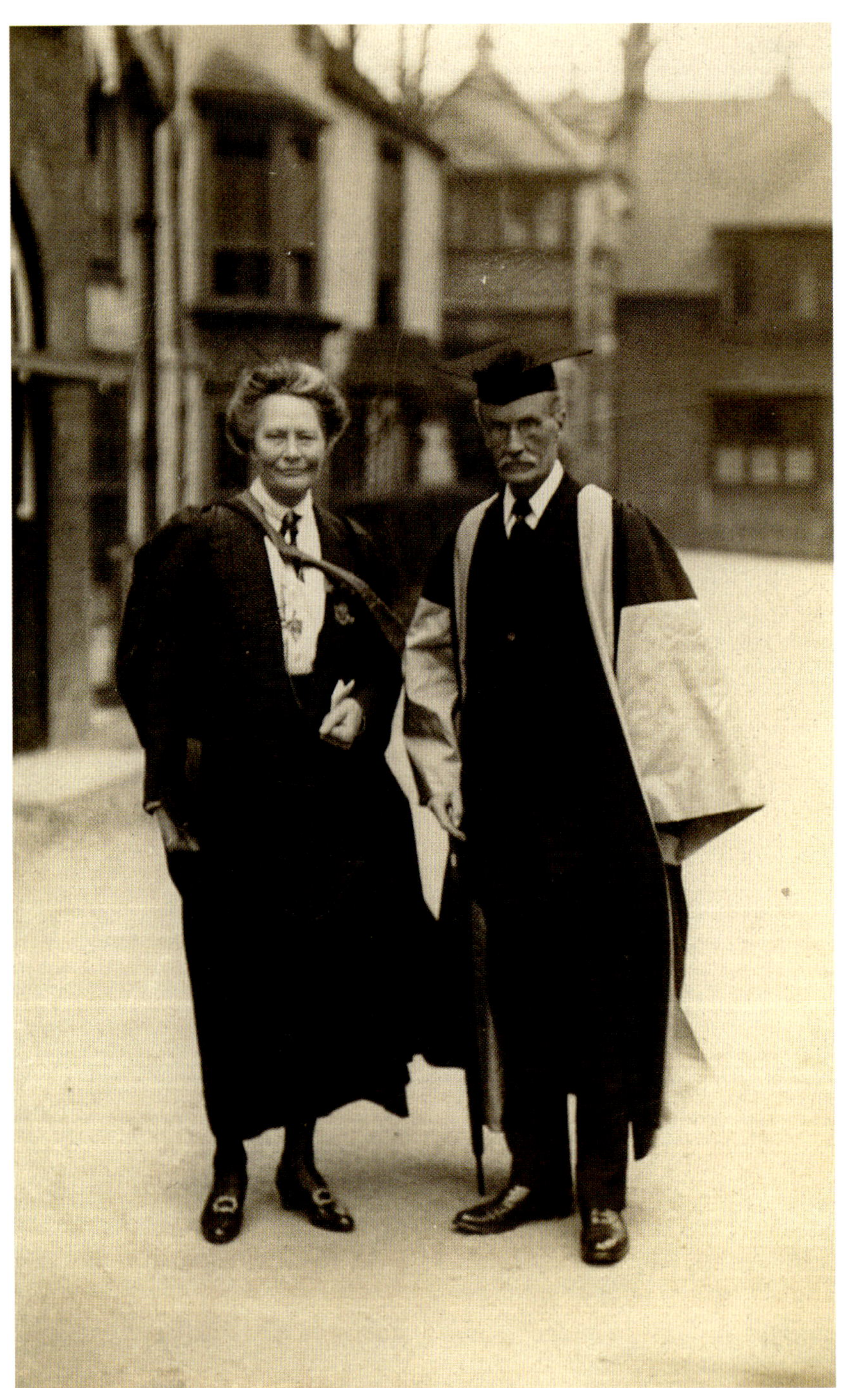

5a

First Year Students   June 13. 1921

What I have to say to you tonight does not apply to you all. To some of you I know that it does not apply at all. In some cases I do not yet know how far it applies. But you know. It should not be difficult for each one of you to know how far, if at all, what I have to say is intended for her.

I have been asked, what I have never been asked before, in all the 28 years that I have been the Principal of a College, to speak to a whole year & to tell you that — with some exceptions — for some of you, I understand, have worked admirably — that your Tutors have been seriously dissatisfied with your work & progress. The general impression you have made upon your Tutors — again I say there are exceptions — is that you have been content with the bare minimum of work which you thought would carry you through an easy examination, with the bare minimum of work which you imagined would satisfy your Tutor you were doing well. Some of you, I learn, have not even attempted that. Attendance at lectures & classes has been irregular, vacation work scamped or neglected. You have given the impression that you looked upon your work as a tiresome task to be got through in such a way as to interfere as little as possible with what are to you the more important interests of life, whether the river, or tennis, or tea parties or for whatever amusement you have neglected your work.

I wish to make it perfectly clear that Somerville was not intended for idlers. It was founded to give women the advantages of University teaching and the

61
Speech to idlers

Just reading the words makes most of us shudder. This is a reminder that Somerville is not all about cosy community living and fun. If you don't do the work, your sins (and the Principal) will find you out. In a post-war world, Somervillians were not, it seems, taking their studies as seriously as their pre-war counterparts, and the then Principal, Miss Penrose, was forced to address them on the subject: 'I have been asked, what I have never been asked before, in all the 28 years that I have been Principal of a College'. It should be noted that her reference to 28 years includes her time as Principal of Bedford and Royal Holloway Colleges as well (where she had also been renowned for terrifying students).

Ever just, Miss Penrose makes it clear at several points that her criticisms do not apply to all present. To those who had been 'content with the bare minimum', the effect must have been powerful: 'I wish to make it perfectly clear that Somerville was not intended for idlers'. As far as we know, she had no cause to make another such address.

One of the so-called 'trowelblazers' in archaeology, Katharine Menke (1888–1945) came up to Somerville in 1910 to read Modern History, but health difficulties forced her to leave before her studies were completed. After a period nursing with the Red Cross during the First World War (when she had to conceal her German parentage), Menke married Lieutenant Colonel Bertram Keeling (1880–1919), the Director-General of the Survey of Egypt. Keeling killed himself not long into their marriage, and it was probably after this that Katharine travelled to Poland to work in the camp at Strzalkowo, where members of the army of the Ukrainian People's Republic were interned. This certificate was awarded to her by 'the interned Army of the Ukrainian People' in 'great gratitude ... for the help given through her by the great British People'. In the early 1920s she travelled to Baghdad and began to work on the site of an ancient Mesopotamian city state at Ur with Charles Leonard Woolley (1880–1960), whom she later married. The couple went on to be responsible for numerous excavations, and also for the publication of the *Archaeological Survey of India* in 1939. A bequest from them helps to fund Ancient History fellows at Somerville. It was at Ur that Katharine Woolley interviewed and recruited the archaeologist Max Mallowan (1904–78). Mallowan later married Agatha Christie (1890–1976), who was said to have used Woolley as the model for the murder victim Louise Leidner in *Murder in Mesopotamia*.

'great gratitude ... for the help given through her'

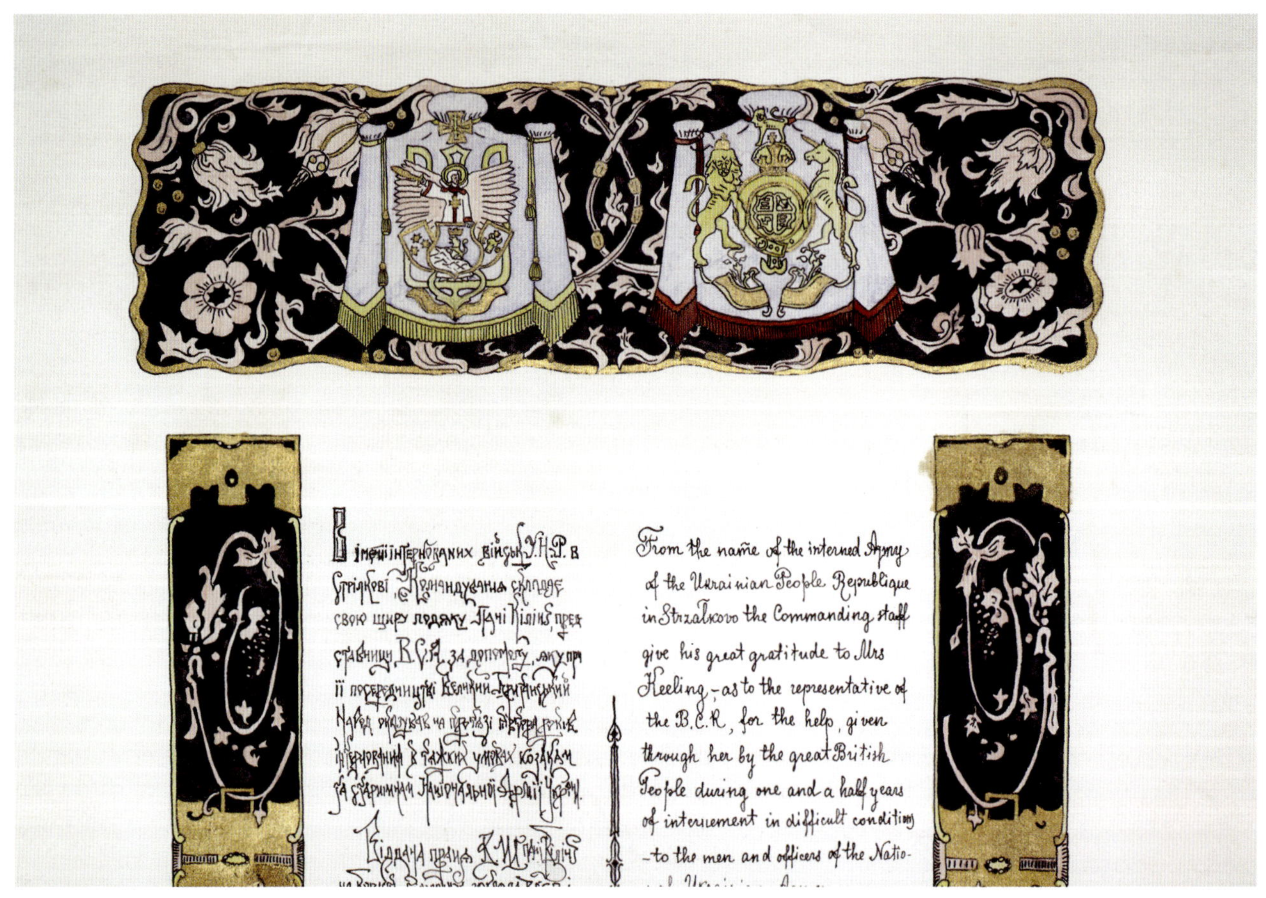

63
Log Book

The college Log Book was kept by
Somerville students to record events
and performances and to keep track
of college societies ('the membership of
the Swimming Club goes up with the
temperature'). Entries often included
sketches or paintings, as well as
newspaper clippings. The pages for
1922 include these costume designs
for the year's Going Down Play [30]
'Donec Rursus Impleat Orbem' [8], a
'Romance of the Troubadour Court in
the 15th Century. The chief threads of
the plot being the quest for the
Endowment Fund, & the fulfillment of
the Somerville Motto.' To win the hand
of the Princess Fleur de Lune, the Prince
sets off on a quest for the Endowment
Fund – 'a dowry for the princess,
wherewith to complete the quad and
fulfill the crescent moon'.

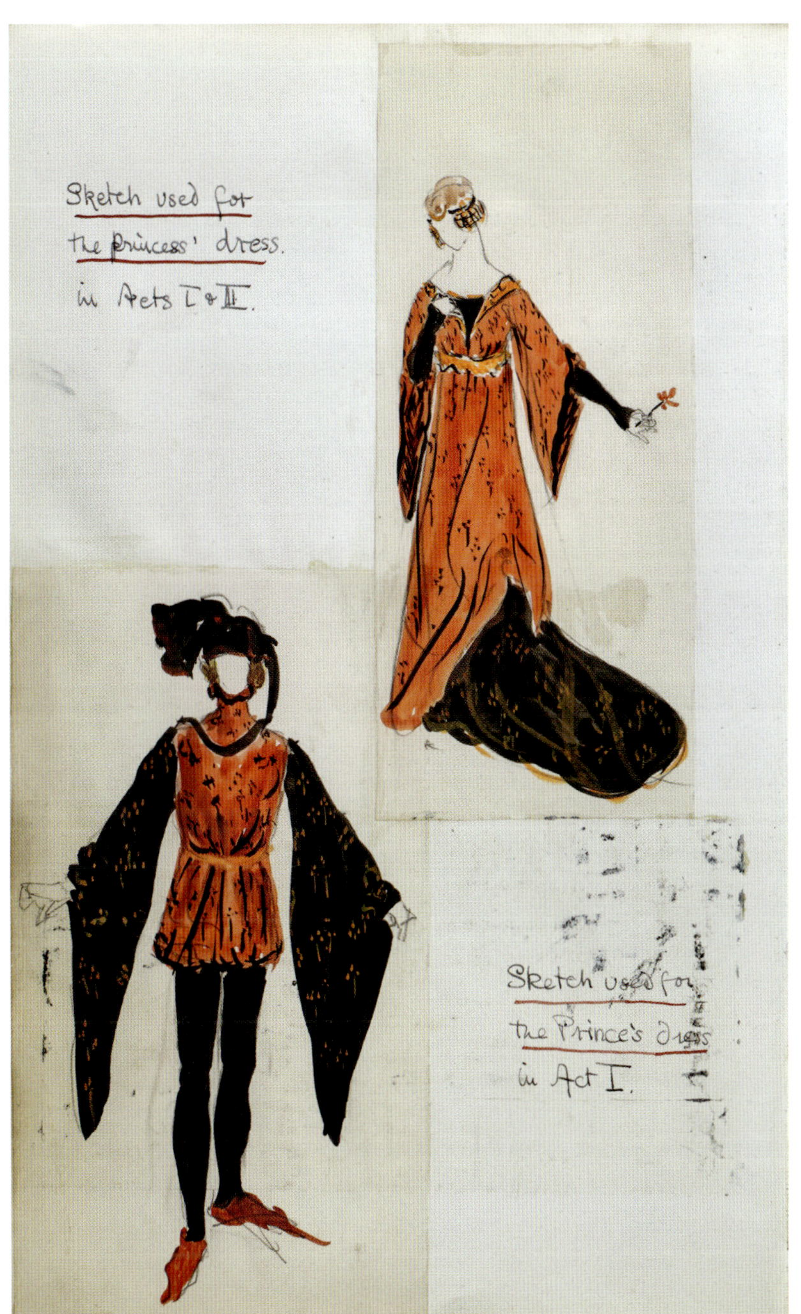

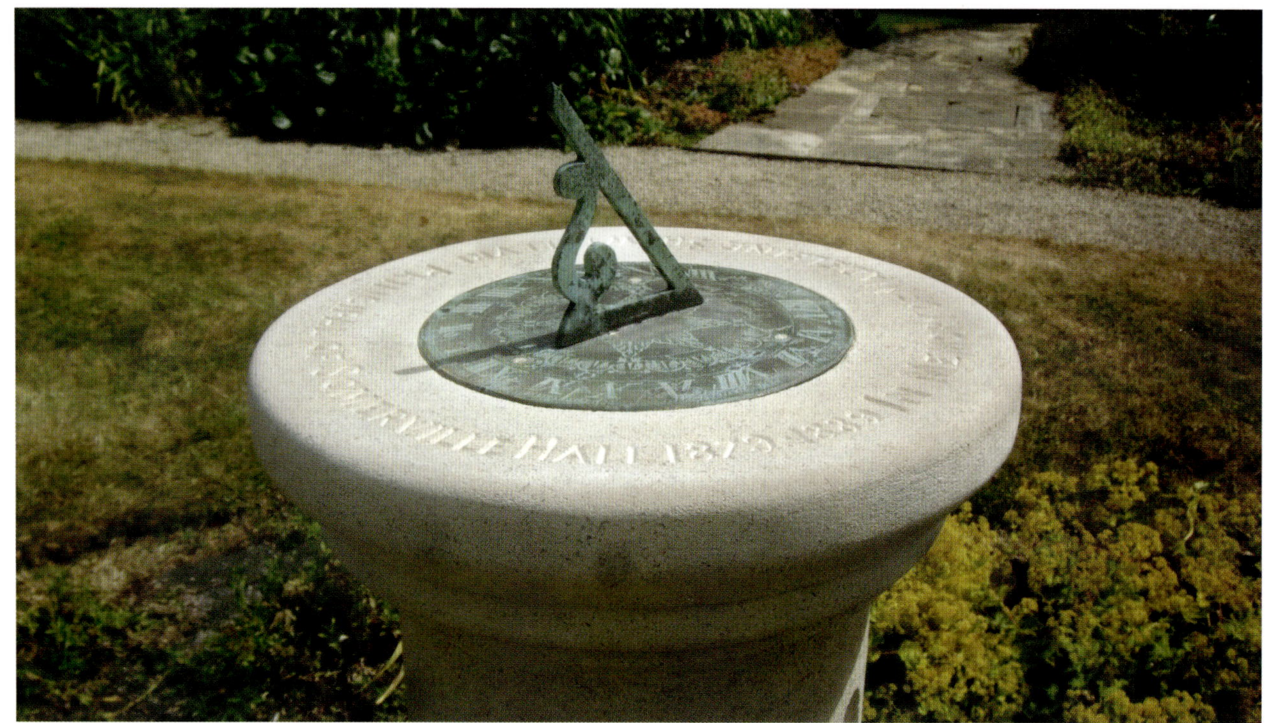

*'Amongst ye flowers
I tell ye hours'*

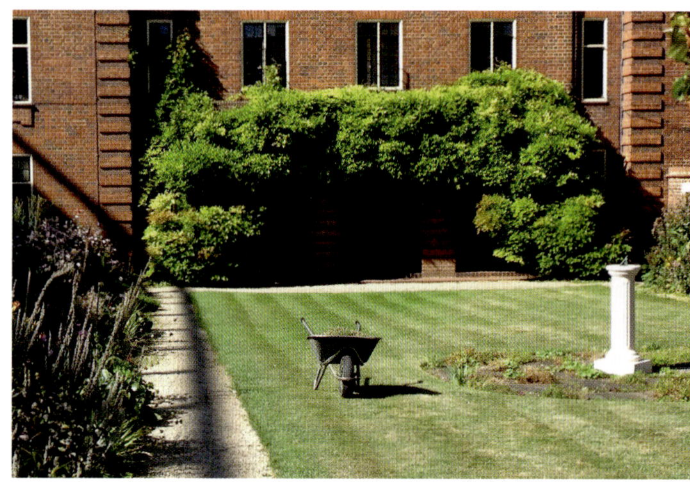

**64
Sundial**

Somerville's first Principal was chosen for her respectability, and her good manners were considered as important as her good judgement. She accepted the post on condition that her appointment would only last for one year, but in the event she stayed for a decade, during which time Somerville Hall grew from 12 students to 35. Madeleine Shaw Lefevre was the sister of a Liberal MP and the daughter of a former Vice-Chancellor of London University: the perfect credentials for a new, non-denominational hall for the higher education of women. Credentials without character would have been little use, and Shaw Lefevre was praised for her 'wise establishment of precedents in the conduct of life in a women's college'. This sundial was set up in 1922 at the centre of a garden built specially to commemorate Shaw Lefevre. In 2013 it was cleaned, repaired and set on a new plinth by sundial maker Harriet James and local stonemason OG Stonemasonry.

Inter=collegiate Rules for Women Undergraduates.

1. A woman undergraduate may not reside in Oxford out of Full Term except by permission of her Principal, and under the conditions laid down by the Delegates of Lodgings.

2. A woman undergraduate may not enter men's rooms either in College or in lodgings without obtaining leave from her Principal. She must have a chaperone approved by her Principal.

It is understood that conversation between men and women undergraduates before and after lectures is not encouraged.

3. A woman undergraduate must obtain leave from her Principal before accepting invitations for the evening, or for mixed parties. She may not go out after dinner without permission, and must always be back by 11 o'clock and must report her return.

4. A woman undergraduate may invite men friends to tea in the public rooms or grounds of the College or Hall to which she belongs, after obtaining permission from her Principal, provided that there are at least two women in the party. A woman undergraduate may receive her brother in her room, but not other men.

5. A woman undergraduate may go to matinees with men friends if leave is obtained from her Principal, provided that there are two women in the party.

6. Mixed parties may not be held in cafes, restaurants, or hotels without a chaperone approved by the Principal.

7. A woman undergraduate may not attend a subscription dance.

8. All Joint Societies must be approved by the Principals, and such approval must be renewed annually. Meetings of such societies may not be held in undergraduates' rooms, and may only be held in men's colleges with written permission from the Dean of the College, provided that a woman senior member is present.

9. A woman undergraduate may not go for walks, bicycle or motor rides alone with a man undergraduate other than her brother. Permission for mixed parties may be given at the discretion of the Principal.

10. A woman undergraduate may not boat with men (other than her brother) without a chaperone approved by her Principal.

11. A woman undergraduate may only be present at football or cricket matches or boat races under conditions approved by her Principal.

12. Women undergraduates are not allowed to play mixed hockey.

65
'Inter-collegiate Rules for Women Undergraduates'

The rules about being accompanied by a chaperone evolved during the first years of the women's halls in Oxford. They were not in fact needed at the very start, when women could not attend the same lectures as men and went to repeat renditions of the same lectures. The change came, not from liberal sentiment, but when the dons giving lectures began to refuse to give them twice; but it was not until the outbreak of the First World War that women were allowed to attend lectures independently. Even then, 'conversation between men and women undergraduates' before and after lectures was 'not encouraged'. As time went by, the operation of the 'Chap. rules' (as they inevitably became known) therefore centred more and more on who could be in whose room, and when. Rules around 'mixed parties' remained especially strict. The 'Chap. rules' soon began to creak, but were only abandoned in 1925, in favour of a raft of other regulations about signing in guests and abiding by curfews.

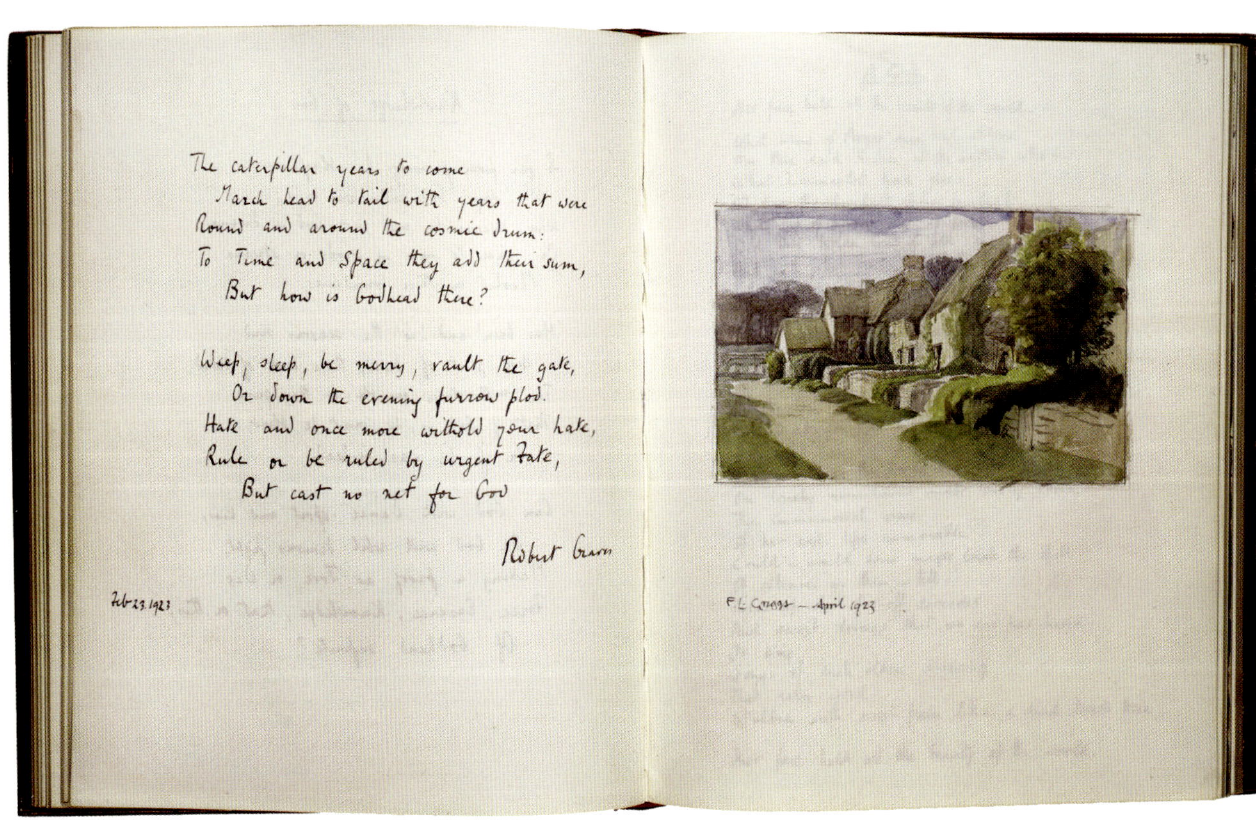

66

'Paradise of Dainty Devices'

This is a showcase of talent and creativity, but above all, it is an extraordinary testament to friendship. It was the property of Percy Withers (1867–1945), a Manchester GP whose wife Mary (1870–1947) and daughter Audrey (1905–2001) [68] both studied at Somerville. Percy Withers had some literary ambition himself, but his chief talent was for friendship. A.E. Housman, Walter de la Mare, Max Beerbohm, Laurence Binyon, E.M. Forster and John Galsworthy were all friends and correspondents. The 'Paradise of Dainty Devices' is a glorified cuttings-cum-visitors' book, which includes paintings by Paul Nash (1889–1946) [68] and a poem by W.B. Yeats (1865–1939). Shown here is a double page from 1923 with a poem by Robert Graves [56] opposite a watercolour sketch by F.L. Griggs (1876–1938, the etcher who was part of the Arts and Crafts movement in the Cotswolds). The book came to Somerville in the late 1970s as part of a donation from Withers's two daughters.

Christina Rossetti, 'Goblin Market'

'Goblin Market' by Christina Rossetti (1830–94) tells the story of two sisters, Lizzie and Laura, who are tempted by the fruit ('sweet to tongue and sound to eye') that is sold by goblins ('Who knows upon what soil they fed / Their hungry thirsty roots?'). Laura succumbs, and only Lizzie's bravery saves her from death. Written in 1859 (while Rossetti was volunteering at a penitentiary for 'fallen women') and published in 1862, 'Goblin Market' has tempted critics into explanations that dwell on everything from temptation and capitalism to feminism and homosexuality. The poem, which appeared in Rossetti's first published volume, was acclaimed by contemporary critics and readers (except for Ruskin [14], who considered Rossetti's irregular use of metre to be a 'calamity of modern poetry'). This copy came to Somerville as part of the Withers collection of art and writing [66], and originally belonged to Christina's brother, Dante Gabriel Rossetti (1828–82), drawn here by William Rossetti (1829–1919), in a sketch also held in Somerville's collections. Dante Gabriel made notes in the volume, recording his feeling that his sister's poem 'A Birthday' ('My heart is like a singing bird…') was 'a torrent of delight'.

'For there is no friend like a sister
In calm or stormy weather'

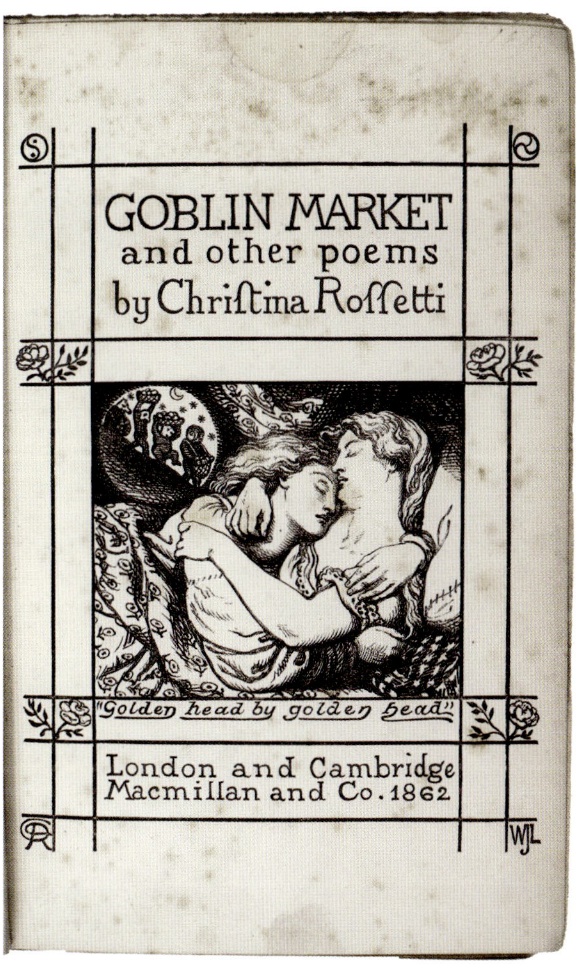

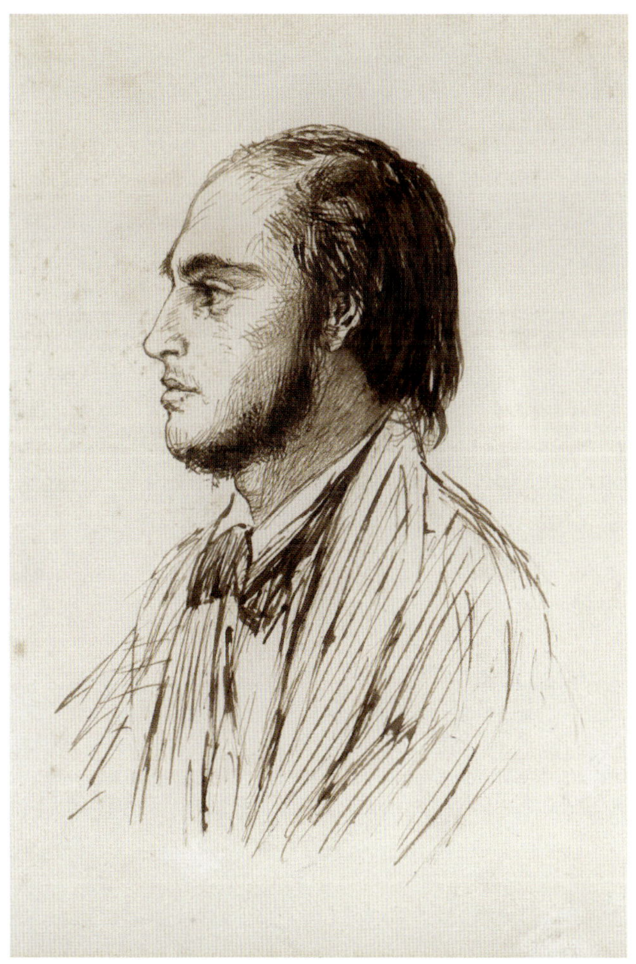

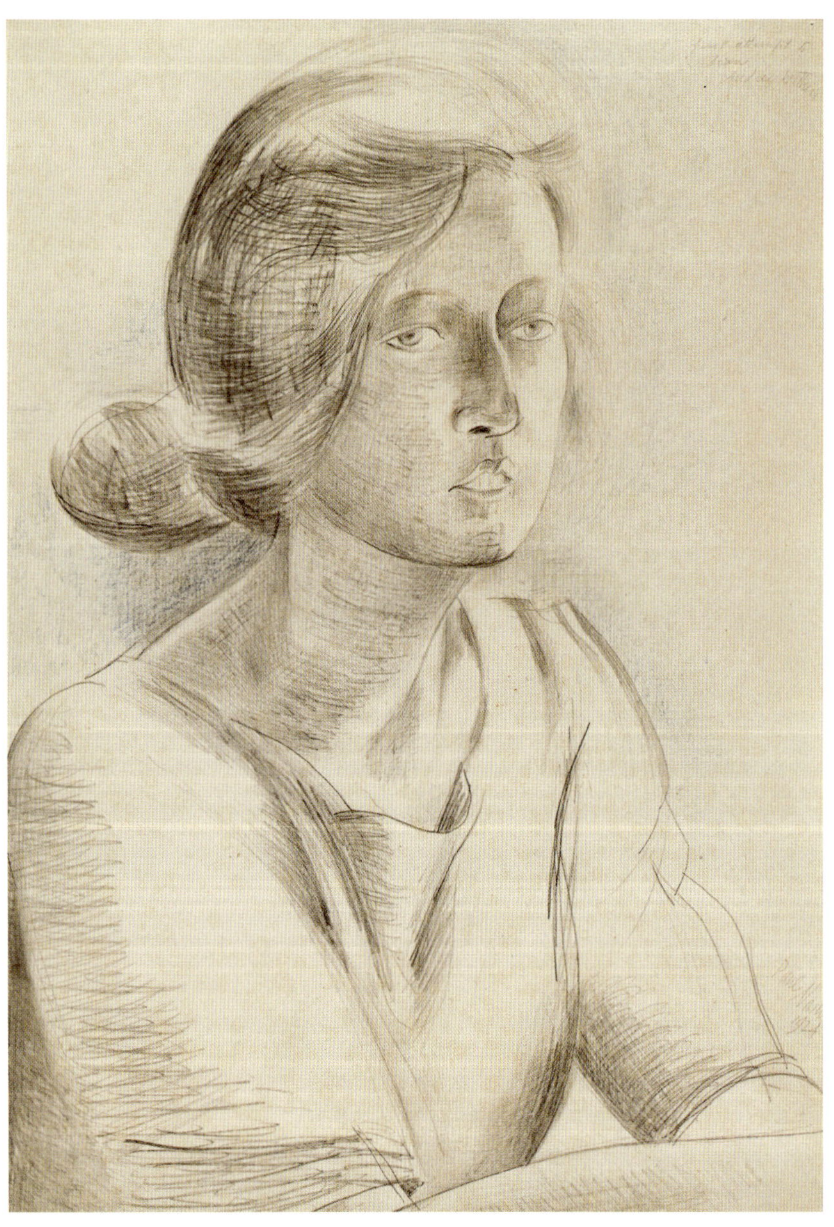

68
Paul Nash, drawing of Audrey Withers

Audrey Withers came up to Somerville in 1924. Her mother was also a Somervillian. Paul Nash was one of the wide circle of literary and artistic friends of Audrey's father, Percy Withers [66]. Renowned for his war art and his landscape paintings, this is a rare example of Nash's drawing from the early 1920s. He was clearly in contact with Audrey Withers at that time: his 1925 woodcut *Head of a Girl* is dedicated 'for Audrey'. Withers (later Audrey Kennett) went on to become the Editor of British *Vogue* from 1940 until 1960. She herself said she had little feeling for fashion, but she did have a feeling for the *Zeitgeist*. Under her editorship *Vogue* became a powerful tool of post-war culture, and she was responsible for persuading both Kingsley Amis (1922–95) and Elizabeth David (1913–92) to write for the magazine. In 1977 Audrey Kennett and her sister Monica donated a substantial collection of artwork and correspondence belonging to their father to the college.

'One day I mean to make a lot
of money by a real best-seller'

69
Letter from Winifred Holtby

It is for *South Riding* [88] and for her great friendship with Vera Brittain [79] that Winifred Holtby (1898–1935) is principally remembered now, although in her lifetime she was known more for her journalism than for her fiction. Born and brought up in Yorkshire, Holtby came to Somerville in 1917 to read Modern History and then took a year away for war work before returning to her studies. In this letter of 1923 she responded to an appeal from Somerville for funds, sending a cheque for £10 ('really from my father & mother'). She goes on to write: 'I wish it were more. One day I mean to make a lot of money by a real best-seller, & then perhaps it might be possible.' Holtby died from Bright's disease (sclerosis of the kidneys) at the age of 37. The money accruing from her published work was for many years the chief source of scholarship funds in Somerville, and in 1956 the new extension to the library was named in her honour.

Statute on Limitation of Numbers (Women).

Congregation, June 14, 2 p.m.

The Statute on Limitation of Numbers which comes before Congregation next Tuesday is spoken of by its opponents as an "attack" on Women's Education in Oxford. I write as one of those, and they are a considerable number, who have worked for Women's Education here in the past and who have helped to secure its present position, but who are supporting the Statute.

It is greatly to be regretted that the present controversy could not be settled by negociation. Those who promoted the petition which is the basis of the present Statute, offered to accept limitation imposed by the byelaws only of the existing societies, provided that the principle of the Proportion of Numbers was affirmed in the University Statutes. They even offered to leave the question whether this proportion should be fixed absolutely or only for a term of years, to the decision of Congregation, provided that the remaining terms of their proposal were accepted as they stood.

To their great surprise this offer, which was a last effort to avoid an open struggle, and which was strongly disapproved of by some of the petitioners whom they represented, was declined. The reason given was, "We cannot agree not to oppose a proposal to amend Sect. II. of Tit. XXIII. by imposing conditions as to the formation of a new Society other than those already contained in the Statute."

This answer means that the opponents of the Statute deny the right of the University to alter the conditions imposed in 1920, when women were admitted to the University.

The struggle thirty years ago was for the admission of women to degrees; this was the proposal of Lord Curzon in his famous book on University Reform (1909), and he was unwilling to go further. When, however, the Statute of 1920 was passed, much fuller University privileges were given to women students here, and only this term I myself suggested the Statute declaring that women were eligible for Professorships and all teaching posts.

But it was never even suggested in 1896, in 1909 or in 1920 that the Women's Societies were to enjoy the unrestricted rights of men's Colleges. Oxford was to remain a Man's University, to the full membership of which some women were admitted. I hope that Congregation on Tuesday will affirm that this principle is still the principle on which we welcome women students here.

JOSEPH WELLS,
Warden of Wadham College.

June 10, 1927.

'Oxford was to remain a Man's University'

70
Statute on Limitation of Numbers (Women)

This is a salutary reminder of the conditions in which Somerville was managing to flourish. By 1927, when this contribution to an Oxford University Congregation debate was penned, women had been admitted to degrees. That was a huge achievement, but it was very much not the end of institutional discrimination against women in the University. Here the then Warden of Wadham, Joseph Wells (1855–1929), explains at length that he has been a great supporter of 'Women's Education in Oxford', taking pains to point out that he has recently proposed a Statute to make women eligible for Professorships and all teaching posts. He goes on:

But it was never even suggested … that the Women's Societies were to enjoy the unrestricted rights of men's Colleges. Oxford was to remain a Man's University, to the full membership of which some women were admitted. I hope that Congregation on Tuesday will affirm that this principle is still the principle on which we welcome women students here.

Congregation decided to limit the number of women admitted to Oxford, and the limit was not lifted until 1957.

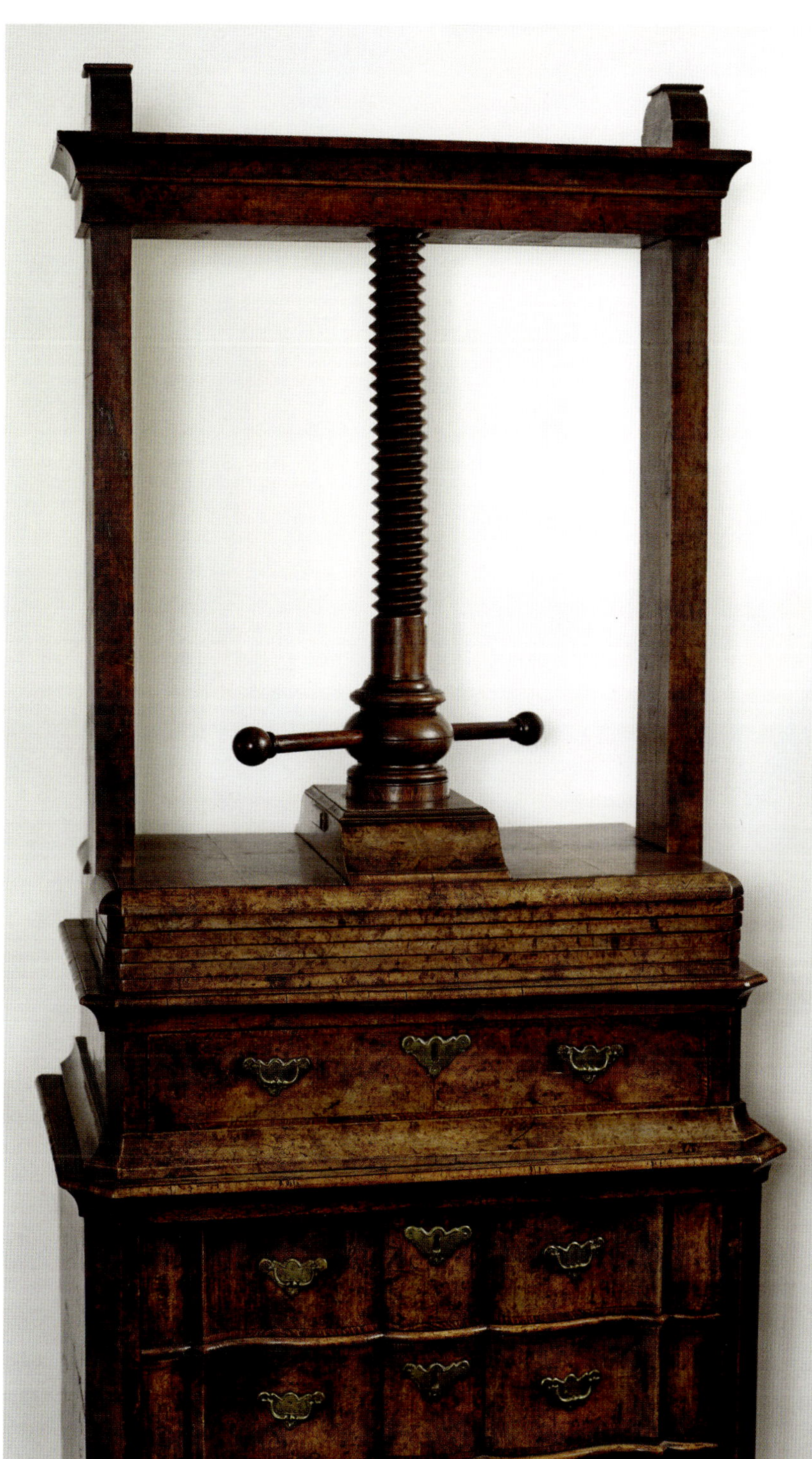

71
Book/linen press

This handsome piece of eighteenth-century Dutch furniture (walnut, with an oak mechanism) was purchased from the belongings of Sarah Smithson (1844–1928). Smithson was active in the suffrage movement and in the promotion of women's education and equality more generally: she left money to establish a garden 'limited to women and girls' in Hitchin – home of the College for Women that would go on to become Girton College, Cambridge – and she also bequeathed money to Somerville 'for the promotion and study of Modern Languages', which helps to fund Modern Languages fellows today. Furniture of this sort was used as an early ironing mechanism for linen or in the process of binding books: pressure on the wooden leaves is increased by turning the handle to tighten the large wooden screw. Many examples, though (of which this is probably one) were purely decorative.

'Frequent raids should be made on private property'

72
Vera Farnell's notes for the Librarian

This is a handover document of the old school. The note on the first page (dated July 1928) reads 'intended merely as a possible saving of time and in no sense as a set of measures to be carried out!' A detailed exercise book's worth of notes follows, and the themes are those that would, doubtless, still be close to a college librarian's heart today. Chief among them is the war on 'the untidiness of students'. 'Frequent raids should be made on private property, correspondence, books, clothes etc. left in the Library and cluttering up the tables.' Vera Farnell (1889–1976) came up to Somerville in 1911. She later became Tutor in English and French, and also the college's Librarian and Dean, as well as holding a host of other college offices. In her introduction to her memoirs of the college, *A Somervillian Looks Back* (published in 1948, shortly after she had retired), she states that the particular character of Somerville 'is based upon an idea of intellectual integrity and independence, of wide toleration and of a liberal attitude', though she goes on to note wryly that a 'certain tendency to eccentricity may sometimes accompany these admirable qualities'.

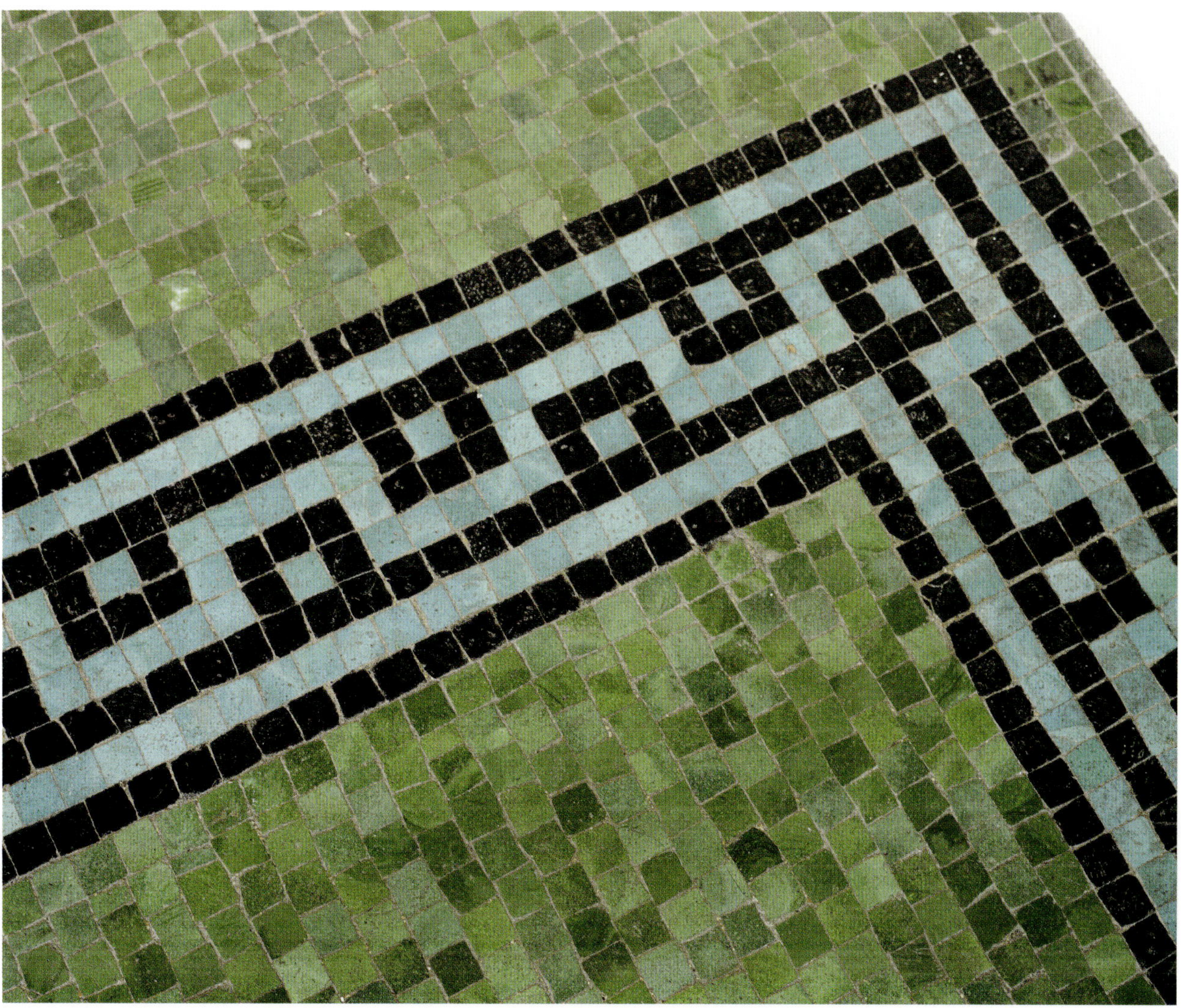

73
Mosaic floor tiles

Unusual, calming and sea-like, these mosaic tiles are remembered by everyone who has ever walked through the ground floor of House, and that means every Somervillian. Sourced from Italy by Margery Fry and installed by Italian workmen in 1929, they now set a Mediterranean tone matched by the paintings on the wall, the work of Margery's brother Roger [76]. At the time when they were installed they must have looked startlingly modern, and they still stand out. Margery Fry often encouraged Somerville's 'students' (as she called them, where others still insisted on 'undergraduates') to flout the aesthetic conventions of the time: she once suggested that when at home they should decorate their parents' fireplaces in gold paint.

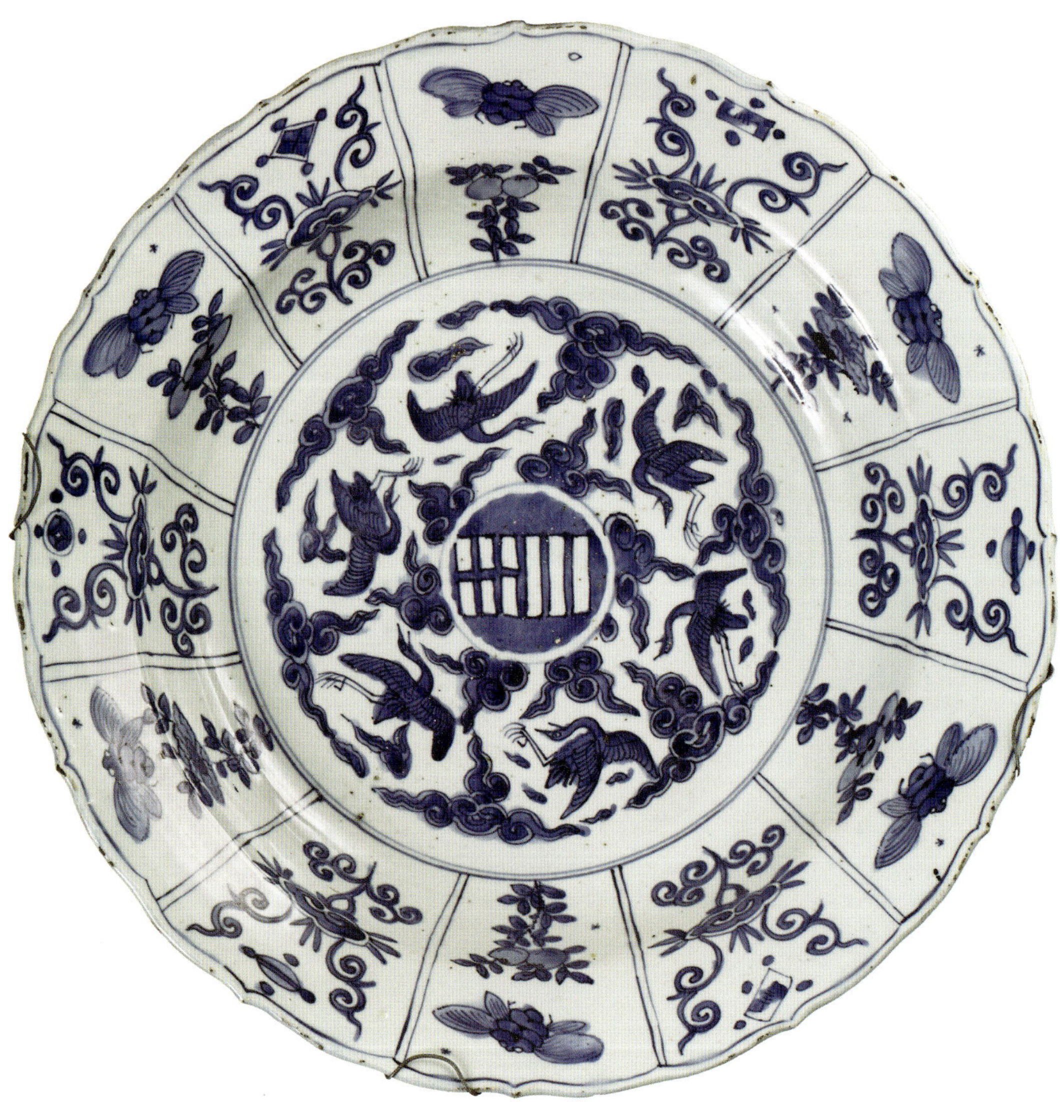

74
Kraak ware dish

Margery Fry was Principal of Somerville from 1926 to 1931. Nationally and internationally she is remembered for her pioneering work on prison reform. Her long-standing links to the visual arts are perhaps less well known, and came not least from her brother, the artist and founder of the Omega Workshops, Roger Fry [76]. Roger Fry was in large part responsible for the resurgence of interest in Chinese and Japanese ceramics in England in the 1930s, and this aesthetic inspired much of the pottery produced in his workshop. Margery Fry held a large collection of her brother's work and of pieces by other members of the Bloomsbury Group, and she also had a number of his ceramics and those of the kind that had inspired him. Here, we see one of Margery Fry's gifts to Somerville [76, 83], a Chinese blue and white kraak dish from the Wanli period (c.1600). It is still displayed in Margery Fry and Elizabeth Nuffield House, the building that was completed in 1964 to accommodate Somerville's growing number of graduate students [107].

It looks from the outside as though it must have been built at the same time as the hall, but the Reading Room was in fact constructed in 1930. This becomes obvious when you step down into it from the hall and move from an Edwardian space into something that feels a bit like one of the University of London's buildings. The resemblance is more than coincidence: the architect of the Reading Room, Percy Morley Horder (1870–1944), designed the School of Hygiene and Tropical Medicine. He was not the easiest man to work with, and the then Principal, Helen Darbishire, recalled 'stormy Committees' as the building was discussed. She conceded that 'if you choose an architect of genius you must expect storms', and Somerville chose Morley Horder to design the new East Quadrangle (later Darbishire) shortly after the Reading Room was completed. The room is an ingenious piece of infill work, and it was made possible by a generous gift from a wealthy student. At the time the donor wished to remain anonymous, and in that spirit we do not name them here.

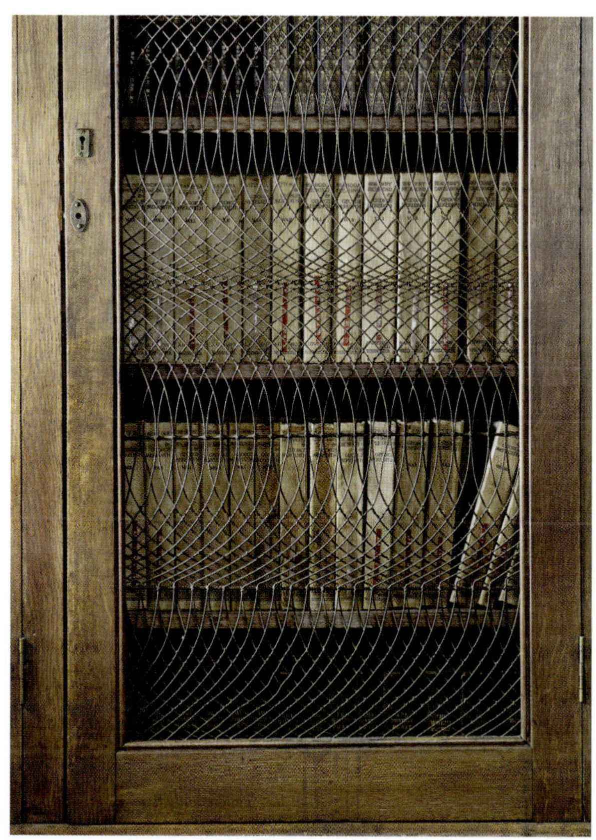

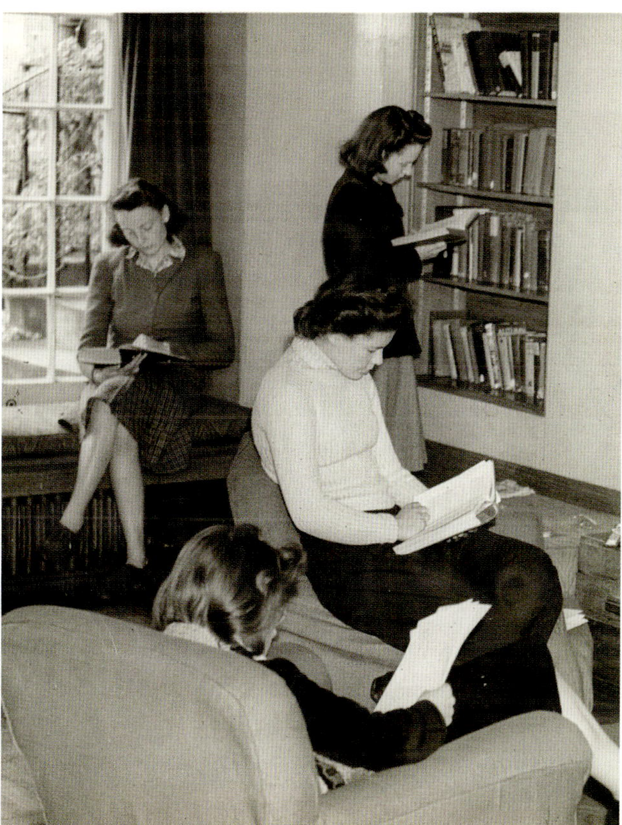

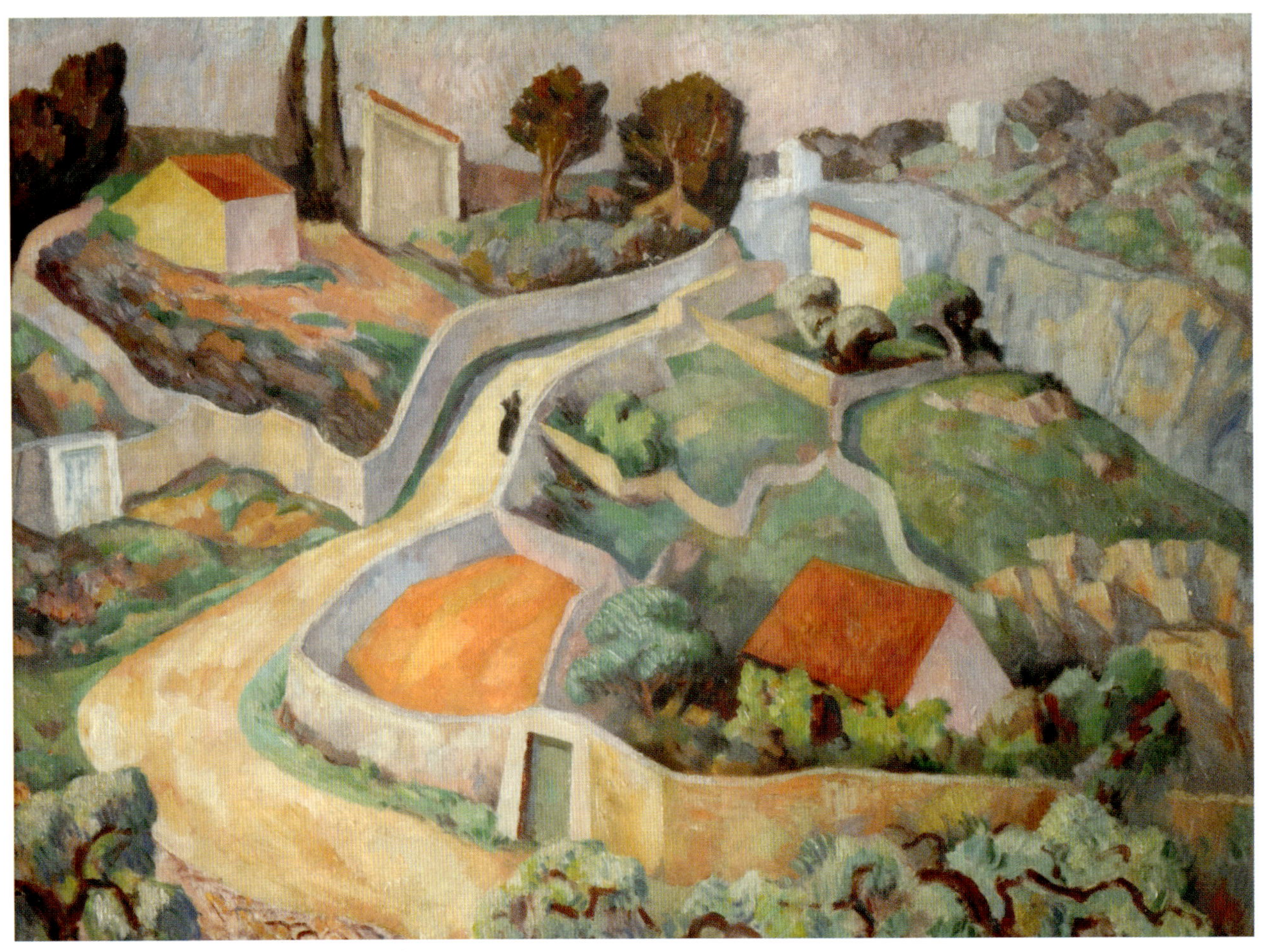

76
Roger Fry, *Near Nîmes*

Roger Eliot Fry was the brother of Margery Fry, Principal of Somerville from 1926 to 1931. His own expertise began in Italian Renaissance art: he taught art history at the Slade School of Art, and in 1906 was made Curator of Paintings at New York's Metropolitan Museum of Art. Roger Fry was also an accomplished painter in his own right, although he was far more renowned as a critic. Margery Fry gave *Near Nîmes* to Somerville in 1931, and it now hangs above the green Italianate tiles she had installed on the ground floor of House [73]. In his work as a painter and, more influentially, as a critic, Roger Fry brought to the attention of the English the French style of painting he himself dubbed 'Post-Impressionism', and *Near Nîmes* is very much in that mode.

Jacob Epstein, cast of *First Portrait of Louise*

Jacob Epstein (1880–1959) was one of the pioneers of modern sculpture. His work – a strong influence on Henry Moore (1898–1986) and Barbara Hepworth (1903–75) – often displayed a 'primitive' style. Born in the US to a family of Polish Jewish refugees, Epstein moved to Europe at the turn of the century and became a British subject in 1911. This is a cast of

First Portrait of Louise, conceived in 1932. It stands at 20 cm high, and is now outside Hall. Its verdigris picks up the colour of the Italianate tiles on the ground floor, which can be seen through the stairwell [73]. Epstein used friends and acquaintances as models, and he produced many images of writers, artists and politicians. He was also known to ask strangers to sit for him;

'Louise' has not yet been identified. The sculptor Clare Sheridan (1885–1970), who modelled for Epstein in 1919, said: 'He did not model with his fingers, he built up planes slowly by means of small pieces of clay applied with a flat, pliant wooden tool … it is his method of building up that gives Epstein's surfaces their vibrant and pulsating quality of flesh'.

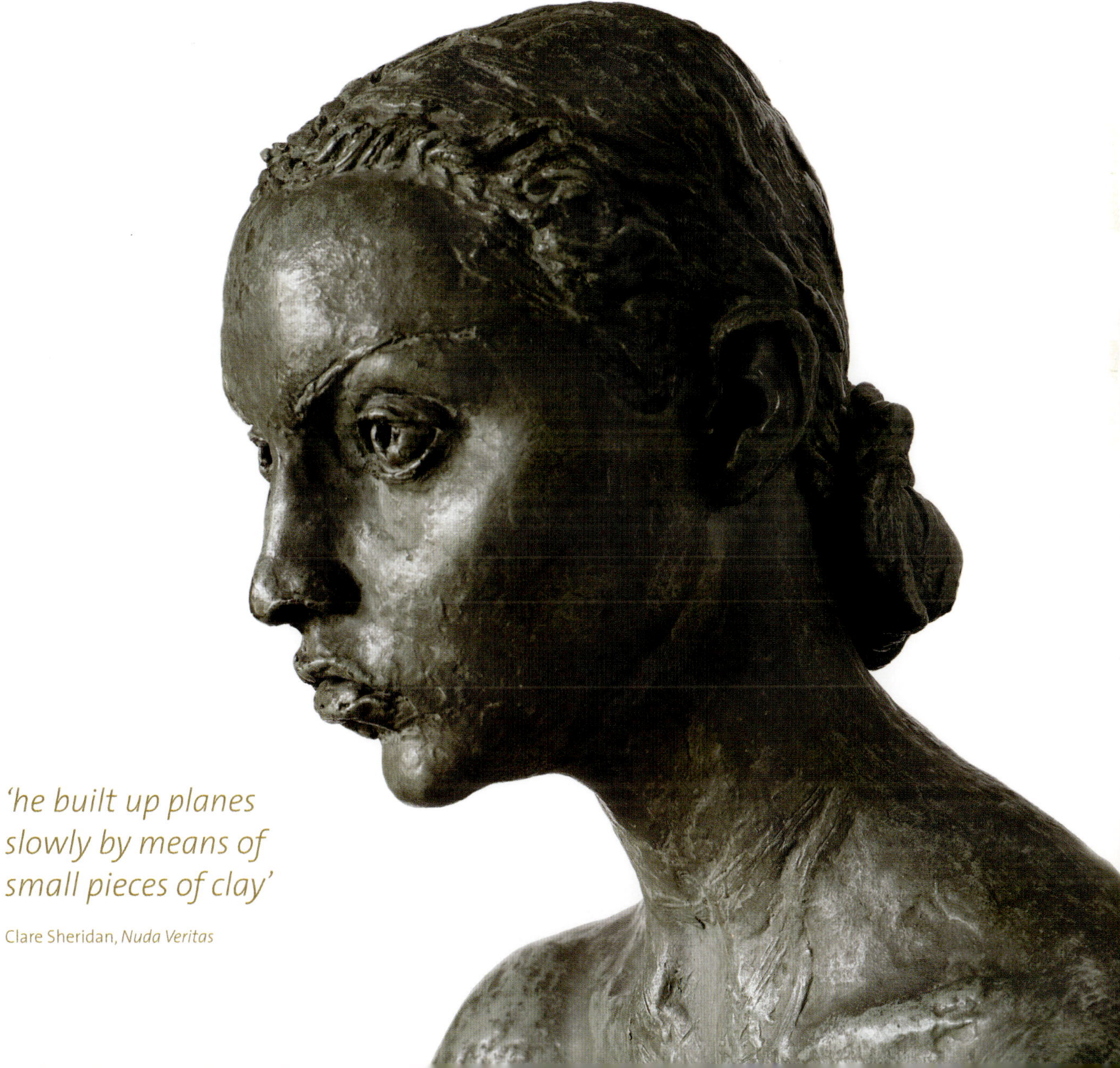

'he built up planes slowly by means of small pieces of clay'

Clare Sheridan, *Nuda Veritas*

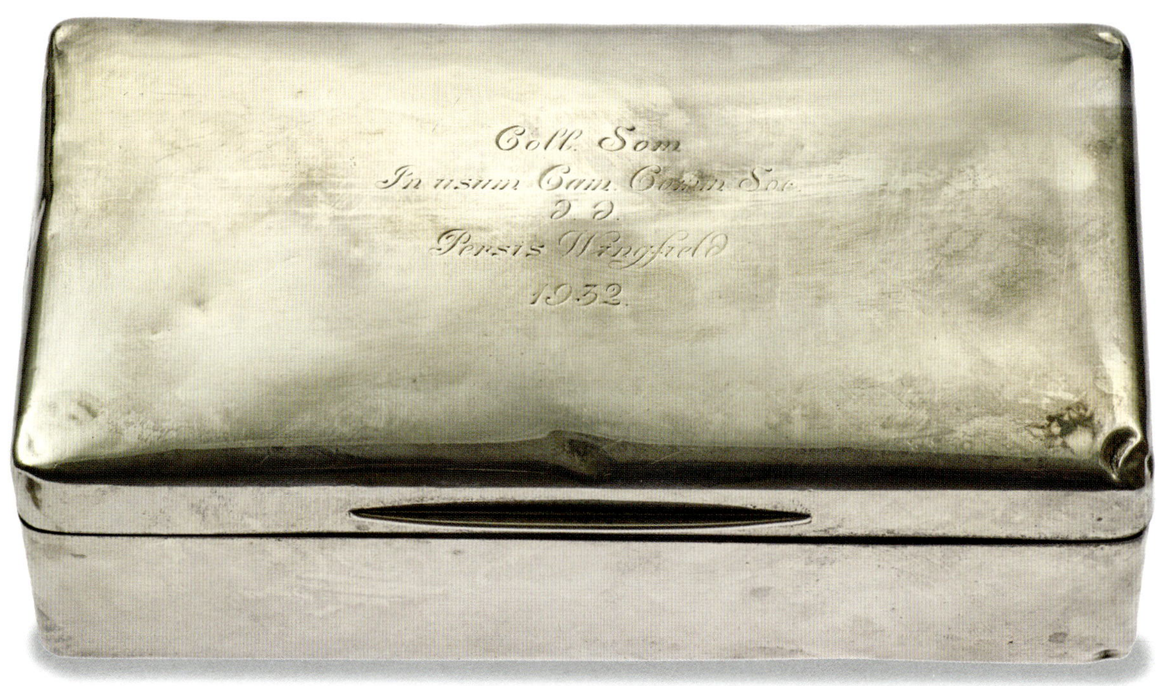

78
Cigarette box

Now, it looks a quaintly old-fashioned thing, like seeing people smoking in black and white films, and it is odd to consider how many of the respectable ladies of Somerville were in fact drug addicts (though it doesn't do to be pious: there is still the SCR coffee machine, after all [116]). In Somerville's early years, smoking was discouraged, although not formally prohibited as it was in some of the women's societies in Oxford and Cambridge, but by the 1920s it was rife. The gift of Persis Wingfield (assistant to the Treasurer, and also a member of the college's jiu-jitsu society), this silver cigarette case remained in use in the SCR (Senior Common Room) until the 1980s. Inside, its wooden dividers retain the scent (and stains) of stale tobacco. In 2007, when the ban on smoking in public places came into force, all college rooms became non-smoking zones. And so, reaching into one's gown for one's cigarette case (as Harriet Vane does in *Gaudy Night*, only to find the first of the novel's poison pen letters) has joined sherry parties and gramophones on the river as something belonging to an older Oxford.

MEMORANDUM OF AGREEMENT made this 4th day of March 1933 BETWEEN Miss Vera Brittain, c/o Curtis Brown Limited, of 6, Henrietta Street, Covent Garden, London. W.C.2. (who and whose executors administrators and assigns are where the context permits hereinafter included in the term "the Author") of the one part AND Victor Gollancz, Esq., for and on behalf of VICTOR GOLLANCZ LIMITED, of 14, Henrietta Street, Covent Garden, London W.C.2. (who and whose successors and assigns are where the context permits hereinafter included in the term "the Publishers") of the other part WHEREBY it is mutually agreed as follows respecting a work to be written by the Author provisionally entitled:-

"TESTAMENT OF YOUTH"
----

1. The Publishers shall during the legal term of copyright have the exclusive licence of producing and publishing the said work in volume form in the English language within the limits of the British Empire excepting Canada, subject to the conditions following:-

2. The Publishers shall publish the said work within six months of the delivery to them of the complete manuscript ready for press at a published price of not less than 8/6d (Eight Shillings and Sixpence) or more than 10/6d (Ten Shillings and Sixpence) not in the first instance.. The Publishers shall not, however, be responsible for any delay in the publication of the said work caused by strikes, lockouts, abnormal trade conditions or any other circumstances over which they have no control.

3. The Author warrants to the Publishers that the said work shall be in no way whatever a violation of any existing copyright and that it shall contain nothing libellous or objectionable and will indemnify the Publishers against any loss injury or damage including any legal costs or expenses occasioned to or incurred by the Publishers in consequence of any breach of this warranty.

4. The Publishers shall keep or cause to be kept proper books of account and shall enter or cause to be entered therein statements showing the number of copies produced and sold of the said work. Accounts shall be made up to the 25th day of March and the 29th day of September in each year and shall be delivered or sent to the Author within three months of such making up of account and the amount due to the Author shall be payable within one month of such rendering of account, the Publishers paying the Author as follows:-

(a) On the Home Edition.

A royalty of 10% (Ten per cent) of the published price of all copies sold of the original English edition up to 10,000 (Ten Thousand); 15% (Fifteen per cent) of the published price of all copies so sold from 10,000 (Ten Thousand) and up to 20,000 (Twenty Thousand) and a royalty of 20% (Twenty per cent) of the published price of all copies so sold beyond 20,000 (Twenty Thousand).

(b) On Cheaper Editions.

A royalty of 10% (Ten per cent) of the published price of all copies sold of any cheaper editions published at less than half the original published price.

Please Initial ....

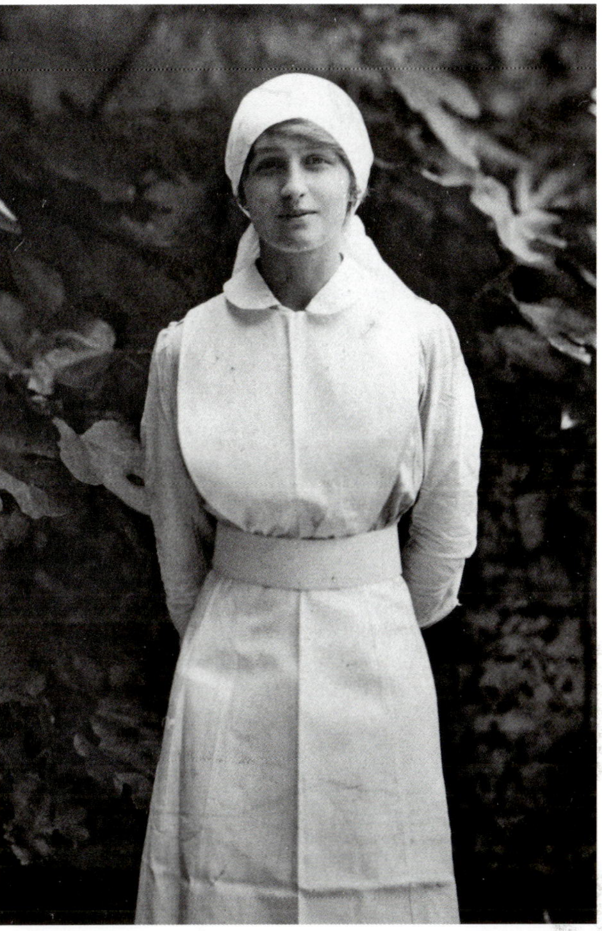

‘I shall remember, always’

Vera Brittain, *Testament of Youth*

79
Contract for *Testament of Youth*

Vera Brittain was born in Staffordshire, and won an exhibition to read English at Somerville. She came up in the autumn of 1914, but left at the end of her first year to work as a nurse with the Voluntary Aid Detachment in London, Malta and France. By the time she returned to Somerville in 1919 she had lost her fiancé, her brother and two close friends in the First World War. *Testament of Youth* was one of the best-known accounts of the war written from a woman's point of view. Brittain's contract for the book, with publisher Victor Gollancz, stipulated that she would receive royalties of 10 per cent for the first 10,000 copies sold, 15 per cent for the next 10,000, and 20 per cent for copies sold above that. The first print run of 3,000 copies sold out on the day it was published in August 1933. *Testament of Youth* sold 120,000 copies over the next six years. It fell out of favour during the Second World War and afterwards, not least because of Brittain's fierce pacifism. In the 1970s Carmen Callil, co-founder of Virago, reissued it, and *Testament of Youth* became a best-seller again. Brittain's daughter, the politician Shirley Williams [101], is also a Somervillian.

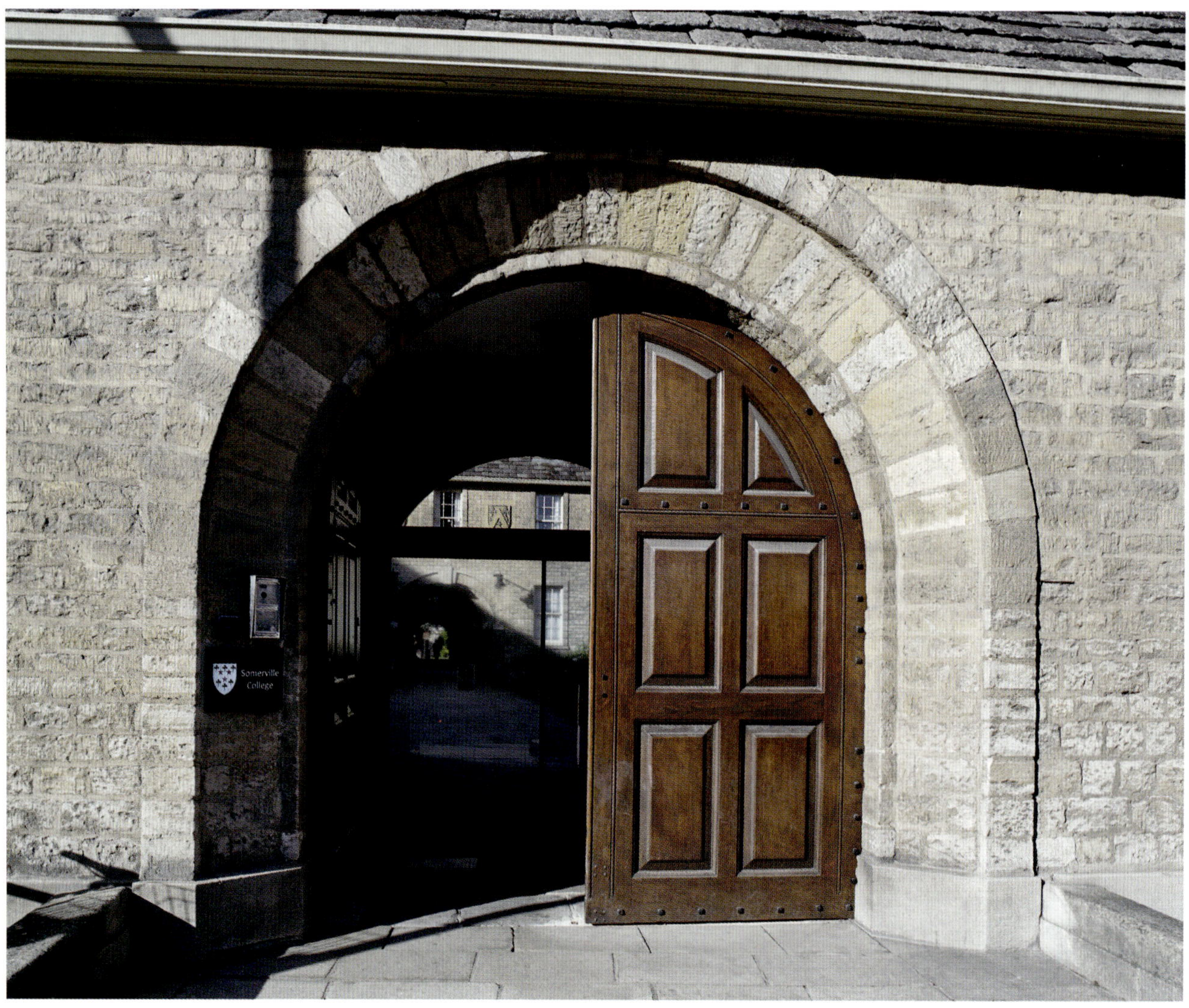

80
Woodstock Road door

The first Woodstock Road gates to Somerville opened on to a simple driveway flanked by a row of cottages leading down to Walton House [9]. In 1891 these gates were replaced by a lodge and arched gateway (the work was partly paid for by a generous donation from the Clothworkers' Company, which had funded one of the earliest scholarships at Somerville). The current entrance was part of the design of the new East Quadrangle (later Darbishire) by Percy Morley Horder, whose neo-Georgian style of architecture can also be seen in buildings for the London School of Hygiene and Tropical Medicine and the University of Nottingham. Morley Horder could be very exacting [75], and his pupils' nickname for him was 'Holy Murder'. One senses from the correspondence that in Miss Beauchamp, the then Treasurer of Somerville, he may have met his match. His designs for the East Quadrangle included a 'Lodge for day portress' and these smart wooden gates. Now they have a sliding glass door set behind them, for security, and Morley Horder's clean lines have, inevitably, become a little cluttered by bicycle racks.

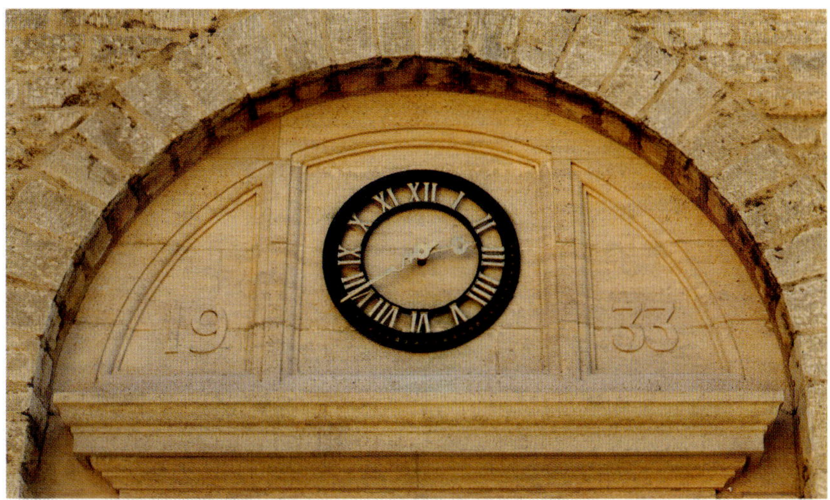

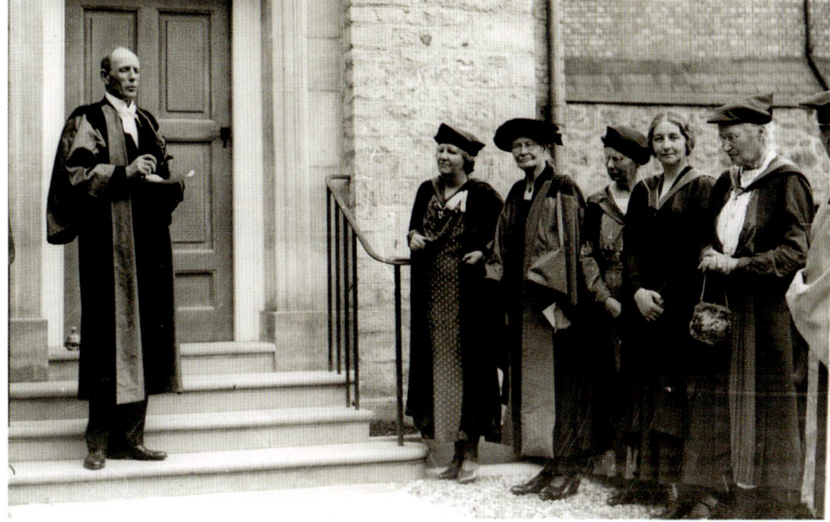

Dorothy L. Sayers, *Gaudy Night*

81
New Council Room clock

In 1932 Somerville's college Council made the decision to construct a new building next to the Woodstock Road. Completed in 1933, the East Quadrangle was later named for Helen Darbishire, Principal from 1931 to 1945. In one corner of this quadrangle stands the New Council Room. Funded by an anonymous gift from an old student, this grand room was used for meetings of the college Council or Governing Body. The clock over its arched entrance was a gift from Eleanor Rathbone [25]. Darbishire was officially opened by the Chancellor of the University, Lord Halifax (1881–1959), on 23 June 1934, and this was the ceremony Sayers borrowed for her fictional Shrewsbury College. Though she tells us that 'Shrewsbury College with its dons, students and scouts, is entirely imaginary', traces of Somerville can be found throughout *Gaudy Night* [87]. The novel's opening paragraph describes a quadrangle that all Somervillians will recognise, with its 'style neither new nor old, but stretching out reconciling hands to past and present' and its 'flower-beds splashed at the angles, and surrounded by a wide stone plinth.'

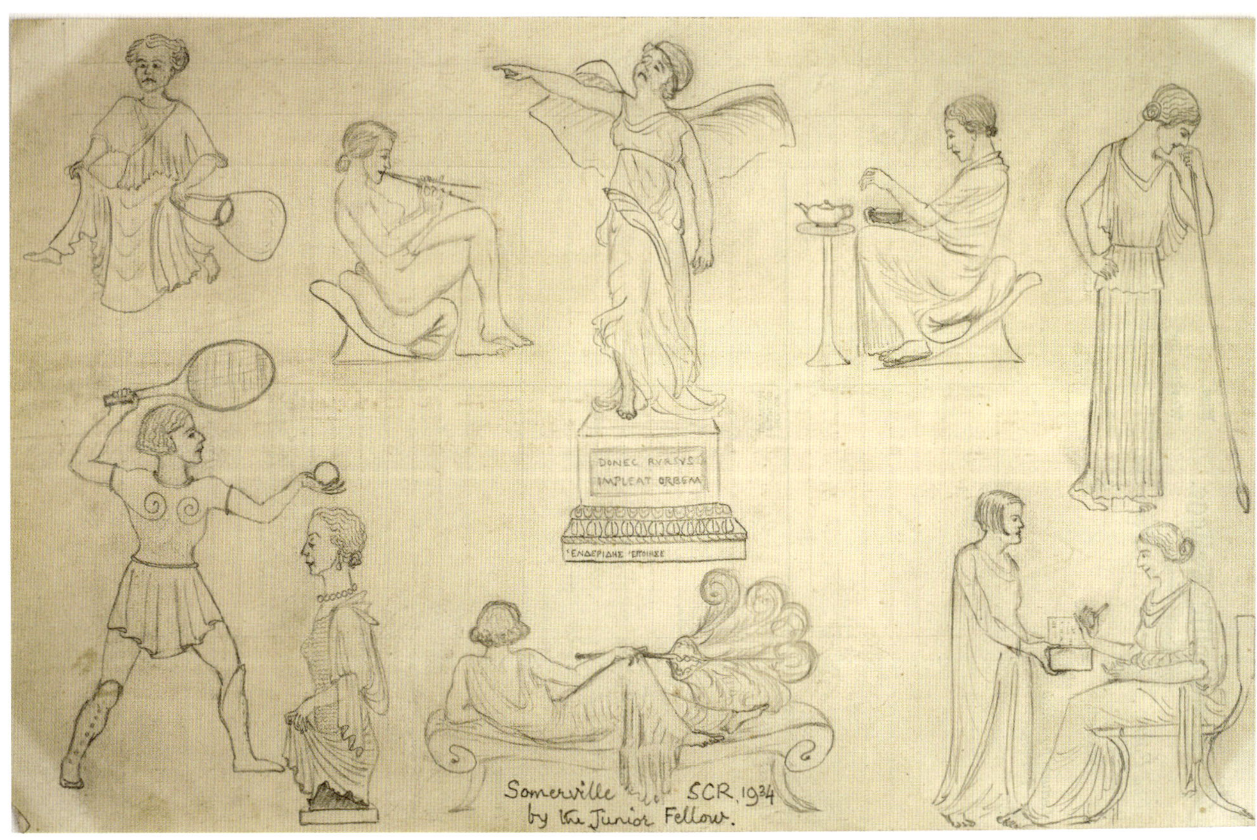

82
Isobel Henderson cartoons

Isobel Henderson (Munro; 1906–67) was Somerville's Fellow and Tutor in Ancient History from 1930 until 1967. Among her pupils was the future Principal of the college, Barbara Craig. Henderson had a wide range of interests beyond her academic work on Roman republican history, including horse racing and Cornish history. She also had an impeccable Oxford pedigree (her father had been Rector of Lincoln) and enjoyed sketching the occasional cartoon. She drew this one in 1934 when she was Junior Fellow, and here are the college's members in classical guise. From left to right in the back row are: Miss Lorimer (Tutor in Classics); Henderson herself; Principal Helen Darbishire (atop a plinth bearing the college's motto [8]); Miss Lascelles (Tutor in English); and Miss Farnell (Librarian [72]). In the front row, left to right: Miss Stonedale (Bursar); Miss Beauchamp (Treasurer); Miss Starkie (Reader in French [100]); Miss Sutherland (Tutor in Economic History and Politics, and later Principal of Lady Margaret Hall); and Miss Clarke (Tutor in Modern History [85]).

Silver inkstand

The Fry family were Quakers. Joseph Fry (1728–87) was, among other things, the founder of chocolate manufacturer J.S. Fry & Sons (drinking chocolate was championed by the Quaker movement as a cheap alternative to alcohol that was also safe to drink, as the water to make it had to be boiled before use). Joseph's great-grandson Edward Fry (1827–1918) did not join the family business, instead becoming a lawyer.

He was eventually a judge in the British Court of Appeal and he also acted as an international arbitrator at the Hague in the early 1900s. In 1859 Fry married Mariabella Hodgkin (1833–1930). They had five children, including Margery Fry, who came up to Somerville in 1894 to read Mathematics (although she took no examinations, as her father did not consider it right for a woman to do so). Fry went on to become the college's

Librarian. She left Somerville in 1904 and became Warden of the new women's residence at Birmingham University, returning to Somerville to become its fourth Principal in 1926. The inkstand was given to Edward Fry in 1908, 'in recognition of his services as Chairman of Royal Commission on Trinity College Dublin and the University of Dublin', and it was then given to Somerville by Margery Fry in 1934.

'in recognition of his services'

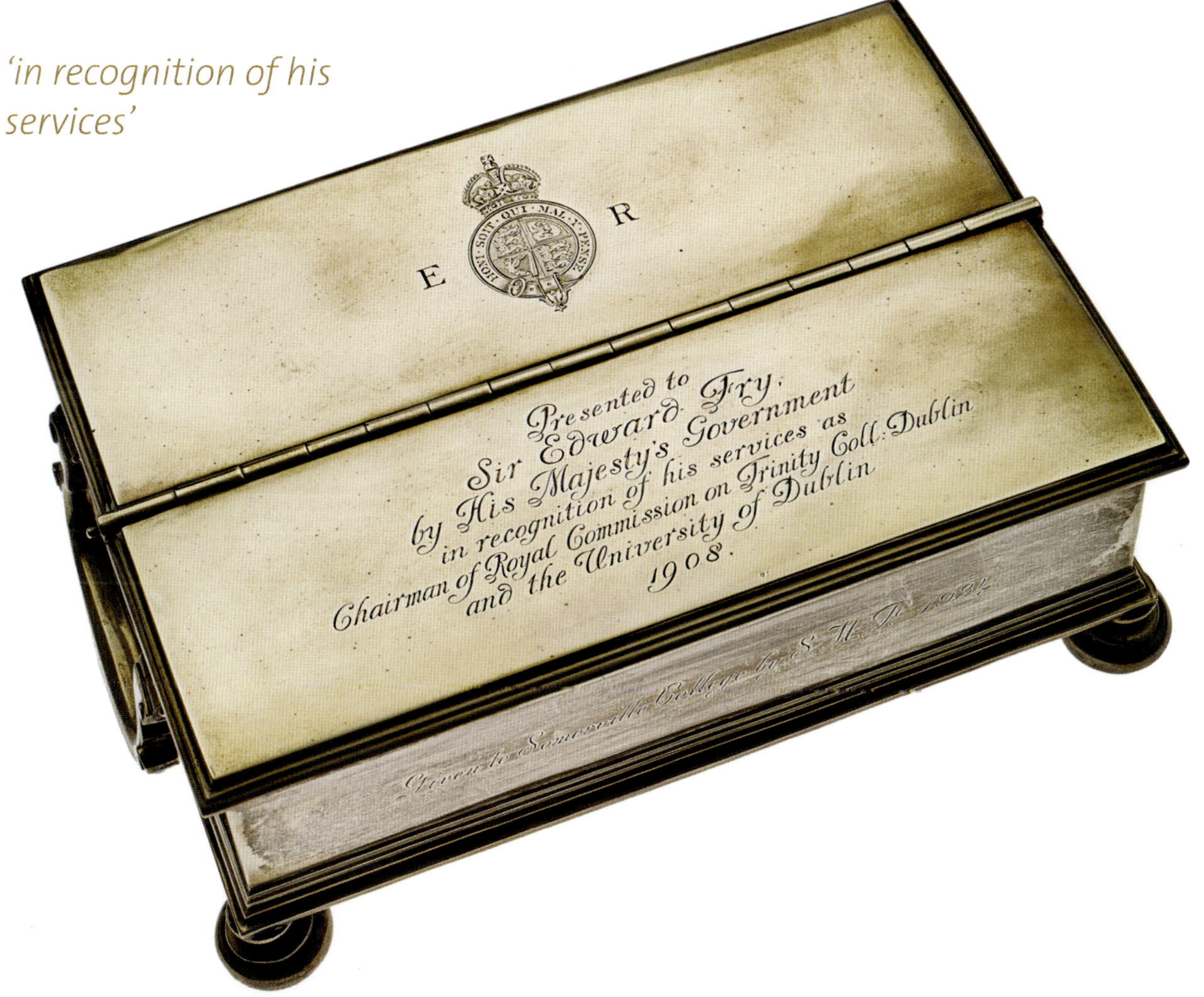

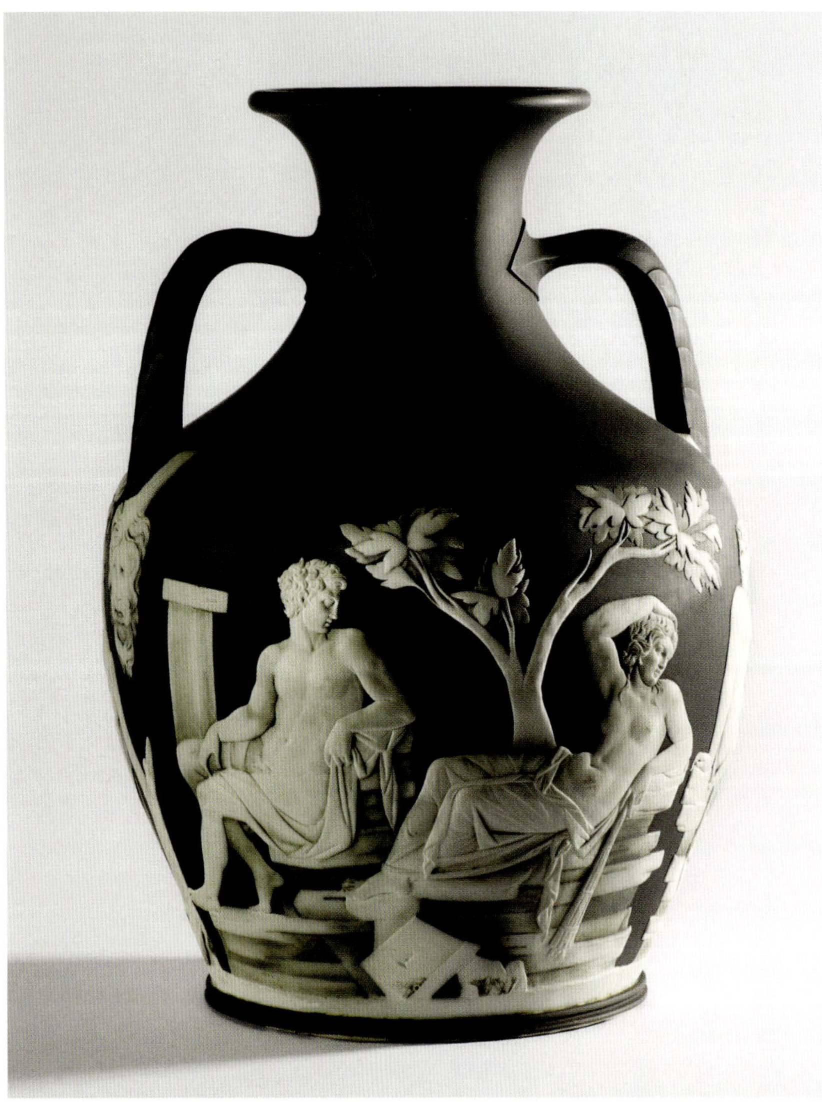

84
Copy of the Portland Vase

In the late eighteenth century the British ambassador in Naples bought a Roman vase made of deep blue glass and adorned with cameos of mythological and historical scenes. He brought it back with him to Britain several years later and promptly sold it. Eventually the vase found its way to William Cavendish-Bentinck (1738–1809), 3rd Duke of Portland, who lent it to Josiah Wedgwood (1730–95). It took Wedgwood four years of trial and error to make a copy of the vase (not in glass but in 'jasperware', the form of unglazed pottery he himself had developed). 'First edition copies' of Wedgwood's piece were issued in 1790 and examples can now be found in the V&A and the Fitzwilliam Museum. Somerville's was part of a gift of Wedgwood items for the New Council Room [81], given by E.R. Cochrane (b. 1908), who came up to Somerville in 1927 to read Philosophy, Politics and Economics (PPE). Theories about the iconography of the images on the vase abound: from the marriage of the sea gods Peleus and Thetis to Mark Antony being lured by Cleopatra (complete with asp). The original Portland Vase was smashed in an act of vandalism in 1845, and only properly reconstructed (though still with some fragments missing) in the 1980s. It is held in the British Museum.

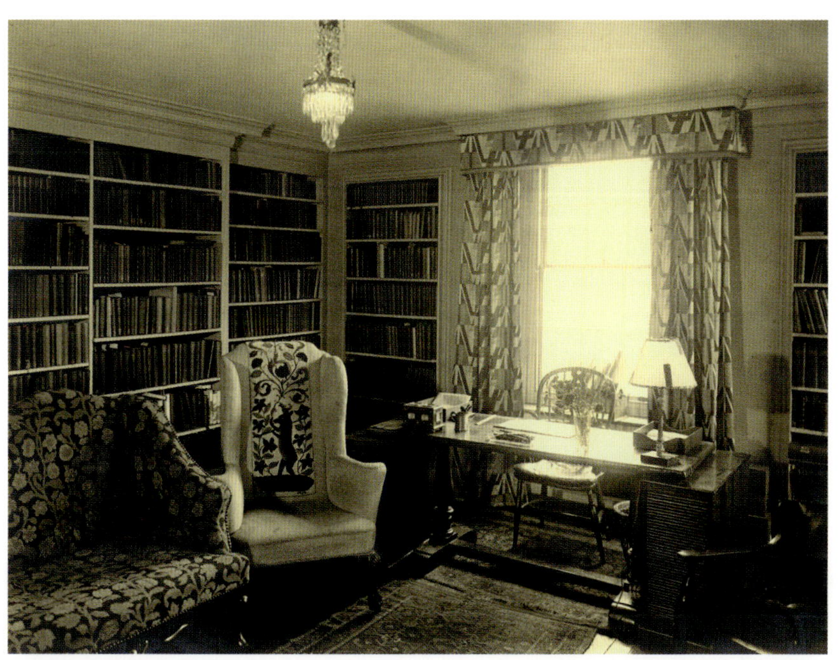

85
Settle

With its seventeenth-century frame, this handsome settle came from the room of Maude Clarke (1892–1935), tutor in history at Somerville from 1919 until her early death. She came to Somerville from a post in another university, which she described as having been 'demoralised by the war', and said that the experience of coming to Somerville was 'like coming from darkness to daylight'. Clarke was a historian of fourteenth-century England, with a particular focus on constitutional history. No wonder, then, that she became adept at college governance and administration. One of her first pupils when she arrived at Somerville was Vera Brittain [79]. A brilliant tutor and one of the dominant figures in the SCR (Senior Common Room) of the 1920s and 1930s [82], Clarke became ill in 1933 and resigned in 1935 (although the Council tried to persuade her only to take a leave of absence). Now on the ground floor of the library, next to the grandfather clock [112], the settle can clearly be seen on the left of this 1934 photograph of Clarke's room in the East Quadrangle (later Darbishire).

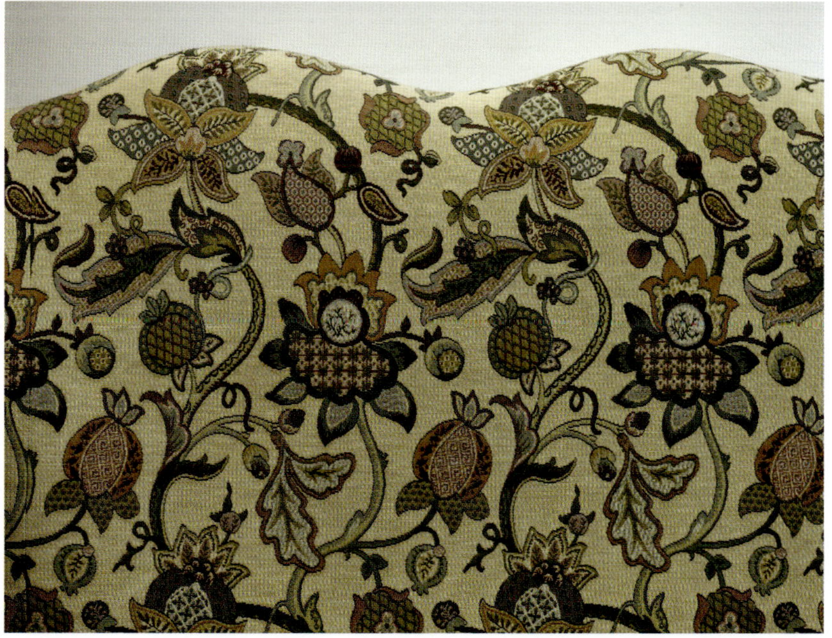

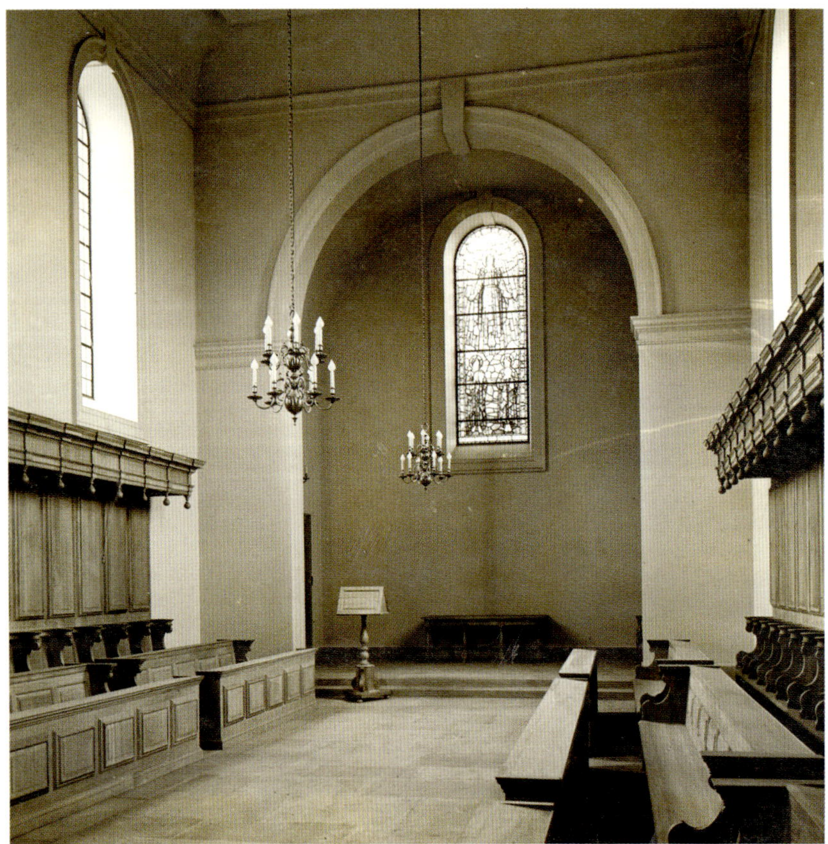

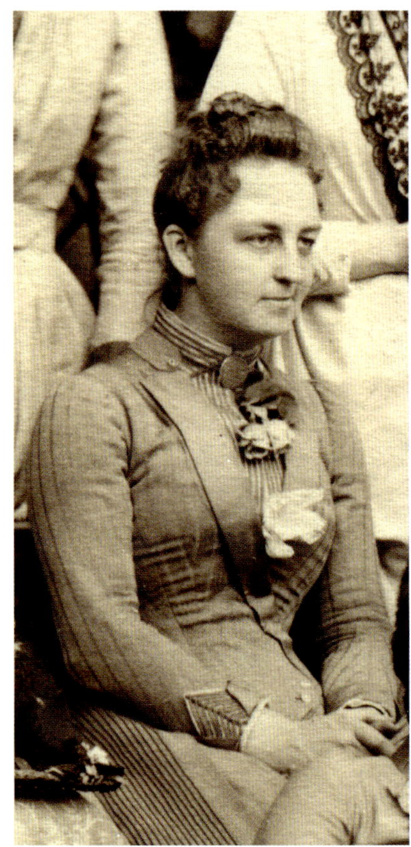

86
Chapel

Almost as soon as it began, the movement for women's education in Oxford split over the question of religion. The founders of Lady Margaret Hall, named for the pious Lady Margaret Beaufort, looked to a life 'modelled on that of a Christian family'. Somerville followed instead the liberal principles of those such as T.H. Green [13], opting for the life of an 'English family' and choosing to be named for Mary Somerville (a Christian, certainly, but renowned principally for her talents in science and mathematics). For almost fifty years at Somerville there was no chapel: prayers were said in the hall but attendance was never compulsory. When in 1932 Emily Kemp (1860–1939), one of Somerville's first students, offered the gift of a building 'for the promotion of the spiritual life, mainly by prayer and meditation for those of all creeds and nations', there was strong resistance. The ASM (Association of Senior Members, or former students) was especially determined to maintain Somerville's non-sectarian character, and Miss Darbishire, the then Principal, went so far as to describe one meeting with the ASM in 1932 as 'lively'. A compromise was eventually reached, and the chapel was carefully situated so as not to dominate the grounds of the college. Pevsner described it as 'bleakly classical'. Some detect echoes of Edwin Lutyens (1869–1944) in the chapel: the architect, Courtenay Theobald (1903–89), was the business partner (and son-in-law) of Maxwell Ayrton (1874–1960), who had been one of Lutyens's assistants. Others see it as the precursor of modern multi-faith prayer spaces. Opened on 16 February 1935, the building proclaims itself 'A House of Prayer for All Peoples'.

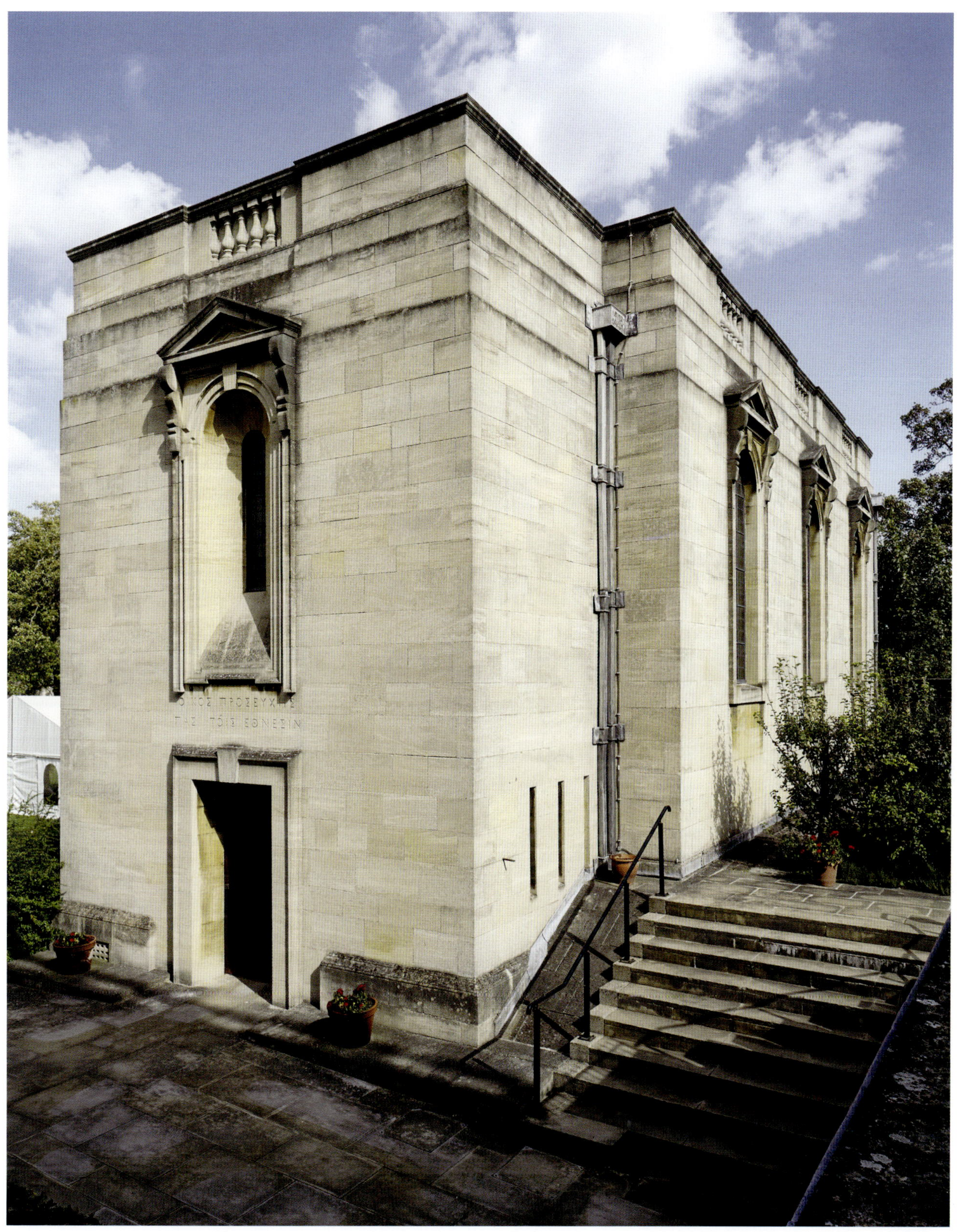

Principali sociisque Collegii de Somerville
in Universitate Oxoniensi
d. d. d.
Dorothy L. Sayers
eruditionem venerata, mansuetudinis memor

a. d. VII. Id. Nov. MCMXXXV.

'at night, the lit lamp and the drawn curtain,
with the flutter of the turned page and the soft
scrape of pen on paper the only sounds to break
the utter silence'

Dorothy L. Sayers, *Gaudy Night*

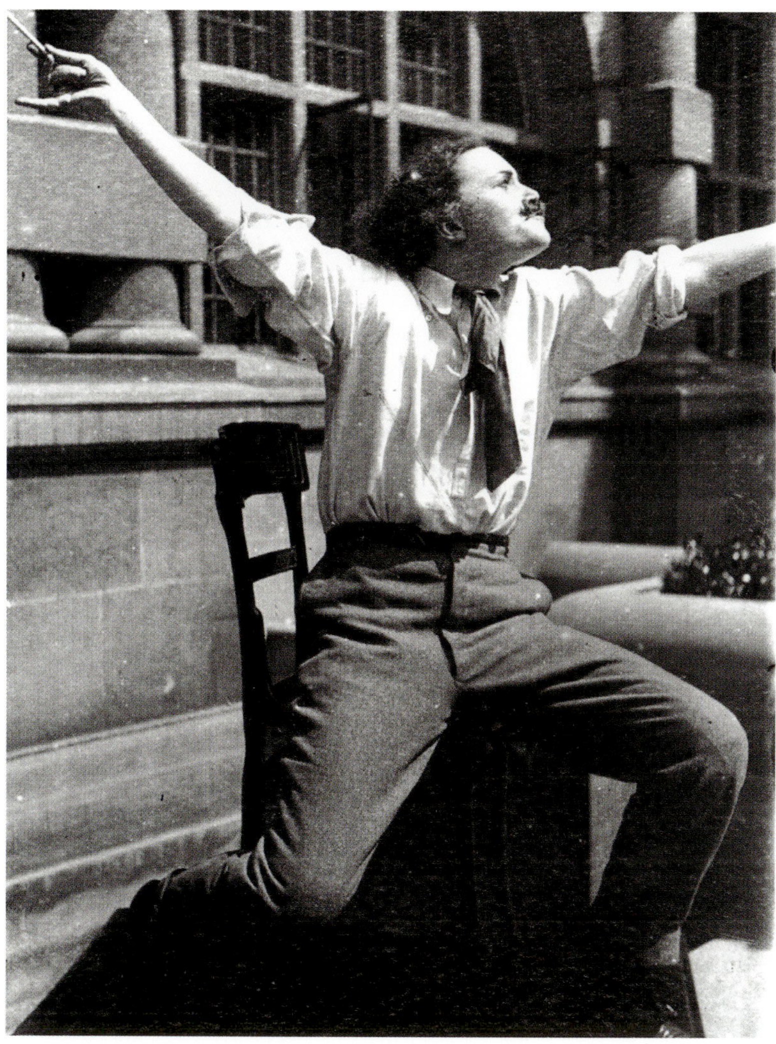

87
Gaudy Night, signed by Dorothy L. Sayers

There are probably many people who feel they know 'Shrewsbury College' without realising that it is based on Somerville. Dorothy L. Sayers came up to Somerville in 1912 (she is shown here doing an impression of Hugh Allen, conductor of the Oxford Bach Choir) and took a First in Modern Languages – later in life she was most proud not of her detective stories, but of her translation of Dante's *Divine Comedy*. After graduating she worked for Blackwells and later for an advertising agency. Of her novels featuring Lord Peter Wimsey, *Gaudy Night* (1935) is surely the most famous, not least because of its wonderful evocations of Oxford in the 1930s. It tells the story of Harriet Vane, writer of detective stories, who had been saved from a murder charge by the intelligent and brilliant Lord Peter Wimsey. She comes to her old Oxford college, first for a Gaudy, and then to investigate a series of poison pen letters. Together she and Wimsey solve the mystery and finally find their way to their own love story as well. Sayers's inscription in this copy translates as: 'To the Principal and Fellows of the College of Somerville in the University of Oxford Dorothy L. Sayers gave this as a gift in veneration of their learning, in memory of their kindness'.

No. 28 of the Limited Edition of
175 copies of "South Riding –"

Presented to Somerville College
in memory of Winifred Holtby
by Vera Brittain.

May 7th, 1936.

88
Winifred Holtby, *South Riding*, signed by Vera Brittain

When they first met at Somerville, Vera Brittain [79] and Winifred Holtby [69] initially failed to get on; but later they became firm friends. After graduation they rented a flat together in Bloomsbury and both began their writing careers. When Brittain married George Catlin (1896–1979) in 1925, Holtby lived with the couple: Brittain called Holtby her 'second self'. It was only due to Vera Brittain's perseverance that *South Riding* was ever published, and it has never been out of print. The novel is a love story set in the Yorkshire landscape of Holtby's childhood and against the struggles of local politics (Brittain's daughter, Shirley Williams [101], called it 'the great epic of local government').

Holtby's mother, the first alderwoman on East Riding's County Council, did not want *South Riding* to see the light of day. Thanks to Brittain's efforts, though, it was published only six months after Holtby's death. Royalties from publication were bequeathed to Somerville in Holtby's will and are used to help fund teaching in History.

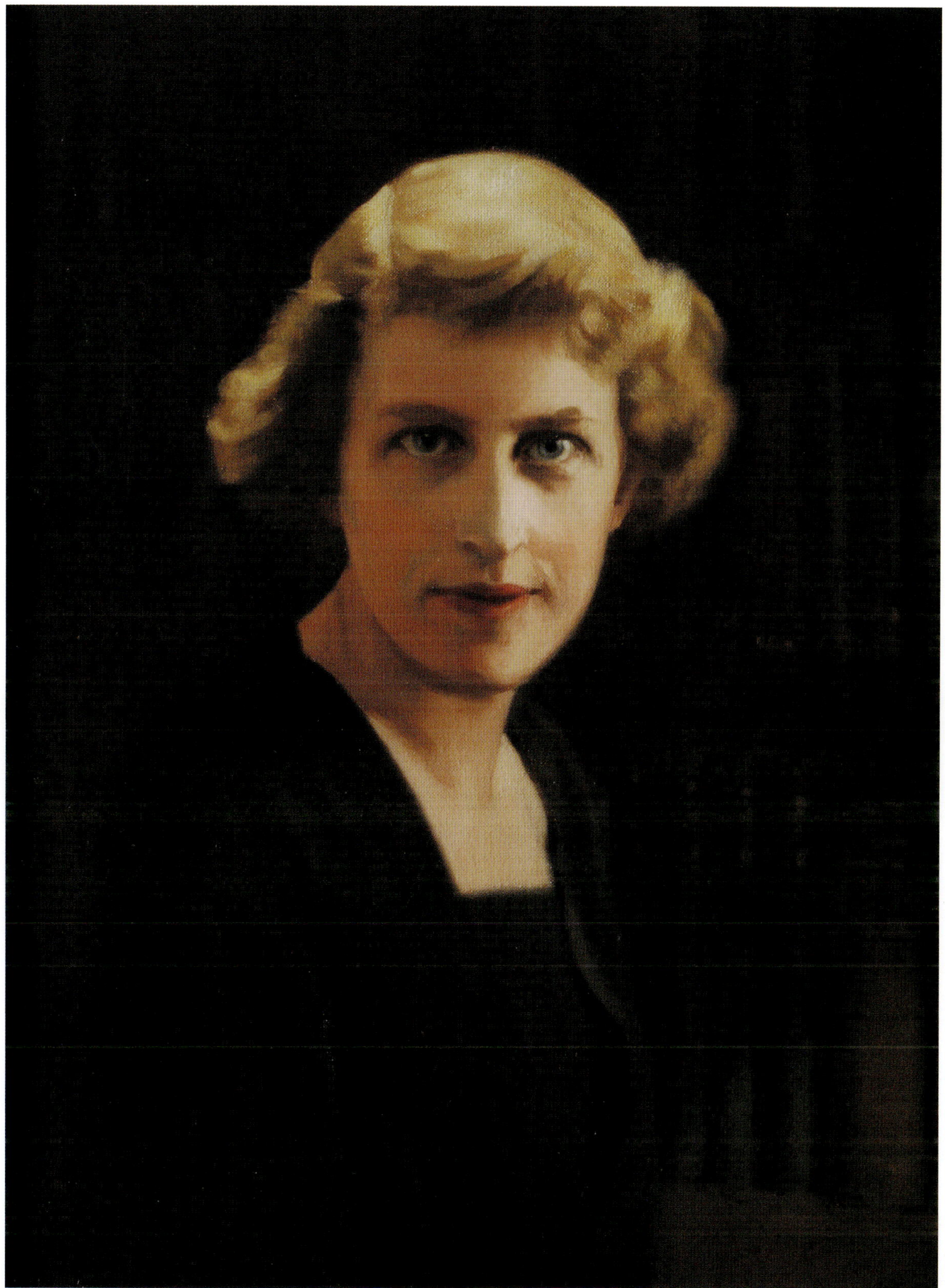

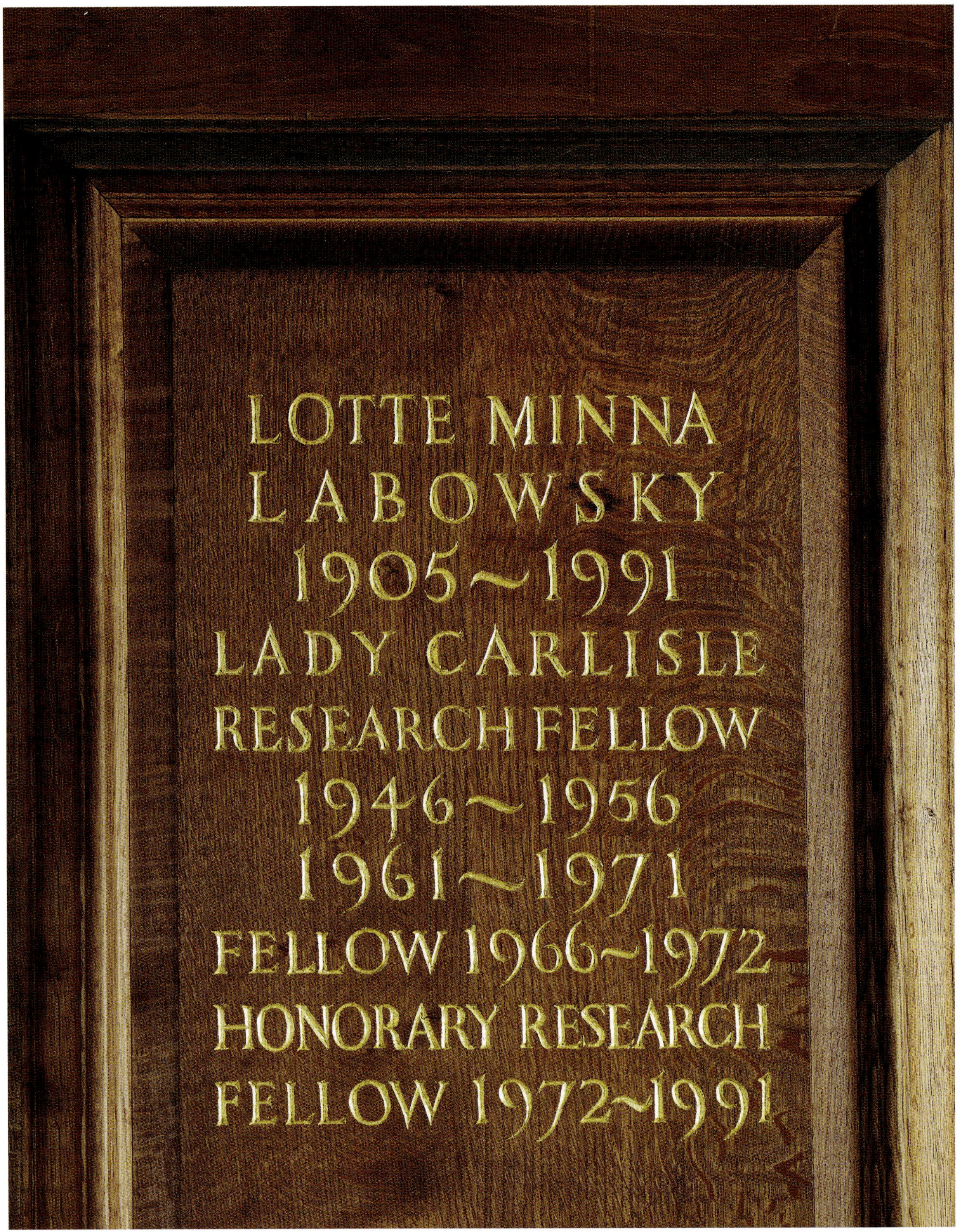

LOTTE MINNA
LABOWSKY
1905~1991
LADY CARLISLE
RESEARCH FELLOW
1946~1956
1961~1971
FELLOW 1966~1972
HONORARY RESEARCH
FELLOW 1972~1991

89
Plaque to Lotte Labowsky

Lotte Labowsky (1905–91) was not the first Jewish exile to be given what Somerville's Council minute called 'hospitality' by the college – Margarete Bieber (1879–1978), former Professor of Classical Archaeology at the University of Giessen, had been offered an Honorary Research Fellowship (and a home in college for three terms) in October 1933 – and nor would she be the last. Somerville offered research grants, meals and accommodation for those fleeing the Nazi regime, including to the Egyptologists Käthe Bosse (1910–98) and Elise Baumgartel (1892–1975), the Hittite scholar Leonie Zuntz (1908–42) and the classicist Gertrude Herzog-Hauser (1894–1953). These arrangements were part of a wider British initiative, the Academic Assistance Council, which asked universities to help persecuted and exiled academics (and which still exists as the Council for At-Risk Academics). Labowsky was a classicist, having studied at Munich and Heidelberg. Born in 1905 in Hamburg, her childhood friends included Aby Warburg (1866–1929), and she worked at the Warburg Library in Germany until the anti-Jewish laws led her to leave her native land. The Warburg Institute had moved to London and Labowsky continued her research there. It was Gilbert Murray and his wife who introduced Labowsky to Somerville's Classics tutor, Mildred Hartley (1904–96), and in 1934 Labowsky moved to Oxford to continue her research. In 1939 she was offered a research grant by Somerville as well as meals in college. During the war Miss Darbishire wrote testimonials to keep Labowsky from internment as a German national. In due course Labowsky became Somerville's Acting Librarian and later she was elected to the Governing Body as an Additional Fellow. Throughout her time in Oxford she continued her work on the texts of Plato read in Latin in the medieval period. On her death in 1991 Labowsky left generous bequests to Somerville, including funding for a Fellowship in English in memory of her great friend Rosemary Woolf (1925–78), and the gift of a painting by Paula Modersohn-Becker (1876–1907 [90]).

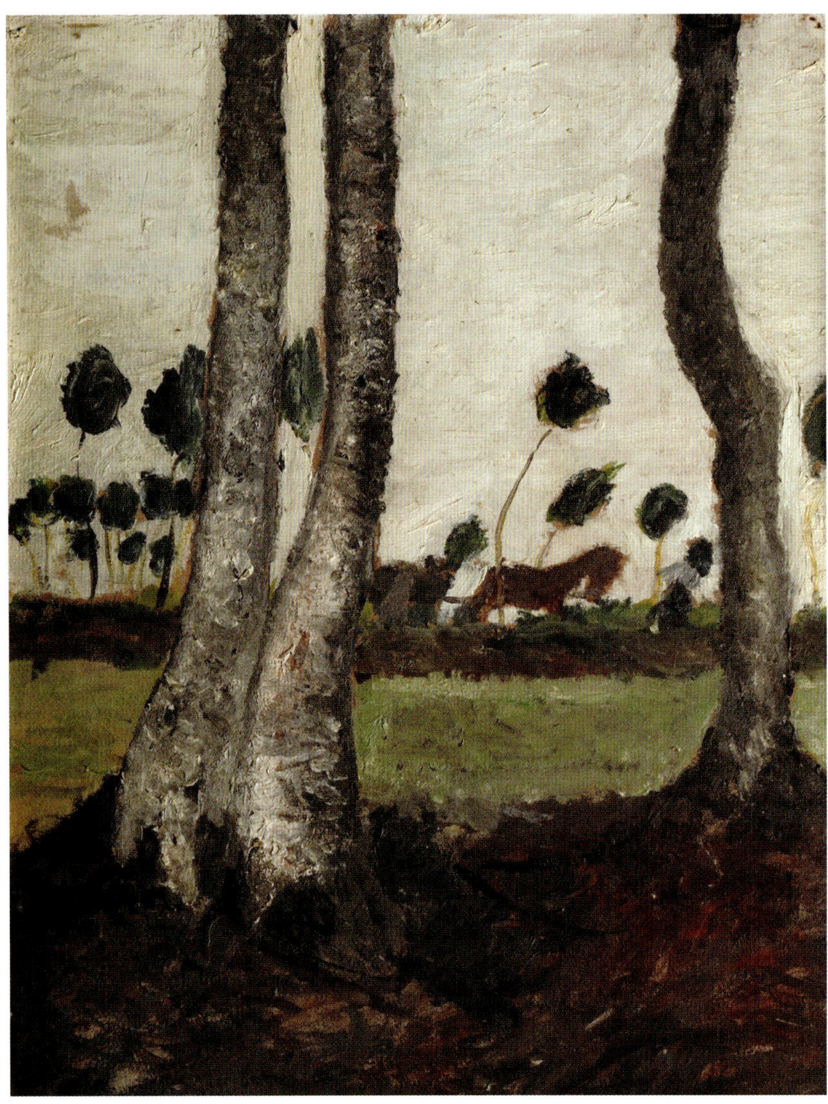

90
Paula Modersohn-Becker, *Landscape with Windblown Trees*

This was probably painted at the very end of the nineteenth century, when Paula Modersohn-Becker was living in an artists' colony outside Bremen. She went on to study art in London, Berlin and Paris, and soon moved her artistic focus from landscapes to the human form. She was (as far as we know) the first woman to paint a full-length nude self-portrait. Modersohn-Becker died at the age of 31 after suffering a postpartum embolism. She had sold only three paintings in her lifetime, but when her mother published her letters, her work became hugely popular. The Paula Modersohn-Becker Museum opened in Bremen in 1927, the first museum dedicated to a woman painter. In 1935 it was attacked by the Nazis, and Modersohn-Becker's work was condemned as 'degenerate art', 'lacking in femininity'. This painting was owned by Lotte Labowsky [89], who bequeathed it to Somerville.

91
Organ

The organ in the chapel was built in 1937 by Harrison & Harrison (founded in 1861 and still going strong), two years after the chapel building [86] was completed. Its handsome oak case was designed by the chapel's architect, Courtenay Theobald, and it was said that the cherubs on the casing were modelled on Theobald's children. A fundraising initiative to cover the full cost of the organ came from some of the very first students at Somerville who called themselves simply '1879'. The archives note that 231 old members answered the call for funds put out by '1879'; we know, too, that the then Principal, Miss Darbishire, topped up the final amount to ensure that the project could go ahead. The organ brought a new grandeur to services, replacing the piano and string accompaniment previously used.

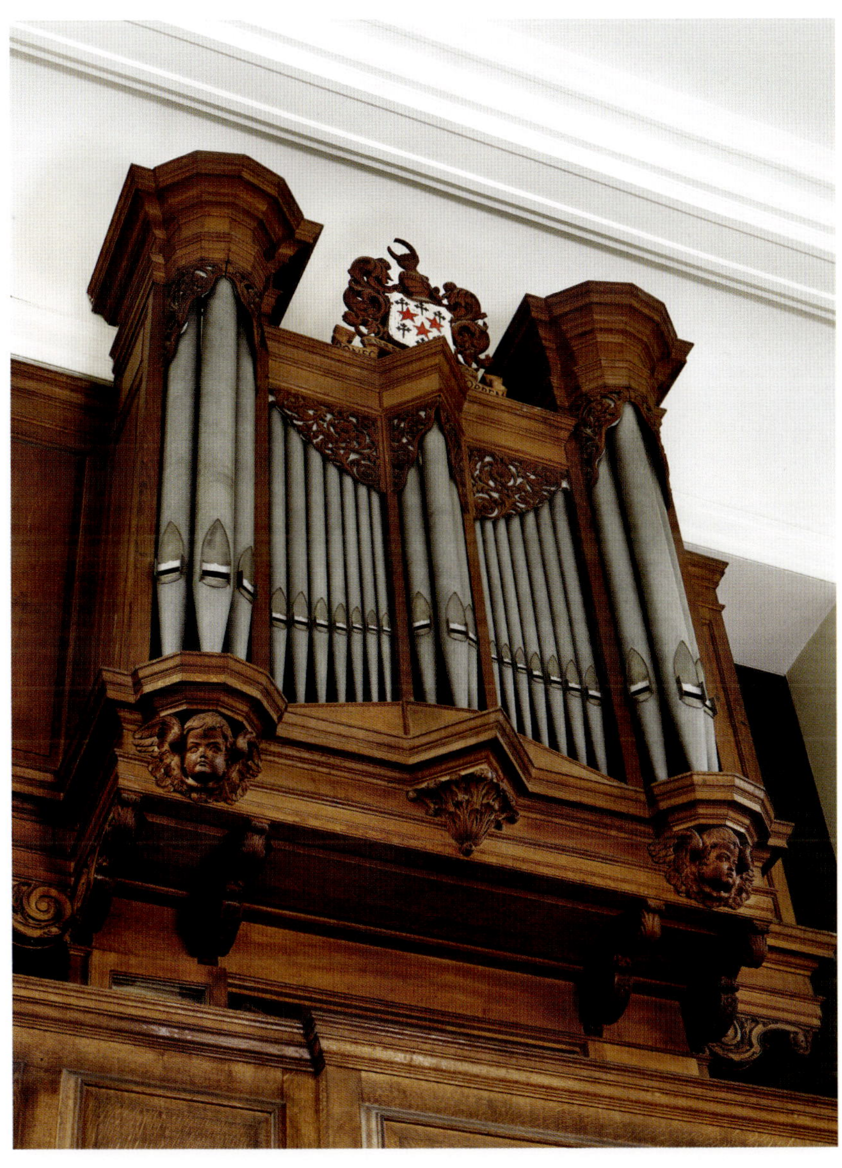

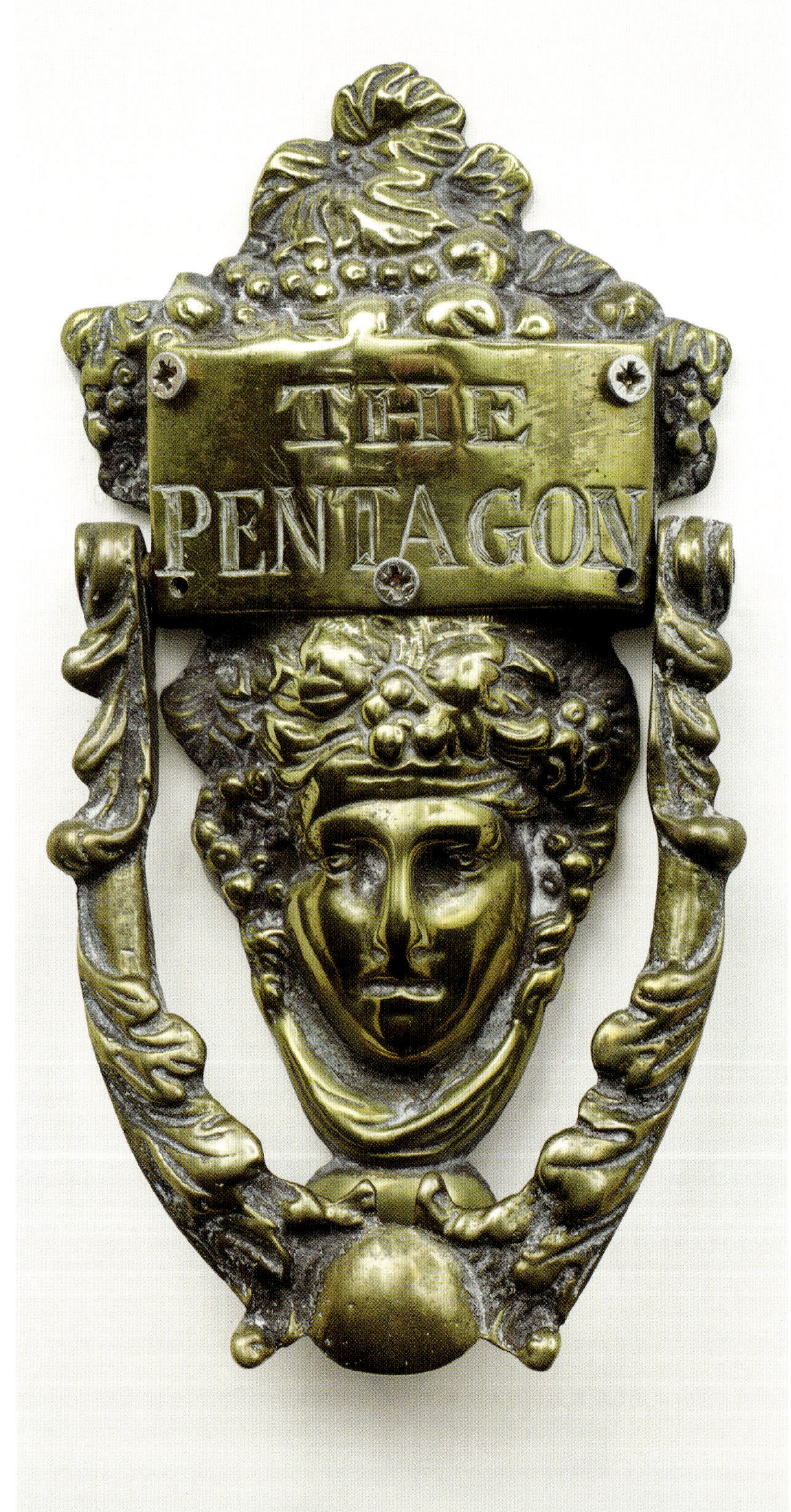

92
Pentagon Club doorknocker

We hope that this found its way to Somerville by lawful means, but there is just a chance that it is an early example of students appropriating trophies, in the same way that traffic cones still sometimes appear in college. 'The Pentagon Club' (so called because its members came from the four women's colleges, plus the Society of Oxford Home-Students – later St Anne's College) was a women's club that had premises on the High, offering overnight accommodation, a reading room and somewhere for (as one member recalled) 'very nice teas, with creamy cakes and sandwiches'. The atmosphere was 'rather prim' but the club could still indulge in behaviour sufficiently daring – it apparently once showed a rather frank film about conception and childbirth – for the authorities of the women's colleges to become occasionally alarmed. Respectability was still an issue, it seems. The Pentagon Club was too ambitious a project to survive financially, and it closed after six years. Presumably this was the point at which its handsome doorknocker appeared in Somerville.

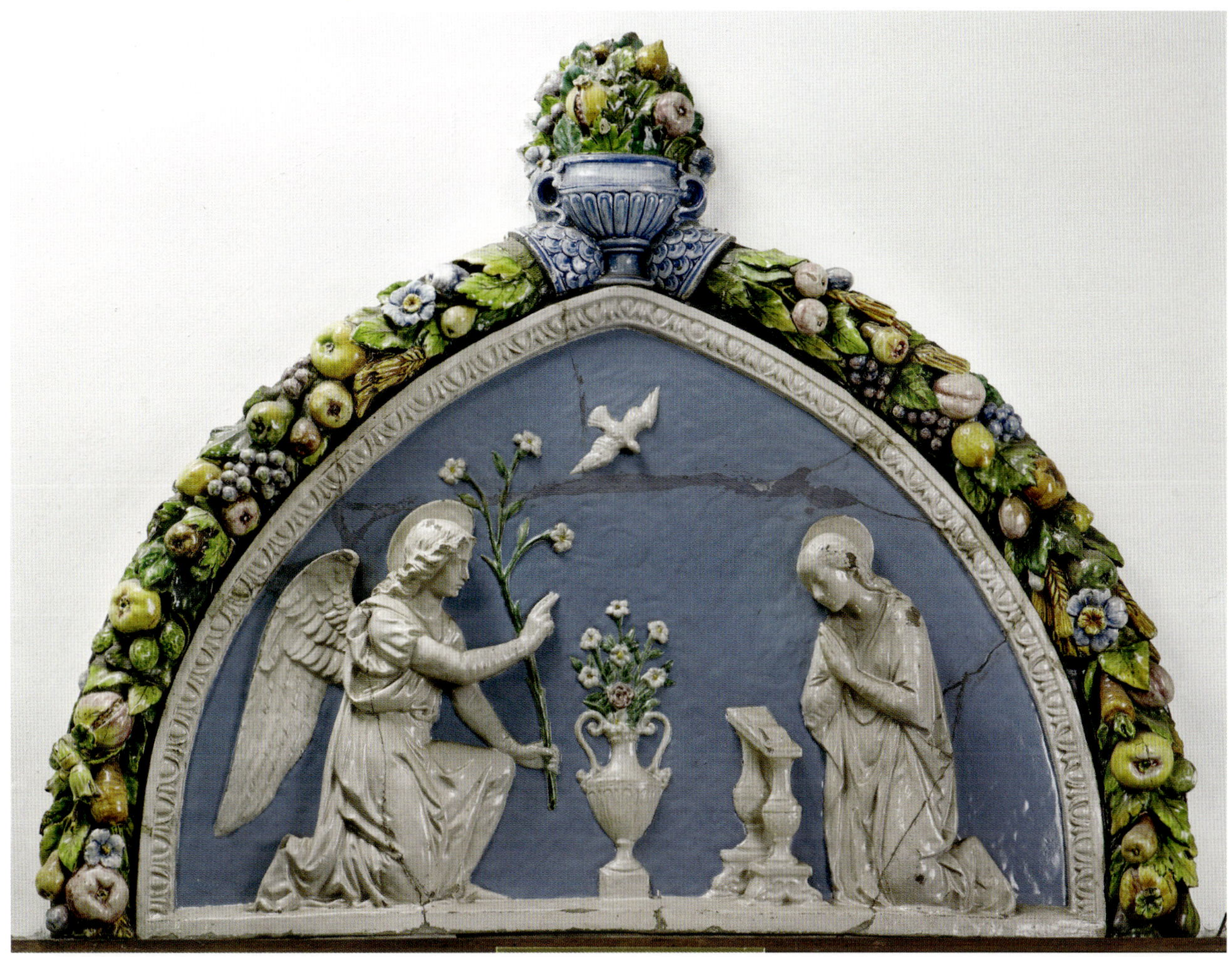

93
Annunciation, after Della Robbia

This nineteenth-century terracotta relief is a copy (or at least 'in the manner of' – its provenance is uncertain) of Andrea Della Robbia's lunette of the Annunciation. Della Robbia (1435–1525) made a series of glazed blue terracotta roundels for the Ospedale degli Innocenti ('Foundlings' Hospital') designed by Filippo Brunelleschi (1377–1446) in Florence, to sit between the arches of the loggia, showing religious scenes relating to children. Here the Angel Gabriel brings God's message to Mary beneath an arch of fruit and flowers, with the dove representing the Holy Spirit and lilies symbolising purity. Somerville's version sits on the north wall of the chapel (over the fire exit, in fact), but its donor, Emily Kemp, had originally wanted it to be housed in a dedicated room where students could discuss their plans for charitable and religious works abroad. Kemp was a great connoisseur of art (she studied at the Slade School) and left the whole of her collection, except for this one piece, to the Ashmolean.

Given by Somervillians Rose Graham (1875–1963) and Lettice Fisher (Ilbert; 1875–1956) in 1944 to commemorate the fiftieth anniversary of their coming up to Somerville, this handsome and intricate silver bowl is inscribed on the base with the names of its makers ('Omar Ramsden et Alwyn Carr me fecerunt 1909'). The names of the ships and the English admiral and captains in the battle with the Spanish Armada in 1588 are to be found on the bowl, and Somerville's archives hold two delicate vellum scrolls detailing 'the most high contending parties' at the battle, complete with pictorial depictions of the disposition of the fleets. Rose Graham recorded that the bowl was bought by her grandfather, Mr D.P. McEwen, from Ramsden & Carr's studio on the Fulham Road. Omar Ramsden (1873–1939) and Alwyn Carr (1872–1940) met at the Sheffield School of Art. The V&A describes the work from their studio as having 'an English decorative quality of historic reference to medievalism' alongside 'a subtle awareness of the sinuous lines of contemporary Art Nouveau'.

'Omar Ramsden et Alwyn Carr
me fecerunt 1909'

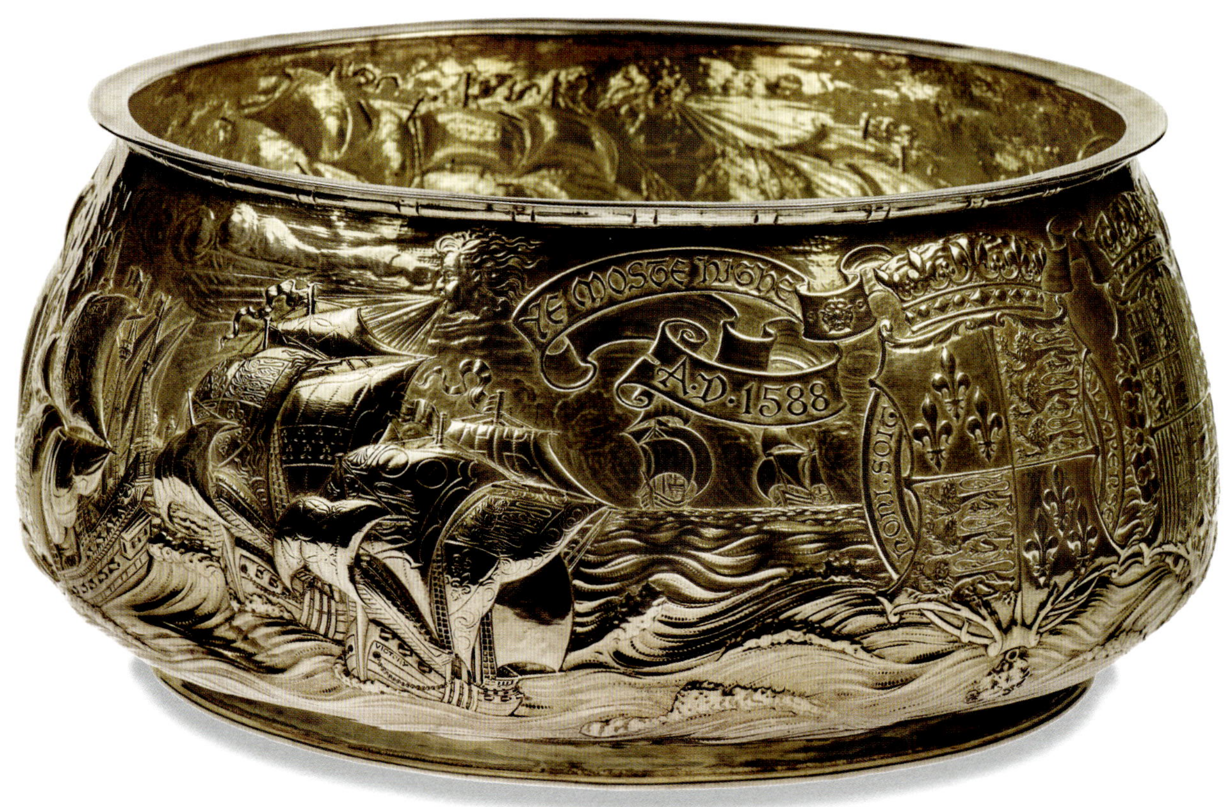

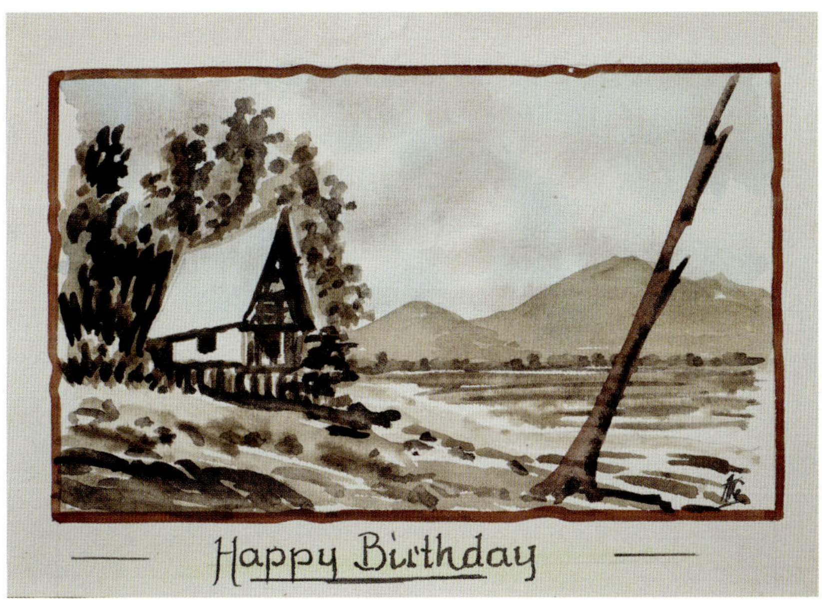

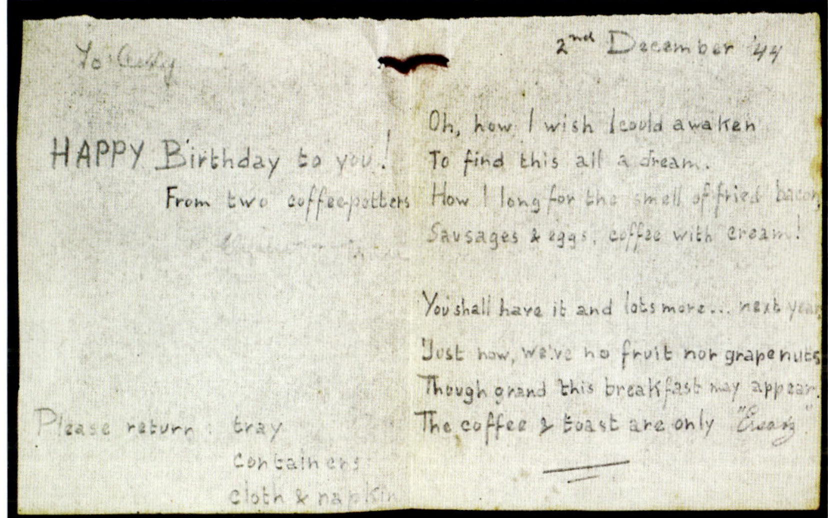

95
Birthday card for
Cicely Williams

Cicely Williams came up to Somerville in 1917 to study medicine. As a woman she found it difficult to obtain a permanent medical post in the UK, and she chose instead to join the Colonial Medical Service as a 'Woman Medical Officer' (a term she disliked, not least as it meant that she was paid less than men doing the same job). Her observation of babies and children led her to develop and publish groundbreaking work on the causes of and cure for protein malnutrition in children. She went on to work in Malaya, but was forced to leave when the Japanese invaded in 1941. When Singapore also fell, she was interned, eventually being taken to the notorious Changi prisoner-of-war camp [58]. This is one of the birthday cards drawn for her by fellow prisoners. She became one of the camp leaders among the prisoners, and for this she was taken to the headquarters of the Kempeitai (the Japanese equivalent of the SS) where she and other prisoners were kept in cages and starved, tortured and beaten. After the war, as head of the new Maternal and Child Health division of the World Health Organisation, Williams worked to promote a focus on local resources and observation in place of relying on solutions from the developed world.

'The whole thing is crying out for just a little initiative'

Cicely Williams, on healthcare provision in 1920s Ghana

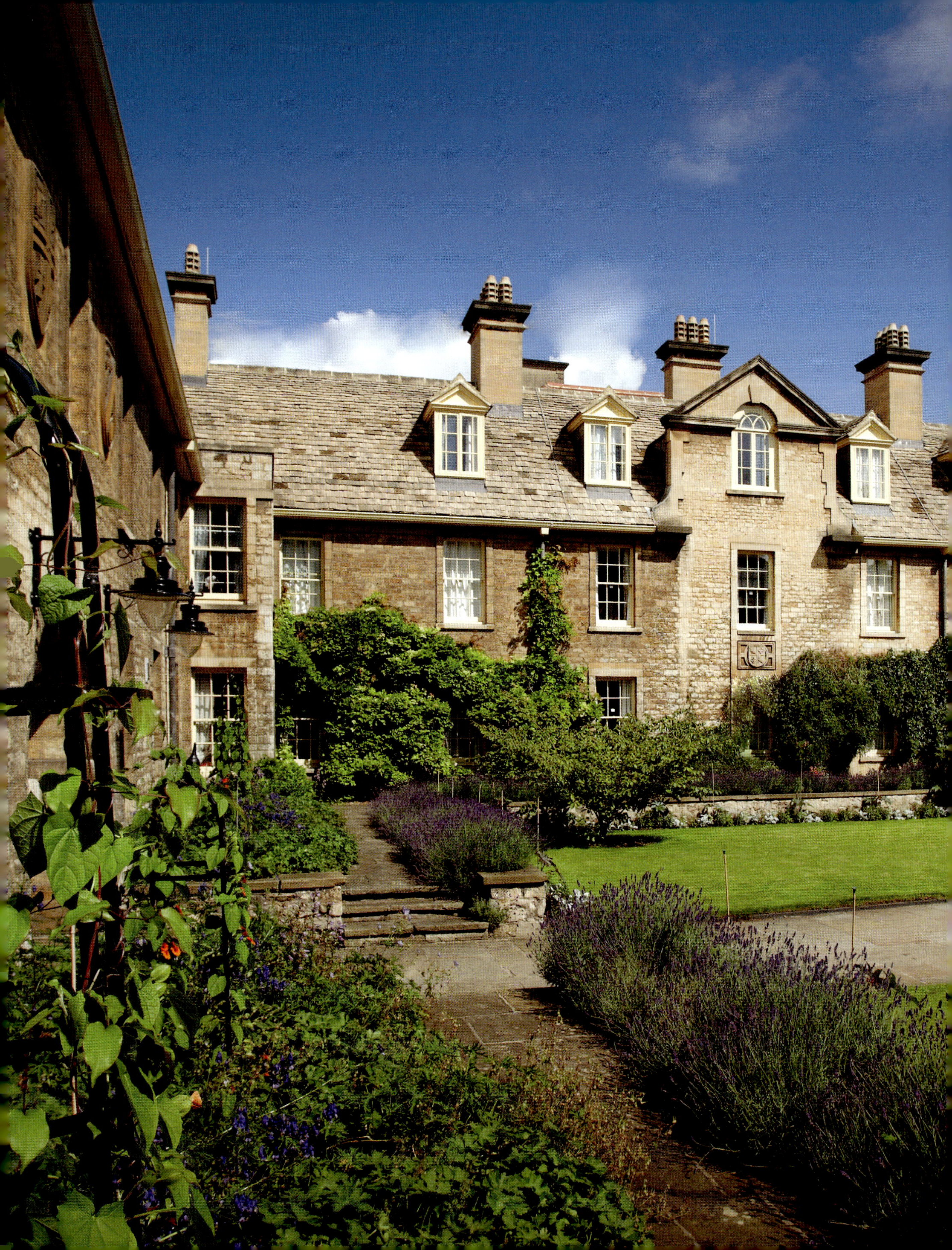

1945–1989
'always have your plans on the drawing board'

The words are those of Janet Vaughan, the first scientist to be Principal of Somerville. She knew that this would be a time of great expansion and change, and that Somerville had to be ready. This was when the numbers of students – both undergraduate and graduate – increased, along with new buildings to house them, and when academic achievement went from strength to strength. As the men's colleges started to discuss the possibility of admitting women, Somerville tentatively began its own exploration of whether to 'go mixed'.

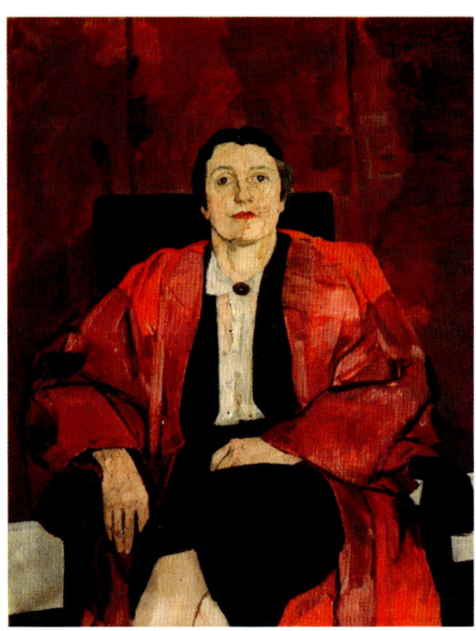

1945–1967
Janet Vaughan

Somervillians remember Vaughan as the Principal of the college between 1945 and 1967, or as the name of the building where many of them had their first-year accommodation. In the history of medicine, Dame Janet Vaughan (1899–1993) is known as the pioneering scientist who made blood transfusion part of regular medical practice in the UK. She arrived as a student at Somerville with what she called 'a little ladylike botany' (one of her headmistresses had once told her she was too stupid to be worth educating), took a first-class degree and trained as a doctor. Vaughan's medical work in London's slums gave her a lifelong commitment to socialism and also inspired her to take up work as a research pathologist looking at blood disorders. As part of the UK's preparations for the Second World War, Vaughan began to develop a system for separating, storing and moving blood that saved countless lives and continues to do so (she herself once used an innovative transfusion technique to save a victim of burns – a girl who later came up to Somerville). At the end of the war Vaughan was asked to go to Belsen to carry out research into how those suffering from starvation could best be treated ('I am here', she wrote, 'trying to do science in hell'). Her experiences only spurred her on to more scientific work. When she returned to Oxford and took up the Principalship of Somerville, she continued to work in the lab and write academic papers, only stopping well into her eighties (a college play portrayed her crossing and re-crossing the stage, murmuring 'Just off to the lab, just off to the lab...').

Vaughan was the first scientist to be Principal of Somerville. She was also, for a time during her Principalship, the only scientist head of house in Oxford. Under her, science developed even further, into one of Somerville's great strengths. It is pleasing to think that no member of Somerville in the 1940s, 1950s and 1960s would have recognised today's concerns about the place of women in science: it must have seemed that the college *was* the place of women in science. Vaughan's interest was not only in science but also in excellence, no matter the subject, and she encouraged the great and the good in all disciplines to visit the college (this was the time when Ludwig Wittgenstein [1889–1951] could be seen visiting the Senior Common Room as a guest of Research Fellow Elizabeth Anscombe [1919–2001]). She significantly increased the intake of undergraduates in science and medicine at Somerville, and also planned the first graduate accommodation in Oxford, as well as using her medical contacts to start the provision of proper services for student health. Her sheer level of energy and output was prodigious, and made her a profoundly influential role model for generations of Somervillians. When she was asked once in a radio interview how she managed to fit so much into her life, Vaughan said simply, 'I never played bridge'.

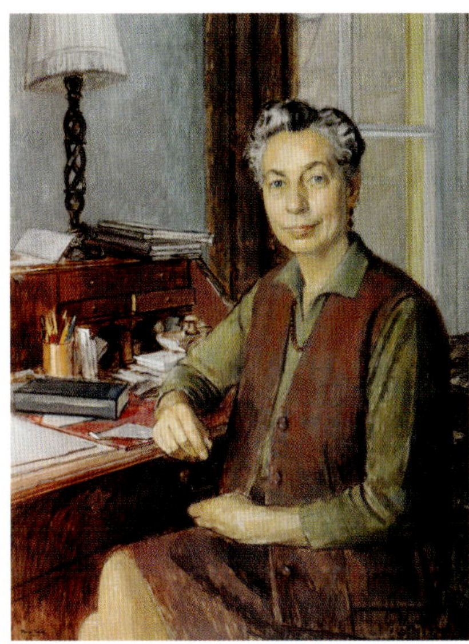

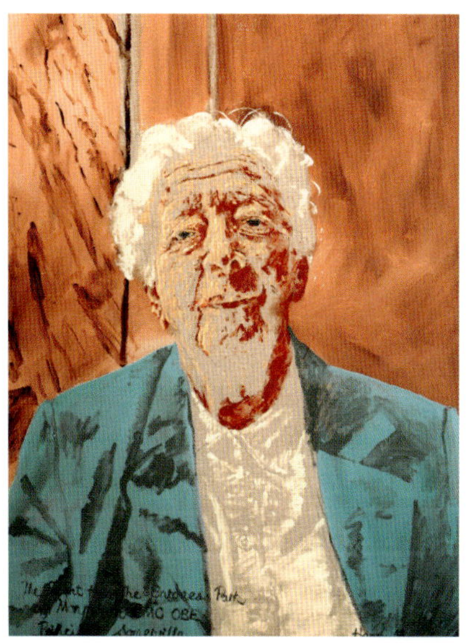

1967–1980
Barbara Craig

Barbara Craig (1915–2005) was a Somerville classicist. Her own work was archaeological, and she had also had wide experience assisting her husband in his work for the British Council. She took the helm at a time when Somerville was larger and more successful than it had ever been. This made her job harder rather than easier, not least as the college (and the University more widely) began to grapple with the question of whether the men's colleges would admit women. Somerville's strength in the sciences continued to grow under Craig's Principalship, with new fellowships established, and there was also growth in other subjects, particularly in Law. The college debated the question of 'going mixed' and decided, for the time being, against it.

1980–1989
Daphne Park

This is Daphne Park (1921–2010), aka 'Queen of Spies' (though few in Somerville realised it until after she had ceased to be Principal). Park was Principal of the college from 1980 to 1989. She came up to Somerville to read Modern Languages (French) in 1940, and also took a Certificate of Competent Knowledge in Russian in Cambridge in 1952. Her diplomatic skills were, as she was the first to admit, enhanced by her almost deliberately unprepossessing appearance. A sort of female George Smiley, her benign looks allowed her to pass unnoticed. During the Second World War, Park was spotted by the SOE (Special Operations Executive). She rose through the ranks ('I must have been arrested and condemned to be shot several times', she said. 'It was a hazard I got used to'), eventually working as senior MI6 controller in Hanoi, Moscow, the Congo and Zambia – the highest position in MI6 of any woman up to that time. The true nature of Park's career was publicly revealed only in 1993, when an edition of BBC's *Panorama* named her as a senior MI6 officer.

Somerville provided a rather safer environment, but still brought its challenges. She found out early on, for example, that it was not done to telephone a member of the Senior Common Room: communication was only via note in pigeonholes (nowadays the telephone has been abandoned again, but this time in favour of email and Twitter). Park's Principalship saw a further discussion of whether the college should admit men. Again, the answer was 'no'. This was not an easy time: uncertainty over university funding and student numbers and the looming question of 'going mixed' called for a Principal of unusual diplomacy and grit.

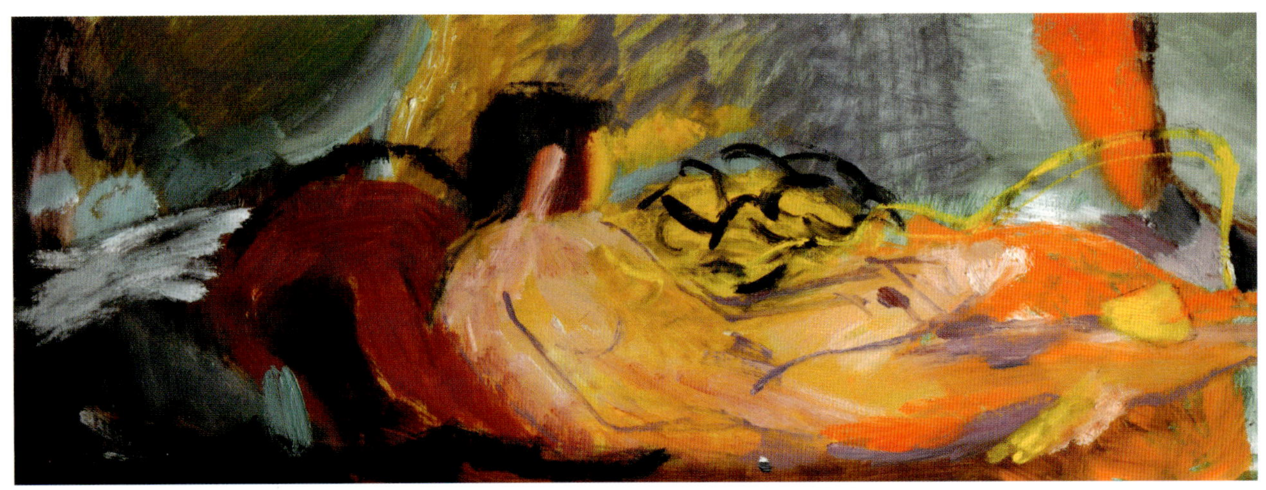

96
Ivon Hitchens,
Nude Algerian Woman No. 2

Ivon Hitchens (1893–1979) was a British artist who began to exhibit his work in the 1920s. He became part of the 'London Group' (founded in 1913 with the explicit aim of exhibiting modern art, continuing the work of the Camden Town Group). Hitchens left London after his house was bombed in 1940 and moved to a temporary home in a caravan in Petworth, Sussex. The temporary caravan became permanent, and Hitchens soon became renowned for his panoramic landscapes. Somerville is fortunate to own a number of his works: they came to the college as part of a bequest from Vera Lucas (Douglas; 1908–71) [97], who came up to Somerville in 1926 to read Modern Languages. *Nude Algerian Woman No. 2* is a perfect example of Hitchens's powerful use of colour.

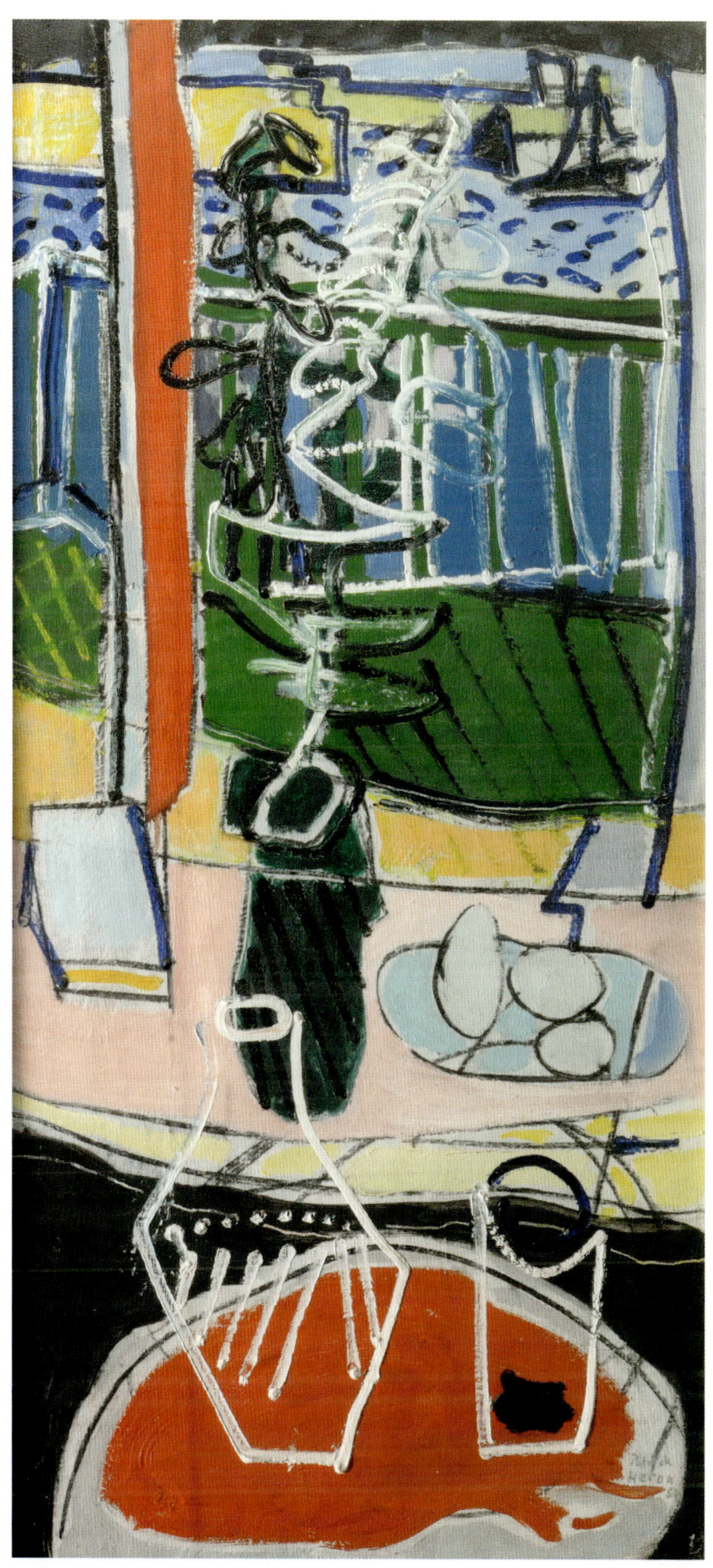

**97
Patrick Heron,
*The Red Table: St Ives: 1950***

Patrick Heron (1920–99) was a British abstract and figurative artist. He was born in Yorkshire but his family moved to Cornwall when he was a child, and much of his work was inspired by the coastal town of St Ives. His still lifes often featured ceramics inspired by Bernard Leach (1887–1979): Heron had worked in the Leach pottery during the Second World War. *The Red Table: St Ives: 1950* came to Somerville as part of a bequest from Vera Lucas (Douglas) [96].

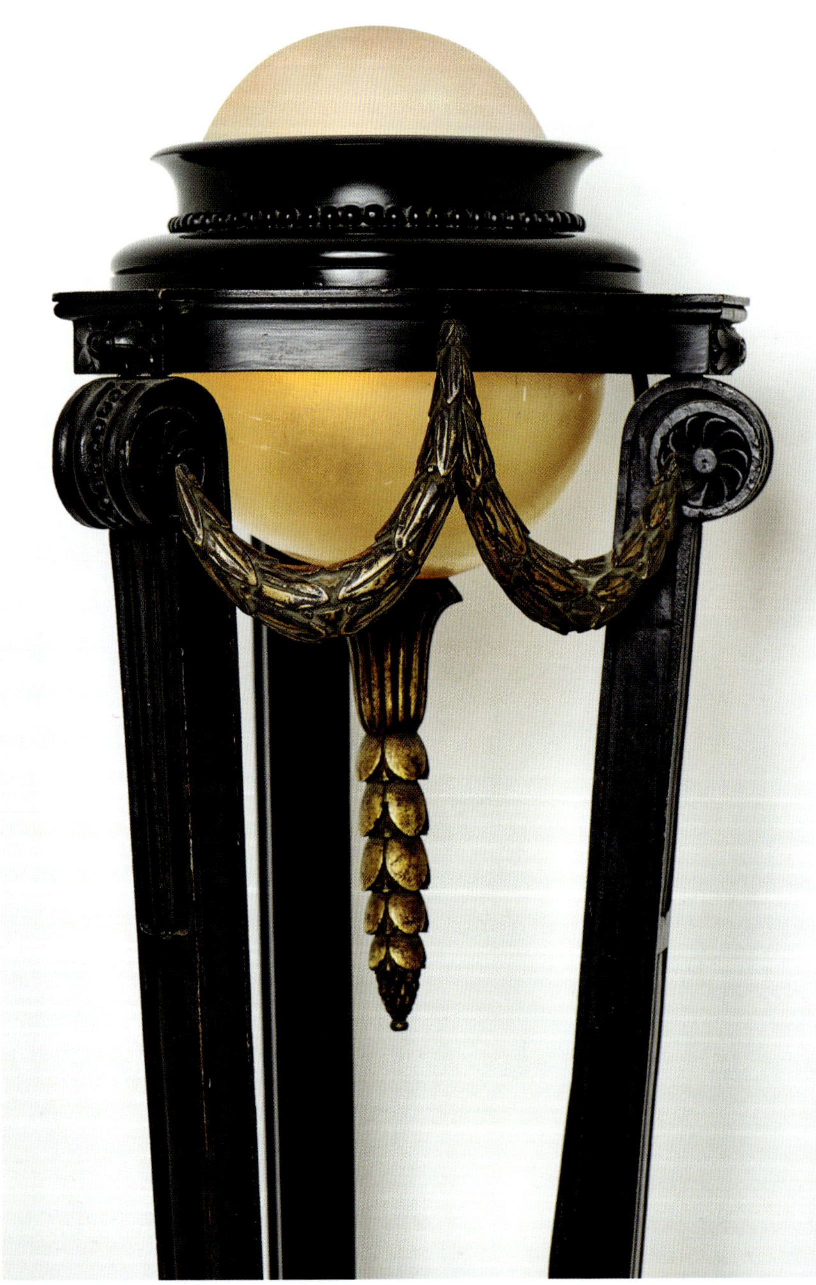

98
Lamps outside Hall

These are not items of great distinction. They flank the Epstein bust [77] on the way into Hall. We are not sure when they were first put into their alcoves, but at least one of them is now beginning to suffer from wear and tear, with a crack in its glass shade and part of its looped foliage missing. Somewhere between Art Nouveau and Art Deco in style, they set a rather cocktail party mood, appropriate for formal dinners in Hall, perhaps, if a little odd at breakfast time.

99
Edgar Degas, horse bronze

For Edgar Degas (1834–1917) the study of horses was a theme that ran throughout his artistic career. In the late 1880s, as his eyesight started to fail, he began to work on a small scale. His bronzes of horses come from this period and may have been inspired by early photography of horses in motion. This example was a gift to Somerville from Alice Horsman (1890–1978), who had come up in 1908 to read Literae Humaniores (or 'Greats', covering Latin and Greek language as well as classical history and philosophy). She was one of the first women called to the English Bar, and later in her life she also became a great traveller (at the age of 65 she sailed from Scotland to Norway, keeping seasickness at bay with occasional doses of Scotch whisky). The Horsman Travelling Scholarship (originally a fellowship, but later opened to students and alumni) was established in 1953 to offer funds to Somervillians undertaking travel or projects to enhance their career prospects.

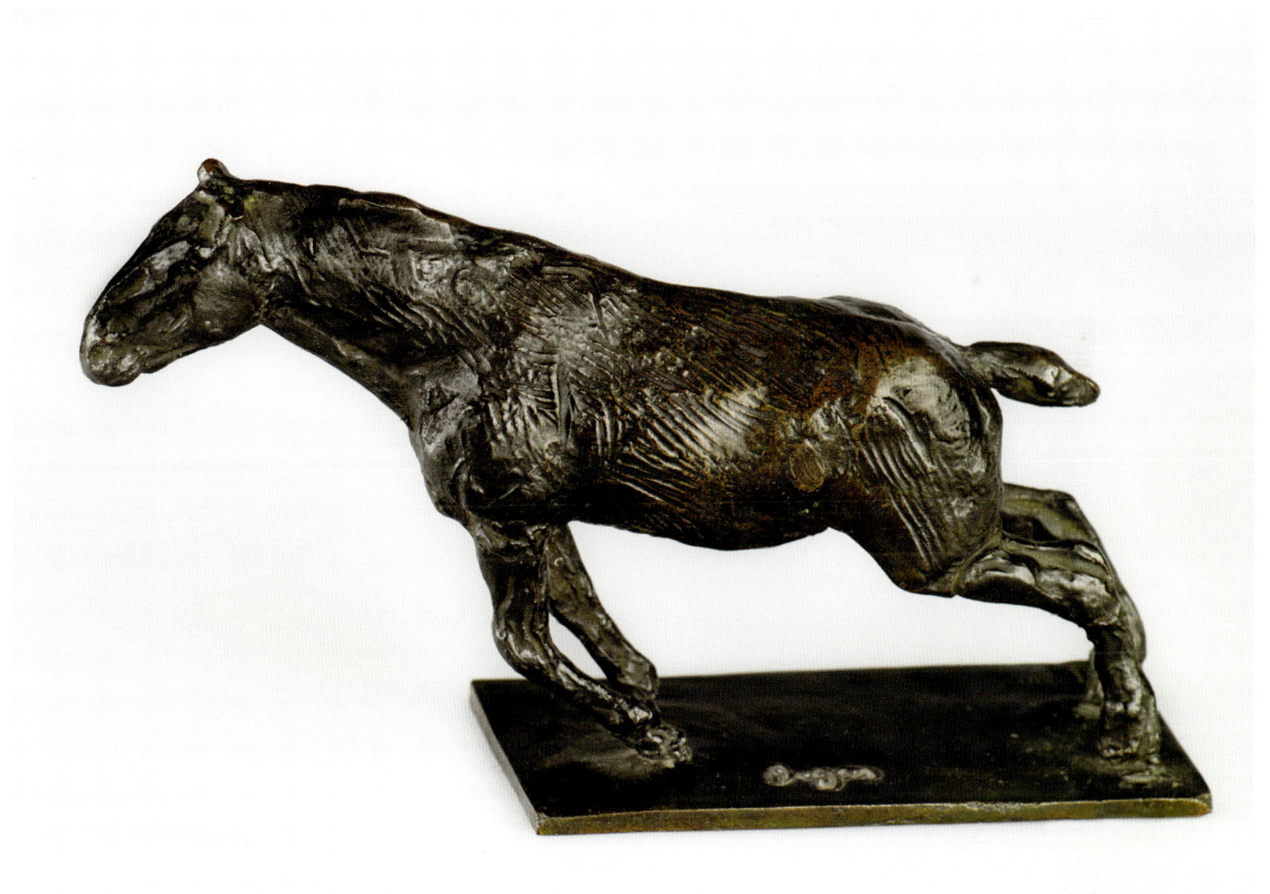

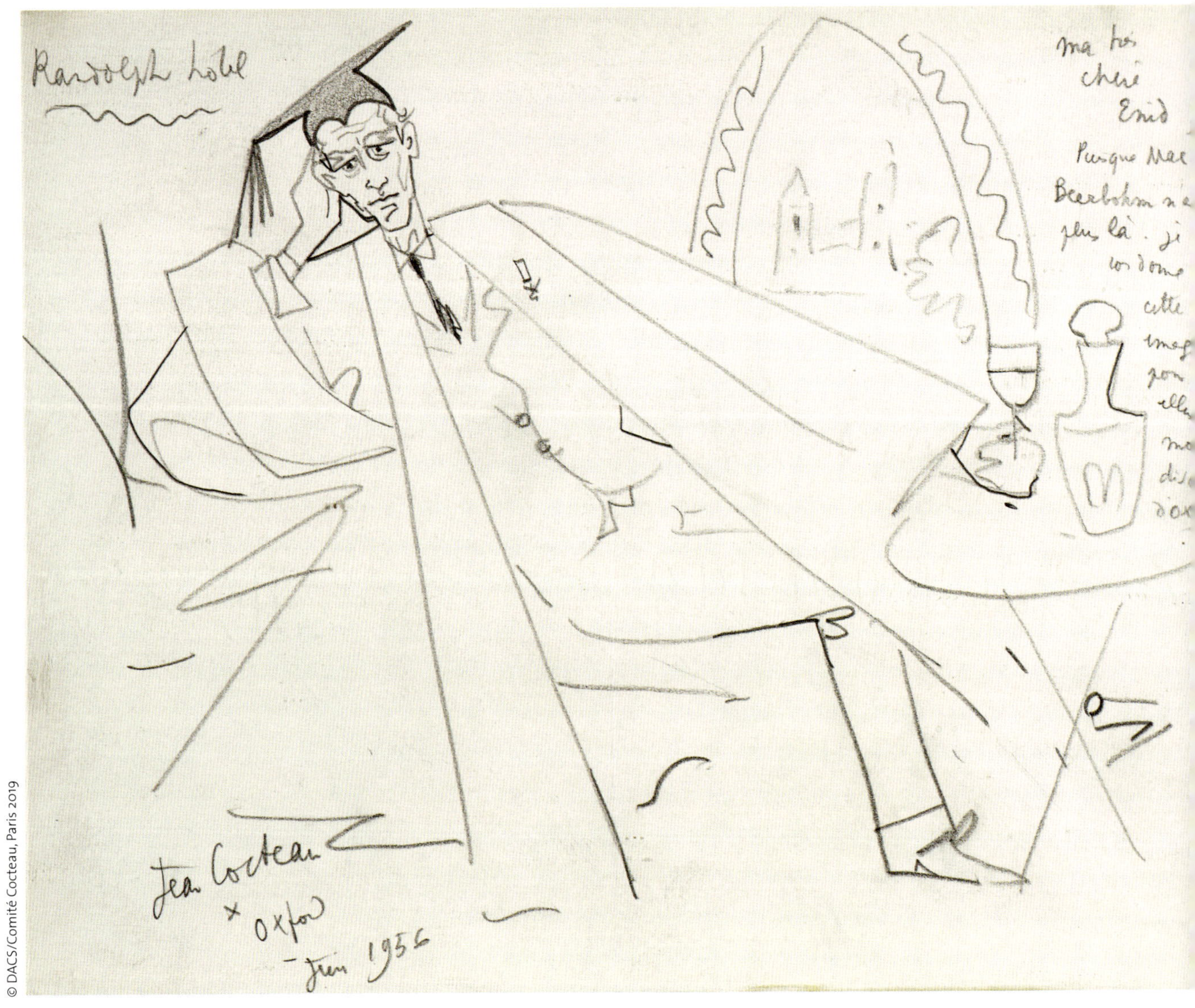

'like an elderly Puck'

100

Jean Cocteau sketches

On 12 June 1956 Jean Cocteau (1889–1963) was awarded an honorary doctorate by the University of Oxford, and these are his sketches of that day. He was enormously proud of what he called his 'honoris causa', which was largely down to Reader in French and Fellow of Somerville Enid Starkie (1897–1970) –

who had also studied at Somerville, exhibiting both academic and musical talent. In March 1956 Starkie wrote to Cocteau to propose that he should give a lecture in Oxford. The lure was the possibility of an honorary doctorate. It took Starkie and others considerable effort to make it happen ('I won, in

the end', Starkie said, 'but don't ask too closely how it was done'). The day of the ceremony saw Cocteau in the lobby of the Randolph Hotel, 'like an elderly Puck' (as the magazine *Picture Post* had it), 'wrapped around in a leaf-green cloak'. He was met 'in a cloudburst of French by a brilliant little lady wearing

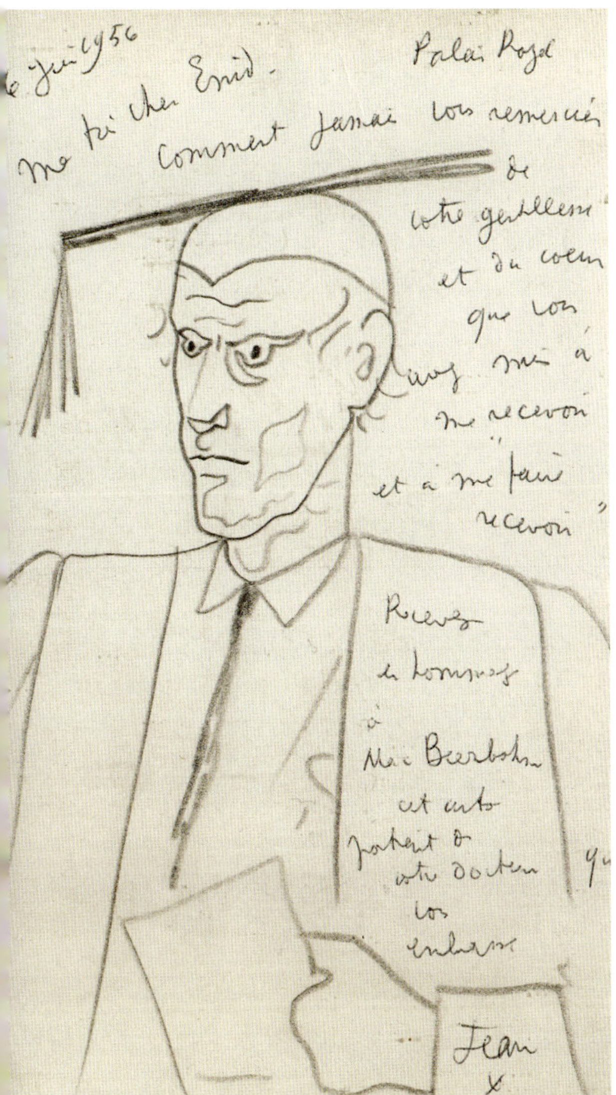

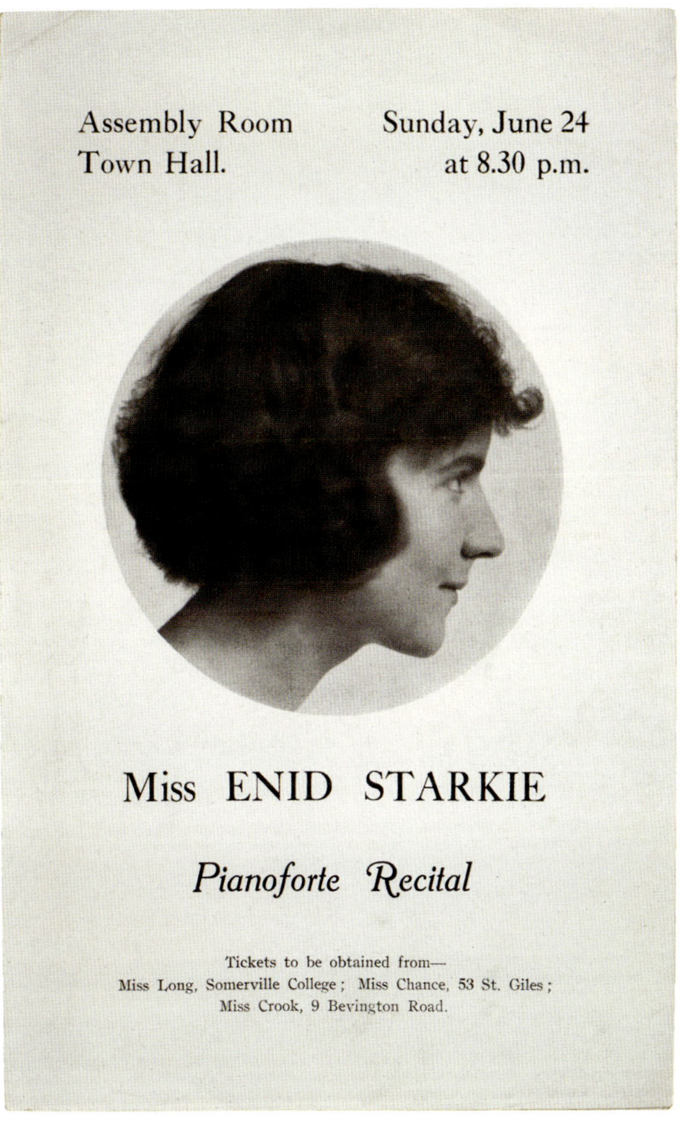

scarlet slacks, beret and duffel coat'. The 'brilliant little lady' had also been instrumental in the appointment of W.H. Auden (1907–73) as Professor of Poetry, and Auden gave his first lecture that afternoon. In the evening Starkie held a party: 'Visite chez Enid Starkie', Cocteau wrote, 'en kimono' and 'saoule' ('drunk' – and who can blame her after a day like that?). The sketches were given to Somerville by Robert Shackleton (1919–86), Bodley's Librarian from 1966 to 1979 and later Professor of French Literature.

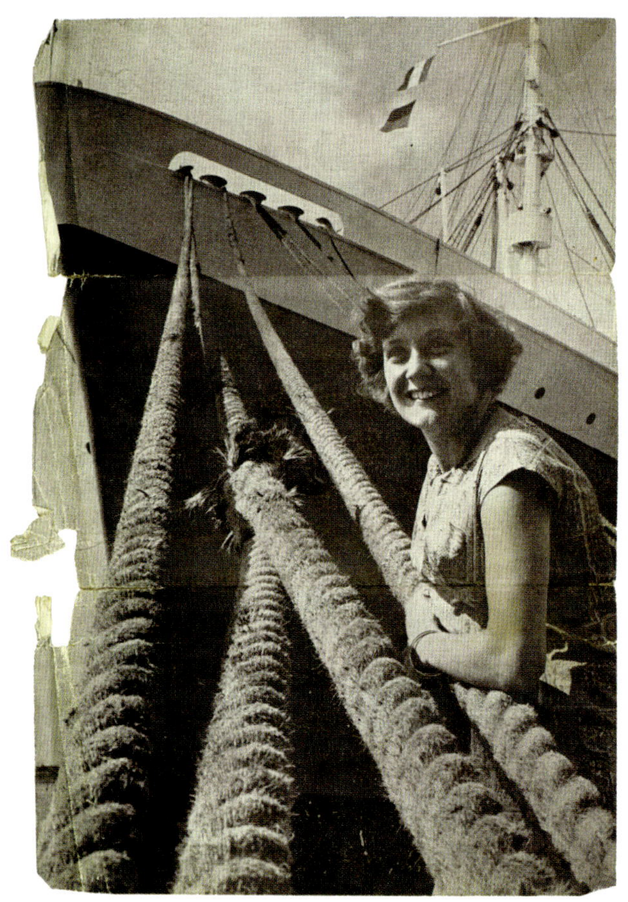

To-day's
THE Day . . .
TO VOTE
LABOUR

for

SHIRLEY WILLIAMS

(Yes . . . that IS Shirley on the other side of this leaflet)

at your usual
Polling Station

which will be open from 7 a.m. to 9 p.m.

TO-DAY

Published by H. T. Willcock, 54 Henstead Road, and printed by Shirley Press Ltd., Church Street, Southampton

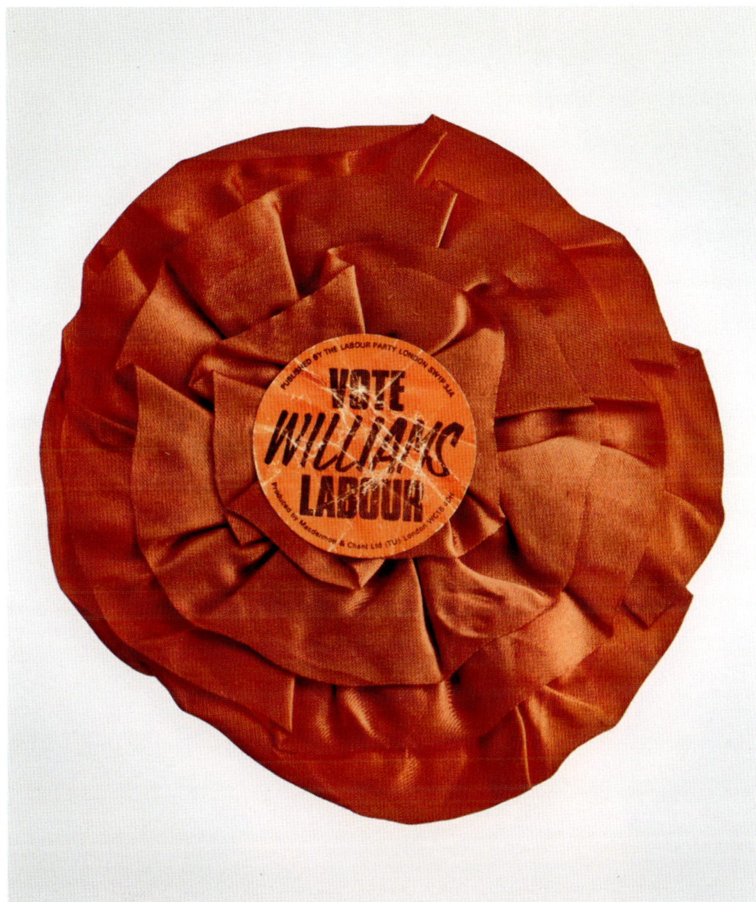

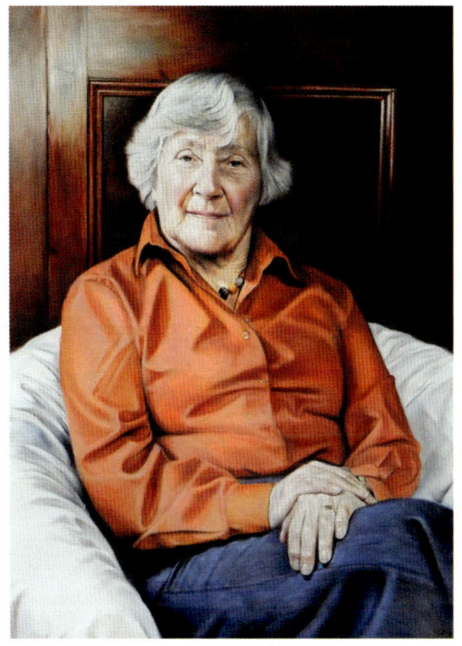

'The best Prime Minister this country never had'

Lord Dholakia, Presidential Address to the Liberal Democrat Conference, 2004

101
Shirley Williams election rosette

Born in 1930, Shirley Williams (Catlin) came up to Somerville to read PPE (Philosophy, Politics and Economics) in 1948. Her mother was the writer and Somervillian Vera Brittain [79]. Williams was the first woman Chair of the Oxford Labour Club and went on to win a Fulbright Scholarship and study at Columbia before working as a journalist. She then stood for Parliament a number of times before being returned as Labour MP for Hitchin. This rosette and leaflet are from her campaign for the constituency of Southampton Test in the 1959 General Election. Williams served as Shadow Home Secretary, becoming a member of Harold Wilson's (1916–95) Cabinet. In 1976, under James Callaghan, (1912–2005), she was Secretary of State for Education and Paymaster General. Disaffected with Labour, Williams was one of the 'Gang of Four' who founded the Social Democratic Party in 1981. In 1988 she moved to the US and took up a professorship at Harvard's John F. Kennedy School of Government. Created a life peer as Baroness Williams of Crosby in 1993, from 2001 to 2004 she was leader of the Liberal Democrats in the House of Lords. Williams retired from the House of Lords in 2016 and is now Professor Emerita of Electoral Politics at the Kennedy School.

Telephone kiosk

A vital lifeline: the cure for homesickness, or something to make it even more acute. The telephone kiosk in the corner of the ground floor of House was, for most Somervillians, the only way to talk to their families during term time. Letters to pigeonholes and the occasional lunch were the other ways to stay in touch. And of course for many students the freedom not to have to report in too often was one of the great joys of university life. Installing telephones in student rooms was an expensive business and rarely done (even the Principal's office had no direct telephone line until the time of Janet Vaughan), so it was only with the rise of the mobile phone in the late 1990s that the use of public telephones like this one began to wane. Now students can ring or message their friends and family whenever they like (payment plans allowing, of course), and House's kiosk is out of use, though it makes a handy storage area.

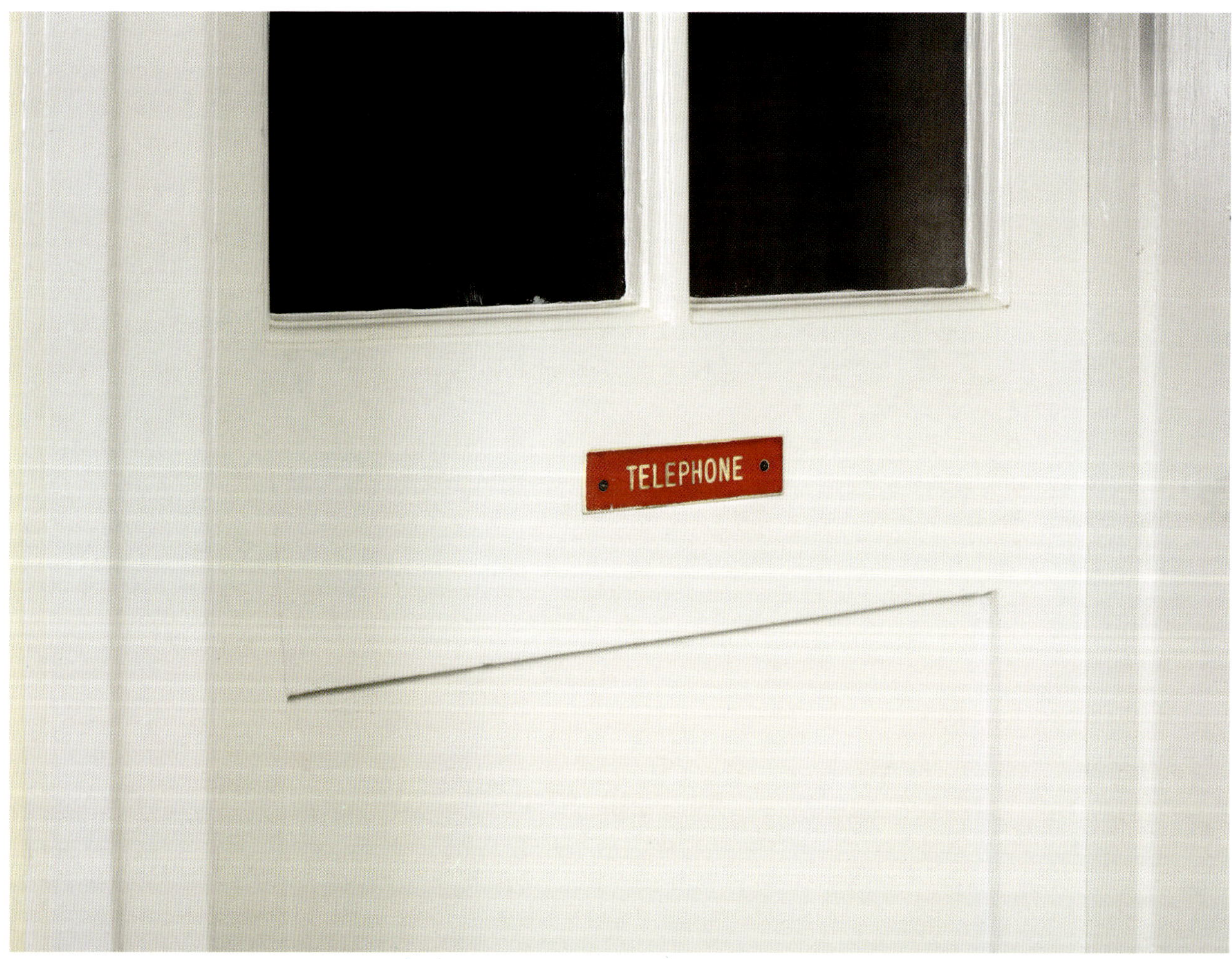

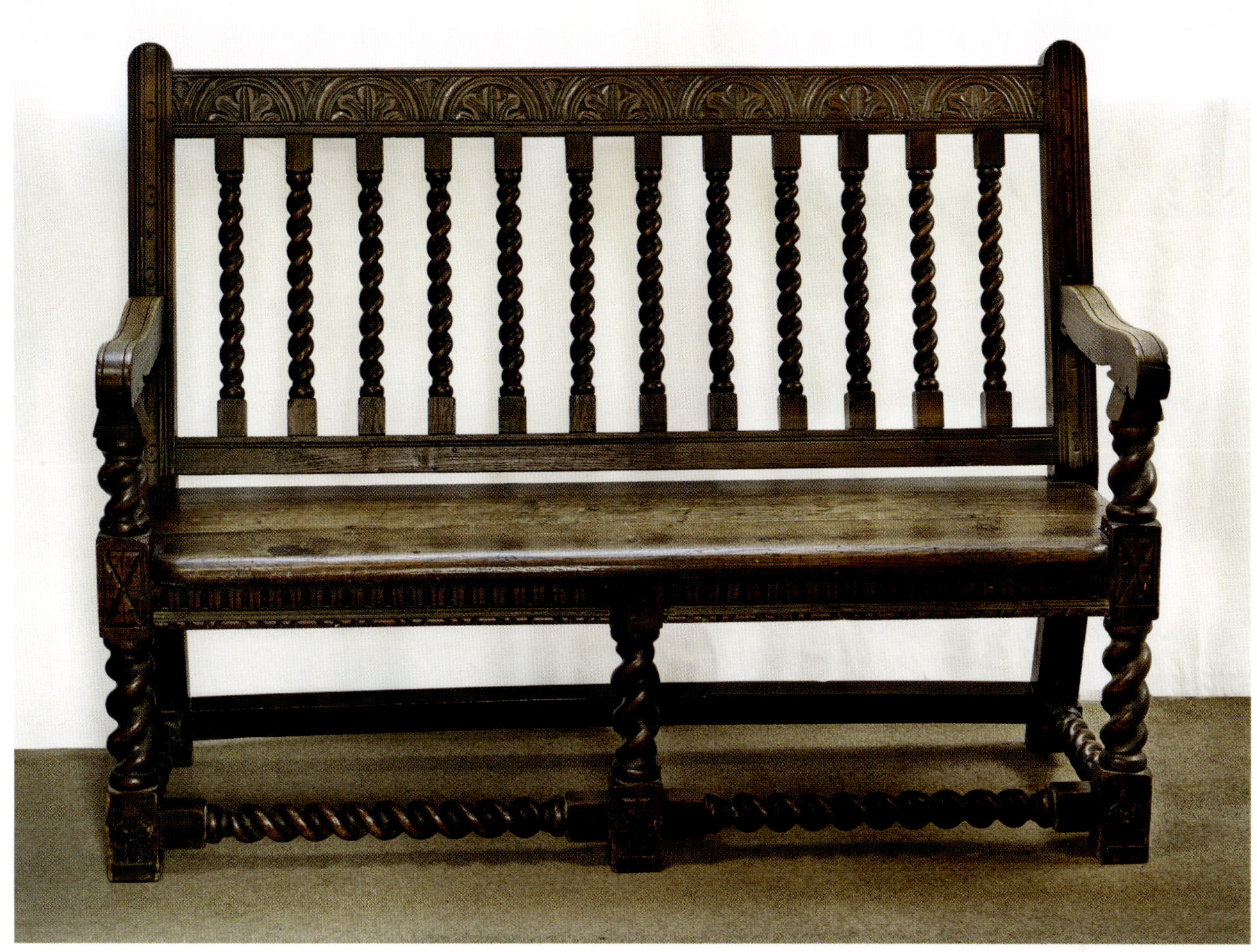

103
Bench outside the
Principal's Office

Handsome in its way, though not an especially significant piece of furniture. Unless, of course, you've ever had a Principal's collection. One of those Oxford terms that means something else in the rest of the world (as opposed to meaning nothing to almost the whole of the rest of the world, like 'battels'), a 'collection' is either a written examination in college at the start of term, or a meeting with the Principal and your personal tutor. Both are very good at showing exactly how much work you've done, and, of course, exactly how much you haven't quite managed to get to yet. Waiting on the bench outside the Principal's room, looking at the half-moon table and the paintings, overhearing a conversation coming from one of the offices next door, is as much a part of academic life at Somerville as a late-night essay crisis in the library. Everyone knows why you're there, of course. And then, with any luck, you go in to find that it's not as bad as you thought. In fact, it may even help you out of whatever jam you've got yourself into, in your work or in any other part of your Somerville life. The bench reminds you that you're taken seriously: and once a Somervillian, always a Somervillian.

'Oxford housewife
wins Nobel'

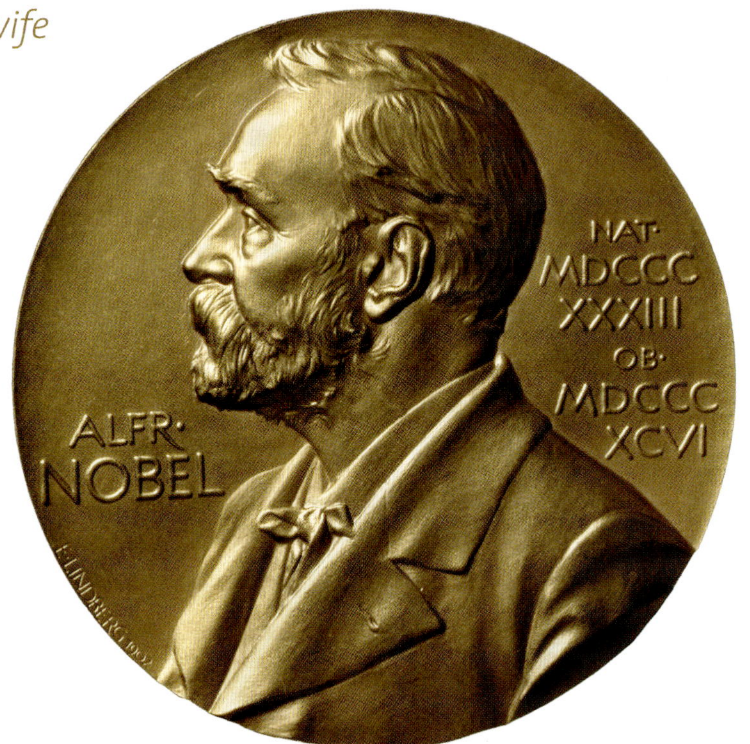

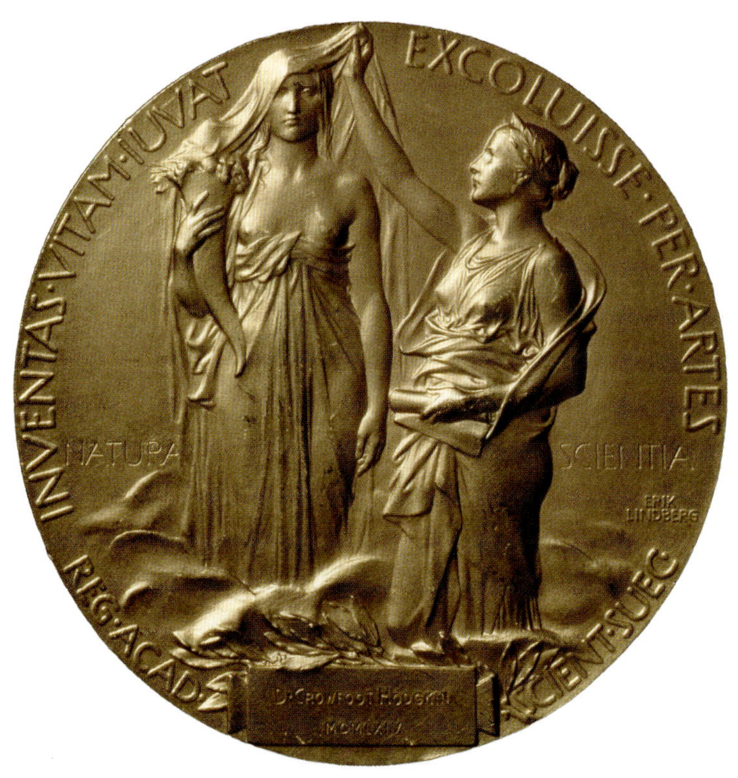

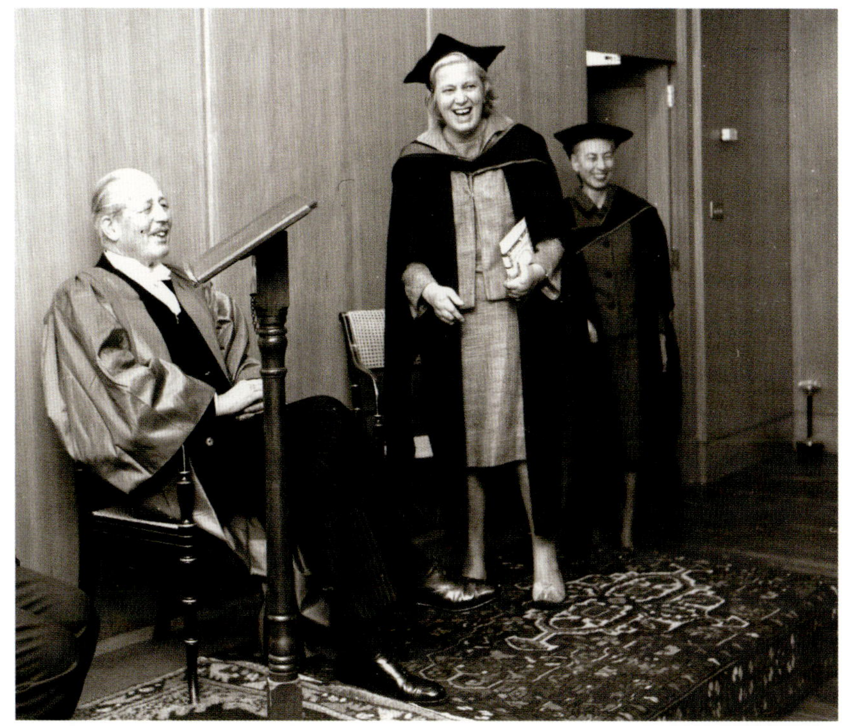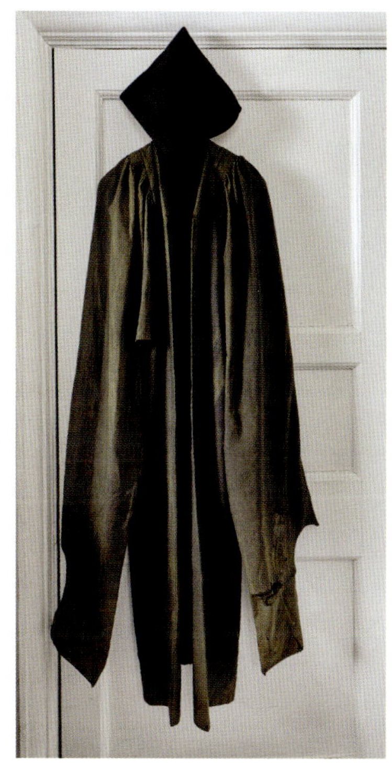

104
Dorothy Hodgkin's Nobel Prize Medal

'Oxford housewife wins Nobel' was the *Daily Mail*'s headline in 1964, when Dorothy Crowfoot Hodgkin (1910–94) became the first (and so far the only) British woman to win a Nobel Prize for science. One struggles to imagine similar headlines about Francis Crick ('Twice-married man honoured for scientific work', perhaps?). Fortunately, Hodgkin's upbringing, education and intelligence were such that she was not deterred by these kinds of attitudes. Dorothy Crowfoot came up to Somerville to read Chemistry in 1928. She went on to doctoral study in Cambridge and returned to Oxford when Somerville offered her a research fellowship in Chemistry. She was appointed the college's first Tutor in Chemistry in 1934, and she stayed in Somerville until her retirement in 1977. Hodgkin advanced the technique of X-ray crystallography to the point where

she was able to use it to confirm the structure of vitamin B12, and it was this part of her groundbreaking experimental work on protein crystallography that won her the Nobel Prize. She is also the only woman to date to win the Copley Medal, the Royal Society's oldest and most prestigious award, given for outstanding achievements in research in any branch of science.

Hodgkin used a large part of her prize money (which totalled £18,750 – roughly equivalent to £400,000 in today's money) to fund the establishment of a nursery in Somerville, and she left her Nobel Prize Medal to the college (it is currently kept in the Ashmolean Museum). Her generosity to Somerville was a symptom of her strong streak of practicality: she knew how much these gifts could do for a college with relatively little by way of permanent endowment. It was also a way of thanking

Somerville for the support it had given her: Hodgkin had been the recipient of the first ever maternity pay in Oxford, arranged by Principal Helen Darbishire (and described at the time as a kind of extended 'sick pay'). Here, alongside the Nobel Prize Medal, we can also see Hodgkin's well-worn gown: an inspiring reminder that her crowning achievement – solving the complex structure of insulin – was the result of a dogged perseverance over 35 years. The gown can be seen in its glory days in this photograph of Hodgkin at the opening of the Wolfson Building [107] with Harold Macmillan [110] and Barbara Craig. Following a successful fundraising campaign (including a strong crowdfunding strand), Somerville and Oxford University have established a five-year science fellowship in Hodgkin's name, with the aim of supporting early career women scientists.

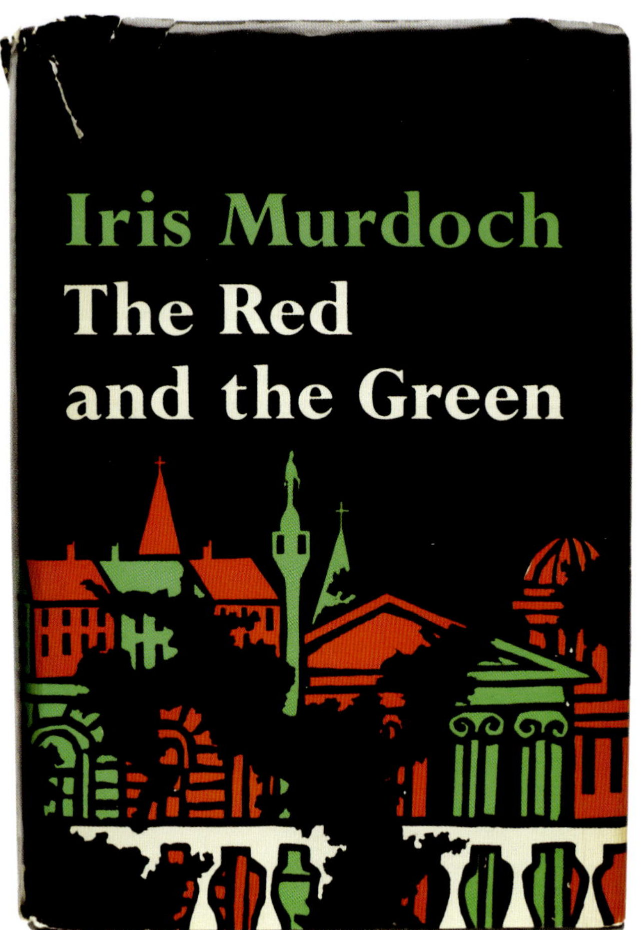

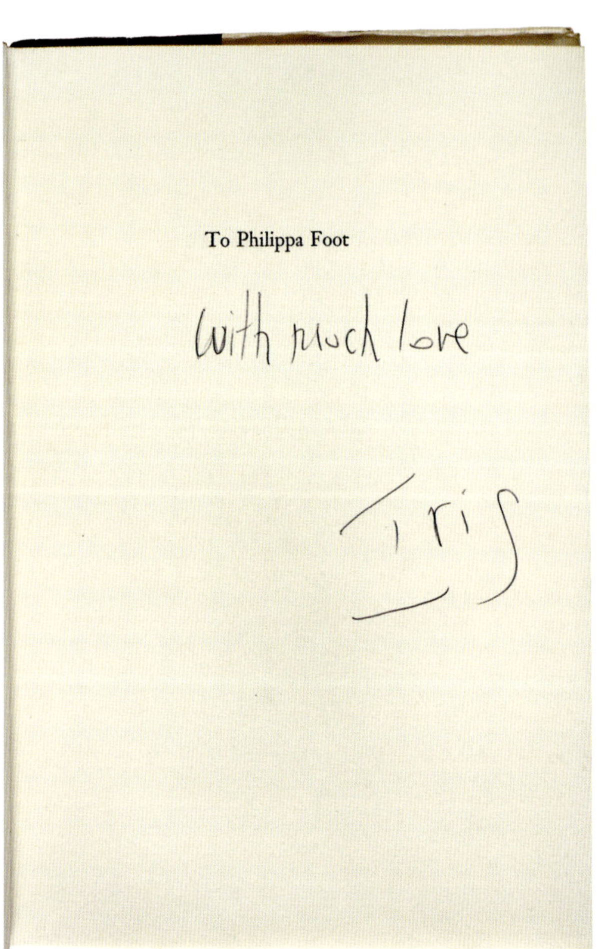

105
Iris Murdoch, *The Red and the Green*

Iris Murdoch (1919–99) came up to Somerville in 1938. She began reading English, but changed to Literae Humaniores (or 'Greats', covering Latin and Greek language as well as classical history and philosophy). It was, of course, philosophy that would become the subject of her academic work and a prevalent theme in her fiction. This first edition of *The Red and the Green* (set in Dublin at the time of the Easter Rising) was given by Murdoch to Philippa Foot (Bosanquet [1920–2010]), her fellow student at Somerville, her close friend and, for a short time, also her lover. Foot went on to become an eminent philosopher and a fellow of Somerville. She famously posited the 'trolley problem', a thought experiment in ethics. Imagine you can pull a lever to divert a runaway railway trolley onto a side track, away from the five people it would otherwise certainly kill. The dilemma? One person is lying on the side track...

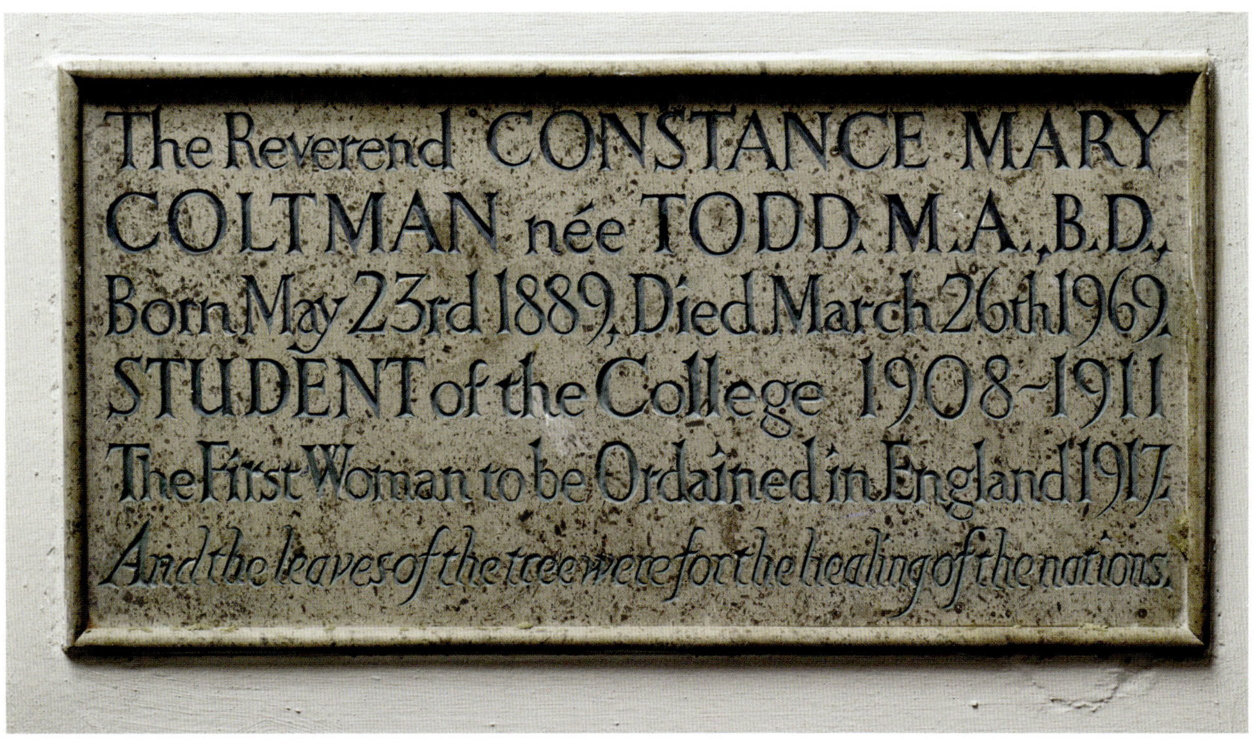

106
Plaque to Constance Coltman

2017 saw the centenary of the ordination of Constance Coltman (Todd; 1889–1969) as a minister of the Congregational Church. She came up to Somerville in 1908 to read Modern History, and felt her call to ministry while she was at Somerville. She initially sought ordination in the Presbyterian Church (in which she had grown up) but was told that this was impossible. She went on to study at Mansfield College, Oxford (at that time a Congregationalist college). There was still no certainty that she could be ordained, but her vocation remained firm and on 17 September 1917 she became the first woman to be ordained in a mainstream church in the United Kingdom. Coltman was a lifelong pacifist and a supporter of women's suffrage and women's reproductive rights, and she helped to found the Fellowship of Women Ministers and the Society for the Ministry of Women.

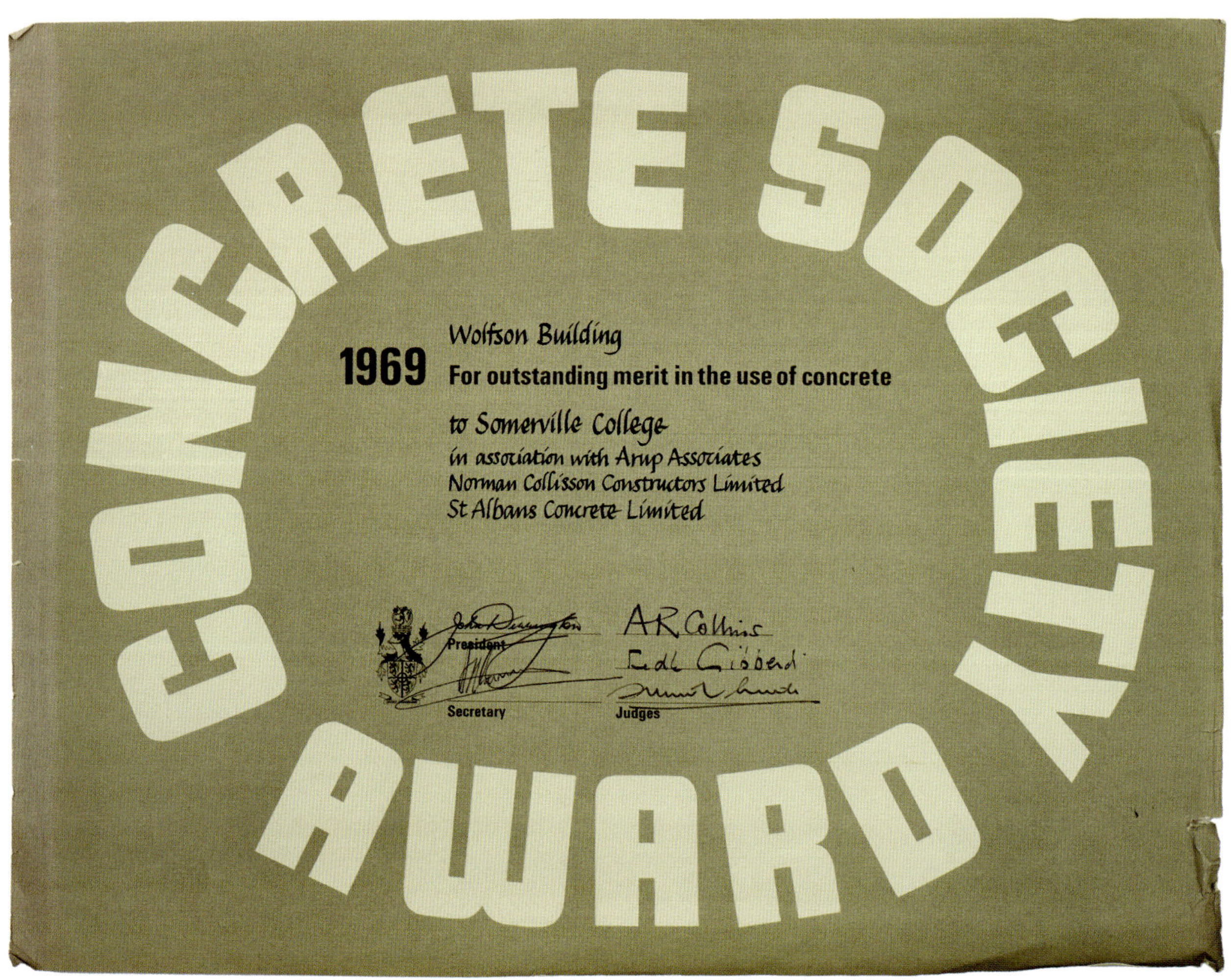

107
Concrete Society Award

In the late 1950s and 1960s Oxford colleges began to expand their numbers, offering more places for postgraduate study, and this shift is marked across the city in concrete buildings. For some they are carbuncles on the beauty of Oxford's historical complexion. For others, and especially for those who lived in them, they were and are a hugely welcome source of comfort, light and heat, bringing the best of modernity to the aid of scholarship and learning. Somerville launched ambitious plans to construct three such new buildings, and their success was recognised in 1969 by the Concrete Society (founded in 1966). Just as the two concrete buildings on Little Clarendon Street were completed, Principal Janet Vaughan announced a major grant from the Wolfson Foundation. Designed, like the Fry/Nuffield and Vaughan Buildings, by Philip Dowson (1924–2014), the accommodation in Wolfson is cellular, with its sheets of glass echoing the oriel windows of the West (later Park) Building. Wolfson was opened in 1967, the ceremony presided over by new Principal Barbara Craig and attended by Harold Macmillan (1894–1986 [110]) and Lord Wolfson (1927–2010), as well as Dorothy Hodgkin [104] (who was a friend of Philip Dowson). In 2012 the building was extended by Níall McLaughlin Architects, who provided an addition to the ground floor hall, named the Brittain-Williams room in honour of two of Somerville's most famous alumnae, the writer Vera Brittain [79] and her daughter, the politician Shirley Williams [101].

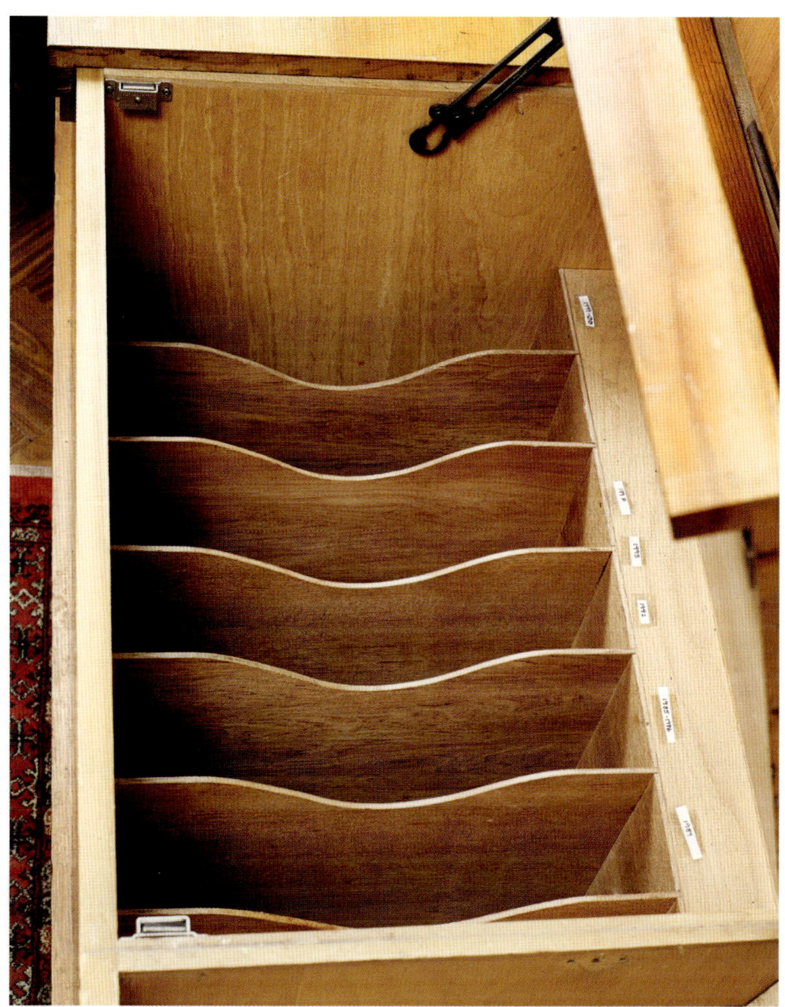

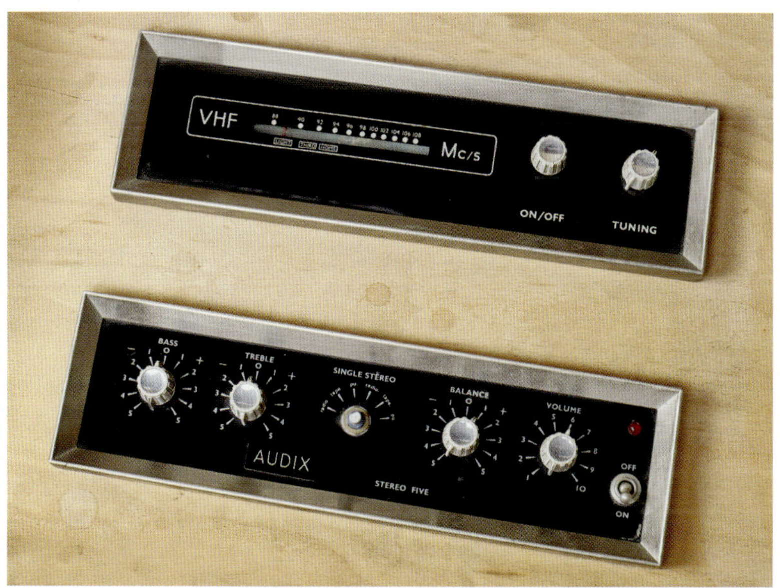

108
MCR stereo cabinet

The college grew rapidly in the 1960s. Undergraduate numbers increased, but just as notable, if not more so, was the increase in the numbers of students staying on or coming to Somerville to read for graduate degrees [107]. The MCR (Middle Common Room) existed, as its name suggests, somewhere between the world of undergraduates and that of the fellows and tutors, and this purpose-built common room space in Margery Fry House reflects that status. Somerville's graduate students had their own small dining room here, as well as a space where they could enjoy the modern luxury of LP records and a turntable. The cabinet in the MCR was designed with compartments specifically measured to hold LPs. When those fell out of fashion, their place was taken by copies of the *TLS* and the *New York Review of Books*. And now that those are easily accessed online, the slots in the cabinet are usually populated with controllers for the MCR's very own Xbox.

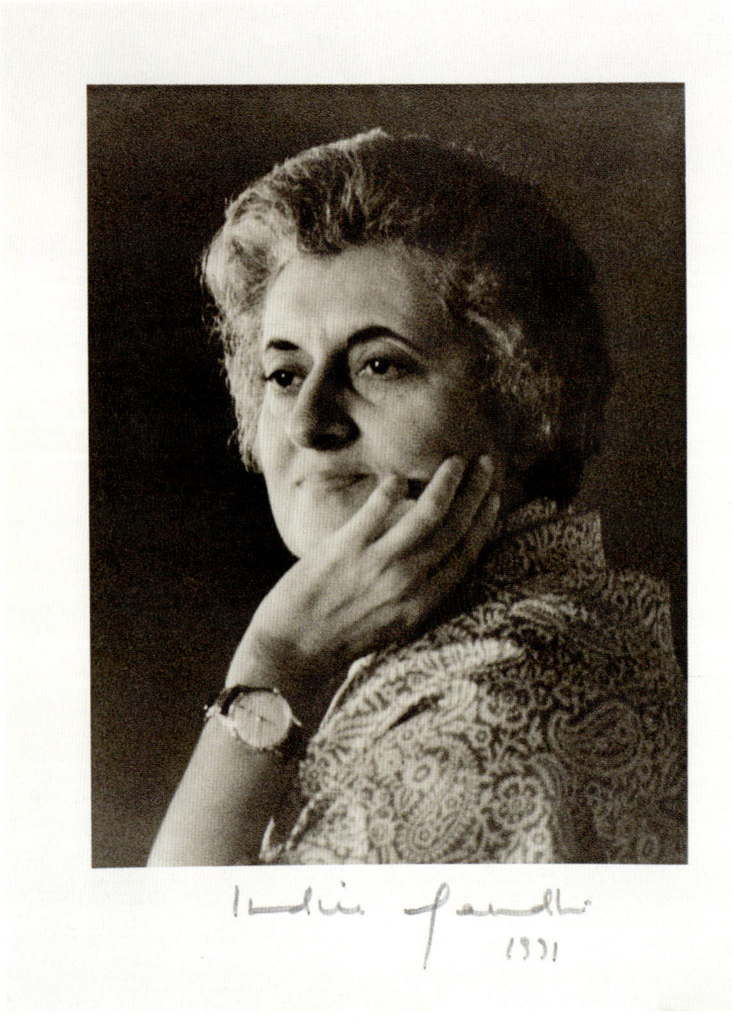

109
Signed photograph of Indira Gandhi

Indira Gandhi (Nehru) came to Somerville in 1937 to read Modern History. She was only able to stay for one year: ill health forced her to leave. Her memories of Somerville were powerful and emotionally warm (if not meteorologically so: she found her room appallingly cold [36]). Her tutorial partner, Kathleen (Kay) Davies (1919–2017), remained a lifelong friend and correspondent, and their letters show Gandhi's wit and lightness of touch alongside her steely political will. Gandhi was elected India's first woman Prime Minister in 1966. She visited Somerville in 1971, and this signed photograph was a gift from her to the then Principal, Barbara Craig. Gandhi was undoubtedly a controversial figure: in June 1984 a violent clash between government forces and Sikhs at the Golden Temple led to an intensification of feeling against her. Later that year she was assassinated by two of her own bodyguards. In 2012 the college, the University of Oxford and the Government of India launched a joint initiative, establishing a centre to promote the study of sustainable development in India. As part of that initiative Somerville and the University of Oxford now offer a series of scholarships in Gandhi's name for Indian students, supporting study in public policy and sustainable development, with a particular focus on India-related projects [123].

Cedar tree

Harold Macmillan was instrumental in the rise of perhaps the most famous Somervillian: it was as a junior minister for pensions in Macmillan's government that Margaret Thatcher [113] took up her first front-bench post. Macmillan himself came to Somerville a number of times (he was Chancellor of Oxford from 1960 to 1986, and he also served as the college's Visitor). In May 1976 he inaugurated the college's centenary celebrations by planting a cedar tree. The choice was far from arbitrary: early pictures of House are dominated by a huge and beautiful cedar tree, but it was blown down in the New Year storm of 1976 (fortunately, away from the hall and not onto it).

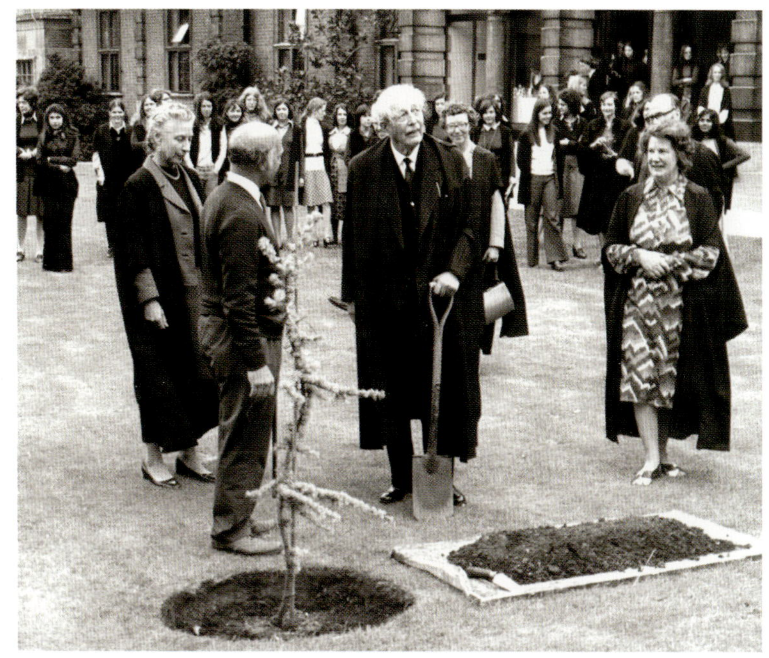

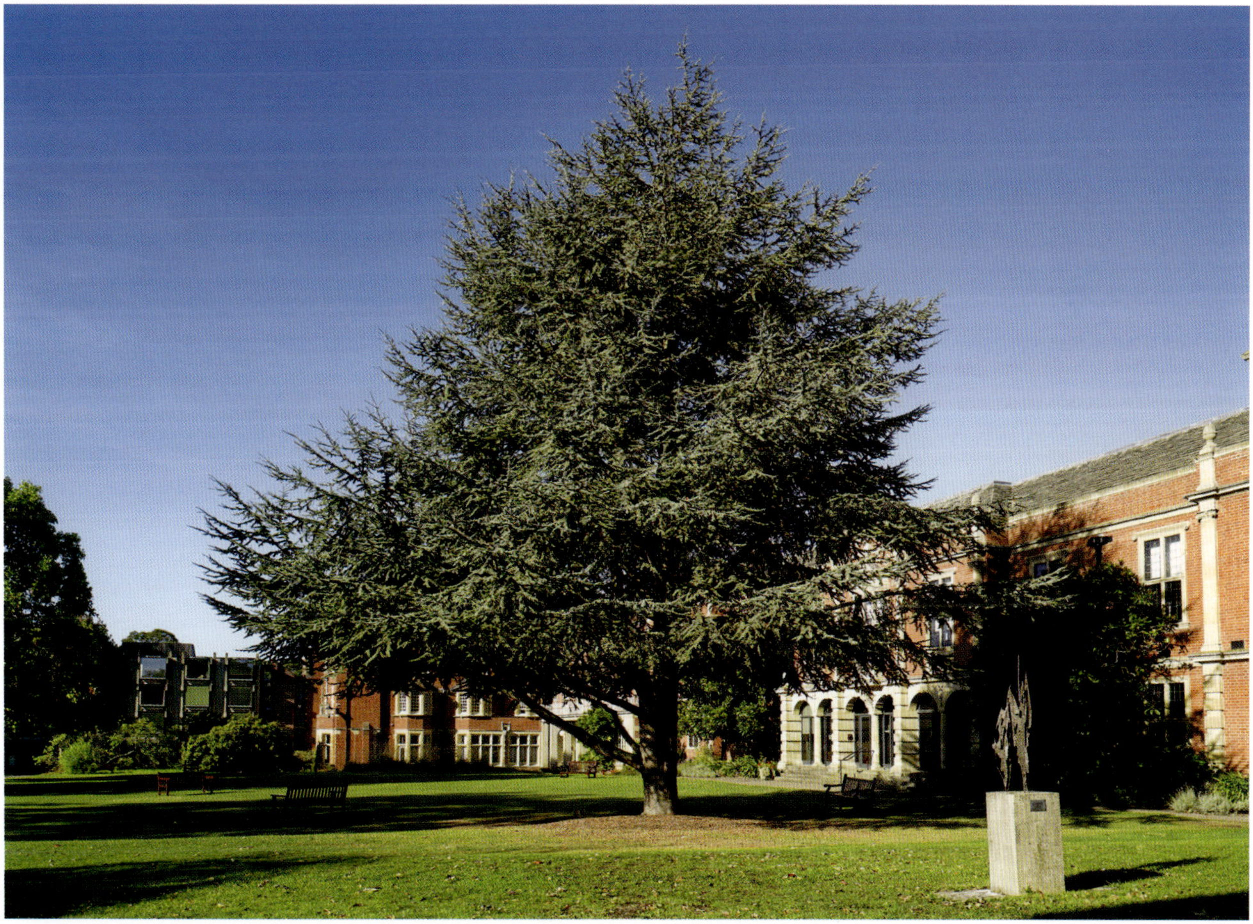

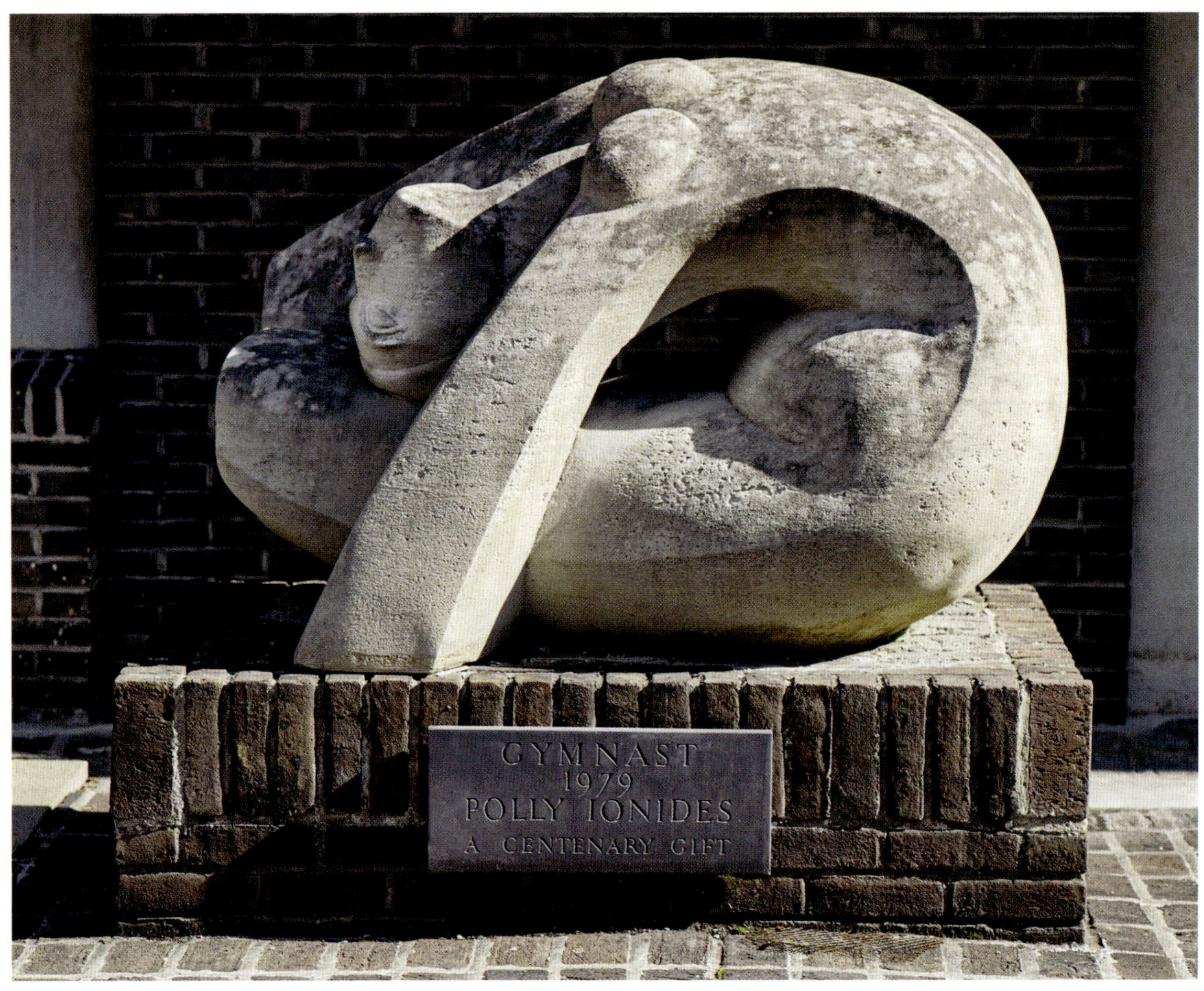

'silent frozen grace'

111
Polly Ionides, *Gymnast*

Polly Ionides (Richter) came up to Somerville in 1961 to read Zoology. She was a leading member of the JCR's Art Committee and went on to study at the Slade School of Fine Art, modelling in clay and carving in wood before she began to work in stone. *Gymnast* took six months to make, and is carved from a four-ton block of blue and cream Clipsham stone (a Jurassic oolitic limestone from a Leicestershire quarry, over 140 million years old). The lettering on the plaque of purple Bangor slate is by Heather Harms. Somerville had for some time wanted a sculpture for the terrace outside the new Vaughan building, and *Gymnast* arrived on its plinth a few days before the centenary Gaudy, having been lifted over the parapet wall from Little Clarendon Street by crane. For Ionides, the 'silent frozen grace' of *Gymnast* showed a body stretched in the same way that Somerville stretches the mind. Sculpture is important to Somerville: other permanent pieces include *Triad* by Wendy Taylor and *Elipsodrome* by Friedrich Werthmann, and in the 1960s the Art Committee successfully arranged the temporary installation of Henry Moore's *Falling Warrior* and Barbara Hepworth's *Core*.

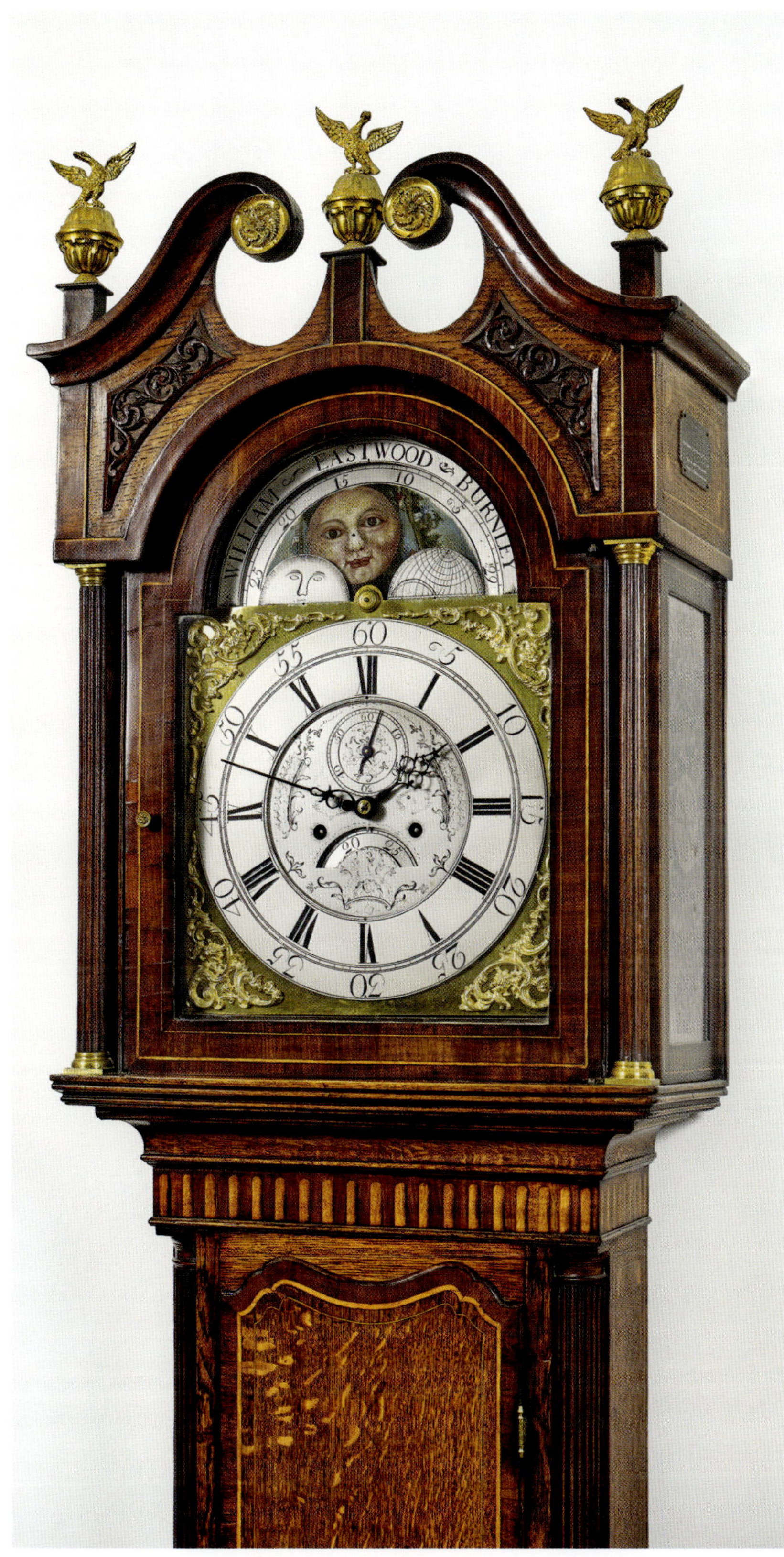

112
Grandfather clock

This was a gift to the college from a former Librarian, Norma Dalrymple-Champneys (Lewis; 1902–98) in 1981. Norma Lewis came up to Somerville in 1921 to read Modern History, and after graduating trained as a librarian before taking a post with the League of Nations Union. She came back to bibliographical work in the 1930s, cataloguing a number of important libraries. In 1952 she returned to Somerville as Librarian; she later also became a Research Fellow and was elected a member of the Governing Body. Her third husband, Sir Weldon Dalrymple-Champneys (1892–1980), was the nephew and godson of Basil Champneys, the architect of the library [32] and the original owner of this beautiful clock, whose dial dates from around 1790.

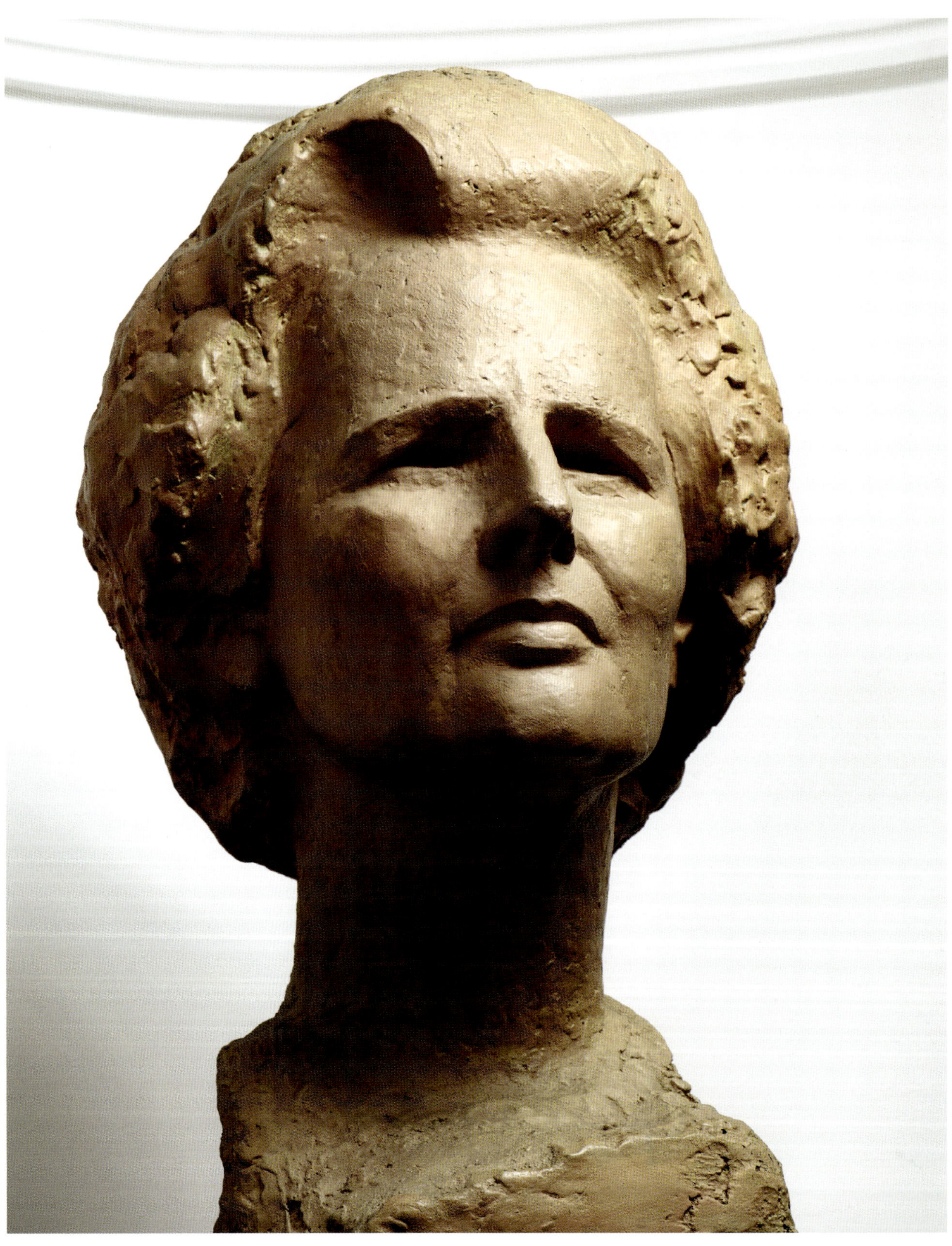

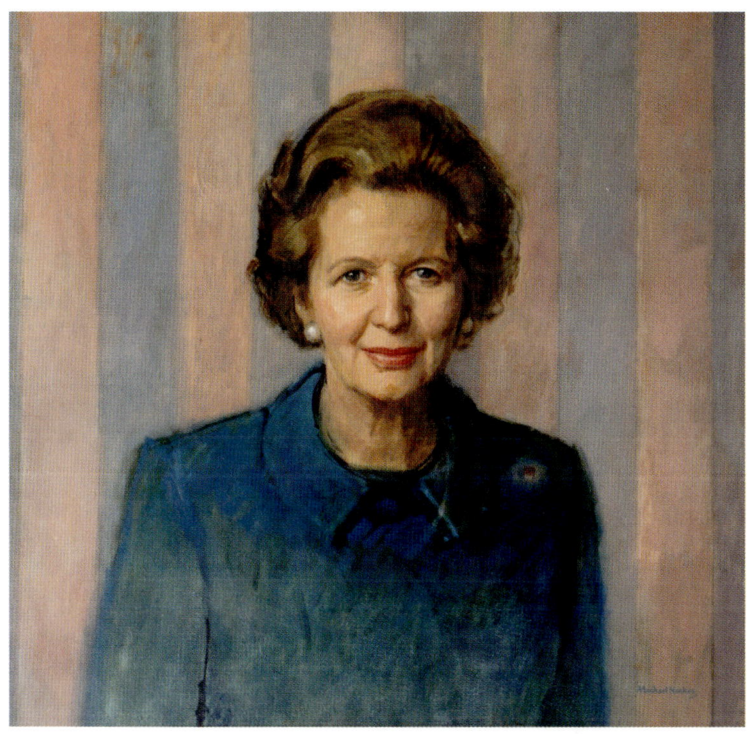

Margaret Thatcher, open letter to Somerville, 1980

113
Oscar Nemon, bust of
Margaret Thatcher

Somerville is spoiled for choice when it comes to choosing an object that tells the story of Margaret Thatcher. This bust was made by Oscar Nemon (1906–85). Born Oskar Neumann in 1906 in Osijek (then part of the Austro-Hungarian Empire, now in Croatia), he studied and worked in Paris and Vienna before escaping the Nazi regime and coming to England in 1938. The subjects of his sculptures are a roll-call of the famous, and he was perhaps most renowned for his series of statues of Churchill. He offered this work to Somerville after it was shown in an exhibition of his work at the Ashmolean ('This was an unexpectedly sudden gesture which I hope all Fellows will welcome', wrote Principal Daphne Park in a memo). Thatcher visited Somerville on 3 February 1983 to unveil the sculpture, arriving to a backdrop of demonstrations (to

which, one assumes, she must have been well used). When she left Oxford, demonstrations against her likeness continued. The Nemon bust was vandalised on at least two occasions, once being covered in green paint.

Margaret Roberts came to Somerville in 1943. Her background was not one of wealth and the then Principal, Helen Darbishire, quickly spotted that Roberts was struggling financially and arranged a bursary for her. Roberts read Chemistry; one of her tutors was Dorothy Hodgkin, who would later win the Nobel Prize for her work in X-ray crystallography [104]. The two remained in contact, though Hodgkin's politics were firmly left wing. Hodgkin would occasionally visit her famous pupil in Downing Street, using the opportunity to lecture Thatcher on nuclear disarmament. It is said that Thatcher would be nervous for

days before each such visit, frantically 'revising' by reading about the latest developments in chemistry.

The personal stories are fascinating but Thatcher was, and remains, a sharply divisive figure. The champion of a new economic individualism? Or the assassin of the welfare state? Whatever your view, you would have to agree that she defined 1980s Britain. The college's connection to Lady Thatcher continues following the establishment of the Margaret Thatcher Scholarship Trust, which provides a number of full scholarships to undergraduate and graduate students. For the holders of these scholarships, many of whom were not even born when she was in power, Thatcher is a figure from a GCSE course: interesting and important, but hardly someone to inspire acts of vandalism.

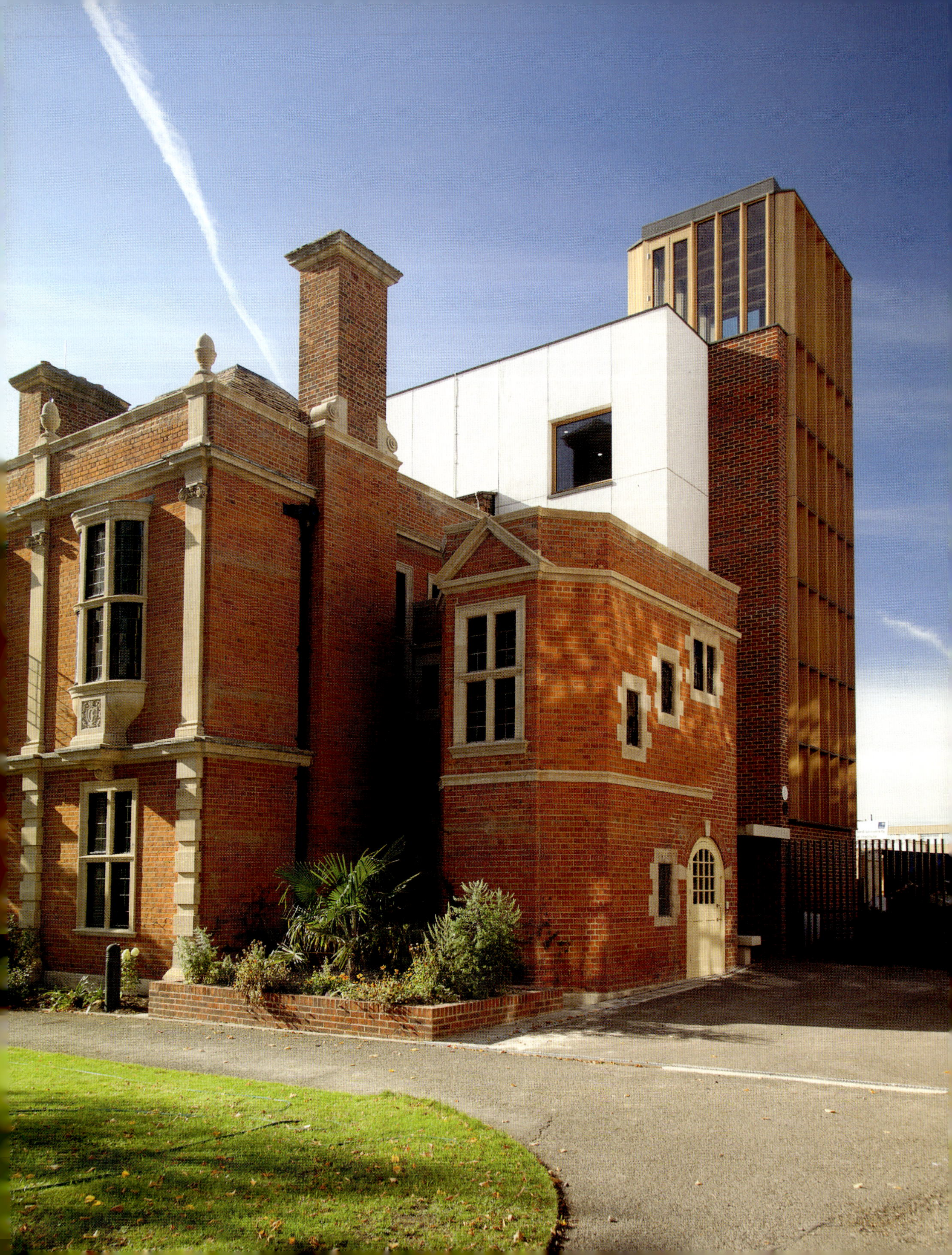

1989–2019
'a college looking forward'

The 1990s saw the biggest alteration in Somerville since its foundation. There were those who objected to the admission of men, but there were also those who felt strongly it was the right step for the future of Somerville. In recent years, the college has enjoyed renewed and expanded connections with India alongside a push to improve diversity in Oxford. The pressing questions now are the same as those when Somerville began. How can a university education be opened up to all who could take advantage of it? And how will those educated by Somerville contribute to positive change in the world? Answering them means building the future on radical foundations.

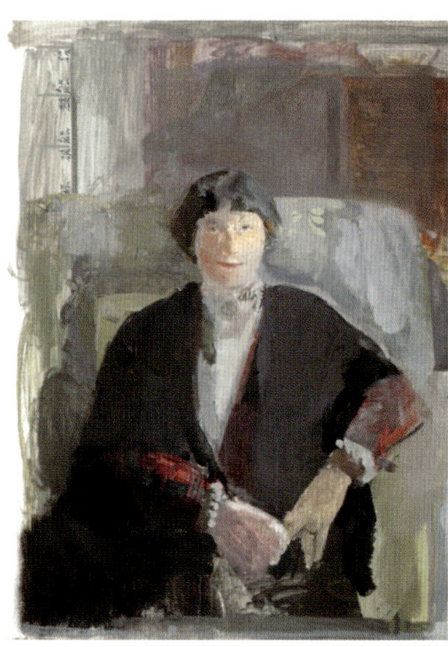

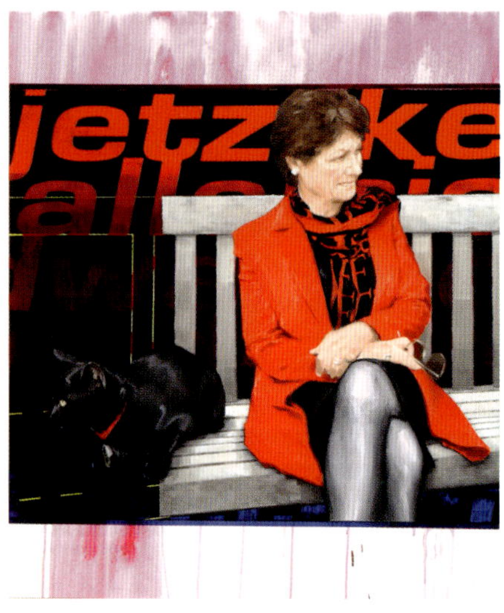

1989–1996
Catherine Hughes (Pestell)

Catherine Pestell was a diplomat and senior civil servant before she was elected Principal of Somerville in 1989. She was also the first non-Somervillian to be elected to the post since Agnes Maitland. A graduate in History from St Hilda's, Pestell brought the ideal combination of skills to the college at a time of great change. Somerville's fellows were achieving the highest positions and honours (two were elected to University readerships, with another two elected to fellowships of the Royal Society) and the college's first ever Proctor was elected in the University. But a legal storm was brewing about whether the appointment of academics to single-sex colleges could feasibly be maintained. Somerville's Governing Body discussed again the question of admitting men, and concluded that the time had come. The JCR in particular was not happy with the decision, and a period of legal challenges and tense negotiation followed. It was eventually agreed that the first cohort of male students would be admitted in 1994. The first male fellows arrived one year before that. 'I think it is already a college looking forward', said Somerville's Principal when the decision had been made. It was a statement typical of her positive outlook, and it set the tone for Somerville's new era. Pestell had also cast light on the college's statutes for more personal reasons: in 1991 she announced her engagement to the acting Warden of Green College, Trevor Hughes. Perusal of the statutes made it clear that while a married woman could be elected Principal, an unmarried one needed to resign her position upon marriage. Pestell duly resigned, was married in the college chapel [86] and returned after a two-week hiatus to be re-elected as Catherine Hughes.

1996–2010
Fiona Caldicott

In Fiona Caldicott, Somerville again had a medical woman at its helm. Caldicott had studied at St Hilda's, as Catherine Hughes had. Her specialism was psychiatry, and she served as President of the Royal College of Psychiatrists and Chair of the Academy of Medical Royal Colleges before taking up the Principalship of Somerville. 'The experience of living in a college community and making life-long friends who were reading a wide range of subjects, as well as medicine, has been a cornerstone of both my personal and professional progress', Caldicott said, and it was a powerful combination of professional and personal presence that she brought to the college. During her time at Somerville she chaired the 'Caldicott Commission', investigating how patient data is used in the NHS, and also took on a number of roles in the wider University, including Pro-Vice-Chancellor for Personnel and Equality, while continuing to oversee the integration of male students and fellows into the college. After her term as Principal, Caldicott went on to chair the Oxford University Hospitals Trust and work as the National Data Guardian for Health and Care.

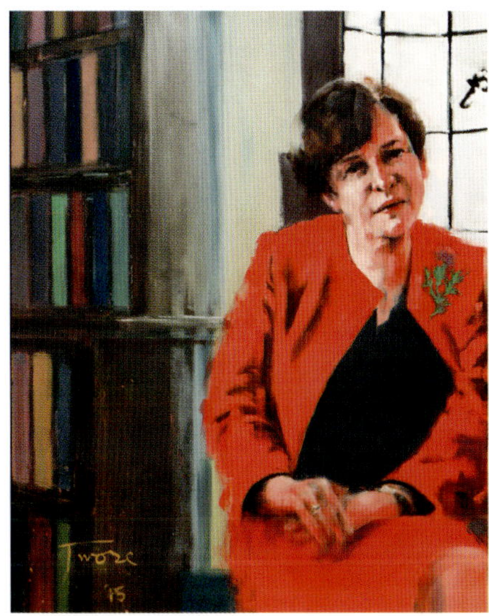

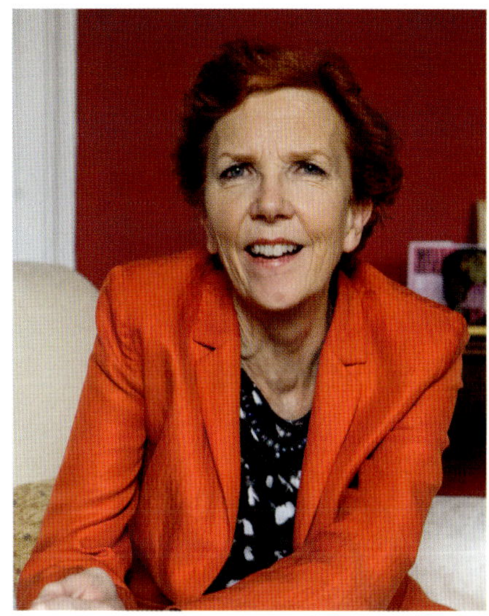

Alice Prochaska

Alice Prochaska came up to Somerville in 1965 to read Modern History, going on to take a DPhil before beginning her career as a curator, archivist and librarian. Prochaska worked as Director of Special Collections at the British Library and director of the library at Yale University before returning to Somerville in 2010 to take up the Principalship. Prochaska was energetically involved in fundraising for the college, and during her tenure as Principal the endowment more than doubled, growing from £36 million to £73 million. She was also instrumental in establishing the major new initiatives of the Oxford India Centre for Sustainable Development and the Margaret Thatcher Scholarship Trust. Prochaska wedded the management of large-scale change to a concern for the everyday details of college life that harked back to the earliest Principalships of Somerville. Her many achievements, including her care for the welfare of college members, led Somerville's students to line up in front of the library in Prochaska's last term, bearing huge sheets of cardboard that spelled out 'Thank you, Ali P'.

Janet Royall

Baroness Royall of Blaisdon came to Somerville as the college's twelfth Principal following a distinguished career in politics. She worked as a senior adviser in the European Commission before heading its office in Wales. When she was appointed to the House of Lords, Royall became a Government Spokesperson for Health, International Development and Foreign and Commonwealth Affairs. She went on to be Labour Chief Whip and Leader of the House of Lords. Firmly in Somerville's traditions of public service and including the excluded, Royall remains an active backbencher with particular interests in education, young people, diversity, health and social care, women and social justice. She is Chair of Trustees for the People's History Museum, Vice President of the Party of European Socialists and a member of the Fabian Executive.

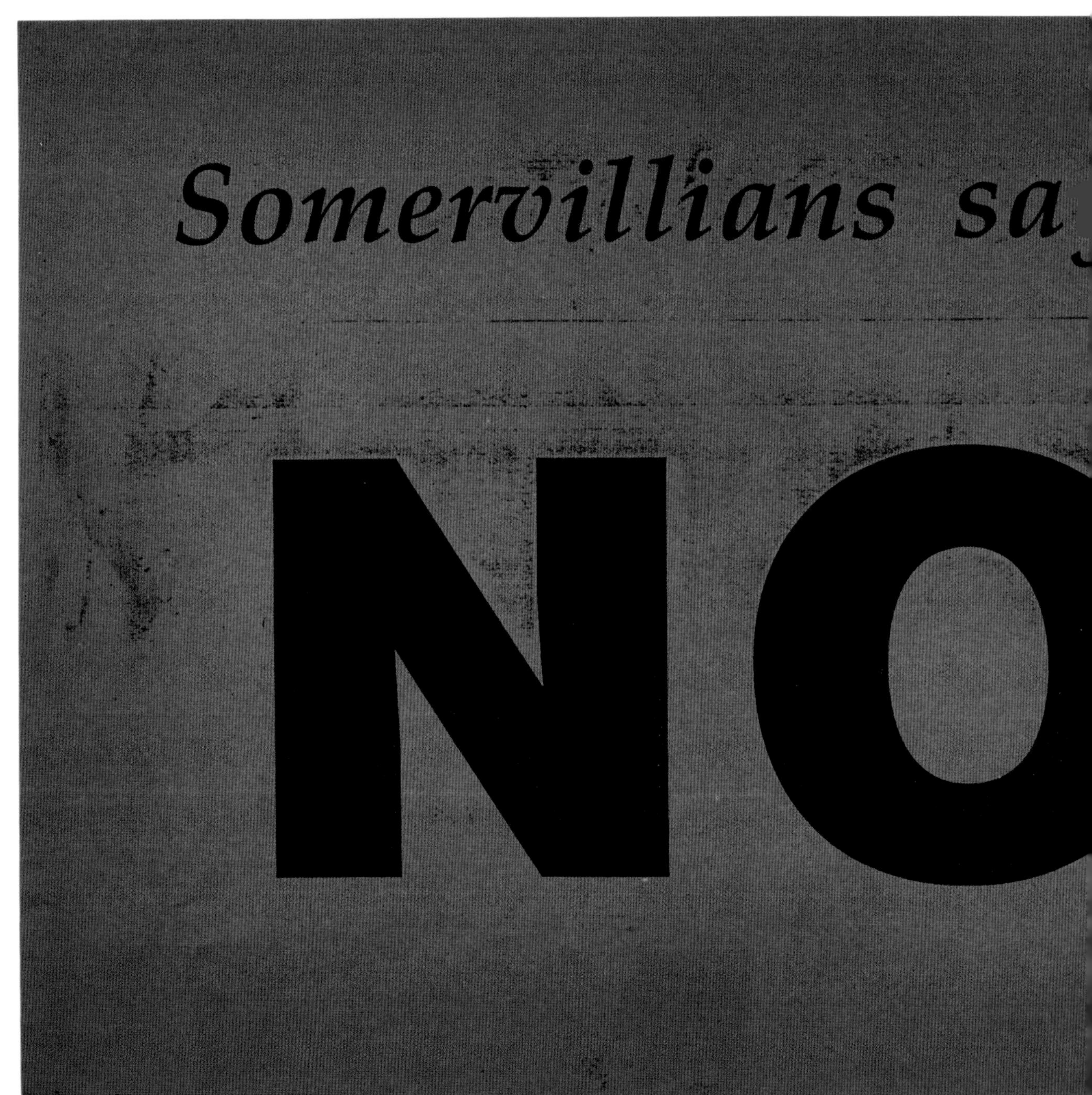
Somervillians say
NO

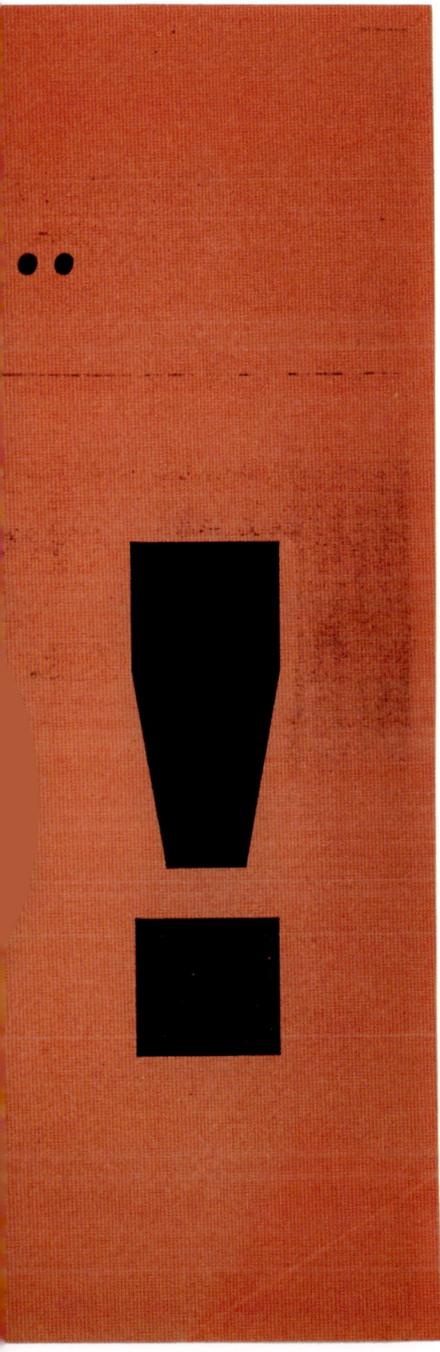

114
Protest poster

What is the biggest change that Somerville saw in the second half of the twentieth century? It has to be 'going mixed'. In 1879, of course, the idea of mixed tutorials, let alone mixed accommodation, would have been enough to shut down a hall before it had even opened. It would be 1974 before any men's college would vote to admit women, with the bulk of colleges following suit in the late 1970s. The move was a welcome one in most quarters, but it posed a threat to the women's colleges. Mary Bennett (Fisher; 1913–2005), a Somervillian who later became Principal of St Hilda's, summed up the risk starkly: men's colleges might 'skim the cream' of female applicants as they sought to get 'stupid men out and clever girls in'.

It may seem inevitable to us that this change would mean the women's colleges too would eventually 'go mixed'. To many Somervillians in the 1980s the idea was anathema. They believed that as the college had been founded to protect and promote the education of women, Somerville should stay single-sex until full equality was reached. The college had its first debates about admitting men during the 1970s. The result was that Somerville said 'no'. The then Principal, Barbara Craig, was so careful to remain neutral that no one was able to discover her views on the matter. The question surfaced again in the early 1980s and it was again decided that Somerville should remain for women only. It took a new decade and a new Principal, Catherine Hughes, to bring the issue back to the table, not least because of the question of whether Somerville would need to admit male fellows in order to fill a number of posts that had fallen vacant. Hughes made it clear that she felt it was time to 'go mixed': 'One of the virtues of having an all-women fellowship in an all-women college is in providing role models', she said. 'But there is something condescending in having a mixed fellowship and an all-women junior membership.' This time the Governing Body voted 'yes', but a vocal student protest, 'Somervillians say... NO!', caught the attention of the national press. The change went ahead but was delayed after a ruling from the Visitor [115]. The college changed its statutes in 1992 and the first male fellows were elected and arrived in 1993. The following year saw the arrival of the first male students.

STRICTLY CONFIDENTIAL

Principal of Somerville

copy (with one copy of each enclosure): Mr Munby

Somerville College: Visitor's ruling

A signed copy is enclosed of the ruling made by Lord Jenkins, as Visitor of the College, following the hearing on 11 May 1992.

The ruling (under cover of this note) is being delivered to the lodge at Somerville College at 9 a.m. on 2 June, and is made available to the parties **on the strict understanding** that its content will not be disclosed to anyone else (i.e. to anyone other than the members of the Governing Body of the College on the one hand or to the Petitioners on the other) before **0001 hours on Thursday 4 June 1992**.

The Visitor has made arrangements for the release of the document direct to the press - namely to *The Times*, the *Financial Times*, *The Independent*, *The Daily Telegraph*, *The Oxford Times*, *The Guardian*, and *The Higher* - subject to the same embargo. In order to ensure that the parties are not asked by the press for comments before they have had an opportunity of studying the ruling, the document will not be transmitted to the press until Wednesday morning, 3 June (and then of course subject to the embargo to 0001 on 4 June).

One spare (unsigned) copy of the Visitor's ruling is enclosed.

Also enclosed are two copies of the transcript of the hearing on 11 May; this is subject to the same conditions, as to confidentiality, as apply to the ruling. *

A note is being sent in identical terms to the President of the Somerville Junior Common Room (with a copy to Mr Evans).

1.6.92

* The transcript is not being sent to the Press.

115
The Visitor's ruling

When Somerville's Governing Body made the decision to 'go mixed', the JCR took the extraordinary step of appealing to the college's Visitor to overturn it. Their argument was that the decision was in breach of the objects of the college's charter and in breach of natural justice.

The Visitor, Lord Jenkins (1920–2003), decided that that Governing Body had acted 'responsibly as well as legally', but he also stated his view that he thought it had acted very quickly, and that the student members did have a right to be consulted. He urged the Governing Body to delay the admission of men as students for at least a year and preferably longer. The Governing Body agreed, and although a significant number of JCR members remained opposed to the admission of male undergraduates, a negotiated position was eventually reached.

SCR coffee machine

Not an object that most students will remember, but for those who were members of the Senior Common Room (SCR) in the 1990s, this represents a revolution almost as earth-shattering as the admission of men. Now the SCR is unthinkable without it (and, indeed, a good number of the fellows and lecturers would probably admit that they cannot think without it). The call for a 'proper' coffee machine came from a group of fellows who had lived and worked on the Continent, and thus had known coffee that was coffee, as the fellows in *Gaudy Night* would have said. The college responded in typically careful and consultative fashion, by constituting a small working group to act as a 'coffee committee'. It duly reported to the Governing Body with the necessary solemnity for an issue of such weight (a written paper, obviously), and the machine was purchased, generously funded by Anna Morpurgo Davies (1937–2014), a fellow of Somerville and Professor of Comparative Philology. This is, it should be said, far from being the first model of the coffee machine (which soon collapsed under the strain): like Dr Who, it is reincarnated as the need arises.

'Here's coffee that is coffee'

Dorothy L. Sayers, *Gaudy Night*

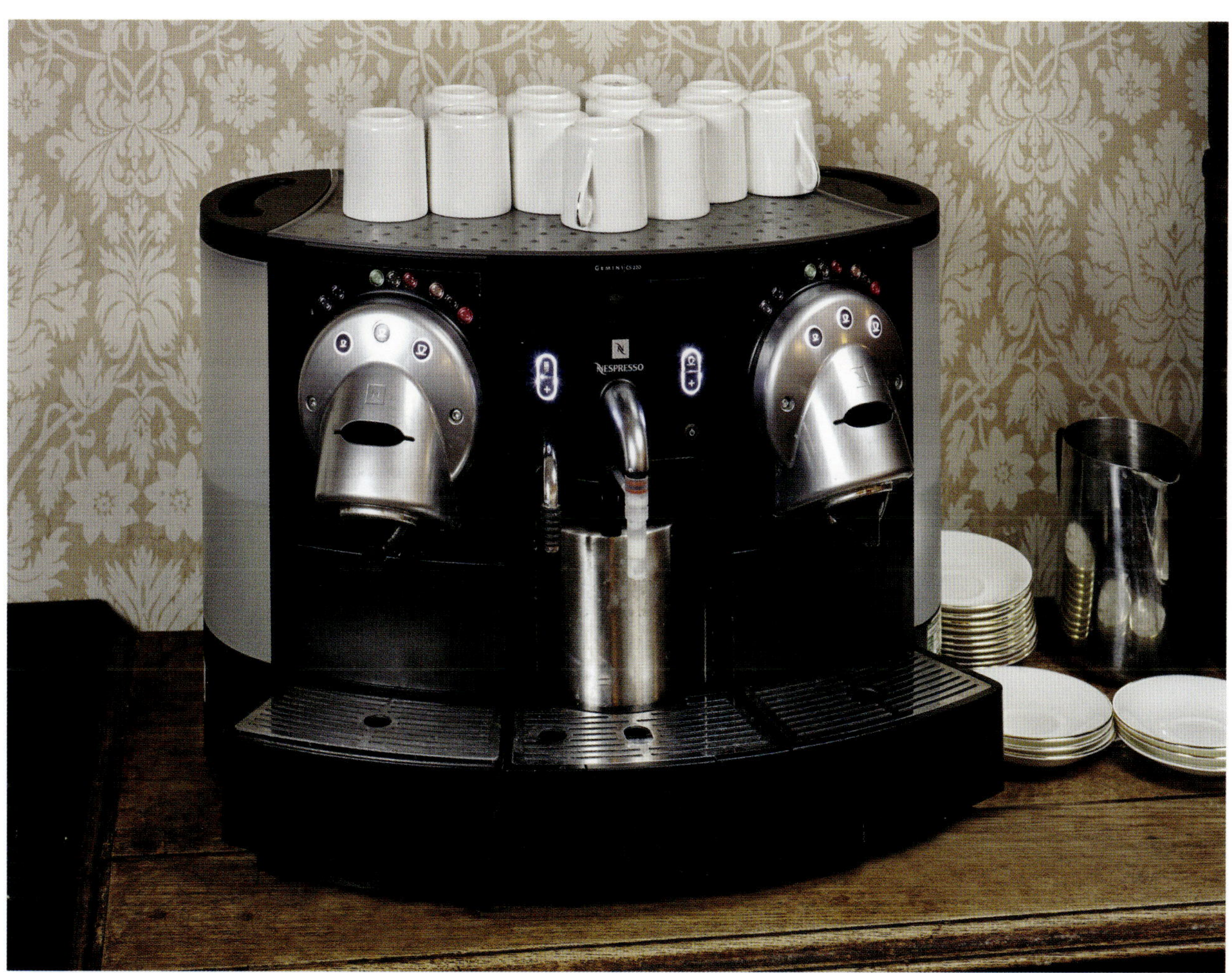

Bar and terrace

In 2007 the *Cherwell* newspaper singled out Somerville's bar for its bright red walls, its murals of the seven deadly sins and 'its very own cocktail, the "stone cold Jane Austen" – a sickly sweet mix including cider and Southern Comfort'. Somerville's 2014 student guide ('Welcome to the Ville') proclaimed its signature cocktail 'a truly authentic Somerville experience'. The bar has since moved to a new bright, light space next to the terrace. Café by day and bar by night, it offers a fine view over the college gardens as well as a place to meet friends or put the finishing touches to an essay. The current status of the 'stone cold Jane Austen' is not known.

'Welcome to the Ville'

2014 Somerville student guide

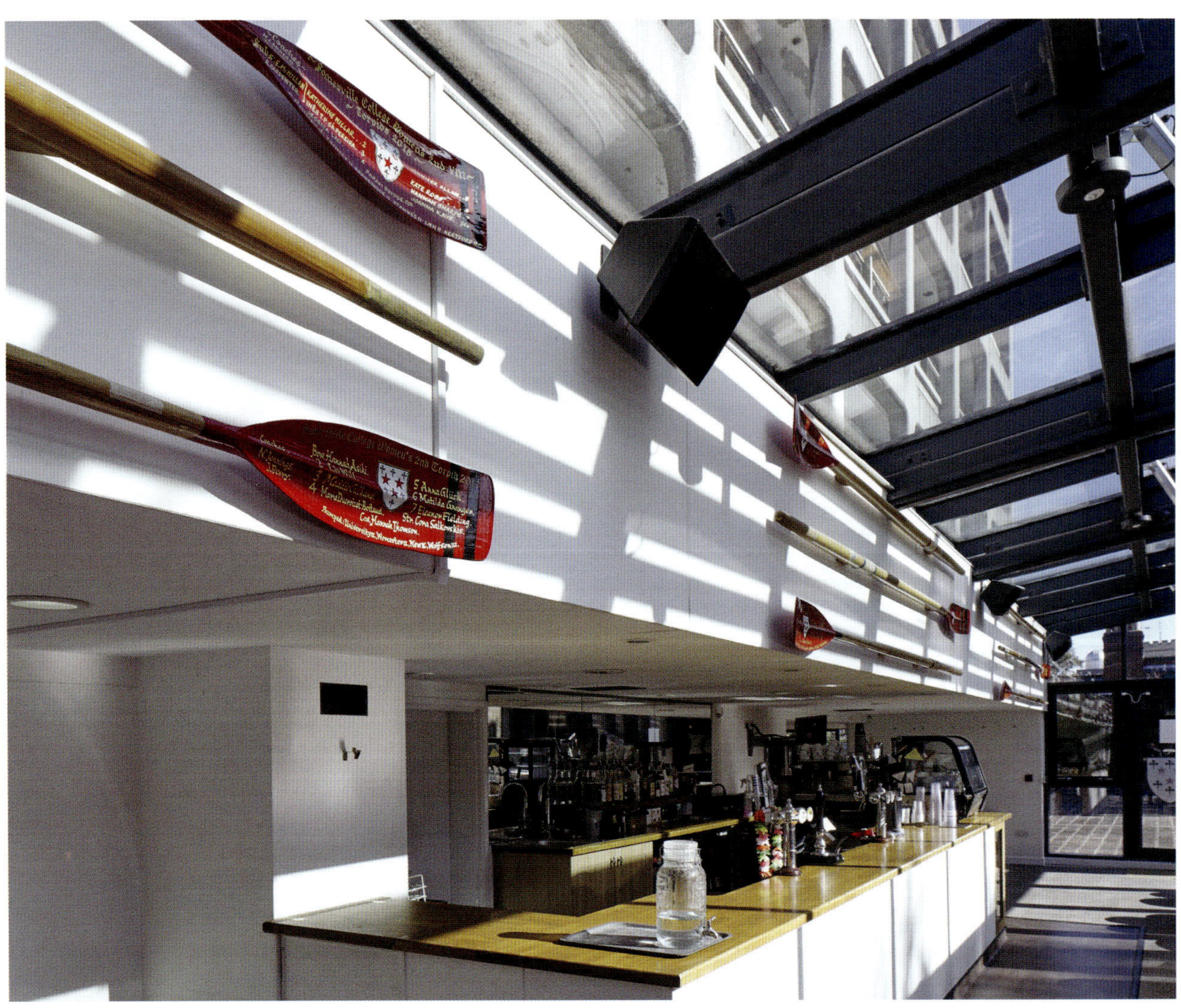

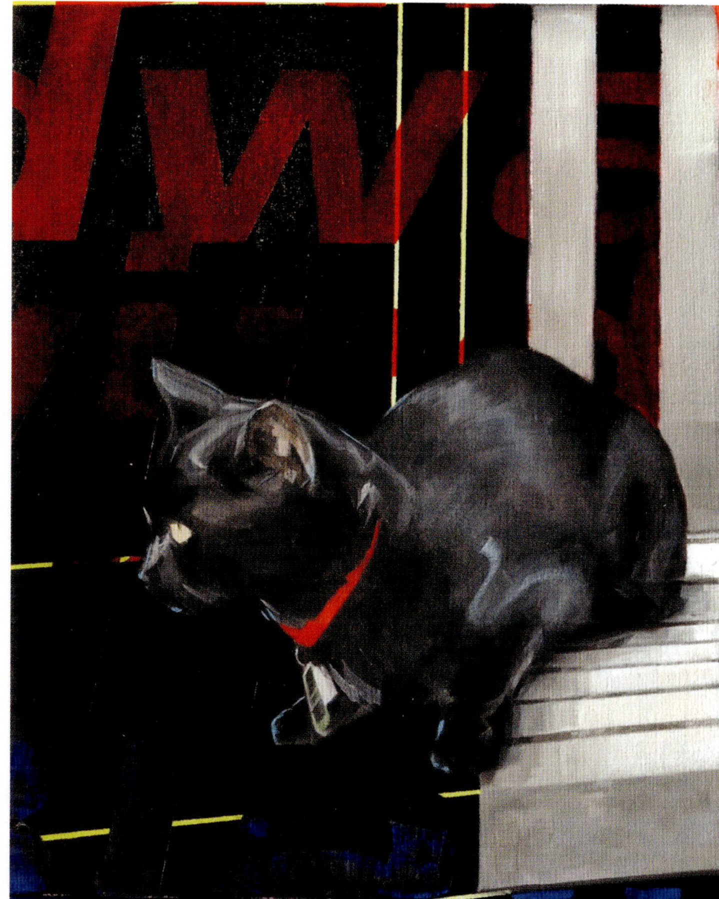

118
Pogo the cat

Cats and Somerville have a long-standing connection, and there is a fair chance (given his ego) that the college's most famous recent feline thought he, and not his owner, was running the place. After all, he even managed to get into the Principalian portrait (which is why he counts, just, as an object). Pogo, beloved pet of Somerville's tenth Principal, Dame Fiona Caldicott, has now been immortalised in literature.

The 2006 children's fantasy novel by Somervillian Matthew Skelton, *Endymion Spring*, begins in St Jerome's College, a version of Somerville whose library houses Mephistopheles the cat. Pogo continued to receive good levels of service on leaving the college (including a sardine with which to celebrate his twentieth birthday). At a 2018 Gaudy, the mere mention of Pogo's name prompted a standing ovation.

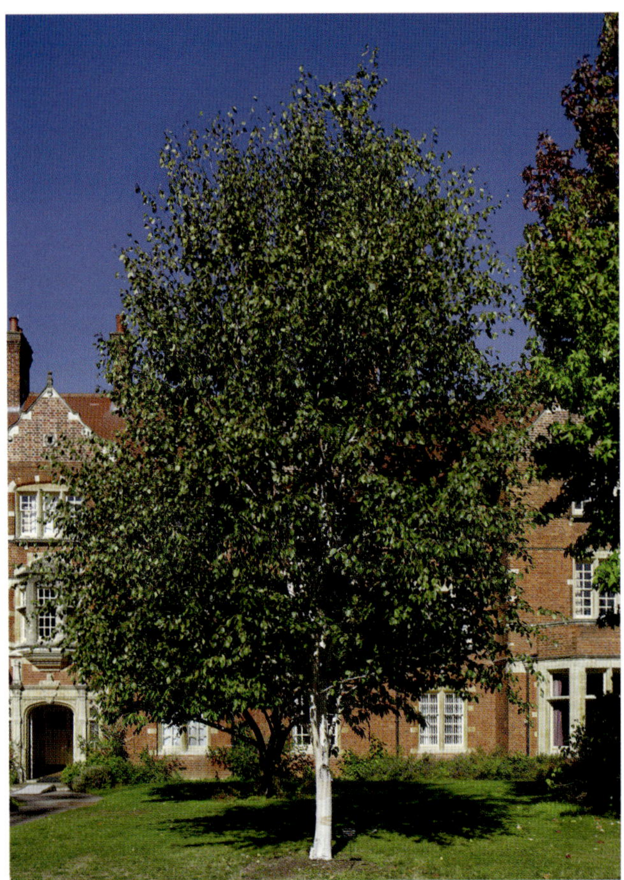
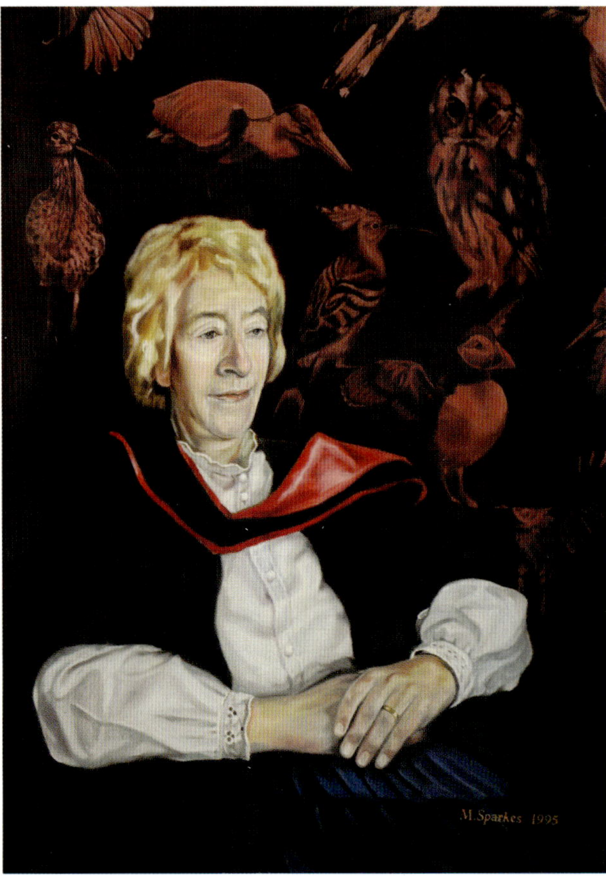

119
Birch tree

Somerville has a proud tradition of planting trees in memory of members of its community [121] or to mark particular occasions or events. This lovely birch (*Betula utilis var. jacquemontii*) was planted to commemorate the life of Nan Dunbar (1928–2005), Fellow and Tutor in Classics at Somerville for thirty years from 1965. The choice of a tree to mark her life was especially apt, as her work on Aristophanes' *Birds* led her to become an expert on matters ornithological as well as classical. Her edition of the play, which came out in the year that she retired from her post at Somerville, dealt with 150 species of birds (twice the number in the play itself) and constituted, among other things, an enormous advance on previous studies on Greek birds.

120
Book of Hours

This manuscript (given to Somerville as MS 1) dates from the middle of the fifteenth century and is likely to have been produced in Bruges, possibly for the use of the Priory of Wenlock in Shropshire. It is a small Book of Hours containing Latin prayers and Psalms. Designed to be held in the hand, it would have been intended for use in personal devotion. Such Books of Hours were expensive to produce and would have been owned by religious communities or by wealthy, educated members of the laity. They were particularly popular among women, for whom they formed an important part of a daily intercessory routine. This image, one of 14 in the manuscript as a whole, is found on folio 22 verso. It marks the beginning of the Hours of the Holy Spirit, which is a series of devotions focusing on the attributes and activities of the Paraclete. The floral border frames an image of the Virgin Mary, clothed in blue, seated in the middle of a spacious room at Pentecost. With an open book on her lap and a right hand raised in instruction, she can be observed teaching the apostles, who sit at her feet in rapt attention.

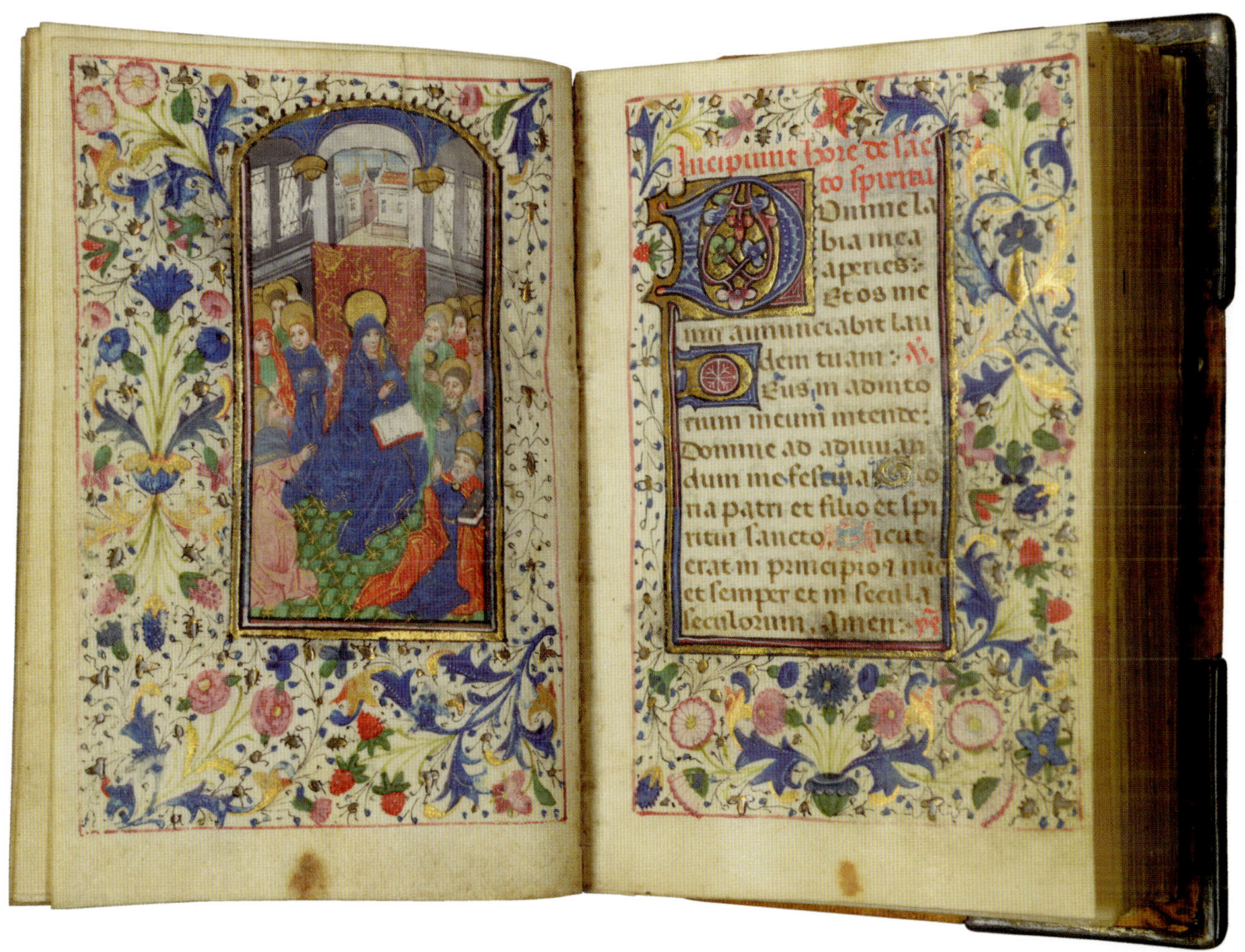

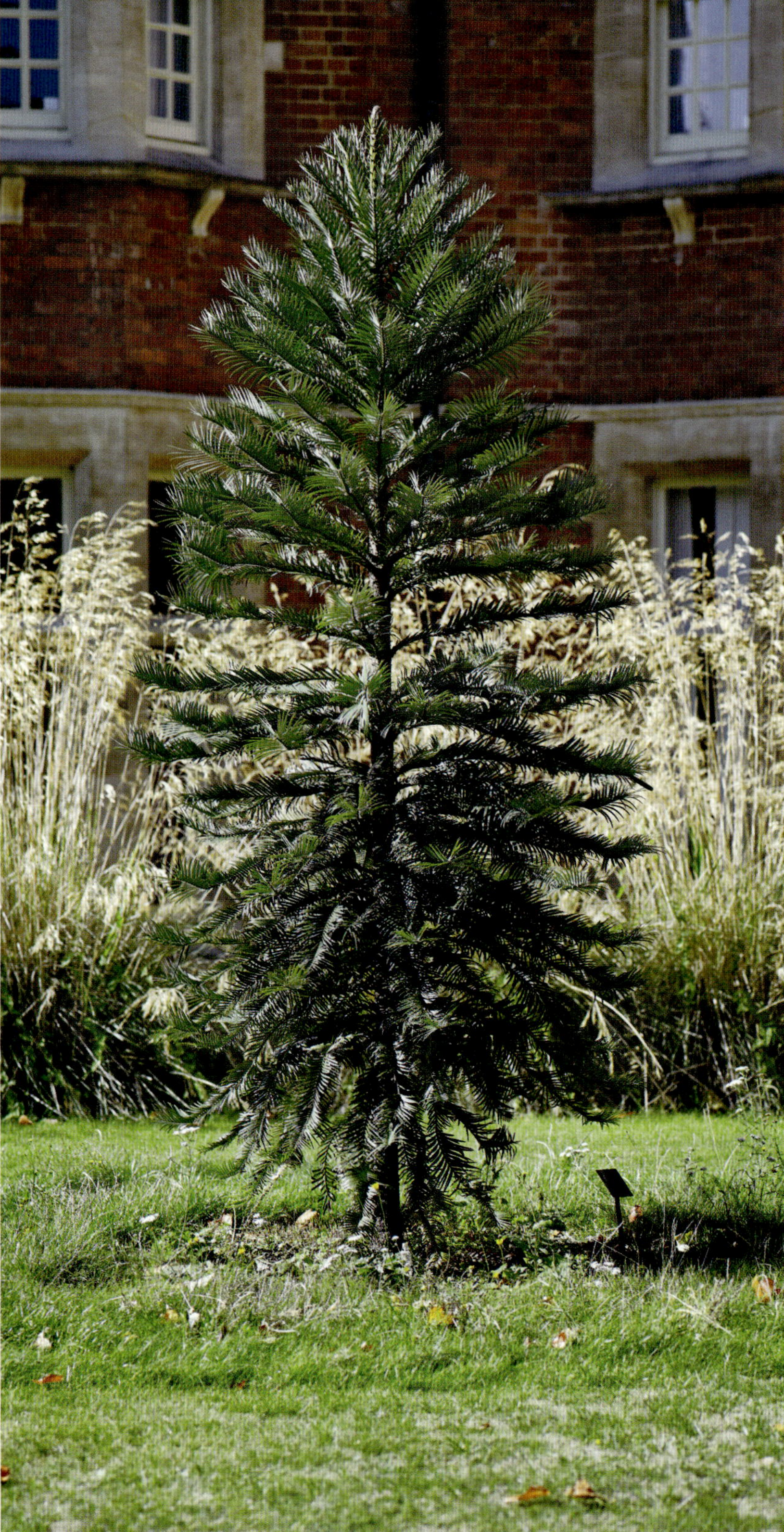

121

Wollemi pine tree

Colleges welcome their students and become a backdrop to their intellectual and personal development over the course of their studies, before they then graduate, ready for the next stage of their lives. Or that is how it is supposed to be. Thankfully it is very rare for a student to die during their time at Somerville, but when it happens, it shakes the whole community, and the whole community has to find a way of trying to mark that loss. This rare species of pine was planted in memory of Jonathan Roberts, who came up to Somerville in 2010 to read History and was killed in a road accident in 2011. His memory lives on in Somerville in other ways, too. Jonathan's family set up the Jonathan Roberts Charitable Trust, which generously offers a 'Jonathan Bursary' to support a student at Somerville.

Margaret Monk and Geoffrey Dawes

They met at Oxford in 1936, graduated in 1939 and were married in 1941.

Margaret read Modern Languages (French) at Somerville and Geoffrey read Animal Physiology (medicine) at New College.

In 1947, Geoffrey was appointed Director of the Nuffield Institute for Medical Research, which then operated in the Tower of the Winds, now part of Green Templeton College. They lived in Oxford for the rest of their lives. Margaret worked during World War II in SOE at Bletchley. Later in life, she co-wrote two books, called 'Country Banks of England and Wales' and 'Women who made Money: women partners in private country banks 1752-1906'. Margaret and Geoffrey had four children. One daughter read PPE at Somerville, one son (who went to Trinity) married a Somervillian, and another son's wife did her MA at Somerville.

Named for her parents by Harriet Maunsell (née Dawes) 1962.

'They met at Oxford in 1936, graduated in 1939 and were married in 1941'

122
ROQ room plaque

Potentially confusing to new students, the habit of placing name plaques above rooms is about recognising support for the college. All colleges ask their old members for support, but the tradition of fundraising in the women's colleges has been especially important for their development and survival. What prompts alumni to give usually comes, at least in part, from a combination of happy memories and the understanding that a Somerville education has given them something enormously important. Sometimes alumni give to 'name' the room they themselves occupied. Here, Somervillian Harriet Maunsell (Dawes) has funded a new room to commemorate her mother (Margaret Dawes (Monk) [1918–2012], who was also a Somervillian) and to tell the story of how her parents met. Somerville's Director of Development, Sara Kalim, remembers taking a guest to view the name plaques in the new ROQ (Radcliffe Observatory Quarter) building, only to encounter a student tumbling out of the door to one of the rooms. 'My mates and I look at those plaques every day', he said, 'and we talk about what we will write on our own plaques in the future.' For Kalim, the plaques serve as 'a reminder for our students that someone before them gave for them'.

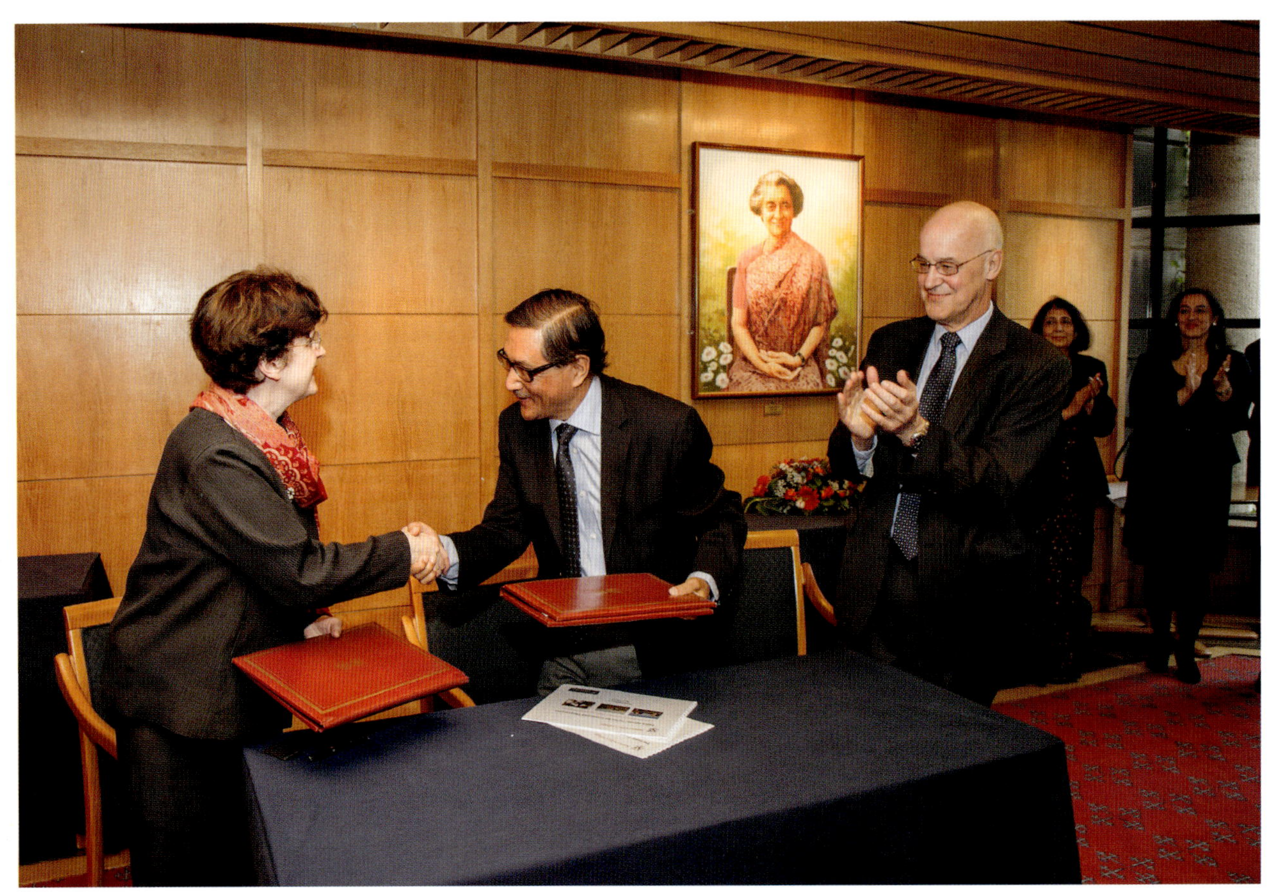

123
Indian Government
Scholarship contract

Somerville's connections with India run deep, and they are long-standing. In 1889, the college welcomed Cornelia Sorabji, the first Indian woman to study at any British university [24]. The first Prime Minister Somerville produced was India's first woman Prime Minister, Indira Gandhi [109]. In the twenty-first century Somerville moved to recognise its connection to India more formally. As a result of a generous grant of £3 million from the Ministry of Human Resource Development in India, matched by Somerville and the University of Oxford, five permanently endowed scholarships were established at Somerville in 2013, providing funding for talented Indian graduate students at Oxford. At a ceremony with then Principal, Alice Prochaska, and Oxford Vice-Chancellor, Andrew Hamilton, Mr Ashok Thakur, Higher Education Minister, signed the contract on behalf of the Indian government. Somerville is now home to the Oxford India Centre for Sustainable Development (OICSD), a multidisciplinary research institute that aims to develop future leaders in India and to translate academic research into practical schemes to support sustainable nutrition, the environment and health. In 2016 the Cornelia Sorabji Scholarship in Law was launched at the OICSD and Somerville, and this has now been joined by the HAS Advocates Scholarship and the Ratanshaw Bomanji Zaiwalla Scholarship, both also for Indian students of Law.

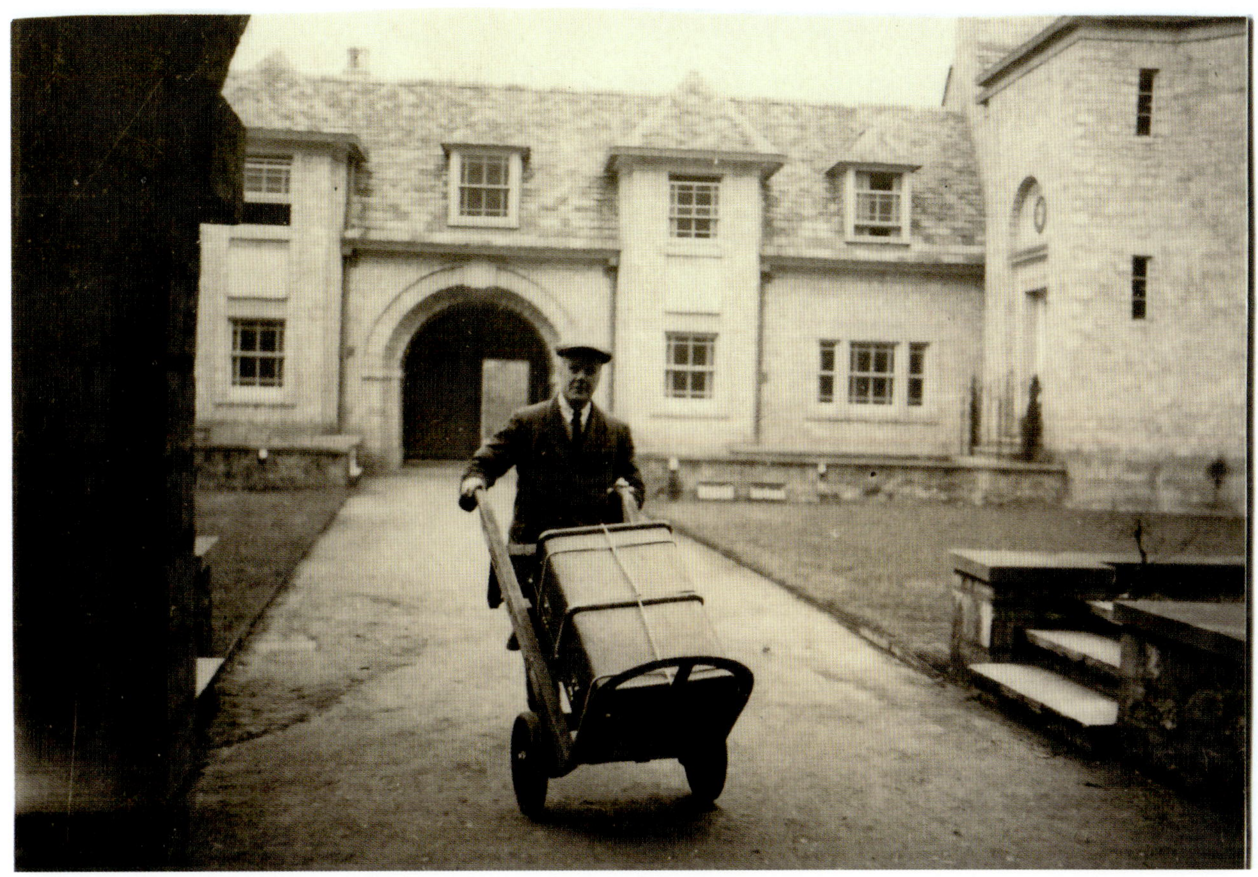

124

Lodge

In colleges, all roads lead to, and from, the lodge. And of course it's far more than directing the traffic: without the lodge, the college would simply grind to a halt. Students, fellows, conference guests and visitors stream through, day and night. Add to that that the lodge staff are running a post office, a telephone exchange and a system of keys and access cards that would give Langley a run for its money, and you begin to have a sense of the importance of this operation. Somervillians know

precisely the feeling you get when you enter the lodge, whatever kind of day you've had in labs or the library, or even if you've been away from college for years: it's that wave of relief when you realise that someone has got it all under control. There is no problem that cannot be solved by the lodge, and it has always been so: this postcard shows Walter Payne, College Porter at the time when the current lodge was opened as part of the East Quadrangle [81].

*'In general terms,
we direct the traffic'*

Agnieszka Rzad, Deputy Lodge Manager

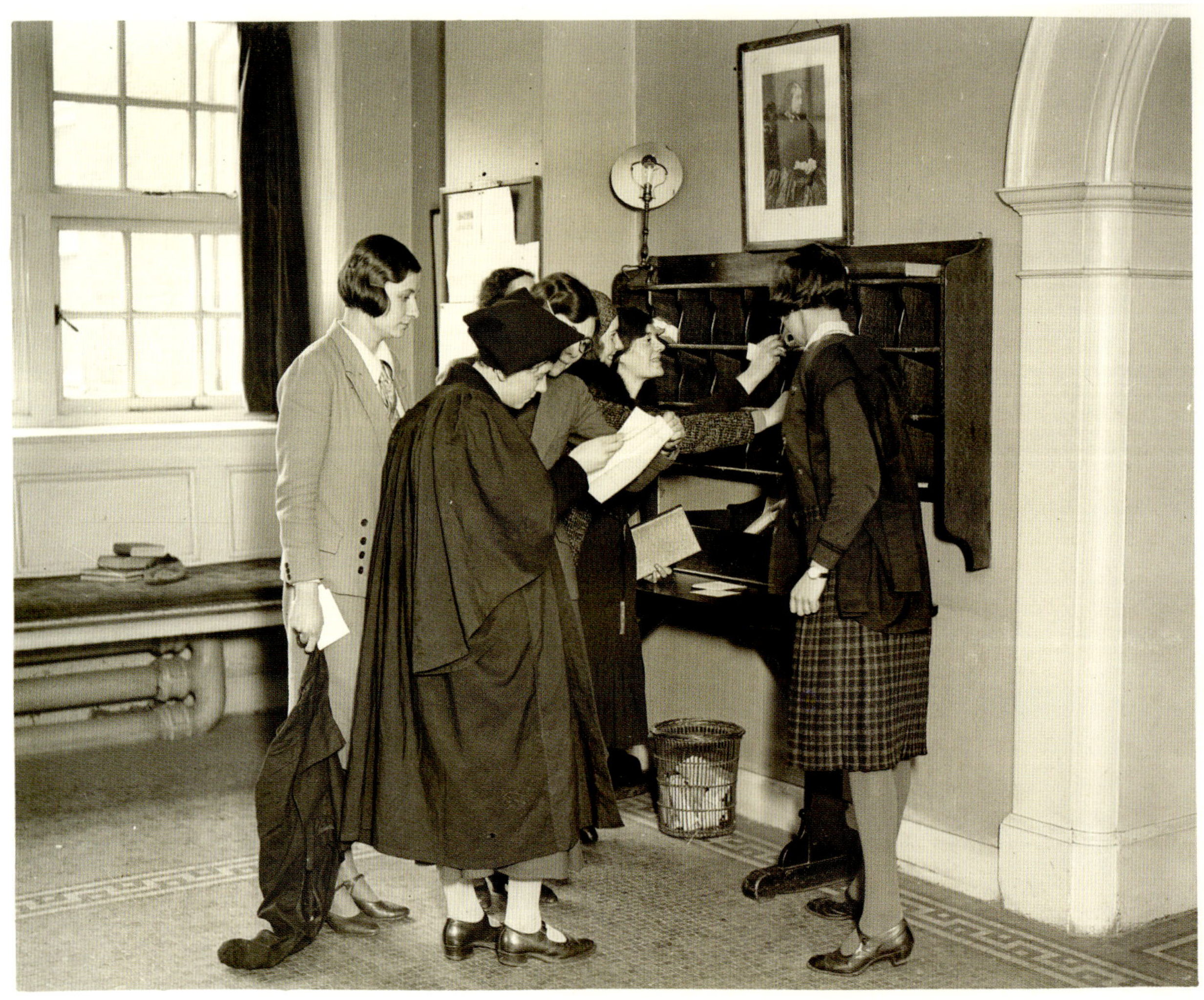

125
Pigeonholes

Pigeonholes were originally just that: small compartments in a pigeon loft or 'cote' where the birds could rest. The word has existed since Elizabethan times. By the late eighteenth century it had come to refer to the slots in wooden cabinets that were used to file papers. Pigeonholes in this sense play a very large role in Oxford life. Your feelings about them change according to the role you have. As a student you long for your pigeonhole to have something in it, and you might find yourself sidling up to the lodge or the mail room several times, hoping that the more you look, the more likely there is to be something. To come home to college after a day in the lab or the library and find an empty pigeonhole is not cheering. If you're a fellow or tutor, then an empty pigeonhole is a thing to be desired. Essays and committee papers are important, of course, but every time a new piece of paper lands in your pigeonhole, it's another thing to do. Email means that personal notes in pigeonholes are fewer and further between, but that doesn't mean that students check their pigeonholes much less assiduously. If anything, 'snail mail' has become more prized than ever, and certainly the abbreviated version of the noun ('pidge') is still going strong, as is its accompanying verb (as in, 'I'll pidge it to you').

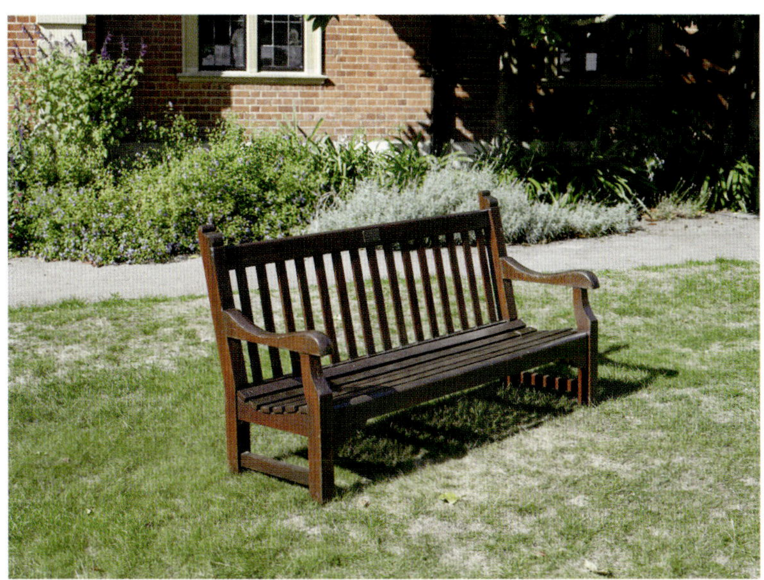

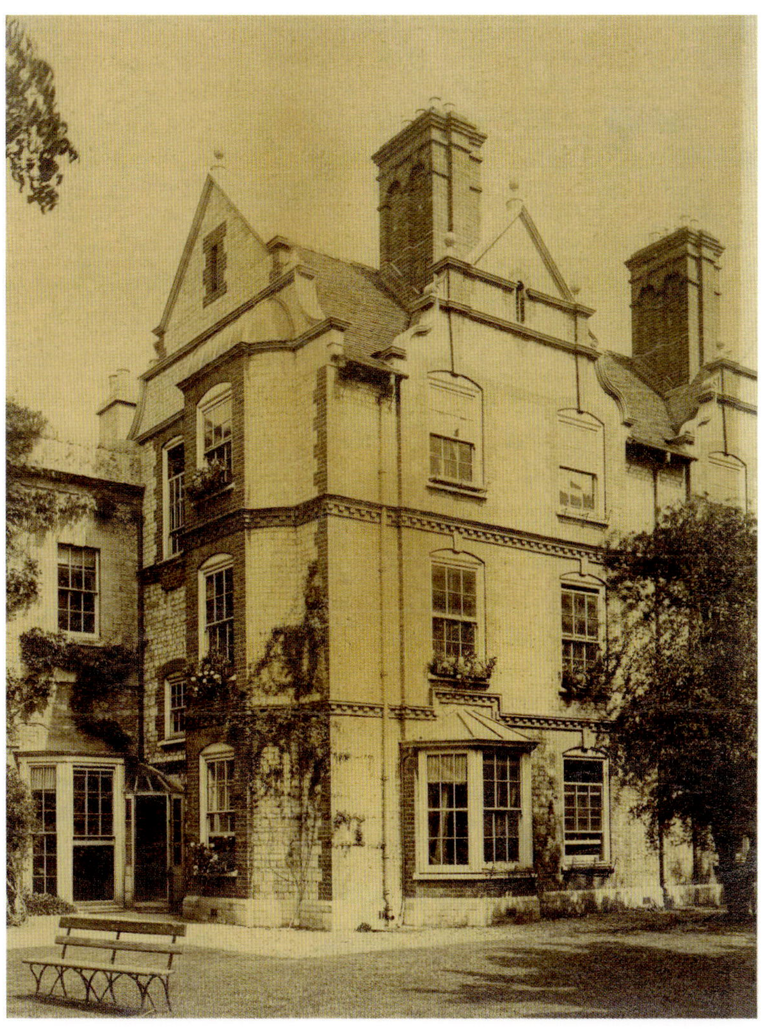

126
The missing object

You will find it in almost every other college in Oxford. And if you were to try to ignore it in those places, you might be accosted by a gang of furious porters. That would never happen in Somerville, where officious 'Do not walk on the grass' signs are notable by their absence. Nor is the college remotely bothered about whether its grass is graced only by fellows, or by those accompanied by fellows, or whoever else. The benches on the grass quad are a long-standing tradition, well used by all members of the college and anyone else who chooses to visit, unless, of course, they prefer just to sprawl on the grass itself.

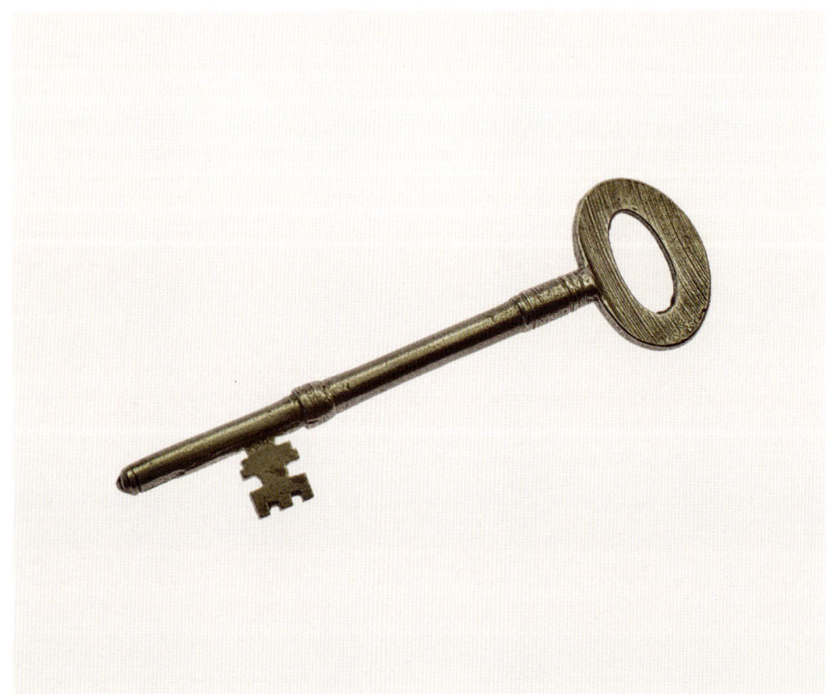

127
Key to the wine cellar

Probing journalists occasionally send Freedom of Information requests around all colleges demanding to know how much is spent on wine. The former women's colleges are probably something of a disappointment when responses are collated (after all, Somerville can hardly compete with some of its neighbouring colleges, one of which is rumoured to have cellars running all the way under St Giles).

This is a relatively new key, sadly not from the time in the 1930s when the college took a decision to start a 'cellar of wine'. Somerville's archives hold a wonderful letter from the husband of a Somervillian, recalling a gift of wine to the college when the cellar began, and offering a further gift in the 1950s: 'I am very touched by your letter with its very generous suggestion', wrote Principal Janet Vaughan in response.

'The Schloss Johannisberger that came to us in 1934 has become one of the College's traditions ... the Wine Steward is very excited at the prospect.' Things were occasionally more abstemious in the college's early days. Professor Gilbert Murray [60] and his wife were prominent supporters of the temperance movement, so that toasts in the college when he and Lady Murray visited were drunk in lemonade.

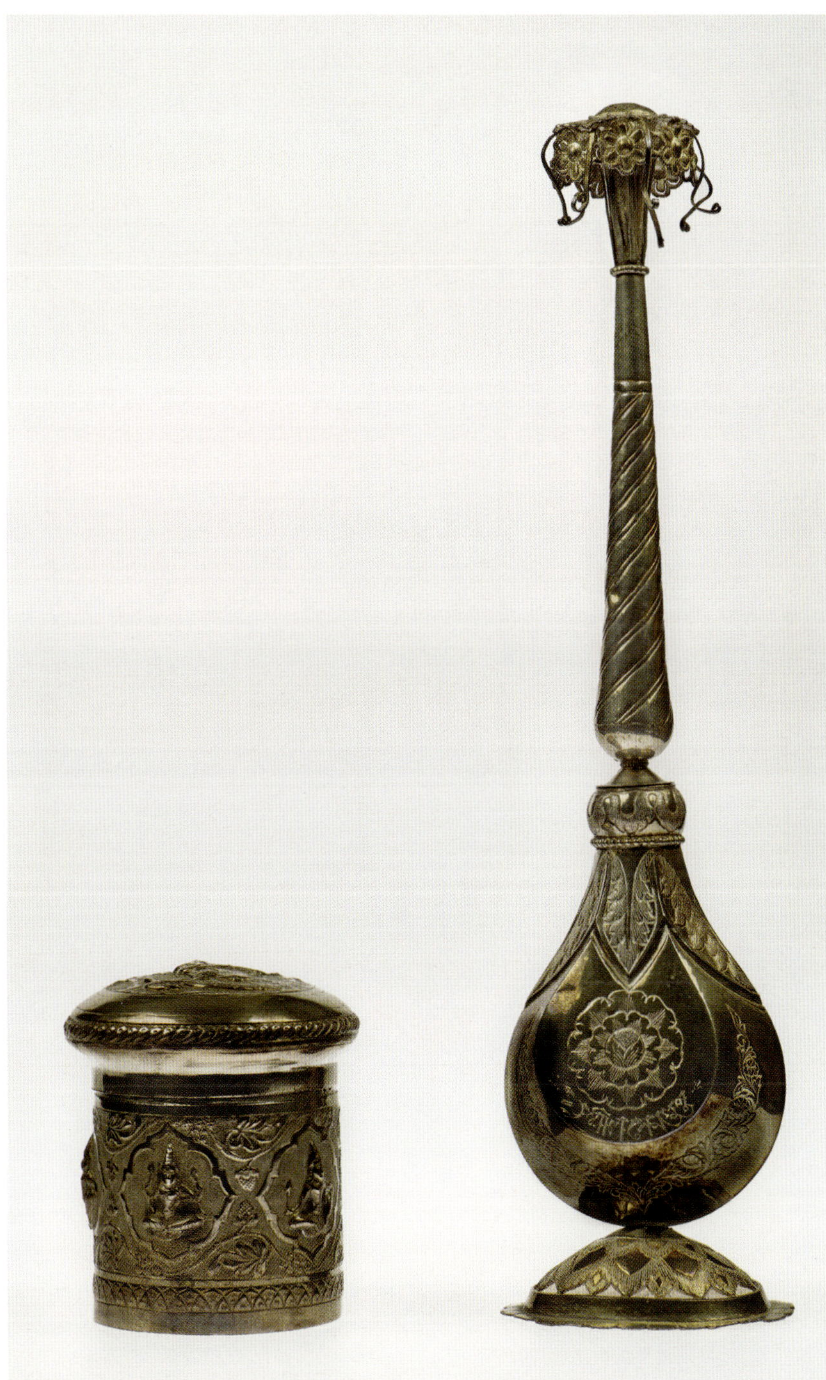

128
Indian silver

These ornate pieces were a gift to Somerville from Professor Aditi Lahiri, who became Professor of Linguistics at Oxford and a fellow of Somerville in 2007. In the tradition of Somerville's pioneers [24], Lahiri is the first Indian woman to hold a Statutory Chair at Oxford. She remembers both pieces from her childhood: the box held her mother's scented body powder, while the taller piece (originally with a glass top) was a sprinkler that belonged to her grandmother. It stood on the large round marble table in the hall, and her mother mentioned that at an earlier time it had been used to spray guests lightly with rosewater as they arrived as a way of greeting. The museum catalogue for Harvard University (which holds a similar piece) notes that 'the tradition of using rosewater came to Mughal India from Iran where, in the festival of Ab Pashan, rosewater was sprinkled to invoke the memory of rainfall, which would put an end to famine'.

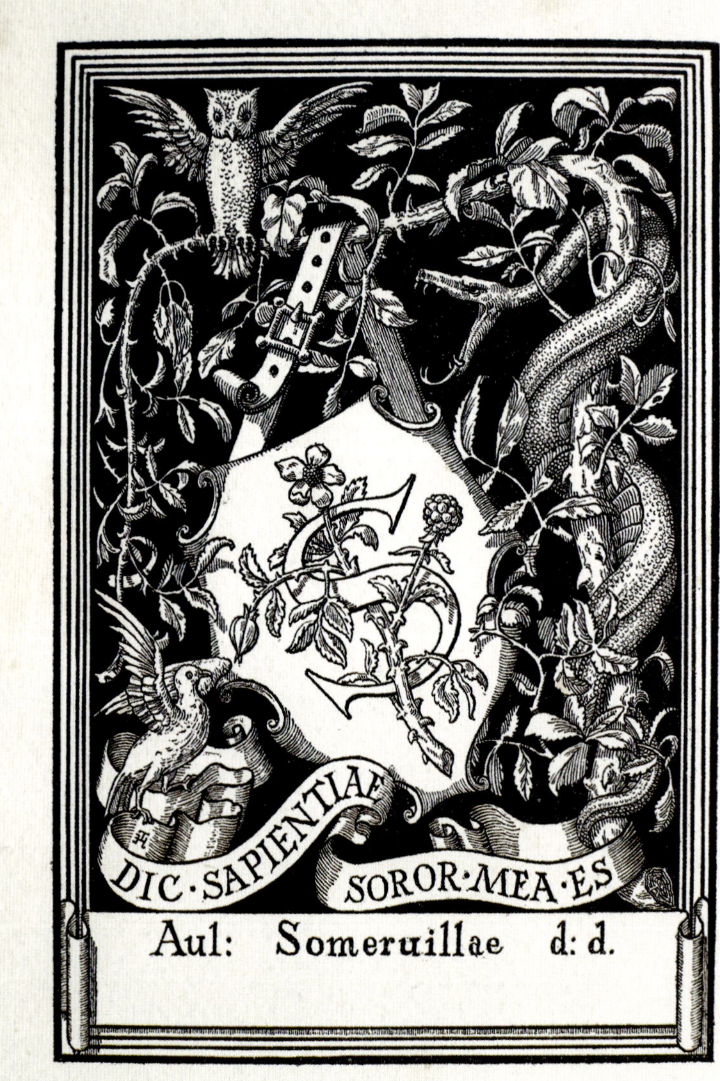

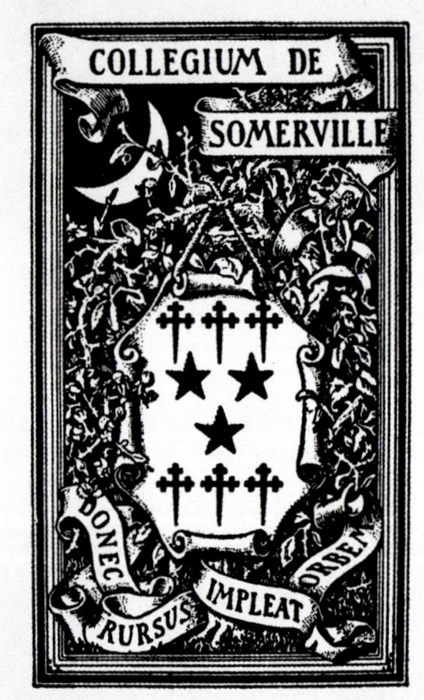

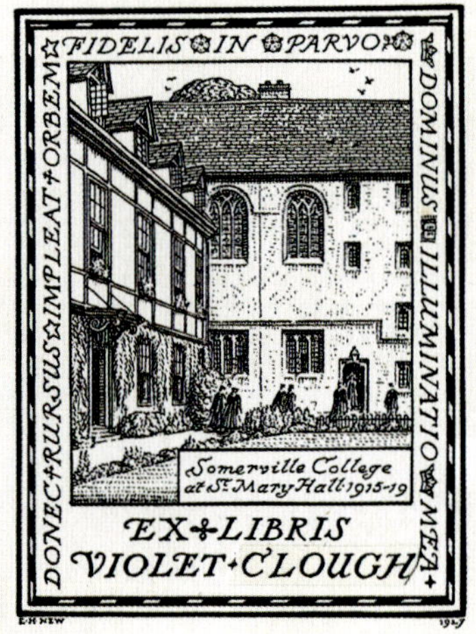

'Say to wisdom: you are my sister'

129
Bookplates

Bookplates are one of the many ways in which Somerville has expressed itself creatively over the decades: the college holds a range of designs, a number of which play fast and loose with the college's coat of arms and motto [8], or abandon them altogether. Here we see one of the earliest designs, noted in the gift book [10] for the year 1885/6 as a gift from Mrs Yorke Powell, with the motto chosen by her ('Design of Shield by Miss Howard', and engraved by Mr G.C. Harrison). The motto comes from the Book of Proverbs: 'Say to wisdom: you are my sister'. Next to it is the bookplate currently used in the library, with the correct motto and coat of arms firmly present, and an example of a student's own bookplate, made for Violet Clough (1895–1985) while Somerville was temporarily resident in St Mary Hall [58].

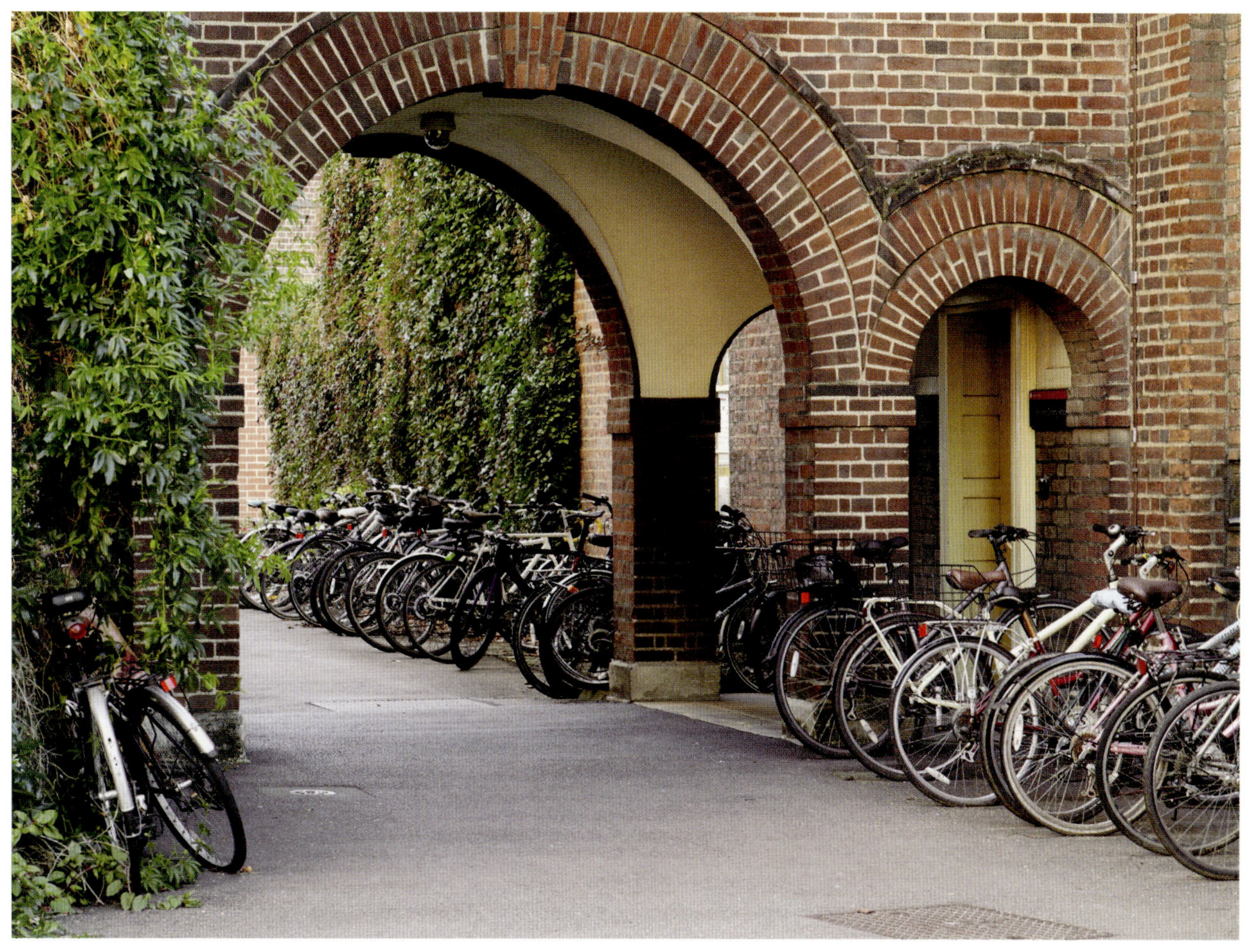

Dorothy L. Sayers, 'The Bicycle Secretary's Song', 1915

130
Bicycle racks

No matter how many racks there are, there are never quite enough when you arrive, late for a tutorial and desperate to lock your bike and get going. It was always so, with the result that then, as now, stray bikes were a subject of swift and merciless justice. In the 1915 Going Down Play, *Pied Pipings*, Dorothy L. Sayers [87] penned 'The Bicycle Secretary's Song' (to be sung, naturally, to the tune of 'I've got a little list' from *The Mikado*), which noted that abusers of the college's rules 'deserve to be interned'. She wrote from the heart, having herself held the position of Bicycle Secretary. Nowadays the punishment falls on the bicycles themselves, and they are cast somewhat in the role of farmed animals: old or unloved specimens are dealt with in the college's annual 'cull'.

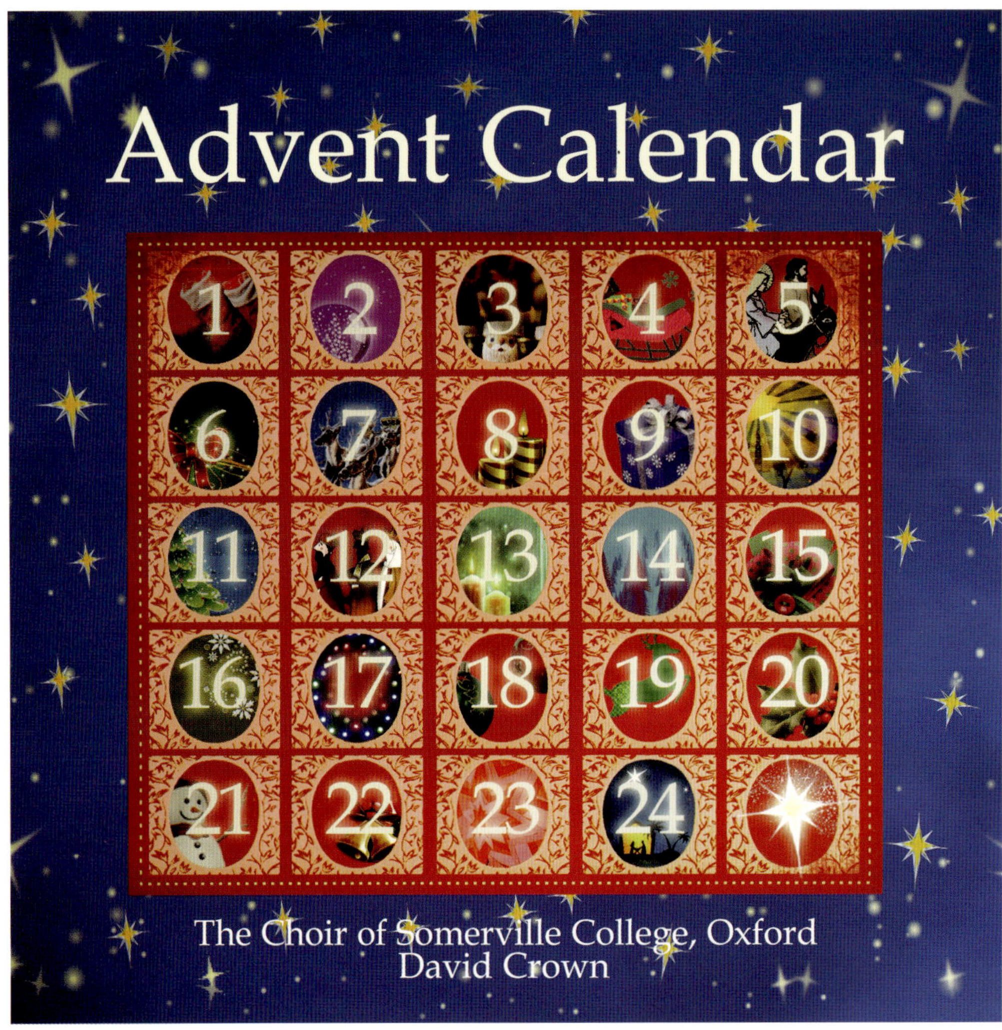

'Lusty performances'

BBC Music magazine, review of *Advent Calendar*

131
Choir CD

Somerville has a rich musical tradition. In the 1920s it began to outpace other colleges in both the number and quality of its concerts. 1935 saw the inauguration of the annual carol service, which still continues, and in 1964 the Somerville Musical Society hosted a recital at which both Julian Bream and Peter Pears performed. Distinguished musical alumni continue to play a part in the life of the college (soprano Emma Kirkby, who came up to Somerville in 1966 to read Literae Humaniores, is now an Honorary Fellow). Somerville's choir is now overseen by a professional Director of Chapel Music. It sings for the Sunday evening service in the college chapel during term time and offers concerts throughout the year, with Choral and Organ Scholarships available to students. It has also made a number of successful recordings, including this festive offering from 2013. In 2018 the choir became the first from an Oxford college to tour India, and used the college's online crowdfunding platform to raise money for the trip, which included outreach work with schools and NGOs.

View of the Observatory

Is a view strictly an object? It is if it has one of Oxford's most beautiful buildings in it. And this one is especially prized in Somerville because it was, for so long, obscured. Opened up with the construction of the ROQ (Radcliffe Observatory Quarter) buildings (West and East, in a nod to Somerville's first ever houses), the space here now shows the Tower of the Winds of the eighteenth-century Radcliffe Observatory (used as a dining and common room space by Green Templeton College, when it isn't appearing in episodes of *Endeavour*). Most Somervillians will recall the view before the ROQ site was developed: a rather run-down set of buildings forming the hospital complex of the original Radcliffe Infirmary. The site was bought by the University in 2003, the last of the hospital buildings closed in 2006, and grand plans were launched for the area. The plain brick wall of Somerville's library was not considered quite modern or lovely enough to act as the boundary to this ambitious new space, and Somerville took advantage of the situation (under the guiding hands of Principal Fiona Caldicott and Treasurer Helen Morton) to negotiate a 999-year lease for a long strip of land bordering the site and running east to west. Níall McLaughlin Architects offered a design of brick and timber, with up-to-the-minute sustainable technologies (so effective that the heating controls had to be turned down soon after the buildings were opened). And between the two buildings, a new gate for Somerville and a new, or at least renewed, view.

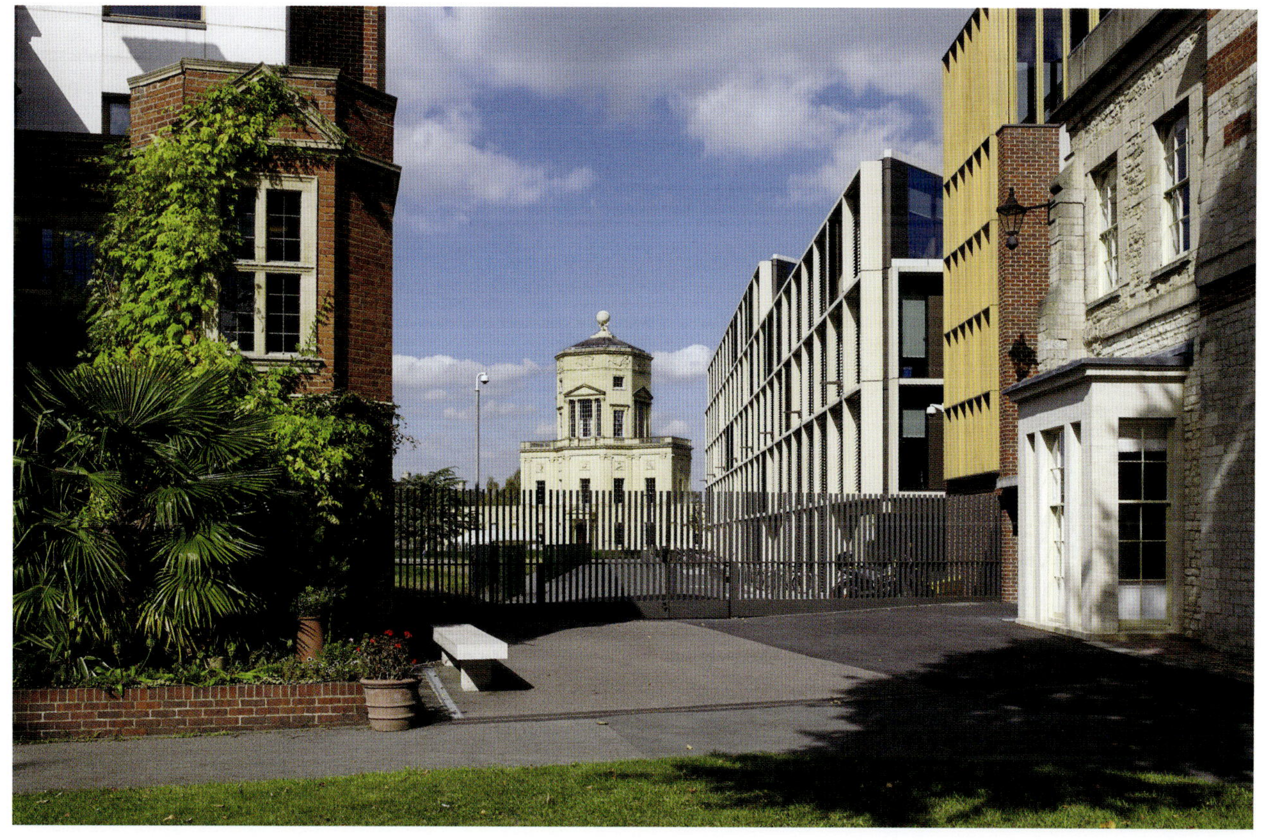

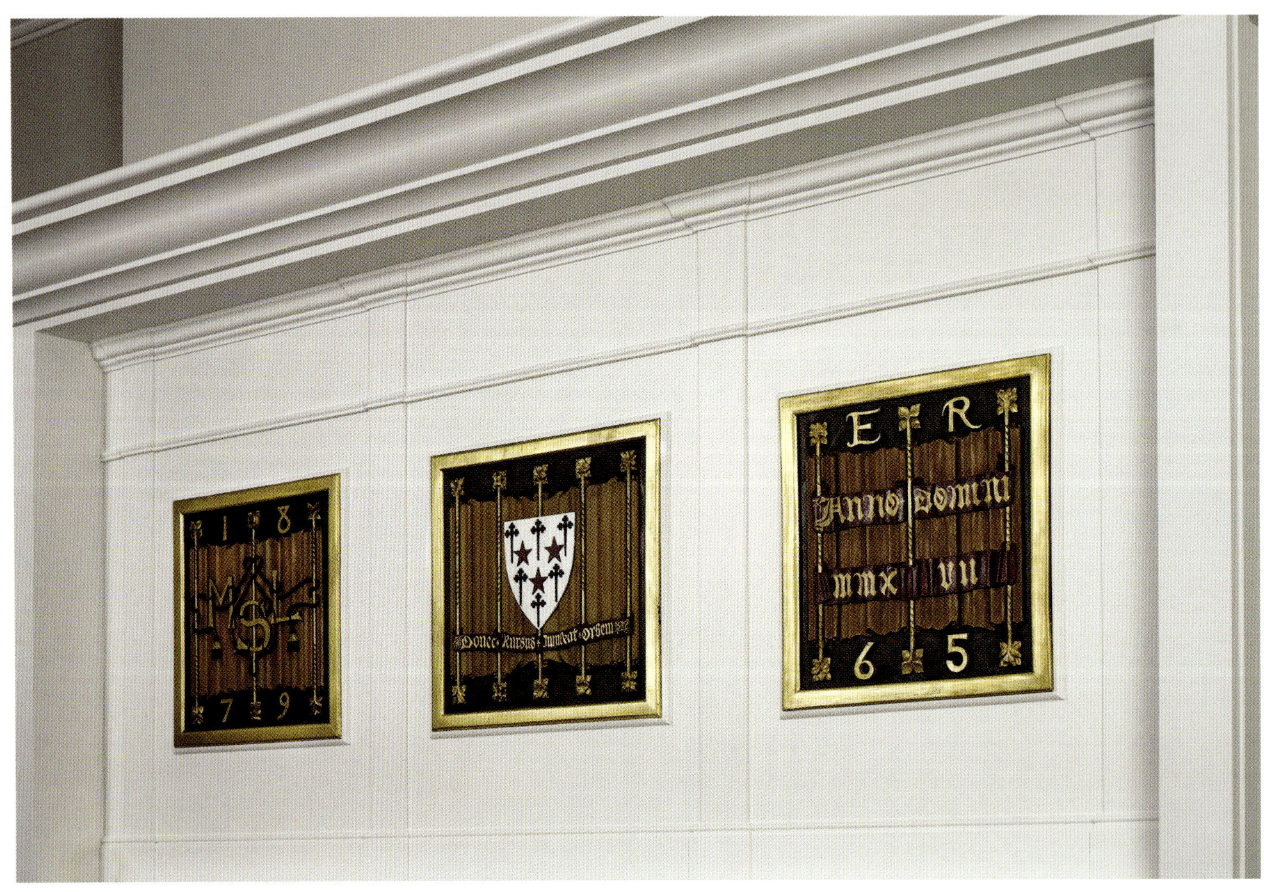

133
Gold-painted panels

At a distance you might mistake them for decorative ventilation grilles of some kind, carefully constructed to be in keeping with this light and elegantly furnished room. They were made for this room, which was at one time the college bar but for a much longer period was the JCR. No one is quite sure when two of the original panels were stolen. One of them later reappeared at the Lodge [124], handed back anonymously. A fit of conscience? We may never know, but fortunately the panel had suffered few ill effects, and it and its companions were restored. One of those we see here was made to replace the panel that is still missing. The set of three were then reinstalled when the room was refurbished and named for Mary Somerville in 2017 (following a generous bequest from Honorary Fellow Ruth Thompson [135]). The remaining missing panel would be welcomed back with open arms: anyone handing it in at the Lodge will be guaranteed their anonymity.

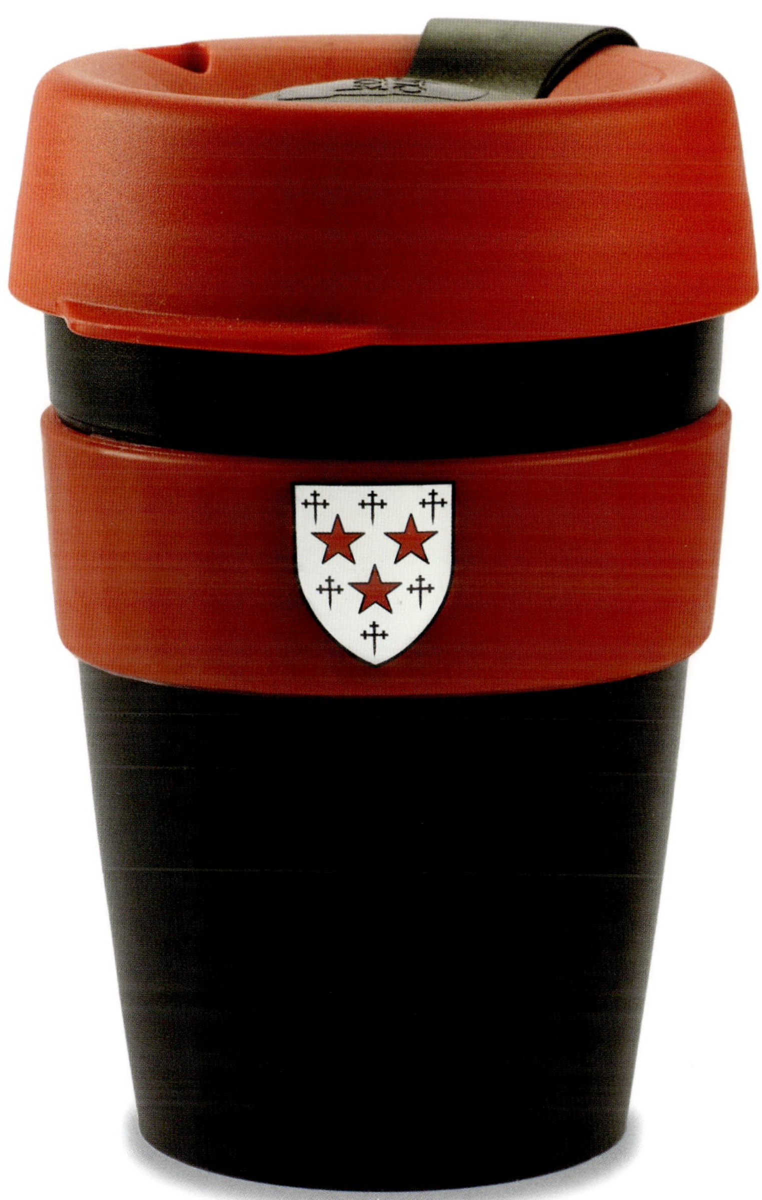

134
Keep cup

From silver teapots in the Edwardian
era to today's stimulant of choice, made
portable. Colleges offer a range of
souvenirs, from key rings to teddy bears
wearing gowns and mortarboards, but
the two things that are actually used by
students are the hoodie and the keep
cup: both vital weapons in the weekly
essay crisis. The college's first keep cup
was produced in 2017, by Somerville's
JCR, who consulted widely and took
great care to match the college colours
accurately (colour codes have become the
modern equivalent of heraldic language,
it seems [8]. For those who are interested,
Somerville's striking red translates to C17
M100 Y97 K7). The beauty of this object,
apart from its ability to keep your coffee
hot, is that it is permitted in the library.
Now there's no need to leave your desk
at all, unless you feel like standing for a
while [136].

135
Ruth Thompson Room

Named for an undergraduate who later became an Honorary Fellow, this room is used by students who want to work in groups, and is especially popular with scientists bringing their collective brainpower to bear on weekly problem sheets. Ruth Thompson (1953–2016) came up to Somerville in 1971 to read Modern History and went on to a distinguished career in the civil service, with a particular focus on education. She came back to college often, and was always eager to talk to students about their interests and experiences. Thompson supported the college generously, acknowledging the role it had played in her own life and saying that when it came to money, she trusted Somerville 'to do the right thing with it'. The room now holds books written by Somervillians (including works by fellows of the college, such as *The Long, Long Life of Trees* by Fiona Stafford). It is an impressive roll-call: Rose Macaulay, Lucy M. Boston, Dorothy L. Sayers [87], Vera Brittain [79], Margaret Kennedy [50], Winifred Holtby [69, 88], Penelope Fitzgerald, Iris Murdoch [105], Nina Bawden, A.S. Byatt, Victoria Glendinning, Margaret Forster, Hilary Spurling, Maggie Gee, Michèle Roberts, Matthew Skelton [118] and Frances Hardinge, to name only a selection. For the Booker Prize alone, Somervillians have been nominated 17 times, with three winners (Murdoch, Fitzgerald and Byatt). In 2018 Somervillian Daisy Johnson became the youngest author ever shortlisted for the Booker Prize, for *Everything Under*.

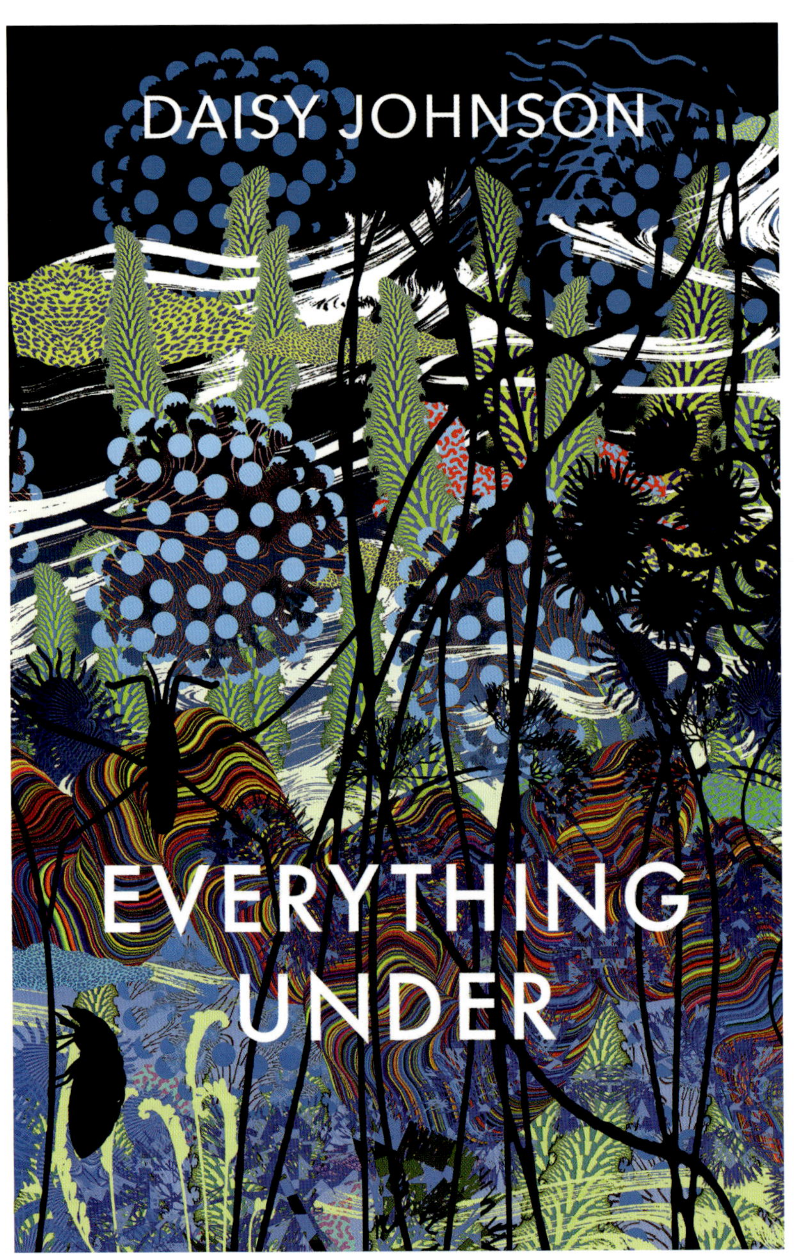

Dr Ruth Thompson (1953-2016) read Modern History at Somerville from 1971 to 1974. For more than 30 years she was a civil servant, her final post being Director General, Higher Education. In 2010 she was elected an Honorary Fellow of the College.

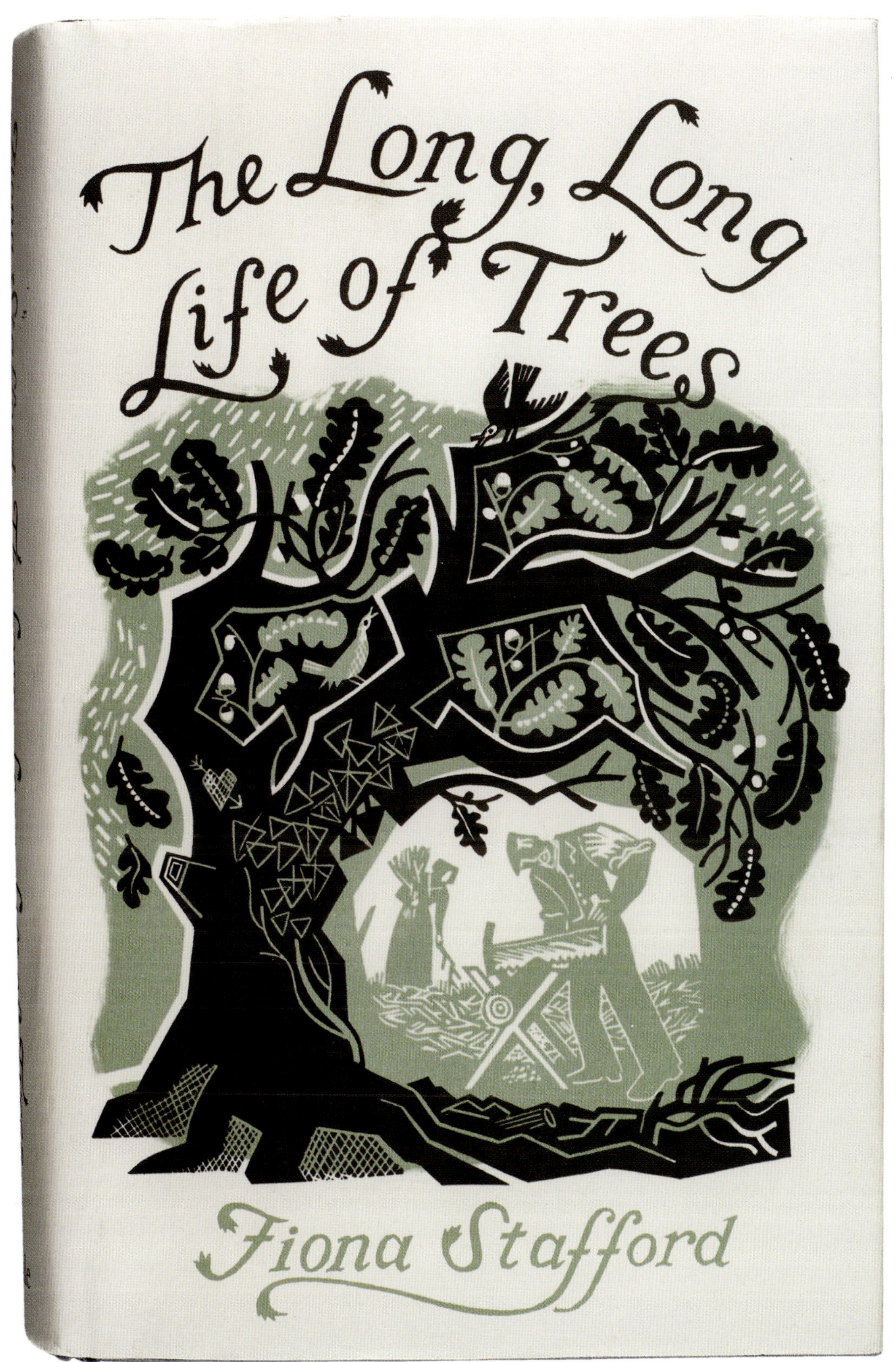

The Long, Long Life of Trees
Fiona Stafford

When the library opened at the start of the twentieth century [32], it was the first purpose-built library space in an Oxford women's college, and one of the first college libraries designed principally for use by students. It was, and remains, perfect for long periods of reading, with ample light, wide bays, and even pull-up easels [35]. Design moves on, and as more and more studies tell us that we should be standing and moving rather than sitting for too long, work can now be done in a healthier, upright posture. It's not one for a long run of study, perhaps, but it's the ideal place to take your laptop if you want a change of scene and to relieve your spine without losing vital intellectual momentum. This one arrived in 2017 after a student survey yielded a request for ergonomic intervention in the library.

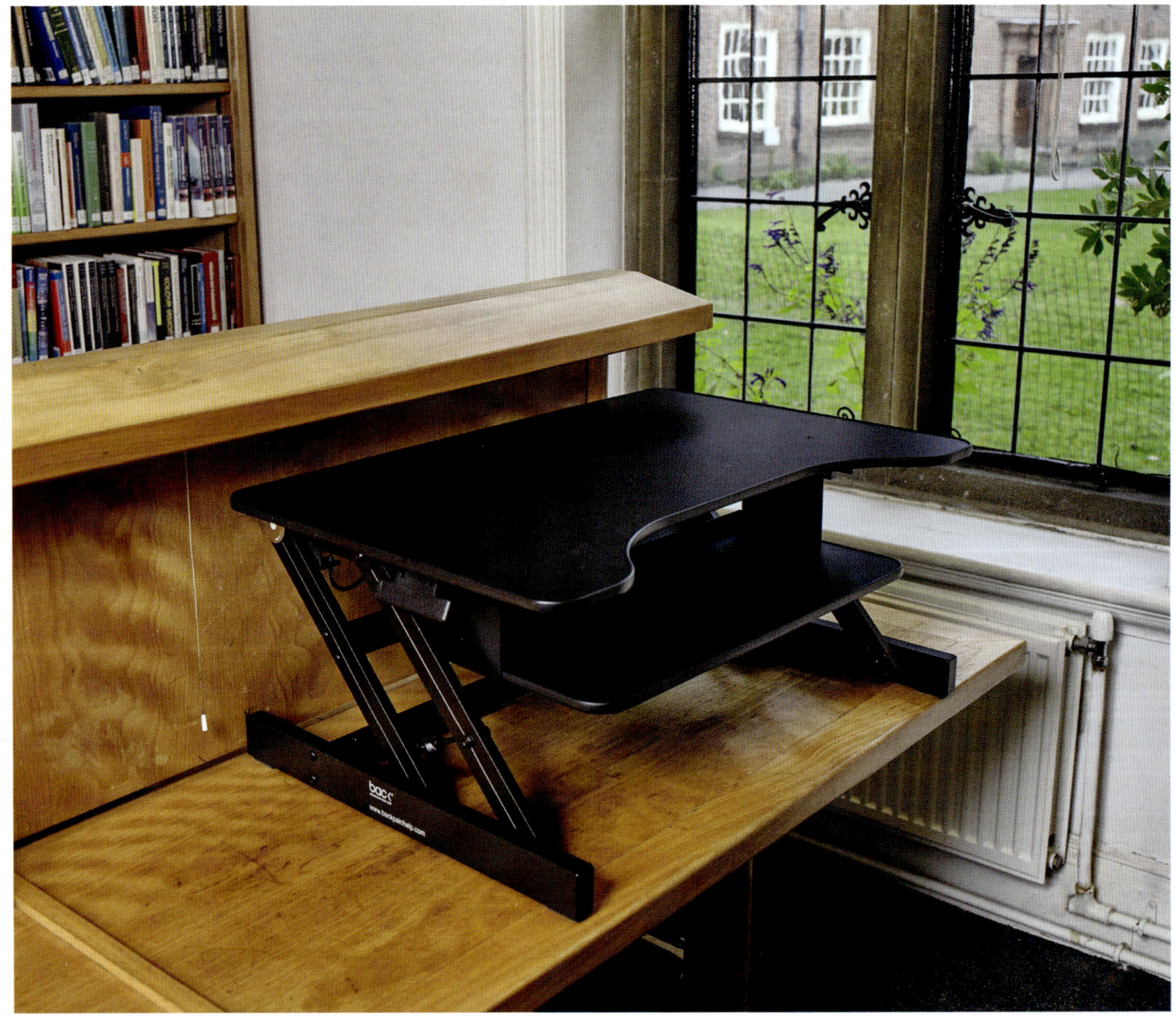

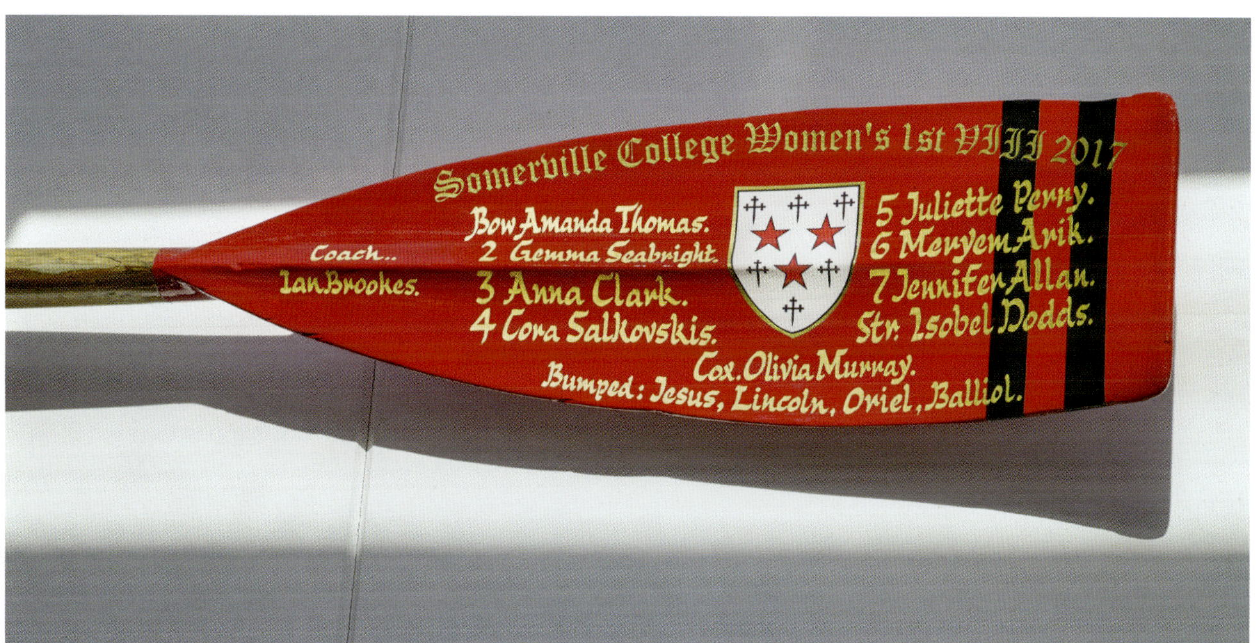

137
Blade in the bar

Does it seem odd to display monuments to physical fitness in a bar? Perhaps, but in Oxford, as elsewhere, sport and socialising are hardly strangers. Here, you'll find a record of the college's considerable successes on the river, but it's also worth noting that Somerville has made up its fair share of blue boats during its history. The 1965 boat must take the prize (though it lost out to Cambridge on the day), with Somervillians at bow, stroke and cox. It was the first year that women's rowing was recognised as a blues sport [30]. Somerville went on to be Head of the River eight times between 1980 and 1993.

The scale and the technology may have moved on from the 1908 dance [55], but the principle is very much the same: a chance to dance, and to celebrate, with fellow students. Now college balls are often collaborative ventures (not least to ensure financial success), and in 2019 Somerville again joined forces with Jesus College, this time for a Hollywood-themed ball. Publicity promised guests 'a taste of the glitz and glamour of this iconic era', and the logo, specially designed for the ball by Somerville student Sophie Kuang, draws on the theme of the golden age of Hollywood. And the title of the event? 'It's a Wonderful Life', of course!

'glitz and glamour'

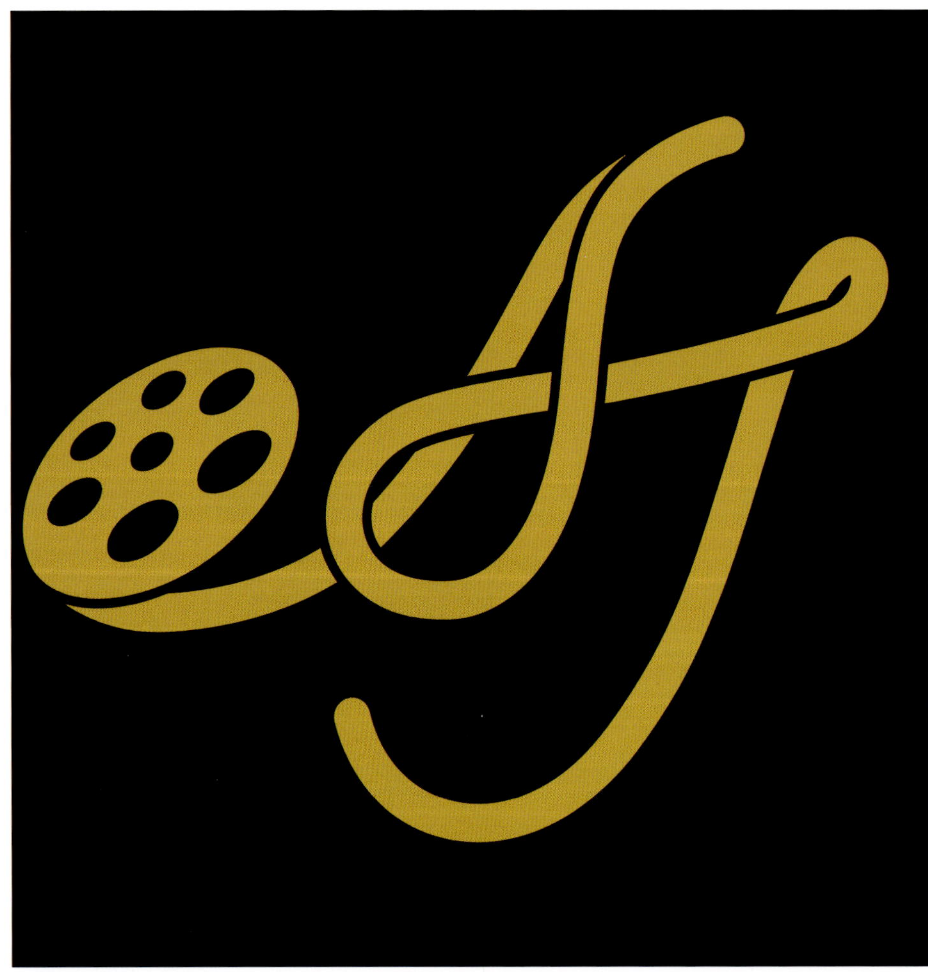

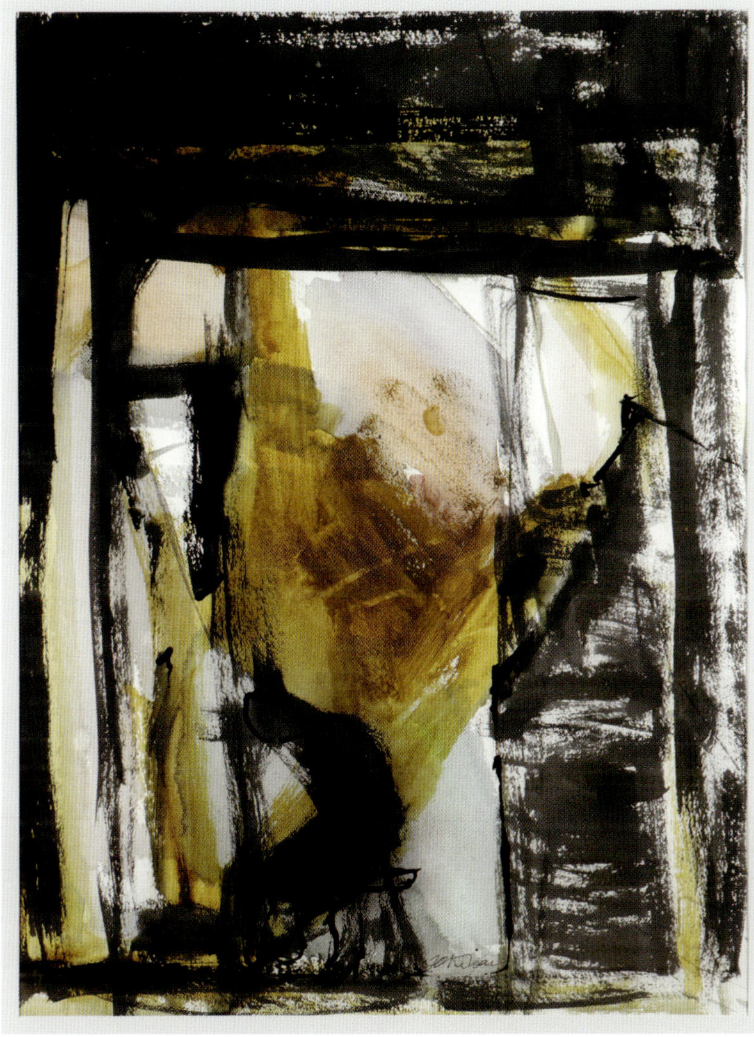

139
Janet Treloar,
The Fateful Meeting

Janet Quintrell Treloar was born in West Cornwall and studied at the Penzance School of Art before coming up to Somerville in 1958 to read Geography. As well as painting landscapes and still lifes, she finds inspiration in themes including 'The Romanesque Arch as a Language of Europe', the war sites of 'Russia's Hero Cities' and the poet Anna Akhmatova (1889–1966). In 2018 Treloar held an exhibition of her work at Wolfson College, focusing on those of her paintings dealing with the meeting in 1945 in Leningrad between Anna Akhmatova and Isaiah Berlin (1909–97). 'I visited the Akhmatova Museum', says Treloar, 'and read her life story and poetry, which has left an indelible impression on me. As the translator D.M. Thomas said, Akhmatova is "one of those few people who have given meaning and dignity to our terrible [twentieth] century".' *The Fateful Meeting* now hangs in the room of Somerville's Principal, Janet Royall.

'Akhmatova is one of my favourite poets', Royall says. 'She was an extraordinarily intelligent and resilient woman, who countered the worst excesses of Soviet brutality with a beauty and profundity of expression that takes my breath away. To find such a wonderful painting of her by a Somervillian is, I think, no coincidence. The qualities I have always admired in Akhmatova – brilliance and resilience – are those I have already seen in so many Somervillians as well.'

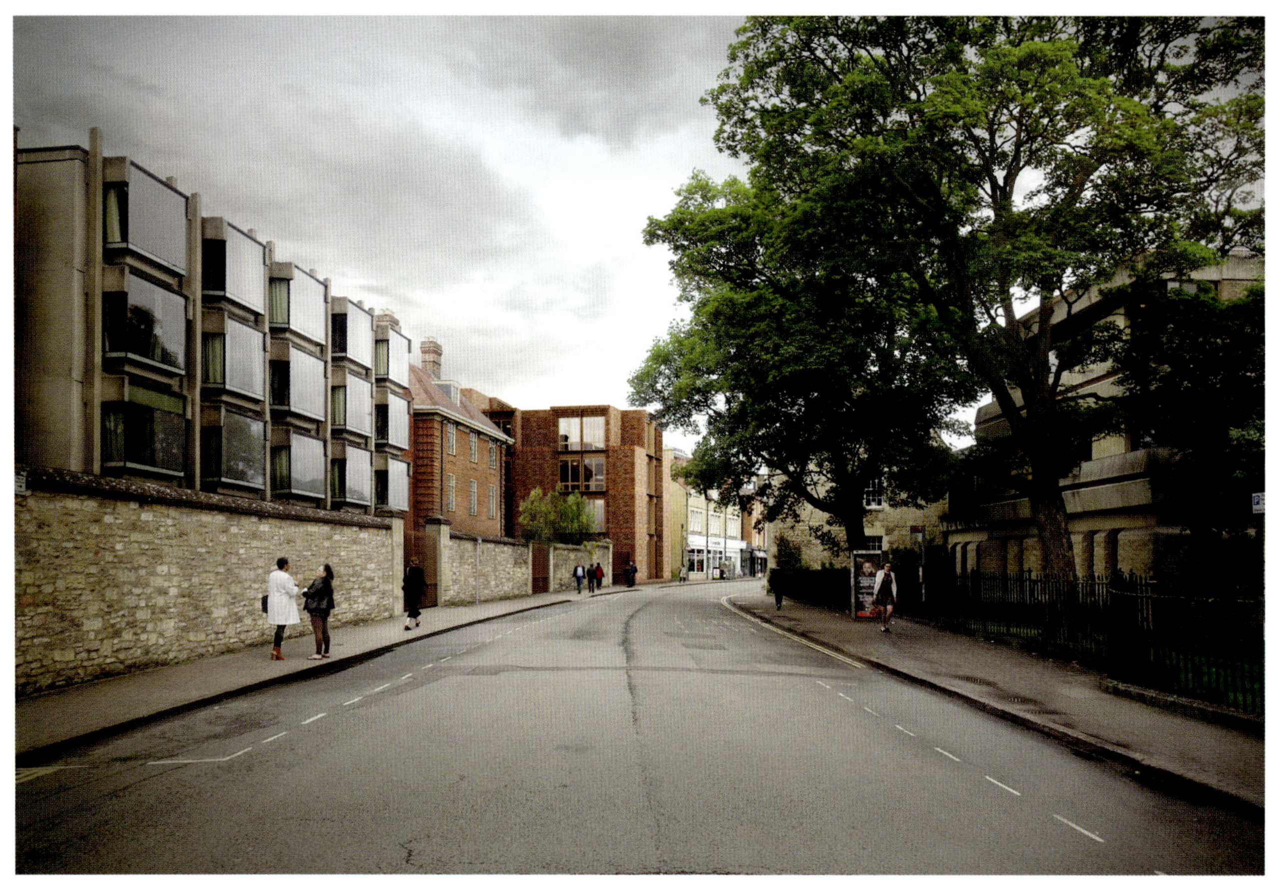

140
Catherine Hughes Building

We end with an object that is not quite complete at the time of going to press. Somerville is marking its 140th anniversary by honouring former Principal Catherine Hughes. How best to do it? Given Hughes's particular interest in student wellbeing, the college took the decision to construct a new block of accommodation behind Penrose. In the spirit of Somerville's foundation, the Catherine Hughes Building will allow the college to offer accommodation on site to all its undergraduates. Fronting onto Walton Street, the red-brick building picks up on the architectural styles that Somerville has used since it began. It will offer 68 en suite student rooms, a study area for graduate students and also a space for local community events. It is the next stage in the life of the Somerville family, and we hope that Hughes would have been proud of it.

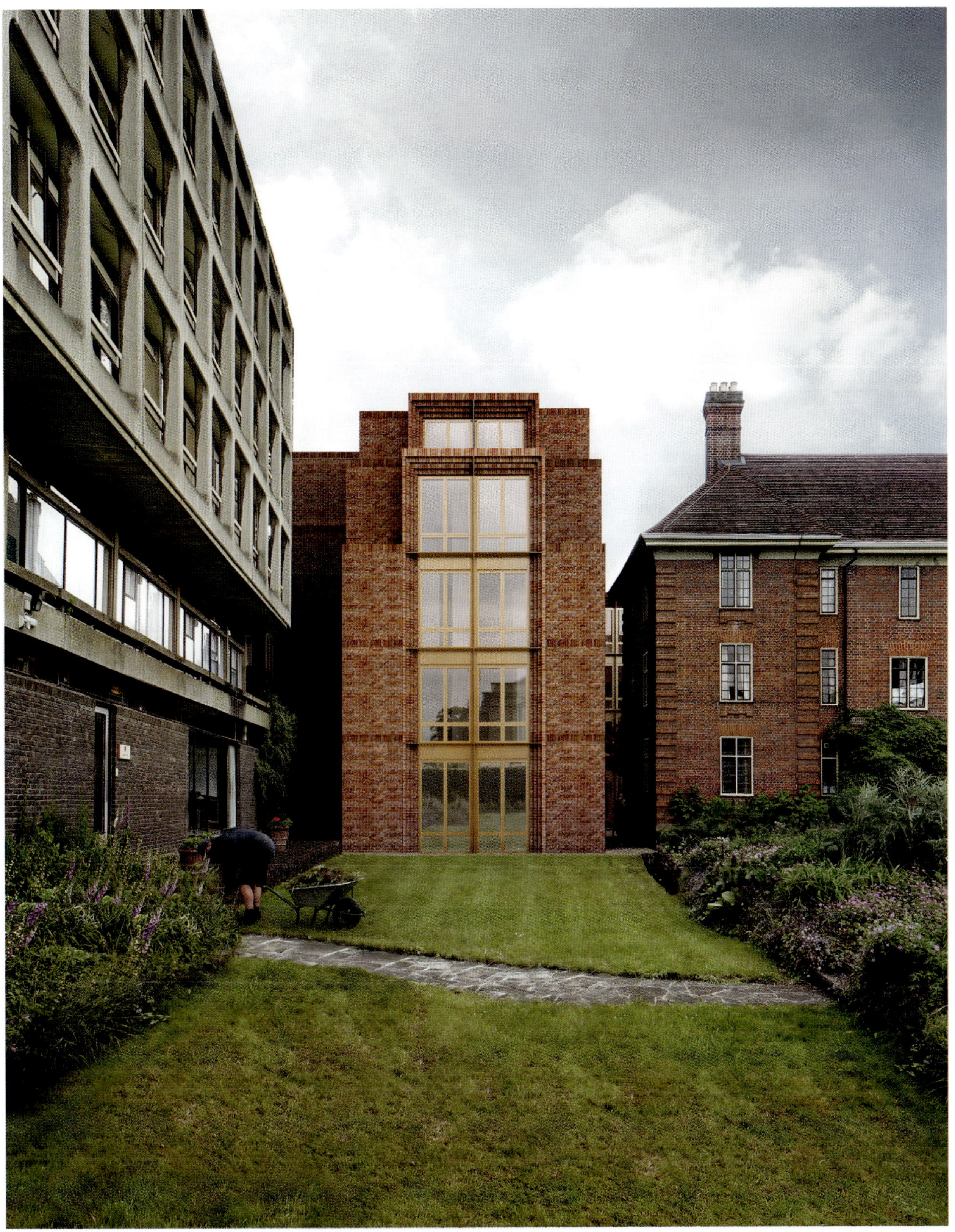

Afterword

Baroness Wolf of Dulwich, CBE
President of the Somerville Association

J ust a month before writing this Afterword, I walked into the entrancing Dublin building that is home to the Royal Irish Academy. And there was Mary Somerville. Not in the flesh, of course. It was her portrait, the first object in these pages, enlarged and copied as part of a display. It was instantly familiar and also reassuring. I was there to give a public lecture, and not at all sure if I had judged its content right. But anywhere that was honouring Mary Somerville had to be friendly.

I looked at that portrait quite a lot as an undergraduate. It is excellent: the painter captured intelligence, and a strong personality, along with genuine beauty. Of all the 140 fascinating objects in these pages, for me this is not just first, but favourite.

I came up to Somerville knowing nothing whatsoever about why it bore its name. What I did know was its reputation as the most intellectual of the women's colleges, so going there meant you were aiming very high. Reading this book reminds one again of how extraordinary a good many Somervillians have been, often in spheres beyond research and academe, but as world-class academics too. The objects, and their stories, also remind us of the barriers and difficulties of the early days.

However, I think my undergraduate self was so attracted by the Mary Somerville portrait for slightly different reasons. Even though she had been an amazing and brilliant pioneer, a mathematical and experimental scientist and astronomer, she had also been pretty, and obviously cared about her clothes and hair. She had married, and had a family, and travelled and entertained, and was a celebrated member of the more intellectual parts of London, and European, society. Some of that was obvious from looking at her – the rest I found out later. If having a full, complex life was possible for someone born female in 1780, surely it could be for us too.

In the contemporary world we are bombarded and preoccupied with immediate issues and concerns: Brexit, #MeToo, obesity, populism of the left and right, terrorist attacks. Once, an Oxford term could be a bubble for students, on which the outside world barely impinged. It can't be like that for anyone now. But our 140 objects can remind us, as that portrait does for me, that there are real continuities and that we are the direct and very fortunate heirs to a remarkable period of human history.

Higher education for women followed from the Enlightenment, and necessarily so. Enlightenment ideas made it obviously ridiculous to treat half of humanity as intellectually inferior, barred from developing its talents just because it was female rather than male. Enlightenment values were and are those of reason and scientific inquiry, of individualism and equality among people. Slavery was seen as perfectly normal and acceptable throughout most of human history, but viewed through Enlightenment and post-Enlightenment eyes it is utterly intolerable and totally wrong. The values and ideas that made this obvious were also the ones that gave us Somerville.

English universities did not have much to do with any of this to start with. Eighteenth-century Oxford was sunk in torpor and sinecure (though Scotland was very different and Mary Somerville herself was Scottish). Institutions like the Royal Society, and other learned societies and associations, were key, whether in London or in Edinburgh, Newcastle, or of course Dublin – hence the Royal Irish Academy with which I began. Similar institutions were founded in many other European cities. Then as Enlightenment ideas spread, the modern university also emerged. The women's colleges were founded in the wake of reforms in Oxford and Cambridge and the spread of higher education across the country.

Somerville was and is an Enlightenment endeavour. I was delighted to read about Mrs Thatcher desperately 'revising' her chemistry before meetings with Dorothy Hodgkin. And quite right, so she should have. To create major new knowledge and understanding, as Dr Hodgkin did, is surely the greatest individual achievement to which someone can aspire.

Will Somerville still be living by these values 140 years from now? I hope and believe it will, and that Somerville in 280 objects will tell an equally fascinating story.

ACKNOWLEDGEMENTS

The Principal and fellows of Somerville College would like to thank all those who have given permission for images and text to be reproduced here, and those who have contributed their time and expertise to this project. Text by Lizzy Emerson (text for Book of Hours by Annie Sutherland), edited by Johanna Stephenson, Anne Manuel and Katherine O'Donnell, with additional help from Pauline Adams and Jane Robinson. Text for 'Part One: in memory of the late Mary Somerville' corrected and supplemented by Brigitte Stenhouse (Open University). Particular thanks are due to the 2018 MCR and JCR Presidents, Connor Scott and Emmanuel Amissah-Eshun. Unless otherwise credited below, information about Somerville's history is taken from Pauline Adams, *Somerville for Women: An Oxford College 1879–1993* (Oxford 1996), from Anne Manuel, *Breaking New Ground: A history of Somerville College as seen through its buildings*, and from material held in Somerville's archives. Design by Heather Bowen. Contemporary photographs of objects by Angelo Hornak unless otherwise credited. Contemporary photographs of the college by Keith Barnes, John Cairns, Christopher Cornwell, Angelo Hornak, Steve Johnson or Rob Judges unless otherwise credited. Historical photographs taken from Somerville's collections. Photographs of oil paintings by the Public Catalogue Foundation for BBC Your Paintings. Every effort has been made to trace the copyright holders and obtain permission to reproduce material. Apologies are offered for any errors or omissions.

1780–1872
pp. 25–9 Martha Somerville, *Personal Recollections, from Early Life to Old Age, of Mary Somerville. With Selections from her Correspondence* (Boston, 1874) can be found at https://archive.org/details/personalrecolle04somegoog/page/n9

p. 28 Quotation from Ada Lovelace's letter to her mother (1841) in James A. Secord, *Victorian Sensation: The Extraordinary Publication, Reception and Secret Authorship of* Vestiges of the Natural History of Creation (Chicago, 2000), p. 184

1879–1906
p. 37 Portrait of Madeleine Shaw Lefevre by George Percy Jacomb-Hood (1857–1929)

p. 37 Portrait of Agnes Maitland by Herbert James Gunn (1893–1964), reproduced by permission of the Herbert Gunn Estate

p. 40 Photograph of garden roller from Somerville's collection

p. 48 Edward Lear's letter to Marianne North reprinted by permission of the Estate of Edward Lear

p. 54 *The Memories of Cornelia Sorabji* (London, 1934) can be found at https://archive.org/stream/MemoriesCorneliaSorabji/MemoriesCorneliaSorabji_djvu.txt

p. 56 Information on the 'Associated Prigs' taken from Pauline Adams, 'Associated Prigs (act. 1894–1899)', *Oxford Dictionary of National Biography* (published online 4 October 2007)

p. 57 Portrait of Mary Humphry Ward by Lucy Graham Smith (d.1942)

p. 58 E.H. Edwards, *Fire and Sword in Shanshi: The Story of the Martyrdom of Foreigners and Chinese Christians* (Edinburgh and London, 1903)

p. 58 John Gittings, 'Lost Souls', *The Guardian* (5 August 2000)

p. 59 Photographs of Emily Pfeiffer, *Poems* from Somerville's collection

p. 60 Muriel St Clare Byrne and Catherine Hope Mansfield, *Somerville College 1879–1921* (Oxford, 1922)

p. 64 Photograph of the library (external) from Somerville's collection

p. 66 1954 photograph of *Demeter* reproduced by permission of the *Oxford Mail and Times*

p. 71 Photograph of John Stuart Mill's copy of Emerson's *Essays* from Somerville's collection

p. 71 Photograph of the John Stuart Mill Library from Somerville's collection

p. 72 Photograph of Harriet Taylor Mill, 'The Enfranchisement of Women' from Somerville's collection

1907–1945
p. 78 Portrait of Emily Penrose by Francis William Helps (1890–1972)

p. 79 Portrait of Margery Fry by Roger Fry (1866–1934), reproduced by permission of the Estate of Roger Fry

p. 79 Portrait of Helen Darbishire by W.M. Coldstream (1908–87), reproduced by permission of the Estate of Sir William Coldstream/Bridgeman Images

pp. 80–1 Details of the Amelia Edwards Collection from the catalogue compiled for Somerville by Amanda Sharp

p. 90 Margaret Kennedy, 'Suffragets' March' reproduced by permission of English PEN

p. 96 Siegfried Sassoon, *Siegfried's Journey 1916–1920* (London, 1945)

p. 104 Photographs of Madeleine Shaw Lefevre sundial from Somerville's collection

p. 106 Image of poem by Robert Graves reproduced by permission of the Robert Graves Copyright Trust

p. 116 Roger Fry, *Near Nîmes* reproduced by permission of the Estate of Roger Fry

p. 116 Virginia Woolf, *Roger Fry* (London, 2003)

p. 117 Jacob Epstein, *First Portrait of Louise* © The Estate of Jacob Epstein

p. 117 Clare Sheridan (Frewen), *Nuda Veritas* (London, 1927)

pp. 67, 119 Cover of Vera Brittain *Testament of Youth* (London, 2009) reproduced by permission of The Orion Publishing Group, © Mark Bostridge and Timothy Brittain-Catlin, Literary Executors of Vera Brittain. Photograph of Vera Brittain reproduced by permission of the Vera Brittain Literary Estate
Contract for *Testament of Youth* reproduced by permission of the Vera Brittain Literary Estate

pp. 121, 128–9, 173 Dorothy L. Sayers, *Gaudy Night* (London, 1935)

p. 126 Architectural information about the chapel taken from Daniel Moulin-Stożek and Fiona K.A. Gatty, 'A House of Prayer for all Peoples? The Unique Case of Somerville College Chapel, Oxford', *Material Religion*, 14:1, pp. 83–114

pp. 119, 130 Shirley Williams, 'The tragic story of "South Riding"', *Independent*, 19 February 2011

p. 131 Portrait of Winifred Holtby by Frederick Howard Lewis (1885–1969)

p. 134 Olivia Laing, '*Being Here: The Life of Paula Modersohn-Becker* review – the story of women's art', *The Guardian*, 4 November 2017

p. 136 Penny Griffin (ed.), *St Hugh's: One Hundred Years of Women's Education in Oxford* (London, 1986)

p. 138 Note on Ramsden and Carr from V&A Collections online (http://collections.vam.ac.uk/item/O295510/spoon-omar-ramsden-and/)

p. 139 Natalie Shenker, 'Cicely Williams. A Pioneer for World Paediatrics', *Somerville College Magazine*, 2017

p. 139 Jennifer Stanton, 'Obituary: Dr Cicely Williams', *Independent*, 16 July 1992

1945–1989
p. 142 Biographical material on Janet Vaughan taken from Rose George, 'A Very Naughty Little Girl. The Extraordinary Life of Janet Vaughan, who Changed our Relationship with Blood.' (https://longreads.com/2015/03/10/a-very-naughty-little-girl/)

p. 142 Portrait of Janet Vaughan by Claude Rogers (1907–79) reproduced by permission of Crispin Rogers

p. 143 Portrait of Barbara Craig by Michael Noakes reproduced by permission of the Estate of Michael Noakes (1933–2018)

p. 143 Portrait of Daphne Park by Henry Mee reproduced by permission of the artist

p. 144 Ivon Hitchens, *Nude Algerian Woman No. 2* reproduced by permission of the Estate of Ivon Hitchens

p. 145 Patrick Heron, *The Red Table: St Ives: 1950* © The Estate of Patrick Heron. All rights reserved, DACS 2019

pp. 148–9 David Thomas, 'Jean Cocteau in Oxford', http://blogs.bodleian.ox.ac.uk/taylorian/tag/enid-starkie/

p. 151 Portrait of Shirley Williams by Andrew Kinsman reproduced by permission of the artist

pp. 154–5 Image of Nobel Prize Medal HCR9535 Image © Ashmolean Museum, University of Oxford. 'Nobel Prize Medal' is a registered trademark of the Nobel Foundation. Photograph of the opening of the Wolfson Building reproduced by permission of the *Oxford Mail and Times*

p. 156 Cover of Iris Murdoch, *The Red and The Green* reproduced by permission of Viking Press

p. 161 Photograph of Harold Macmillan reproduced by permission of the *Oxford Mail and Times*

p. 162 Polly Ionides, *Gymnast*, reproduced by permission of the artist

p. 162 Martin Plimmer, 'Rolling Stone', *The Mercury*, 12 July 1979

p. 164 Bust of Margaret Thatcher reproduced by permission of the Estate of Oscar Nemon

p. 165 Portrait of Margaret Thatcher by Michael Noakes reproduced by permission of the Estate of Michael Noakes

1989–2019
p. 168 Portrait of Catherine Hughes by Humphrey Ocean reproduced by permission of the artist

p. 168 Portrait of Fiona Caldicott by Thomas Leveritt reproduced by permission of the artist

p. 169 Portrait of Alice Prochaska by Richard Twose reproduced by permission of the artist

p. 169 Photograph of Janet Royall © John Cairns

p. 172 Unpublished Ruling by Roy Jenkins submitted to Somerville College reprinted by permission of Peters Fraser & Dunlop (www.petersfraserdunlop.com) on behalf of the Estate of Roy Jenkins

p. 175 Matthew Skelton, *Endymion Spring* (London, 2007)

p. 176 Portrait of Nan Dunbar by Malcolm Sparkes

p. 177 Photograph of Book of Hours by Lisa Handke of Oxford Conservation Consortium

p. 180 Photograph of Indian Government Scholarship Contract signing © John Cairns

p. 185 Note on 'Rosewater Sprinkler' (Object Number 2005.23) from Harvard Art Museums Catalogue, https://www.harvardartmuseums.org/art/27294

p. 188 Cover of *Advent Calendar* CD reproduced by permission of Stone Records Ltd

p. 192 Cover of Daisy Johnson, *Everything Under* reproduced by permission of Penguin Books. Illustration © Kustaa Saksi. Design © Suzanne Dean

p. 193 Cover of Fiona Stafford, *The Long, Long Life of Trees* reproduced by permission of Yale University Press. Cover illustration by Clare Curtis

p. 196 Ball logo designed by Sophie Kuang

p. 197 Janet Treloar, *The Fateful Meeting* reproduced by permission of the artist

pp. 198–9 Artist's impression of Catherine Hughes Building reproduced by permission of Níall McLaughlin Architects/Forbes Massie

This edition © Scala Arts & Heritage Publishers Ltd, 2019
Text and photography © Somerville College, 2019

First published in 2019 by
Scala Arts & Heritage Publishers Ltd
10 Lion Yard
Tremadoc Road
London SW4 7NQ, UK
www.scalapublishers.com

In association with
Somerville College
Woodstock Road
Oxford OX2 6HD
www.some.ox.ac.uk

ISBN 978-1-78551-225-4

Edited for Scala by Johanna Stephenson
Designed by Heather Bowen
Printed in China

10 9 8 7 6 5 4 3 2 1